The Gardener's Book of Trees

The Gardener's Book of Trees
Alan Mitchell

Illustrated by Joanna Langhorne

J. M. Dent
London

First published 1981
First published in paperback, with corrections, 1993
© Text, Alan Mitchell 1981
© Illustrations, J. M. Dent & Sons Ltd 1981

Printed and bound in Great Britain by
Butler & Tanner Ltd, Frome and London
for J. M. Dent Ltd
The Orion Publishing Group
Orion House
5 Upper St Martin's Lane
London WC2H 9EA

This book is set in 10/12pt Monophoto Photina

British Library Cataloguing in Publication Data

Mitchell, Alan
    The gardener's book of trees.
    1. Trees
    I. Title
    635.9'77   SB435

    ISBN 0–460–86085–2

Contents

List of Colour Plates *vi*
Some Trees of Prominent Crown Shape *vii*

Introduction *1*
A Brief History of Trees in the Landscape *3*
The Importance of Trees *10*
The Tree as a Plant *12*
Planting a Tree *17*
Tree Care *23*
Landscaping with Trees *27*
Trees for Special Conditions *38*
Alphabetical Lists of Garden Trees
Broad-leafed Trees *55*
The Ginkgo *146*
Conifers *147*

Trees for Special Purposes *185*
Glossary *194*
Notable Tree Collections Open to the Public *197*
Index *205*

List of Colour Plates

Between pages 84 and 85

1 Mixed coloured conifers, Wakehurst Place, Sussex
2 Maples at Winkworth Arboretum, Surrey
3 Sycamore 'Brilliantissimum', Thorp Perrow, Yorkshire
4 The prospect from the House at Batsford Park, Gloucestershire
5 The east end of Mitchell Drive, Westonbirt, Gloucestershire
6 Golden conifers at Sheffield Park, Sussex
7 A screen of great variety at Annesgrove, County Cork
8 Weeping Willow and Lawson Cypresses, Cowdray Park, Sussex
9 Narrowing a vista and making a focal point near its end, Westonbirt
10 Paperbark Maple and Cypresses at Dunloe Castle, County Kerry

Small-leafed lime

Black pine (var. nigra)

Corsican pine

Coast redwood

Female Lombardy poplar

Hungarian oak

Western hemlock

Red fir

Crimean pine   Western yellow   Leyland cypress   Monterey pine
                pine

Silver fir   Low's white fir   Black Italian poplar   Swamp cypress

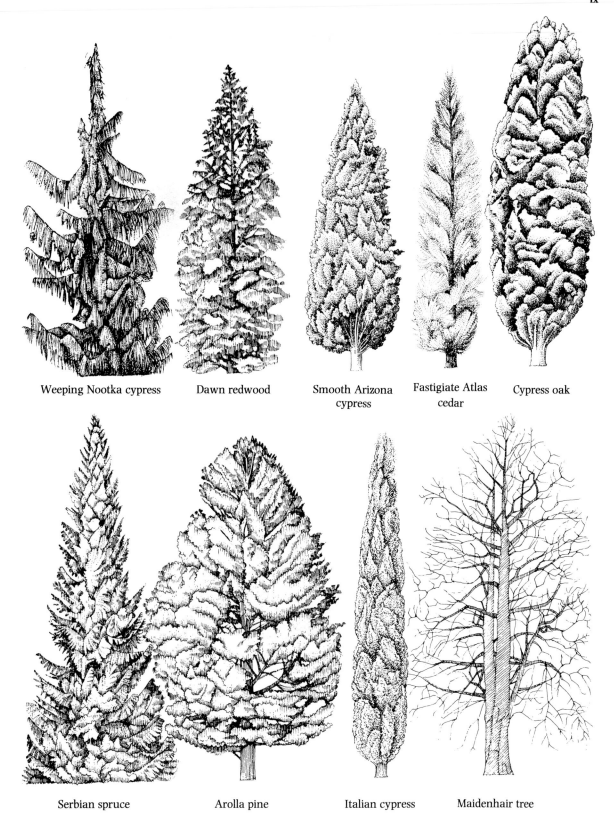

Weeping Nootka cypress   Dawn redwood   Smooth Arizona cypress   Fastigiate Atlas cedar   Cypress oak

Serbian spruce   Arolla pine   Italian cypress   Maidenhair tree

Bolle's poplar   Turkish hazel   Erect red maple   Caucasian lime

Silver pendent lime   Railway poplar   Weeping beech

West Felton yew   Phillyrea   Strawberry tree   Chusan palm

Pillar apple   Cox's juniper   Pyramidal hornbeam   Tulip-tree 'Fastigiatum'

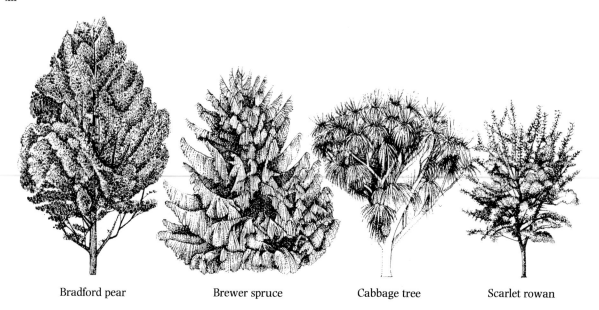

Bradford pear   Brewer spruce   Cabbage tree   Scarlet rowan

Weeping giant sequoia   Pond cypress   Vilmorin's rowan   Syrian juniper

Introduction

Aims and Purposes

Trees are the most enduring living things we handle, and can be prominent features through five or six generations after the death of the planter. Unlike the making of a stone monument or mansion, the planting of a grove of trees requires no special physical skills, no gangs of labourers and no long years of work. It can be done by one gardener in one afternoon. It cannot, however, be made in the form in which it is to endure. Architect and gardener both envisage the final effect for which they aim; but whereas the architect can ensure that this comes about as the work goes on, the gardener has to leave it in the hands of the trees he plants to mature in the way he hopes.

Planting a tree is, or should be, an irrevocable act. It is unwise and difficult to move it even after two or three years, and after thirty or so it is quite impracticable. The only change possible is to fell it.

Trees being the entire framework and background and the largest-scale features of all large gardens and parks, the choice of the right tree for each position is vital at the outset. Mistakes will live on and affect the overall design for its lifetime, for the removal of a wrong tree results in an unplanned gap followed by years with a tree smaller than that intended at each subsequent stage.

The aim of this book is to make such mistakes less likely, by provoking thought and airing ideas on patterns of planting and what to avoid, and to show the great diversity of tree which can be used for the different requirements. Every planting is unique in the details of its situation; aspect, altitude, soil and climate will rarely all be similar, while local topographies can never be the same. Precise recommendations are therefore of less value than general ideas and guidance as to the merits and demerits of each species. Most of the prime considerations in landscaping and planning a garden are simple and, once they are pointed out, obvious, but they do not always occur to those beginning to plant, and need to be stated.

A subsidiary aim, but an important one, is to remove the great discouragement to tree-planting enshrined in the commonly held fallacy that trees grow very slowly. This leads to the idea that the results of planting are appreciated only by one's grandchildren and that newly planted trees must be big, staked, ugly and expensive. None of these things is true and this cannot be said too often.

It is hoped, also, that by describing a proportion of the huge number of trees to be seen in this country, a greater interest in them will be aroused in the reader and he or she will realize that tree-watching is a rewarding pastime in towns, cities and suburbs as well as in rural areas and one that can be pursued every day even when one cannot be visiting the well-known gardens and collections. By giving brief historical details about the discovery and introduction of some of the world's trees, it may be that trees will come to be seen as individual personalities with a romance behind them. The trees generally seen in this country are not just remnants of the old native woodland; they have mostly been brought here by colourful characters, often in diverse circumstances, from all parts of the temperate world.

The Scope of this Book
Inclusions and Exclusions

It will be expounded elsewhere how our benign climate and our history combine to make these islands the finest and most varied assembly of trees in the temperate world. At least 1500 species, and 900 forms of them, can be found in collections and gardens. This book cannot therefore be comprehensive and must select rigorously. To merit mention, the following criteria must apply: the tree must be a tree, not a shrub (see below); it must either be gardenworthy and distinctive with positive merits or, lacking these, have been much planted nonetheless and so worthy of mention, if only as a warning against further planting; and it should not, in general, be so rare that only one or two specimens are known in specialist, often private, collections. Some trees only a little less rare will be included where they are of special merit and really ought to be better known, for unless they feature in books like this they will never be more widely planted. There is a conflict here, since readers do not like being inspired to plant a tree they cannot obtain and nurserymen do not relish being asked for something they cannot supply. But this must be the case if the position is ever to improve, for the market system only really works when supply arises to meet demand. Today, the position is deteriorating on many fronts as large nurserymen are persuaded by their financial advisers to stop growing those lines which do not reach a certain high minimum sale and increasingly the plantsman relies on newly established, small, one-man nurseries not so afflicted. It may well be too late to save the rarer stocks in big nurseries but it is vital to encourage the enterprising individual who is willing to risk raising plants which at present are known to, and required by, few.

The range of plants deliberately omitted from this book is as follows:

1   Shrubs. Some masquerade as trees – the Wayfaring tree is an example – and they are firmly excluded because all the space available is needed for the inclusion of proper trees. There are plenty of books devoted entirely to shrubs and all too many books supposedly on trees into which shrubs have infiltrated. If one is admitted, the line between shrubs and trees becomes hard to draw, and before long the book will be deep in rhododendrons. A definition is therefore required to which to adhere, or from which to depart, with reasons why. A suitable criterion for a tree is a woody plant which is commonly capable of growth to over 6 m on a single stem.

2   Dwarf conifers. A vital part of garden design, especially in the smallest gardens, this subject must be omitted as it is one on its own with its own literature, and would, if included, displace too many trees.

3   Trees so rare as to be found only in a few botanic gardens or specialized private collections, or too tender to be grown except in a very few gardens.

4   Trees with no particular merit, the planting of which would displace a tree better suited to parks and gardens. There are very few in this category; Red horse chestnut, Downy birch and Pissard's purple plum are the obvious examples.

A Brief History of Trees in the Landscape

Only 12,000 years ago there were no trees in Britain as we know it. The ice was at its greatest extension, reaching south to the Chiltern Hills, to the south and west of which was glacial outwash and tundra. There was then land south and west of Cornwall and Ireland which was a refuge for a few species, like the Strawberry tree and, possibly, the Cornish elm. With the retreat of the ice the Strawberry tree migrated into western Ireland and, unless brought there by a tribe in the Iron Age, as has been put forward, the Cornish elm moved into the valleys of south-western Ireland where it is now common. The rest of the land that is now England will have been growing nothing but dwarf willows and dwarf birches. The first pioneers will have been the Downy and Silver birches and the Scots pine, which advanced rapidly northwards. The birches left large populations on sandy and heath areas but the Scots pine populations were crowded out during subsequent climatic changes and those now flourishing on Lower Greensand in Surrey and on Bagshot Sands and other recent beds in Hampshire, Berkshire and elsewhere derive from recent reintroductions, probably in 1663 in Surrey and in 1777 in the New Forest.

Also early to arrive were the Aspen, Bay willow, Rowan, Sallow, Juniper, Hazel and Sessile oak. Pollen analysis cannot distinguish between the two native oaks, but the present distribution with the Sessile oak predominant in the north, west and (with the exception of Dartmoor) at higher altitudes, suggests that the Sessile preceded the Common oak which is found mainly in lowland areas and more in the south and the east. During a warm early period, the Small-leafed lime was dominant over large areas and spread north,

and the Wych elm and Bird cherry were other early arrivals. The Ash, Field maple, Yew, and Hawthorn arrived with time to spare, probably with the Wild cherry and Crack willow, but the Channel was now threatening the land-bridge. This was of chalk, and apart from Holly and Hornbeam, the last trees to cross were those which thrive on chalk, and are often now found wild only near chalk hills – the Wild service tree, Whitebeam, Beech and, probably last, the Box.

The total complement of native trees (dismissing any that cannot grow to 6 m on a single stem as shrubs) was about 35. Europe was unfortunate during the Ice Ages because the great mountain systems run from east to west, from the Cantabrian Mountains in northern Spain, through the Pyrenees, Alps, Sudeten Mountains, Tatra and Carpathians. The flora and fauna were somewhat trapped between the northern ice and the mountain ice. The Mediterranean Sea also prevented access to Africa as a refuge. In Canada and the northern USA, which experienced the same Ice Ages, the mountains run north to south. Trees migrated southwards along mountain or valley at their preferred climate, and afterwards migrated back again. Hence there is an immense wealth of species, broadleafed and coniferous, in North America. Britain could be recolonized only by species hardy enough to survive on the plains from France to Germany and even then only by those near enough and sufficiently fast-moving to migrate back in the 6000 years available before the Channel opened.

The native trees here will have covered all the country except the highest peaks and some swampy valleys, before man made his inroads. Increasingly the forests were cleared for agriculture, the making of charcoal, the smelting of iron, for fuel, and for building ships. Although the remnant forests in the north and west, and a few others, probably redressed the balance, it is evident from engravings and pictures, and plans by Kip and others, that much of the lowlands was by the eighteenth century far more denuded of trees than it is now. Beyond the complex parterres and knot-gardens, the patterned orchards and parkland, lies a landscape of the utmost desolation. Whilst this may have been partly a desire on the part of the designer of the parks and gardens to emphasise the contrast between his well-treed demesne and the windswept surroundings, it is probably true that at this period there were fewer trees in southern England than there had been since the Ice Ages. By 1920 only four per cent of Britain was under woods of one sort or another, and this included the parks and plantations made in the eighteenth century and the copses and spinneys valued as game coverts. At the present time about eight per cent of the land is under managed forest.

By 1700, a small and growing proportion of woodlands was not of native tree species. The exotic Sweet chestnut made up large areas of coppice and Norway spruce and European larch formed many coverts, shelter-belts and plantations, while parklands increasingly used a wide range of exotics and the Sycamore had long spread wild. Today the production-forests of the west and north are almost entirely composed of exotic species and others are accepted as part of the landscape. In large parts of the south-west and near all coasts the Monterey pine and cypress from California and the Holm oak from southern Europe are a dominant part of the scenery. In British gardens, native trees are rare or almost absent. A grove of beech, a big old oak or ash, may be part of the garden, but there are entire vistas in famous gardens without a native tree in sight. This is fine – gardens are meant to be decorative and should not be restricted by the vagaries of ice 12,000 years ago and the grain of the European mountain chains. We have one of the very best climates in the world for the development of a huge variety of plants. It would be a gratuitous waste of a superb asset were British gardeners not to take advantage of this and create some unique landscapes by judicious blending of the floras of the temperate parts of the world. In using this extended flora, we are enabled to select the best species in the world for particular sites or features; there is no need to try and make do with the minute proportion of trees which made their own way here.

The Invasion of Exotic Trees

The first additions to the native tree flora were the English elm and the various forms of the Smooth-leafed elm from the Continent brought by Iron Age tribes. Elms were used as boundary-markers and for fodder, and the immigrants no doubt brought the type which grew in the area from which they came. Dr. R. Richens at Cambridge has identified numerous forms in East Anglia, basically Smooth-leafed elm, and traced tribal boundaries thereby. The English elm is thought to have been planted first in the Vale of Berkeley, Gloucestershire, and spread through the Midlands and south but did not reach peripheral areas. East Kent has a typical small-leafed Smooth-leafed elm; much of East Anglia has large-leafed forms as well; the north Midlands has scattered pockets of Plot's elm, a small-leafed form with sinuous bole and sparse, arched branches; and west of a line from Bideford through Okehampton to Plymouth is all Cornish elm, a smooth-leafed form with ascending and arched branches and bright green leaves. The English elm did not extend beyond York and Cheshire in the north or into Wales.

The Grey poplar and the White poplar may also have been brought here during this time, but the Romans are credited with the introduction of the Sweet chestnut and the Walnut and possibly the Fig. The interest in trees was strictly medicinal or culinary from Roman times until after 1500, so it is unlikely that a tree would have been brought here just for its timber, with so much virgin woodland around. Hence the Romans are unlikely to have brought the Sycamore, although this too has been suggested, because its value lies entirely in its timber, and the shelter it gives on coasts and high land. The True service tree may have been introduced by the Romans for its fruit, or it may have come later, but it is hardly to be considered a native on the strength of the single apparently wild tree found in the Forest of Wyre in 1678.

There is a period of 1500 years between the Roman introductions and the first with known or accepted dates. Until writers began recording trees either as long grown or known, or as new, there was no way of knowing when they came. William Turner, writing in 1547, was the first important source of information, but only to confirm that many trees from southern Europe were already here by then, including the Italian cypress, Maritime and Stone pines, Bay, Almond and Peach, and the Norway spruce. The Cherry-laurel, Black and White mulberries, the Judas tree, Oriental plane and Holm oak were here by 1600 but their precise dates of arrival are not known. The 'Turkey Merchants' were trading actively from Aleppo at about this time and a number of trees from Asia Minor are thought to have come along the trade routes. Four species from this region have, however, presumed precise dates: Common laburnum, 1560; Turkish hazel 1582; Scotch laburnum 1596 and Phillyrea 1597. The rather few trees of central Europe arrived at long intervals afterwards – Silver fir 1603; European larch about 1620; Norway maple before 1683; Arolla pine 1746 and Grey alder 1780. Surprisingly, the Austrian pine so common now, was not in cultivation until 1835.

Eastern North America shares with China an early flora able to escape Ice Ages by migrating southwards. Magnolias, tupelos, Kentucky coffee trees, tulip-trees, hemlocks and hosts of other genera unknown in Europe proliferate in both these countries, while locust trees and swamp and pond cypresses are only found in America. A few American trees came before 1600 and increasingly they came after. John Tradescant brought the Swamp cypress in 1640 and his son the Red maple in 1656. There were two periods of intensive introduction, the first from about 1675 to 1713 when Henry Compton was Bishop of London. His friend John Banister was an ardent collector and Compton put him in charge of

missionaries in the Carolinas. Together these two arranged the Atlantic crossings of returning missionaries so that plants could be brought at the right time – a critical matter in the days of no fungicides and rat-infested ships. Hickories, maples, oaks, Sweet gum and many more American trees stocked the Bishop's garden at Fulham Palace. The cause was continued from 1730 or so until 1771 by Peter Collinson, planting at Mill Hill and receiving plants from the Bartrams, father and son, in Philadelphia. From 1785 to 1796 André Michaux sent large numbers of trees from America to France, some of which were then sent on to England. With John Fraser bringing trees back from his dozen or so journeys to America before 1811, most of the eastern American trees were growing here by 1820. Two notable late arrivals are Snowdrop tree, 1897 and Western catalpa, 1880.

The Caucasus Mountains are the home of a choice small group of endemic trees (trees found nowhere else) which grow exceptionally vigorously here, mostly with handsome, glossy leaves. The Caucasian zelkova was the first to arrive, in 1760, and one of the five original trees is a big tree in Syon Park, by the 'Flora' lawn. The rampant Caucasian wing-nut followed via France in about 1785 and the elegant Caucasian ash came in 1815. The Chestnut-leafed oak was first sent, to Kew, in 1846 and this original tree is now a monumental specimen. The vigorous and variable Caucasian alder came in 1860 and Van Volxem's maple, with large, sycamore-like leaves, in 1873.

China was a closed country until about this time except for a few coastal areas, but some trees had come along the old trade routes to the Middle and Near East in or before the Middle Ages. The Peach and the White mulberry, for example, were widespread in those regions before plant-mapping began. Between 1751 and 1753, d'Incarville, a French Jesuit missionary, had introduced from northern China the Tree of Heaven, the Chinese thuja and the Pagoda tree as well as the first Ginkgo. From the treaty ports on the south coast – still the only parts of China generally accessible to foreigners – came the Chinese privet in 1794, brought by Sir Joseph

Banks; the Cunninghamia and Chinese juniper in 1804, brought by John Kerr; the Chusan palm in 1836, the Cryptomeria in 1849 and the Golden larch in 1854 by Robert Fortune. But the amazing abundance of plants in China, particularly in the centre and west where they are most concentrated, remained unknown until other French Jesuit missionaries began to describe some of them after 1860.

In 1885, Augustine Henry, a doctor with the Customs Service, travelled in Szechuan and Yunnan in south-west China and introduced a few of the trees he discovered. The Japanese had long cultivated many Chinese trees and the Paulownia was first introduced from there to France in 1834 and thence to Britain in 1840.

In 1898 it was decided that the time had come for some serious collecting in China, to follow up the tales and specimens brought back by the Jesuit Fathers like David, Farges and Delavay and from Augustine Henry, and in 1899 Ernest Wilson was appointed collector by Veitch's Nurseries, trained and sent to China. In four journeys between 1900 and 1911 Wilson discovered and sent 400 new species of trees and shrubs and 800 others. Every suburban road has plants owed to Wilson and among the more notable species are Paperbark maple, Chinese tulip-tree and Sargent spruce. George Forrest made seven expeditions from 1904 to 1932, approaching from the Burma border, and collected in areas slightly further south and west; he sent back numerous silver firs, spruces and other conifers, and vast numbers of rhododendrons. Joseph Rock and Kingdon Ward collected in the same areas and beyond from 1923 until 1958. Further collecting expeditions are planned, for there is still much to come.

The Himalayan slopes are botanically an extension of China and many of the genera of trees found only in North America and Eastern Asia extend along them, notably the magnolias and hemlocks. The first tree from this region was received in 1818 when Dr. Govan was sent cones of the Morinda spruce by his son and gave the seed to the Earl of Hopetoun; at his home near Edinburgh the two original trees and an early graft of one of them on to a Norway spruce still flourish. The Bhutan pine followed in 1823 and

the Deodar in 1831, the Himalayan hemlock in 1838 and other trees rather sporadically afterwards.

Japan is horticulturally important for two reasons. It has a great array of endemic species, many of genera with species familiar elsewhere, like the oaks, maples and birches, but some, like *Sciadopitys* and *Trochodendron*, not closely related to any other plant in the world. It also has a very long history of intensive horticulture; both from its own trees and from some long imported from China, Japanese gardeners have raised cultivars which by long selection are more diverse and extreme than those elsewhere. The best-known are some of a host of maples and the 'Sato' or decorative cherries.

Japan was a country closed to the West until 1854 so that little was known of the wealth of plant forms there. A few trees came to Europe from a botanic garden established on Java, in 1843. A few filtered out with occasional travellers. The most important of these was Philipp von Siebold, a German eye-surgeon whose wanderings were tolerated from time to time as his services were so much in demand. It was he who brought to Europe the (Smooth) Japanese maple in 1820, and much more. After 1854 the collectors arrived and the sudden eruption of Japanese plants dates from 1860. In 1861 numerous conifers and cultivars of maples were sent back by Robert Fortune and John Gould Veitch. But the interior still was not open and naturally these collectors concentrated rather on nurseries, so the wild species in the mountains were less collected than the cultivars. When the country was fully available to collectors, a flood of species of maple, oak, birch, silver firs and others was sent here by Charles Maries and J. H. Veitch between 1877 and 1892 and, via the Arnold Arboretum in Massachusetts, by Charles Sargent.

Korea has a tree flora which includes some found otherwise only in Japan, and some which range far to the south in China and to the north in Mongolia. The trees tend to be small, very hardy and attractive. Charles Oldham first collected there, for Kew in 1860–2, and Ernest Wilson was there in 1917.

Taiwan has a flora of mixed Japanese and

Chinese origin together with some endemics like *Taiwania*. Wilson visited the island in 1917 but the Formosan cypress, which grows quite well in all parts, had already been introduced in 1910 by Admiral Clinton-Baker.

South America has, with Tasmania, the only temperate Southern Hemisphere forests and it has provided many fine trees. The first to be introduced, the Chile pine or Monkey-puzzle, arrived in 1795 brought by Archibald Menzies who had sailed with Captain Vancouver along the west coast of the Americas north to Alaska. He took five nuts from the table during a banquet in Valparaiso and raised the trees on the voyage home. This is ironic, for it was also Menzies who first saw many of the giant conifers of the north-west, like Douglas fir and Coast redwood, but at that time could neither collect seed nor store it on the voyage home. As for the one tree he did introduce, the Chile pine, he never saw it growing wild. In 1843 and 1849, Sir Joseph Hooker and William Lobb collected in Chile and the Argentine, and quantities of Chile pine seed as well as seeds of many other trees like *Fitzroya* and *Saxegothaea* were sent back by Lobb. The most vigorous South American trees, the Roblé and the Rauli, were much later imports, in 1902 and 1913 respectively.

The Pacific slopes of the northern and middle Rocky Mountain system, including the Siskiyou Mountains and the Sierra Nevada, are the home of the finest forests in the world. Nowhere else are conifers consistently growing with the main canopy trees all over 60 m tall, and in places 90 m tall; a dozen species easily exceed a height of 60 m. It was Menzies who first saw these trees and collected foliage for description in 1792, but the first man to collect seed of the giant conifers was David Douglas. He travelled mostly alone and in two journeys, 1825–1827and 1829–1833, he sent back Douglas fir, Sitka spruce, Sugar pine, Western yellow and Western white pines, Grand and Noble firs, and, when based in Monterey, California, the Digger, Coulter and Monterey pines.

Douglas decided in 1834 to walk back home to Scotland across Siberia and Europe but there was no ship to take him to his starting point, Vladivostok, so he sailed to Hawaii as a first step.

He disembarked as soon as possible to walk across the island over the volcano Mauna Loa, and, his sight failing badly, fell into a buffalo trap and was killed. No other collectors went to the Pacific Coast for a period and apart from the mysterious appearance of an envelope of seed in 1838 on a desk at Kew, which turned out to be of Monterey cypress, no more seed arrived until 1846 when Theodor Hartweg, the German Collector for Kew, sent Bishop pine from southern California.

By 1850 the original Douglas trees were around 20 years old and showing extraordinary promise, especially in the gardens and policies around Douglas's native Perth and further north. The lairds had become great enthusiasts for western American conifers and more were badly needed. In 1849 they formed the Scottish Oregon Association and selected and trained a collector to send to Oregon. He was John Jeffrey and he managed to repeat all the Douglas imports and to find new ones. He sent back ten crates of seed in the next four years, finding and introducing Jeffrey pine, Mountain hemlock, Red fir and others and sent the first Western hemlock, Nootka cypress and Western red cedar but he received little credit for his pioneer work because he fell foul of his sponsors. He failed to provide the stipulated journals with details of the collections with any of his boxes; the amounts of seed became too small and he became elusive and finally disappeared.

In 1849 also the nursery trade saw the potential of these trees and many collectors were sent out to the West Coast. William Lobb of Veitch's sent back many of the same trees as Jeffrey and is given the credit for their introduction, although in some cases Jeffrey was first. Lobb also remained convinced all his life that it was he who first sent the Giant Sequoia in December 1853, but a Scottish landowner, J. D. Matthew, had been there himself and collected seed in August of the same year. However, it *was* Lobb who introduced the Santa Lucia fir, the California nutmeg tree and Low's white fir among others. Several collectors were at work in Oregon and California at this time, sending more seeds of Douglas fir, Sitka spruce and a confusion of silver firs – Red, Low's, Beautiful, Grand, Shasta and

Alpine often arrived under the wrong names – and these all helped to bulk out the supplies from Jeffrey and Lobb which were the source of the plants for the enormous upsurge in the planting of conifers from 1853 to 1860. Many hundreds of our big gardens and pineta owe their biggest trees to these imports.

One major conifer from the Pacific north-west and featuring in this flood of imports had, nonetheless, a very different early history in Europe. The Coast redwood was, it is now known, brought to Portugal in about 1780 by the missionaries who discovered the coast of California. This was even before Archibald Menzies, sailing with Captain Vancouver, saw and took specimens of it as well as Sitka spruce, Douglas fir and others in 1792. David Douglas collected seeds and plants in 1832 but these were lost when a boat was swamped, together with his journals. The Coast redwood was sent by Theodore Hartweg with other discoveries in 1846, but it had already reached England by a roundabout route in 1843. Russia had a colony at Fort Ross where the redwood belt is relatively broad and Russian botanists had taken seed many years before and were growing the tree in the Crimea. Dr. Fischer of Leningrad sent some seed to the London nurseries of Knight and Perry in 1843. Several specimens are known in British collections, planted in 1844 and 1845 from this seed, although most of our biggest trees derive from the other collectors' packets and date from after 1850.

By 1856 all the big trees of the Pacific north-west had been introduced to Britain. A few smaller species from high altitudes like Balfour's, Limber and Bristle-cone pines were sent in the early 1860s. Those from the interior south-west, Arizona and Colorado, followed in the years 1870–1880. The Blue Colorado spruce was brought from a Boston garden by Anthony Waterer in 1877 to Knaphill, where the original tree grows still.

The first tree from Mexico was the Cedar of Goa, which came via Portugal between 1650 and 1700, but the first direct imports were brought by the German collector, Theodore Hartweg, in 1846. These included the Cedar of Goa but were mainly pines, including the Montezuma, Mexican and Mexican white pines. There is a huge assembly of pine species and forms in the mountains of Mexico, and various imports of Montezuma pine have grown in Europe under thirty different names while several more are well marked varieties. Since 1950 foresters in Tropical and semi-tropical parts have found that a number of Mexican pines grow in their areas with remarkable speed and there has been much exploration to find the best areas for seed and to collect new species. In 1962 *Pinus durangensis, P. engelmannii* and *P. cooperi* were introduced to Britain and may be seen in some pineta growing strongly, but *P. maximartinezii*, prized for its huge cones and bright blue-white foliage when young, introduced in 1969, has failed to survive our worst winters since then.

Arrivals from Australasia began in 1775 with *Sophora tetraptera*, but have been sporadic and not well recorded since. The Cabbage tree, so familiar near the west coast of England, on the Isle of Man and in Ireland, was sent from New Zealand in 1823 and the Blue gum from Tasmania in 1829. All three of the King William pine (*Athrotaxis*) group of strange redwood relatives were sent from their Tasmanian mountain in 1857. The Cider gum came in 1846 but other eucalypts have been sent at various times and new ones still arrive.

Trees from South Africa have a poor record of survival in Britain and introductions do not seem to have been noted. However, a few Cypress pines (*Widdringtonia*) grow in Irish gardens.

The Use of Exotic Trees

The parks and gardens in the British Isles rely primarily for their beauty on exotic trees from every part of the temperate world. Many well-known garden vistas have no native tree in sight. These gardens are unsurpassed for the variety and excellence of their trees. Nor has any other country anything approaching the number of gardens with fine trees or tree-collections found in these islands. At least 1000 have been visited before writing this book but there are as many more, if mostly smaller, yet to be seen. In Sussex, five tree-collections among the best in the world are within about ten miles of Haywards Heath, a concentration almost equalled around Exeter, Truro and Crieff in Perthshire. The skill of the designers of British and Irish gardens has been in making full use of the peculiarly benign climate in which they work and achieving blends and contrasts among the great wealth of the world's plants which flourish here. In this way the gardener is circumventing the geological accidents and processes which have prevented all but a tiny remnant of trees from growing naturally in the British Isles. The climate is now eminently suited to most of them, indeed in many cases more favourable than that in which they find themselves in their natural ranges. Some of the trees which are so exotic to us now, like Sequoias and Magnolias, grew naturally in what is now England when it was in the latitude of Florida. This rich and varied flora declined slowly with the northward drift of the land and then rapidly about $2\frac{1}{2}$ million years ago with the start of the Ice Ages.

The probability of finding several good trees for any particular purpose or situation makes the designing of plantings very much simpler than if the gardener were restricted to native species, and the results more varied and nearer the actual requirements. There are, however, grave dangers in using a world flora too liberally, and these are both aesthetic and ecological. The native flora, however restricted in variety, has been the setting of unique country scenery and has supported and grown with the native fauna. The scenery is now very man-made and one typical view unique to England and much admired until disease struck – the wide lowland valley heavily sprinkled with elms – relied in fact on an exotic elm, an immigrant of the longest standing, however. Any unique natural feature is inherently of the utmost value and must be preserved. Most large-scale countryside views are basically of native species and an important feature of contrasting, obviously exotic trees is disruptive and out of place.

Land usage, on the other hand, demands crops over wide areas and these must usually be highly exotic, whether potato-fields or plantations of larch or Sitka spruce, in order to produce the crop required. Large regions under this sort of crop are therefore unavoidable and, to most people, quite acceptable, having their own features and effects on fauna and flora, by no means all negative. In other regions, however, there has not been, and need not be, a big incursion of exotics. All plantings which are a visible part of the landscape need sensitive treatment and should at least appear to be native species or those visually acceptable as native, like Sweet chestnut, Norway maple or even, perhaps in hill-country, European larch. In this connection it is appearance rather than time of arrival which must be the guide. The Horse chestnut has been here over 300 years and is regarded by many laymen as a native but it is visually quite out of keeping with native trees, while the Rauli, new in 1913, fits very well. The general rule is to keep all fancy planting and bright colours to enclosed or small-scale features.

The Importance of Trees

In the Landscape

The British Isles have within small areas uniquely varied geology and scarcely a rock-series from the most ancient to recent is missing. From the Malvern Hills to the New Forest – a distance of only about 130 km – one traverses rocks of every age, from Pre-Cambrian to Recent sands. The scenery is thus likely to be exceedingly diverse and in fact lacks only towering peaks and glaciers, and active volcanoes. Within the great range of scenic features, only cliffs and rugged peaks owe nothing to trees for their appreciation as scenery. Every other form, every other picture on a scenic calendar relies heavily on trees. Pictures of fens or saltings usually include or are framed by an old hedgerow tree or two, to give contrast and aid composition. Even the scenery of bare rolling hills so admired by ramblers and hill-walkers gains immensely from the little patches of trees under bluffs or by becks and burns and without them the scene is bleak, unvarying and monotonous. In regarding a panoramic landscape, the eyes roam over it seeking some prominent feature for relief, from which to distance the components and to which to return. This is so important in our enjoyment of a view that it operates in surprising circumstances. The view from part of the Chiltern Hills in Oxfordshire, for example, is a broad sweep of lowlands, quite featureless except for the cooling-towers of Didcot power-station. Although we may not choose a clutch of cooling-towers as an aesthetic feature, they are the focus to which the eye returns and by which it distances the middle and background. Without these, the view would be of much less visual interest.

Similarly the ramblers' glorious bare hills, which are in fact a man-made semi-desert resulting from centuries of misuse by clearing, burning and over-grazing, gain as scenery if the valley sides are in many places clothed with woods, providing changes in colour and texture and emphasising the form of the land, affording some resting place and distancing reference for the eye. Woods also provide much needed cover for wildlife and increase the number of species of plant, insect, mammal and bird. Many birds which will hunt over moorland need trees in which to breed and roost.

In Gardens and Parks

Trees give a garden style and substance. A single well-chosen tree skilfully sited can transform a scene from one of little visual interest to a vista of great impact. A park or garden may be designed to be a continuation of the surrounding countryside, but it is much more usual for it to define itself and to differ radically from what is beyond, whether open fields or part of a town, and be seen to do so. The outside world should not obtrude but rather than creating a solid screen, views of it should be filtered; even the worst industrial or urban scenery can be interesting as a glimpsed back-drop to the garden. All this is done by trees, which will also define the major features, the glades, vistas and lawns. Trees are thus the backbone of every garden design. They are also, when evergreen, the most important part of the winter aspect.

Trees add a third layer to the structure, above the shrubs and herbs, and increase immensely the varieties of foliage, flowers and fruit. This three-layer structure is best developed and applied in the Cornish-type gardens, many of them in Sussex and other counties where rhododendrons are important in the scheme, and allows the enjoyment of the maximum amount of plant material in the minimum space. Wildlife increases greatly as the trees grow, particularly the number of birds. This is more because of the food and cover provided by the spreading canopy than the greater number of nesting-places, since many of our best songbirds nest only in shrubs or long grass. Tree-creepers, nuthatches and woodpeckers are the important exceptions.

In Towns and Amongst Buildings

The vital role of trees here is to provide welcome change. Change in shape, with the rounded or conic crowns breaking the very rectilinear outlines and features of buildings; change in form, with the light and airy tracery of shoots and crowns in winter relieving the massive solidity of buildings; similar changes in texture and colour, but, above all, change with the seasons.

The use of trees in the downtown areas of clustered skyscrapers in American cities is of relevance and great interest here. The trees cannot hope to screen or compete with 300 m buildings and are not meant to. The Ginkgos, honey-locusts, American and small-leafed limes planted in the canyons between the buildings provide a different environment, on a human scale, where people walk. They give the scenic changes outlined above, shade and relief from monotony, but they also afford fascinating views of the buildings framed by or through their crowns, a new and rather thrilling form of landscape.

Trees in city and town parks and in churchyards also increase the number of bird species in surrounding areas. Greenfinches would be less likely to be found on the suburban nut-bag if there were no Lawson cypresses in which they can breed. The same trees so ubiquitous around towns may have bred the goldfinches sparkling and tinkling over the thistles on the wasteland, and also the great majority of successful early nests of thrushes, blackbirds and dunnocks. More recently, the collared dove has moved into the Lawson cypresses and frequents towns.

The trees in a suburban road, in the street or in front gardens, transform these areas from monotonous rows of similar houses into something more akin to a glade in a garden, and places of real beauty when the cherries and laburnums are in flower.

General

Trees are the most important scenic features which can be added easily, in almost every part of the land. They add diversity in many directions and increase wildlife in general. There should never be any doubt as to whether to plant a tree or not, except where there is obviously not enough room, but only doubt as to which is the best tree to plant. At the worst a tree can always be cut down, but a gap cannot be filled so easily. It may need emphasising that trees, once properly established, look after themselves. They do not need endless attention and they grow just as well when the ground around is deep in nettles and brambles as if it were kept clean. In fact many of the finest trees in Britain are exactly so placed. A herbaceous garden disappears in two years of neglect but a tree thrives on 200 years of it. It is normal for an old tree to carry some dead branches. They need only be removed if the tree is in a public place, for safety reasons. Broken branches look better trimmed back and remedial surgery can save a tree badly damaged by storms, but no amount of care will prevent a tree dying in the end and it will go about it in its own way. No one need refrain from planting trees for fear that they will not be looked after. They will look better if cared for, but they will still survive.

The Tree as a Plant

Definition of a Tree

A tree is a woody perennial plant, a form of growth found in numerous botanical families. It does not, therefore, imply any relationship, and there is no class 'Trees' in the category of 'Mosses' or 'Ferns'. This manner of growth is absent or very rare in such major families as *Compositae*, *Cruciferae* and *Primulaceae*. It is frequent in some families, with many herbaceous species like *Rosaceae*, and it is dominant, almost universal, in *Aceraceae* (maples), *Tiliaceae* (limes), *Fagaceae* (oaks, beeches etc.) and in the class *Coniferae*.

A woody, perennial plant can be a shrub or a tree, depending on where it is growing. Many plants which are trees in the valleys may be shrubs on the mountain-top. Nevertheless, there are many plants which even in the best conditions will never be more than shrubs and others with the potential to grow into trees, and these need to be distinguished by definition.

A tree is here taken to be a plant which is capable of growth on a single stem from the ground, to a height exceeding 6 m. As said earlier, a book on trees should not be cluttered with shrubs because there are already too many real trees growing in Britain to include in a book of reasonable size. Hence the Wayfaring tree, an unashamed shrub, and the Elderberry, will not be found here. On the other hand, the Hawthorn and the Holly, which can be tall trees on a single bole, both qualify for inclusion.

Naming of a Tree

Old-established popular names of trees are usually only *general*. The names Oak, Ash, Elm and Pine do not *specify* which of many oaks, ashes, elms and pines is intended. To be *specific* involves the use of a second name, Red oak, Manna ash, Wych elm or Scots pine. In English, the general name comes second but a list of trees in alphabetic order in that manner would not be helpful as the Red oak would be listed among Red maple, Red spruce and so on, instead of among the oaks. Just as telephone directories would be of little use if subscribers were listed under their first names, so in formal naming of trees the general name must come first and the specific name (or adjective) second. In the course of time, most languages have applied names very loosely; for example, colonists named some of the new trees they found after their homeland trees that they most resembled, and even repeated the process with the same names for other trees found further afield. It was easier to sell a new coniferous timber under the old, well-known name of a highly valued wood like cedar, so the eastern parts of America, explored first, soon had two 'White cedars' and a 'Red cedar'; this last is a juniper, but when the west was opened up, a thuja was also called 'Red cedar' and a cypress was called 'Yellow cedar'. The confusion is great and none of the trees is a true cedar at all. To shed all this ambiguity and to have tree names the same all over the world, the vernacular languages have been discarded and the academically universal language of Latin is used instead.

Early botanists described plants in Latin but

some used descriptive phrases to specify the actual plant in its group. It fell to the Swedish botanist Karl von Linné, writing under the name 'Linnaeus', to implement a concise, more logical arrangement and he named all the forms of life known to him in a work *Systema Naturae* published in 1758. The Linnaean system gave every organism just two names, the generic and the specific, which he consistently included as a summary after the usual long description. The Common oak was *Quercus robur*; 'Quercus' the *genus* (plural 'genera') and 'robur', the rugged, strong one, the specific epithet, the *species* (plural 'species'). With botanists everywhere actively naming plants, it was likely that the term 'robur' could have been used to describe another oak. Confusion could thus return, so the whole subject of naming organisms, the science of taxonomy, evolved certain strict rules, one being that the specific epithet always carries, as part of itself, the author's name. Since Linnaeus's work is the foundation stone, his name is shortened to 'L.', hence the Common oak is *Quercus robur* L., while others are identified by the first syllable of their name or other acceptable abbreviations and, when two or more botanists have the same name, initials need to be added.

Of course, in 1758 neither Linnaeus nor anyone else knew more than a small proportion of the animals and plants of the world. Few conifers were then known, only one Cedar, two Larches, a few spruces and several pines, so it was sensible to consign these woody-coned trees into one genus and the few known scale-leafed conifers into another. Thus Linnaeus has three genera of conifers only, *Pinus*, *Juniperus* and *Cupressus* (apart from the rather different Yew, *Taxus*) and he named the Larch *Pinus larix*, the Cedar of Lebanon *Pinus cedrus*, the Norway spruce *Pinus abies*, and the Deciduous or Swamp cypress *Cupressus disticha*. When it was found that there were several other larches, many other spruces and cedars and more were likely to be discovered, it became evident that this system was inadequate. A spruce was not only a type of pine; there were in fact a large number of spruces and these needed to be distinguished as a group from pines. The Cedar and the Larch likewise had to move up the

hierarchy from being species in the genus *Pinus*, each to be a genus with its own species. *Pinus* was restricted to those conifers that bear leaves arising in a common sheath, in bundles of two, three or five; that is, the true pines as we know them today. The cedars, larches, spruces and others which had been in the genus *Pinus* are now genera in the family *Pinaceae*, of which *Pinus* is the typical genus.

The botanical names had to be altered to reflect the new relationships, and status and names follow the rules of the science of Taxonomy. One basic rule is that a species shall always retain the specific name that was given to it when it was first described and named validly, provided this does not infringe any other rules of Taxonomy. Thus, however later revisions move a plant among other genera, it will always be known from its specific name. The Bluebell, for example, is *non-scripta* whether in *Scilla* or in *Endymion*. However, in dividing a large genus like *Pinus* into many smaller genera, there is frequent conflict with other rules, and the old specific name often has to be dropped and replaced by the second valid published name.

The Cedar of Lebanon was first named by Linnaeus as *Pinus cedrus*. To make the Cedar a genus, the logical step is to promote its specific name to that of the new genus and call cedars in general *Cedrus*. This is straightforward for *Cedrus* and for *Larix* (the larches from *Pinus larix* L.) since *cedrus* and *larix* were used as descriptive nouns, 'the cedar' and (*Pinus*) 'the larch' respectively. It would not do, however, for the hemlocks where the first named was *Pinus canadensis* L. because *canadensis* is an adjective. A generic name must be unique within the Kingdom of plants and, if adjectives were allowed, a commonly used specific name might be given generic status in many different groups. In such cases the first alternative generic name published is adopted, and if there is none available one must be coined. The Eastern hemlock thus becomes *Tsuga canadensis* (L.), the 'L.' in parentheses because Linnaeus did not write this combination of names. Strictly, the author who first published it must also have his name attached to it, so in this case the tree's full name is *Tsuga canadensis* (L.) Carr [for Carrière].

But *Cedrus* and *Larix* run into another difficulty. It would be logical, and would preserve the original names, to make the Cedar of Lebanon '*Cedrus cedrus* (L)' and the European larch '*Larix larix* (L.)'. Zoologists follow this practice and are at home with names like that of the Wren, *Troglodytes troglodytes* (L.). Botanists, however, are still opposed to repetition or 'tautonymy' and will not countenance it, so the next available name for the Cedar of Lebanon is used, *Cedrus libani* Rich. (for Richard); for European larch, Miller's name is used, *Larix decidua* Mill.

It will be noticed that the name *Pinus decidua* (of an early author) which was so descriptive of the Larch when it was among evergreen pines, spruces, silver firs and so on, loses its aptness when named by Miller as *Larix decidua*, since all larches shed their leaves in winter. Taxonomy is concerned only with the correct naming according to its own rules and not at all with distinguishing the plants botanically. Similarly, Linnaeus put the Swamp cypress in his big genus *Cupressus* and distinguished it as *disticha*, with parted leaves, not by its deciduous habit. When it was found to be a redwood, not a cypress, it was made into a genus of its own, *Taxodium distichum* (L.). The Coast redwood, on the other hand, was seen to be closely related to the 'deciduous cypresses', *Taxodium*, but its greatest single distinction was in being evergreen. It was therefore well-named as *Taxodium sempervirens* but when later transferred to the genus *Sequoia*, the term 'sempervirens' lost its significance because the other Sequoia then in the genus *S. gigantea* (now *Sequoiadendron*) is equally evergreen.

Varieties and Cultivars

A species with a wide geographical range is likely to show some minor differences when individuals are compared from remote parts of this range. The Western yellow pine, *Pinus ponderosa*, for example, ranges throughout the vast Rocky Mountain complex within the USA. A specimen from the Oregon coast is, not surprisingly, slightly different from one in the Black Hills of South Dakota and both differ from one by the Grand Canyon in Arizona. The differences are not considered sufficiently fundamental for each population to be made into a full species of its own, nor are the boundaries always definite between such forms, so they are regarded as 'varieties' of *Pinus ponderosa* and need to be named accordingly. They become *P. ponderosa* var. *scopulorum* from South Dakota and *P. ponderosa* var. *arizonica* from Arizona. (Strictly this makes the Oregon form, the one described first as *Pinus ponderosa*, take the addition 'var. *ponderosa*'.) These geographical varieties are named in latinized form, in italics, and (strictly, again) are followed by the name of the author who gave them that name. In each case there is a wild population to provide seed if the variety is needed for growing in a collection.

With 'garden varieties' the case is wholly different. These are forms like weeping, erect, golden or variegated-leafed trees of which there is no wild population. Each has been found as a single oddity, rarely seen again, or as a single shoot growing on a normal tree. Obviously no seed source is there and with very few exceptions any seed produced yields normal trees. These forms are propagated by grafting or from cuttings or layers. They need to be named in a fashion distinguishing them from true varieties. They are called 'cultivars' and they are named by adding a third name to the species name, as before, but in Roman type, in single quotes, or in double quotes after the abbreviation 'cv'. The cultivar name should be in the language of the person who names it, not in Latin, but old-established latinized names given before 1959 are accepted. Hence the Weeping beech can be *Fagus sylvatica* 'Pendula' as that is the earliest correct name, or it can be *F. sylvatica* cv. "Pendula". The cultivar name must begin with a capital letter. Recent cultivars have vernacular names like *Gleditsia triancanthos* 'Sunburst' and *Fraxinus oxycarpa* 'Raywood'.

In some cases with cultivars of unknown origin or very mixed or uncertain parentage, the second botanical name, the specific epithet, is dropped as being misleading and unnecessary. Many of the Japanese cherry cultivars are in both categories and their names become of the form *Prunus* 'Kanzan', *Prunus* 'Taihaku' or *Prunus*

'Ukon'. Many hybrid poplars are in the second category, hence *Populus* 'Robusta' and *Populus* 'Eugenei'.

Brief History of Cultivars

The propensity to run to forms worthy of selection as cultivars is found unevenly among trees, native or exotic. Among the native species, the Beech, Yew and Holly have given many, the Ash, Hornbeam, Rowan, Whitebeam and White willow have yielded several each; the English oak, Sessile oak, Wych elm and Scots pine few, and the Crack willow, Sallow, Wild service tree and Small-leafed lime, effectively none. The main impact on gardens and parks of the cultivars of native trees has been to ensure the continued planting of some species in which the type tree is almost never planted. Very few hornbeams are planted as such, but the neat cultivar 'Fastigiata' or Pyramidal hornbeam is freely used in streets and parks; the Wych elm is on no one's planting-list but the golden-leafed form 'Lutea' and the fully weeping 'Camperdown' were in streets, cemeteries and city parks in numbers, until disease struck them down.

There is no record of the first appearance of some of the cultivars of native species. Some, like the Cypress oak, *Quercus robur* 'Fastigiata', and the Single-leafed ash, *Fraxinus excelsior* 'Diversifolia', crop up from time to time in the wild, the Cypress oak probably only in Europe, especially in Germany. These and the Weeping ash and Red-twigged lime could well have been planted since the sixteenth century when planting trees for ornament really began. A few cultivars of exotic trees may also have been in use at the time. By about 1680 that scourge of the modern village, park and garden, the so-called Copper or Purple beech, was introduced from Germany, and in 1758 the Lombardy poplar was brought from Turin to St Osyth's Priory, Essex, a cultivar of the native Black poplar. The Dovaston yew was planted in 1777 and now is a splendid tree, but propagants from it are fairly rare, whereas another cultivar of yew has had a universal effect on churchyards and large gardens. This is the Irish yew which was found in County Fermanagh in 1780 and was put into commerce in 1812.

The Weeping willow probably came into use before 1800 and soon made its mark in landscapes beside water. It is either a cultivar of the native White willow or a hybrid between that species and the Chinese *Salix babylonica* which is so much planted in Washington DC, for example, but is scarcely known here. Two cultivars of the beech which are common today in towns and parks are the Weeping and the Fern-leafed beeches which both arrived first in 1826 at Waterer's Knaphill Nurseries. The originals are still there and are fine big trees. The Coral-bark willow came from Germany in 1840 and in early spring is a glowing feature of many pond margins. The Whitebeam 'Majestica', arose in 1858 and is much planted by arterial roads, and the Pyramidal hornbeam reached Kew in 1885.

The cultivars of exotic species are legion and being added to all the time. Their effect on decorative plantings is profound but they are rarely suitable for large-scale features. The first to have a specific date appears to be the Corstorphine sycamore which arose in 1600. The leaves emerge a light gold but turn gradually green through July, so except where new growth is made late, which is largely confined to young trees, it is the usual heavy, dull green by midsummer. The Sycamore with leaves densely spotted white, which is frequent in old parks and gardens, was brought here in 1730. The double-flowered horse chestnut, 'Baumannii', was here by 1820 and the popular heavily white-variegated Ash-leafed maple came from Toulouse in 1845. In 1861 the wealth of the gardens and nurseries of Japan became available and by then the Lawson cypress, sent in 1854 from the Siskiyou Mountains in Oregon and California, was about to get into its stride. This cypress has emitted a steady stream of cultivars of almost every colour and form available to a cypress in British and Dutch nurseries ever since.

Looking at Trees

In no country in the world is there anything comparable to the number of fine gardens available here to the public, as we have already seen. Most of our stately homes are set among splendid trees and Scottish castles tend to have huge conifers in the policies and more in a separate pinetum. The botanic gardens are generally open, and a huge number of private gardens are now open on certain days under the various schemes for charities. The Royal Parks in London and many other city parks everywhere are first-class arboreta and most town parks have a number of unusual trees. Many suburban roads with front gardens and street-planting are virtually linear arboreta and it is fascinating to see how many really quite rare trees may be found in them.

To those who have no real interest in trees, it is axiomatic that a tree enthusiast walks the countryside woods and copses to see his trees, but compared with those in streets and gardens he will find little of interest here – only the few native trees and the common exotics like Sycamore, Horse chestnut and Turkey oak, and remarkably few will be well-grown specimens. Little new will be seen or learned of trees, however delightful it is to be in woods, without visiting areas better stocked with a variety of trees.

The visits to large collections and gardens have value in more ways than enjoyment of rare, beautiful or imposing trees. They are essential in learning to identify the less common trees as well as enabling the gardener to see them in various stages of growth and health and in varying climates and soils. To someone who is planting trees, there are great areas of knowledge to be gained in this way: the wealth of species possible for each particular situation; the shapes, growth and health which can be expected; and ideas in design to be gathered and judged. Most major gardens plant continually and these are where the new cultivars can be seen and assessed as established trees used in designs, rather than as young trees in lines or containers in a nursery.

Apart from studying trees with a view to planting them, tree-watching becomes an addictive and absorbing hobby which can be indulged in at any time of the year and in almost any place in the British Isles.

Planting a Tree

Selecting the Plant

The majority of trees make very rapid growth when young. This cannot be said often enough, for the generally held myth that all trees are slow-growing leads to great expense and difficulties in establishing garden trees. If trees did grow slowly there would be some advantage in buying and planting an already tall specimen. Since they do not, this common practice merely proliferates unsightly gaunt, staked cripples scarcely able to grow, where one should see sturdy, unstaked, well-furnished, thriving small trees.

In forestry, tree-planting is on a vast scale, more than one hundred million trees being planted annually. Because the costs of the ground, drainage, clearing, plants and planting are set against the plantations at compound interest, the trees must have a survival rate of about 95 per cent, grow fast from the start and produce early returns from thinning if the planting is ever to be profitable. Forestry land is usually very poor, run-down grazing at fair altitude. Planting is done by simple notching at a thousand plants a day per man. A handful of phosphate fertilizer is often given, but thereafter the trees receive no further attention except weeding for a few years. There is just no place for staking or other after-care.

Surely, then, a gardener in a sheltered lowland site, on rich, prepared soil, giving each tree an elaborate individual planting, watching it every day and with only, say, a dozen trees to care for, should expect to have vastly superior results to the forester, even though the gardener's trees may be decidedly less robust. But who could claim that this often happens? The forester plants trees two or three years old and less than 45 cm tall. The inexperienced gardener, on the other hand, plants his 2 to 2·5 m tall.

In a tree, as in any other plant, the roots feed the leaves and the leaves feed the roots. Without disturbance, this balance is maintained; the roots grow enough to support a sufficient head of foliage to provide them with adequate nutrients to make this growth. If some accident removes part of the crown, the roots, now in excess for the needs of the crown, can provide enough nutrient for extra shoot and leaf growth; big sprouts arise and the balance is soon restored. If part of the root system is destroyed, perhaps by the laying over it of a concrete or asphalt surface, the position is more serious and shows the unstable nature of the balance. The shoots will be fewer and much smaller. This cuts down the amount of nutrient available from the leaves to regrow roots, and if these conditions continue, the growth of the tree is permanently retarded. In transplanting, the situation is inherently unstable. A large tree will have a large root system but must leave a part of it behind. In the new, and usually more exposed, position the new growth requires more, rather than less roots. New shoots are therefore very short, and may not last the full season. Hence the roots, when they also need the most nutrition to regain balance, have a minimum from the leaves. They therefore make little growth and, next season, can support very little more shoot-growth and hence few more leaves and hence again, they can make little new growth. This vicious spiral is seldom ever fully broken and can be crippling for as much as 20 years.

In contrast, a two-year transplant brings all its roots and has but a small crown to nourish. There will be a slight check in the first year as the roots find their new position, but by the next year all will be in balance and long shoots will be grown. The great increase in foliage gives the roots all they need to make a big system to support further big top-growth the following year – and so the cycle continues. The crown is small when it is moved into greater exposure and relatively unaffected by this so it grows good, normal foliage.

Again, a large plant has no chance to grow and retain any tap or sinker roots after being moved, and even if it has a large ball of roots, none is anchored in the new soil and the whole ball can rock. Being a tall plant, it must therefore be staked strongly. There is some evidence that staked stems, freed from recurring strains, fail to thicken and strengthen as they would if free, and problems arise when, after two years, the stake should be removed. A small transplant firmly planted, on the other hand, needs no stake and is quite stable. The roots rapidly grow downwards and by the time the top is big enough to be vulnerable – which, in the rapid growth that can be expected, is in only two years – the roots are adequate to hold the plant.

Lastly, the side-branches of trees arise from lateral buds on the leading shoot, with strong ones at the base of the shoot, or, in many conifers, in strong whorls only at the base of the leading shoot. The basal ones are present quite independently of the length grown by the leading shoot, and laterals on the shoot still arise on a very short leader, if in smaller numbers, but are more congested. Thus a tree planted when 2·5 m tall, scarcely able to grow a leading shoot for years, grows, at 2·5 m up its stem, a dense system of branches. This ruins the shape of the crown and makes it even less stable in the wind. The small transplant, growing its proper 60 cm to 1 m a year, places its branches properly and builds up the correct shape of crown. It is also laying down its crown as it responds to its final position, whereas the tree planted when 2·5 m tall has to grow on from a lower crown grown in response to the conditions of the nursery lines.

There is nothing more satisfying to see, in the world of gardening, than strong growth on small young trees. Only at this stage in their life can trees have more than half the crown composed of new shoots and these have a vigour and freshness all their own. Only at this stage can one handle (carefully) a leading shoot perhaps 2 m long. The annual increase in size is strikingly evident in a way that cannot be seen in a 20 m tree. A group of small, thriving trees growing fast is a delightful feature, full of promise for the future. None of these pleasures is available from trees planted when tall. The staked, guyed and gaunt objects, visibly struggling, give little satisfaction for many years. Their best years have been spent in the nursery, and adding to their cost, too.

In no tree is this early planting out more essential than in the eucalypts. These are very fast-growing trees and resent any check in the growth of their roots. The recommended method is to sow the seed under glass in February, in pans, put them in pots when about 10 cm tall in April and plant them out finally in June or July when 30–60 cm tall. The stronger species then end their first season from seed 1·5–2 m or more tall.

Selecting the Tree

In buying a tree, whatever its size and almost independent of the species, there is one golden rule. There must be a good, strong, single leading shoot. This is the prime indication of healthy growth in the nursery and of strong growth and good shape in the garden. A tree without a leading shoot should be shunned absolutely. Unfortunately few nurserymen are either aware of this themselves or realise that the tree-enthusiast will insist on it, and they seem perfectly happy to recommend a shapeless, leaderless or mutilated bush as 'well furnished'.

Most trees will have one of two careers ahead of them. They will either stand as a single specimen on a lawn or elsewhere or they will be an upper layer to a shrubbery or in a group. The single specimen may, if it is of sufficient character, be left with its foliage to ground level or it may be made to show a clean bole for perhaps 3 or 4 m.

In either case its task is to grow as rapidly and straight as possible as a single stem. This means a good, dominant single leader, right from the start. As part of a group or in shrubberies, a tree's business is to carry its foliage high and not interfere with other plants, pathways, drives or lawns. Trees should not be bushes – there are other species specializing in that. Nor should they, except in rare cases, be on more than one stem – this is an affront to one who likes a tree to be what only a tree can be, and who appreciates a fine bole. The bole should be straight, leading the eye to the crown without taking it around bends or past obvious breaks and changes in direction.

Only plants with single, dominant leading shoots will grow in this desirable way. Some conifers, notably Silver firs and larches, when young will replace a broken leader either by raising a side-branch to take its place or by starting from a new bud below the break, and over the years the slight change in alignment of stem so caused will usually disappear. In pines it remains obvious and in all but the most vigorous broadleafed trees it is also irrevocable. Eucalypts are one exception; they are quite capable of losing 2 m of leading shoot and looking much the same as before in the following year. To buy a maple with three or four equal leading branches is, as one so often sees, to buy one incapable ever of making a good bole and crown. Some nurserymen will cut out the leading shoot of a standard tree and cause a bushy head to develop because some parks like their trees in that form. Since a tree's business is to grow upwards and mop-heads are seldom required in a garden, these trees should be left with the nurseryman. Many of them if left alone would in any case have made only small trees, being chosen for this reason, but of a better shape, having a strong central stem.

The choice of a plant of the right small size can be difficult. It must be ascertained that the small size is not due to lack of vigour but *because it is young*, although of strong growth. A forest nursery is the best supplier of the twenty or so species which are used as forest trees, as it expects to sell these by the thousand at the right age and size and the plants are therefore cheap. With luck it can supply Red, Common and Sessile oaks,

Norway maple. Sycamore, Beech, Silver birch and perhaps Common, Grey and even Italian alder, Ash, and Sweet chestnut. The conifers will be easier to obtain, almost all forest nurseries carrying large stocks of larches, Norway and Sitka spruce, Scots and Corsican pine, Thuja and Western hemlock.

Horticultural nurserymen tend to encourage the planting of large, older trees and may view with disfavour the selection of plants at the right age and size for planting, as they are seen as barely started on the production line. The idea that they could sell more trees to more satisfied customers with vastly less work and use of land, by selling them smaller and cheaper, will not percolate while the average buyer is entranced by sheer size and willing to pay for it. It be may be possible to find a co-operative nursery-man who will sell plants at the right age.

How to Plant the Tree and When

This is very simple and mainly requires common sense and some idea of how roots work. A two to three year-old tree needs only a hole slightly larger than the spread of the roots and some soil enriched with compost or leaf-mould. On very sandy, open soils a much deeper hole is worth while for several buckets of old turf, weeds, compost or leaf-mould sunk in it will provide moisture-holding rooting for many years. A sprinkling of phosphate just below the roots will help some species to establish more quickly.

It is of vital importance that the tree be firmed in really hard. The heel should be rammed into the soil closely around the plant, taking care not to skin its basal bark nor to leave the plant out of the vertical. No stake is required.

A large tree is a much bigger task. Roots in a ball and particularly any curving round a container-edge must, contrary to advice sometimes given, be straightened out to radiate as fully as they can without breakage. Old trees in arboreta are often seen with an old root curving round the bole, usually partly dead, sometimes making an ugly swelling and occasionally constricting the tree seriously. These seem to be the legacy of planting a root-ball unspread. There is, after all, a continual thickening of each root with growth in the same manner as branches although rather more slowly. Also, the stability gained from an undisturbed root-ball is very little indeed whereas the main roots spread into the new soil will acquire some hold. Any damaged root seen when spreading the root-ball must be cut out and any over-long root should be cut back.

The hole for a big tree has to encompass the spread roots with about 30 cm to spare all round. The big tree needs every possible help and must be planted in generous quantities of the best soil available, and this soil must encircle the roots so that their first growth is into it. The hole is deep and will usually reach subsoil at base; this needs breaking up and preferably the addition at the same time of good topsoil. If the drainage is suspect and the subsoil sticky, it needs to be broken up to a depth of 30 cm below the bottom of the hole and then covered with a layer of broken brick or coarse sand. Before the tree is moved in, the stake, which must be stout and sound, will be driven in, near but just offset from the centre. A general fertilizer or bone-meal should be sprinkled in the hole and more mixed with the back-fill. Firming down must be done in layers at intervals of about 15 cm of soil replaced, with care not to pull the roots. Care is also needed to see that throughout this planting and firming, the tree and the stake remain truly vertical and close together. The final level of the tree in the soil must be exactly where the soil-mark shows the depth of the tree in the nursery. Shallow planting will put the upper feeding roots in peril of drying out while deeper planting will deprive them and deeper roots of the aeration they need and may kill them.

It is a sound rule never to let the roots of a tree be open to the air, even for a few minutes. A damp sack or a few handfuls of damp soil should be thrown over the roots even for the few minutes that the tree may be laid beside the planting hole. If the root-tips dry out they soon die; new growth has then to be initiated from farther back and this

takes time. A tree in leaf is losing moisture and cannot survive a long period without active roots.

The best times for planting trees can be deduced from the behaviour of roots and devising ways to ensure the absolute minimum of moisture loss. Roots need a mixture of water and air in the soil; that is, they need to breathe and they give off a quantity of carbon-dioxide that needs to diffuse away. They grow in general from March to the end of October. The part of the root which does the work of abstracting moisture and nutrient from the soil is the root-hair, only found for a few centimetres a little behind the growing tip. Root-hairs live for only a few weeks.

Now the needs of the upper parts of the tree come in. A deciduous tree loses virtually no moisture when it has no leaves. An evergreen tree is always losing some moisture and, perhaps surprisingly, it loses a great deal in very cold weather if there is a dry wind. Both need a maximum of moisture when new growth is enlarging, which in nearly every case is during May and June. Both therefore need as much new root-growth by May as can be made. A deciduous tree will, however, come to little or no harm if it has no effective roots from October until the buds begin to enlarge, in late April, whereas an evergreen needs whatever active roots it can have throughout the winter.

A deciduous tree can therefore be moved at any time after October, as long as periods of frost are avoided, especially if it has entered the soil, and of excessive rain. It is possible to lift the tree just before the leaves fall and have it planted in time for some new root-growth before winter sets in. Any mild, damp spell is suitable and then, as the soil warms up, the new roots can start as early as possible. Unless the planting can be done swiftly, however, and the site has warm, well-drained soil, the new growth will not start, and the tree would be better awaiting a spring planting with its roots intact rather than spending all winter with inactive roots, liable to die back in the hole.

An evergreen can be planted in early October if it is put in well-drained warm soil. After this period, however, there should be no planting until root-growth restarts in March. Then the plant is lifted with new rootlets emerging and these are put straight into good soil to continue growth. The tree is at no time standing about in cold drying winds without a firm root-system. There is some latitude in whether the lifting be done soon after root-growth starts or whether more growth is made before lifting. Again, a well-drained, warm soil is best if early planting is the aim. Some conifers, notably the Monterey and Corsican pines which do not transplant well at normal times, respond well when planted at the time of maximum root-growth in midsummer, even as open-rooted (not containerized) plants.

Small plants genuinely raised in containers or pots (that is, not dug up from open ground and put into them by the nurseryman) can be planted at any time for their roots are almost undisturbed; in the same way, rhododendrons and azaleas will always transplant with open roots, their mass of fibrous feeding-roots suffering no damage if handled carefully and the soil is the open, sandy and leafy sort they thrive in. Big trees also are often planted at any time from containers, but this is a somewhat risky enterprise as the roots usually do suffer some disturbance and the big tree is bound to have a greater struggle because of its size. It needs constant and copious watering in any dry spell for the rest of that season.

In dry soils and on sloping banks, the hole when filled should remain a well-marked depression in all plantings. Otherwise it is not possible for watering to wet the soil below the surface skin. In some cases it is advisable to put a few sticks, 1 cm or more in diameter, in the soil when firming up at planting and to extract them for the purpose of pouring in water. Some people use a length of drain-tile. Without a device of this sort, watering can be most frustrating, creating a mud skin over the surface of the soil. In places liable to flooding or in very heavy soils, the tree can be left on a mound, a dome shape rising in the centre some 15 cm above the general level. This will help some of the superficial feeding-roots to survive.

It may be helpful to know that the feeding-roots of even the loftiest trees are only just below the surface. They can even come on to the surface, as happened with a Serbian spruce growing near some rhubarb, which had a thriving system of roots under a protective covering of old dead leaves. The deep-going roots are the 'sinkers' which strike down vertically from the main spreading roots and anchor the tree firmly as well as finding the water-table. The tap-root is largely mythical in old trees, even in oaks, as its work is done by numerous sinkers and it usually dies away. No roots will penetrate permanently water-logged soil and some trees are very sensitive to this. The Beech is markedly so, and very big beech trees that blow over in damp hollows or above a wet stratum will show vast root-plates, all confined to within 30 cm or so of the surface.

Starting a Large Planting on Open Land

Trees are sociable plants used to growing in company. Even those which are most light-demanding and in need of space, grow naturally into a woodland of an open kind but affording much common shelter. There are several major difficulties in planting specimen trees across an open area and they arise from the sudden increase in exposure suffered by plants brought out from the nursery lines, and the intense competition their roots have to endure, from grass, particularly.

The classic way to start an arboretum avoids all these troubles, and was employed at Dropmore, Buckinghamshire in 1792 and at Westonbirt, Gloucestershire in 1829 and 1855. It may at first seem an expensive and wasteful method but it is in fact neither. The scheme is to plant at once the entire area, right to the rides or glades, with common, rugged trees which are known to thrive in that place, and to include as many beech as possible as soon as possible. (Beech will not establish on their own and need nurse-trees). In an exposed position a great mix of tough fast-growing trees is the first matrix – Sallow, Crack willow, Black poplar, Silver birch, Scots pine, Lawson cypress, Sweet chestnut, Larch –

together with some beech. The smaller and short-lived species fade out when they have done their work.

The advantages of the Westonbirt method are:

1   It marks out the bounds and ride-system from the start with solid ranks of robust, growing trees, giving some immediate appearance of planning and purpose. It makes an interesting place from the outset, helps in visualising later planting schemes and makes mowing the rides easier.

2   From the start it creates some shelter near ground level where new small trees will need it most, and with every year the height and amount of shelter increases. This changes the micro-climate at plant level profoundly, in favour of the young trees to come.

3   It begins at once to weaken the growth of big grasses, and as the beech in the mixture establish themselves, their shade and leaf-fall rapidly changes the sward to smaller herbs and the soil to woodland, humus-rich soil.

4   Unusual specimen tree collections can rarely be acquired all at once. The year or two of waiting for some of the specimens is not wasted since their site is improving each year and the late arrivals will have a better start than the first trees could have done.

5   The matrix trees are planted at or near forest spacing, 2–3 m apart, to have their effect most rapidly. After 20 years at most they will benefit from a good thinning. This will not decrease the shelter but will make pleasing woods in the hinterlands and the thinnings will be useful for stakes, fencing, or firewood if not otherwise marketable.

6   As the specimen trees are planted, they will be along rides (Westonbirt-fashion) or in clearings. Most trees are planted too close to allow for full development in every case after 100 years – and rightly so. But whereas the inevitable crowding will lead to hard decisions and regretted losses if every tree planted were a rare, expensive or otherwise cherished specimen, the chances are that the culprits will be among the common trees if the surrounds are mostly matrix. The removal of a few more matrix trees can free the specimens and the losses will not be noticed if they are part of the plan.

The Beech is the tree best suited generally to all these purposes.

Although the matrix or shelterwood scheme has been described as for an arboretum, which implies an area of many hectares, it is really only an extension of the scheme for planting early shelter trees around and within any garden, and can be used on a very small scale. Birch, willows and larch are excellent disposable trees, cheap and easy to grow. A little belt of these, preferably in a few groups along the weather-side of any new garden in the open, will repay their planting over and over again, not least by removing in their first year the bare and exposed aspect which can otherwise persist for many years.

In public parks, the Westonbirt method will entail fencing off the planted area for a few years and can only be adopted where this is a small proportion of the space open to the public. Some complaints must be expected when the long grass is unmown among the little trees, which will soon subdue it, for many people cannot abide nature taking over. However, every naturalist will applaud the increase in wildlife this always brings.

Tree Care

Fertilizing

In general, trees seldom require fertilizers except for a brief period at each end of their lives, when a judicious application can make a big difference in growth and appearance. A fully established tree can be expected, with its extensive root-system, to find all the nutrients it needs. This is just as well because supplying nitrates, for example, to a large oak would be both difficult and expensive. Garden soils are usually of much better nutrient status than the soils available for reafforestation. It is standard forest practice to plant every tree with a dose of super-phosphate below its roots. Phosphates are important for good root-growth and are notably lacking in peaty and other acid soils but generally adequate in loams and clays. On sandy soils, therefore, it is as well to mix a little phosphatic fertilizer in the bottom of the planting hole and in the back-fill. The one tree for which this is unnecessary is the Lawson cypress and its legion cultivars, for on even the poorest soils this species either finds enough phosphate or does without.

Nitrates, too, are essential for vigorous growth and production of foliage and so are most beneficial in the first few years when the shape and vigour of the young tree are of greatest importance. Nitrates leach out of well-drained soils very readily and only rich loams and clays retain enough. On all other soils, and particularly on open sands and heathy soils, nitrate in some form should be supplied for the first few years. Even on clays, trees of normal vigorous and leafy growth like poplars, willows and wing-nuts will benefit from nitrate. Eucalypts, on the other hand, do not; they have low nutrient requirements and, providing they have a root-run completely clear of vegetation for two or three years, will manage best on their own, as will alders, locust trees and other legumes which equip themselves with bacteria in nodules on their roots for these extract nitrogen from the air. On sandy soils all other trees show clearly the good effects of nitrates. Larches, spruces and many silver firs amongst conifers grow much faster if given nitrate. Leaching away as it does, nitrate needs to be given when it can be taken up immediately by the tree, which is from about early April. The only way in which a tree planted in the autumn can be given useful nitrate at planting is by mixing bone-meal with the soil as this releases the nitrogen slowly.

Four points arise in the use of nitrates. Firstly, grasses, nettles, docks and other weeds will spring up and, if left, will take the nitrate before the tree can, so the root-run must be kept clear of coarse growth. Secondly, because nitrates wash out rapidly a dose in April will not be of great help by late May, when the greatest growth is made by many trees, so there needs to be another dose in early May. Trees with continued growth like poplars and larches, Sequoias and hemlocks will need at least one more dose. If there have been heavy rainfalls from thunderstorms in July, a further application may be needed. Thirdly, an overdose of nitrates can cause serious scorch and death of roots. Apart from keeping strictly to the recommended dose, a safeguard is to place the fertilizer in a band on each side of the tree, leaving a good space between. If too much has been given, the roots in the middle will survive and feed at the edges where the concentration is not lethal. If the right amount is given the roots will forage into the treated bands from each side. Fourthly, tender trees can be kept in growth later than is wise if given nitrogen after early summer, whereas they need to stop before the first frosts to harden off the growth for the winter. Catalpa and Paulownia are probably little affected as they will grow on anyway and lose a varying amount of the tips of shoots every winter so they may as well grow as fast as possible while they can.

The last of the three major nutrients is potash, K, which is needed for flower and fruit production, ripening and hardening off, and resistance to disease in general. It is seldom really short in garden soils except on the poorest parts of Bagshot Sands and Lower Greensand where the little reddish Sheep-sorrel (*Rumex acetosella*) ramps in the flower-beds. On such a soil, annuals like Petunia and Nemesia turn reddish, remain stunted and flower little. It is, however, very noticeable that growth of weeds of a more demanding kind than sorrel is always especially lush around the bonfire site; wood-ash is rich in K.

Potash, it will be seen, in most ways works as a curb on the action of the nitrates, and vice-versa; their effects are opposed. Where nitrates promote shoot and leaf growth at the expense of flowers and fruit, and soft growth, liable to fungal disease, potash promotes flowers and fruit at the expense of foliage, stops late growth and hardens it against disease. This state of affairs demonstrates a vital factor in fertilizing – the nutrients must be balanced. Excess or shortage are equally undesirable for good growth and a balance among the main nutrients, N, P, and K, must be the aim.

This is simple to achieve through the use of balanced fertilizers, which are easily obtained. For general use on a soil not obviously lacking any particular element, a fertilizer like National Growmore does well. For sandy, light soils short of nitrate, a formula relatively high in N is needed for early growth. N is the first of the three figures given in the formula on the pack, so a fertilizer labelled 30, 15, 15 will be high in N content. The K and P content is usually adequate. At planting, bone-meal is highly beneficial because, as explained earlier, the nitrate leaches away more slowly in this form than in the more soluble forms which are given when growth has started, and yields a trace of P as well.

A tree established for a few years is self-sufficient on most soils but on poor sands those with high demands like poplars, Silver firs and larches respond visibly to a high N fertilizer for several more years, whilst the roots are mostly within a circle of manageable size. Later on they may still respond, but grasses will take much of the fertilizer and it becomes expensive to sprinkle the wide area needed to be effective.

Senility can set in at almost any time in the life of a tree. It is when the tree can no longer exploit the site sufficiently to maintain strong growth in the face of conditions of soil, exposure, pollution, poor drainage or other deleterious factors, and the many diseases always awaiting this time, that senility can no longer be held at bay. When a tree looks as if it may soon die, it usually will. It is a big organism to handle and the factors causing the failure are mostly beyond control. If, however, one adverse factor is shortage of nutrient, possibly through long years of closely-mown lawn over the root-run with consequent removal of nutrients without replacement, fertilization may help the tree to better health and growth, and prolong its life. This is given by tree-surgeons, often to Cedars of Lebanon which are so frequently grown on old, much mown lawns. If the fertilizer were spread normally over the root-run, the grass would respond first, taking nearly all the nutrient, and this would be removed as before by mowing. There would be a ring of rich-coloured grass around the tree which would spoil the uniformity desired in such a lawn. The fertilizer, a high nitrogen form, is therefore placed at the bottom of a series of holes drilled in the area of the root-run. The active feeding roots of a big tree are nearly all rather beyond the spread of the crown, and so there is little point in putting fertilizer closer to the bole where drilling holes brings the risk of damaging important roots.

Work by Dr. Alex Shigo throws doubt on the benefits of any fertilizer at planting time or in the backfill, and they are now used less.

Pruning and Not Pruning Trees

Arboricultural pruning is quite different from that done in the orchard and shrubbery to promote larger and fewer flowers and fruit within easy reach, and is very much simpler to carry out. There are only two aims, one of which – to promote a strong single central stem and shapely crown – the tree should be capable of achieving by itself. The other is to achieve rapidly a straight smooth clean stem uncluttered by shaded-out twigs and heavy low branches.

A young tree lays down the future potential of its crown in its first few years. In most trees, and all of large final stature, this depends on the rapid early growth natural to a tree. The main branches will thus be well separated and if, as in many conifers, these are in annual whorls there will be about 1 m between the whorls. The tree must therefore be planted out when small and young and it must have a good, strong leading shoot from the start. Only if the leading shoot fails, or forks into two, or when an extra strong shoot grows out at an awkward angle, does pruning become necessary. Many trees when young will replace a failed leading shoot and only dead wood needs to be cut out. Eucalypts are excellent at this at any age and larches are good at replacement when young but silver firs, spruces, oaks and maples may need some help. Where two or more new shoots compete as leaders, the strongest and straightest (a balance between the two factors may have to be struck) will be selected and the others cut out. Oaks usually benefit from being cut back hard or even to the base if growth is twiggy and without a central stem.

It is essential to keep a tree to a single central stem. Failure to achieve this, and to remove early any heavy low branches, has left us with innumerable monstrous, shapeless, branchy old trees with boles hidden in dense masses of dead shoots and crowns being broken by every gale. They are a travesty of the noble specimens that they could have been with a little attention in their early years.

Nearly all trees grow naturally in groups or in woods and it is normal for the lower branches to be shaded out and die and then to fall, leaving a clean stem. In amenity planting many trees are grown in the open. The interior of the lower branches dies but the tips are still in the light and continue to grow, although often feebly, and this keeps the branches alive and prevents their being shed. The result is a bole cluttered with masses of dead twigs over an area which cannot be reached and which becomes a thicket of nettles, elderberry and brambles and a haven for rabbits. The tree needs help in shedding these useless shoots and the earlier it is given, the better. Even when a tree on a lawn is required to be 'furnished to the ground', it does this best and with more luxuriant foliage when the bottom 2 m of the stem are clean and the branches arising above bend to the ground under their own weight, unhampered by a mass of nearly dead branches beneath them. The bole will then have space around it which can be kept clear of weeds, and the low foliage benefits from the light and air.

Trees other than lawn specimens, and particularly trees grown among shrubs or in groups, need to have their crowns raised and to make the clean straight boles which are their unique contribution to the garden, as soon as possible. It does a tree no perceptible harm to remove a third of its crown and this should be the aim, starting by cleaning 1 m of bole when the tree is 3 m high and probably ending with 3 m clear, from ground level, on a 9 m tree. The advantages are many. The shoots cut off close to (but not flush with) the bole are small and the scars heal within a year and need no treatment at all. The bark can then show its features. Birches, often grown for their bark, smooth over and turn white more quickly when well exposed to sun and wind. Larches attain within a few years attractive clean stems and hemlocks too make smooth boles, whereas if not cleaned they are ribbed and with pockets under the branches. Sequoias and Crytomerias are early to show their red bark on smooth clean boles and in all cases the space around the tree becomes available for planting, mowing or walking. The tree should then mature without further help into a shapely specimen.

Pruning of trees by constant cutting back of branches is a necessity in the shaping of pleached allees, topiary and similar features but in other places the need for shaping is a sign that the wrong tree has been planted. In streets the London plane and the Common lime, being two of the biggest trees we can grow, need some control, but should never have been planted in the first place. The French prune their planes to provide summer shade and an open sky in winter, and some English villages make a feature of mop-headed limes cut back hard every year, but these are special cases. A tree should be chosen for a site where its normal growth will not cause obstruction, and no other form of pruning should be required but the cleaning up of the bole. Dead wood need only be removed where public safety is in danger or where a prematurely dead or broken branch is unsightly or liable to cause damage; it is part of the ecology of woodland and encourages woodpeckers, beetles and fungi which do no harm to the rest of the tree.

Ivy

The growth of ivy on trees causes frequent worry and may lead to well-meant expeditions to cut it away from roadside and other trees. These are inspired by the mistaken idea that ivy kills trees. It is noted that, in general, healthy trees have little or no ivy, sickly and senile ones have a fair quantity depending on how feeble they are, while dead trees are festooned with it. Exactly so. But could this be not because the ivy is killing the tree, but – an equally rational explanation – because a healthy tree shades its bole strongly in the growing season and prevents the growth of ivy? As it weakens it lets in more light, and when it dies the ivy can luxuriate.

In support of this interpretation, it is commonly evident that the Ash with its late and light crown supports a vigorous growth of ivy and the Beech casting heavy shade for longer seldom has more than a few thin shoots, but broadly speaking the Ash and Beech have the same life-span of about 250 years. If strong growth of ivy were lethal this would be unlikely. Ivy is not a parasite, it merely clings to the tree. Its roots offer no significant competition to a tree, and much less than from grass or other trees.

It will be maintained that a tree bound in a corset of interlocked ivy stems is strangled. But when it is recalled how a tree treats a wall, paving or other resistant object pressing on its expanding bole, it seems unlikely that the ivy stems can resist significantly. A Coast redwood strongly invested by trunks of ivy in Ireland increased in diameter in nine years by 19 cm.

Whether or not to remove ivy is a matter of aesthetics, together with a large element of conservation. A fine bole has its looks spoiled; attractive bark is hidden. In general specimen trees should be kept free, especially those prominent on a lawn, but countryside and woodland trees should be left to grow ivy. In a country with very few native evergreens, thick ivy is a vital winter refuge for insects and birds. As well as being important for nesting birds, its late flowers provide insects with the last nectar of the year, enabling fruit to ripen throughout the winter to feed birds in hard times. Deer browse ivy; the trailing stems on the ground hold snow, keep the soil warm and allow small mammals to burrow. Ivy is therefore a valuable plant in woodland ecology.

Landscaping with Trees

Planning

With very few exceptions, trees need full light overhead in order to grow properly and in any case the taller-growing ones will need clear space above into which to grow. A shady corner under other trees is thus not the place to plant a new one, as well as being dry both from the shading and from the mass of roots of the old trees.

The site for a new tree must be able to contain the tree without constricting its natural spread until it is a reasonable age. The spread of a tree at maturity is often given in order to help planters in this way, but only in those trees of fixed, rather formal shape, most of which are conifers, will the figures be of much use. In others, the ultimate spread depends on the individual tree and on its surroundings. It is easily seen that oaks in a wood take up the space available whereas oaks in open parkland, unhindered by any others, vary from being rather less broad than their height to enormously spreading with long low branches and two or three times as broad as tall. Cedars of Lebanon are equally variable, also Sweet chestnuts and many others.

So 'reasonable age' can be interpreted to mean long enough for the tree to show itself as an individual, displaying its unique features before it merges with others to form a patch of woodland and, most important, for it to grow sufficiently tall not to be shaded out and killed. Twenty years of growth without the lower crown tangling and competing with a neighbour seems reasonable for a tree other than one intended to be a solitary feature for its life.

There are two opposing approaches to the spacing of trees at planting. Initial planting can be at the distances required by the trees when they are fully mature, or it can be at very much closer spacing. Planting for the ultimate size usually means leaving a space of 20–30 m clear round each plant, and restricts the number of trees per hectare to 30 or less; but it does permit the tree unhindered growth throughout its life and avoids the possibility of valuable specimens having to be felled for the benefit of the others. It is the course adopted by those managing extensive areas with a future as secure as any can be. It is not attractive as a planting for many, many years but this is remedied by interplanting with numerous shrubs and small-growing and perhaps short-lived trees not intended to form part of the eventual grove.

Those with limited land and a less assured future for their planting will prefer closer planting. One of the purest pleasures of a gardener is to see a tree he has planted growing rapidly into a fine specimen. To limit himself to a single tree where a dozen could be planted, in deference to possible problems 80 years hence, is not so desirable when a new road or his successors may well destroy it before 20 years have passed. There is no better way of knowing and appreciating a species than to plant and tend one, and an enthusiast will wish to grow as many as possible. The pleasures of growing trees for 20 years will overshadow the possible problems of old age. In any case, many of the trees planted will for one reason or another fail to develop as they should. With Ginkgo and Serbian spruce among other trees, it is advisable to plant five or six to ensure having one of first-class shape. Some deliberate close planting is done with the aim of thinning out trees when they begin to interfere with each other, but proponents of wide planting say that this is the weakness of overplanting – the planter tends not to notice when the trees start to crowd each other, and fails in his resolve when at last it is obvious – or has moved on before the plan is carried out. Only where long-term management is assured, as in an established arboretum, is it considered safe to plant closely.

In practice, the plantsman with limited space usually packs in a huge variety of trees and, by judicious placing of erect and small trees among the others, achieves for his lifetime a planting of endless fascination, which may often prove to have been its most important function. Not every garden needs to, or can, last for ever. Nevertheless, great care is required in tree-planting. It is folly to plant a Black walnut within 10 m of a Hungarian oak, for anyone who can appreciate these trees must know that one or other must be doomed within a few years, thus preventing the proper enjoyment of either. Favourite trees should be set as widely apart as possible and the infilling done with the less choice species which can be sacrificed when their time comes.

Placing

The golden rule is that it is where you do NOT plant that makes or breaks a design. Anyone can plant trees that grow into a wood and lose their individual character and fail to make a good picture. Successful vistas depend on the unplanted areas, the glades and lawns and prospects, and these must be kept open. To look its best, a tree needs to be viewed from varying distances and to develop its crown evenly all round, and both requirements imply absence of other trees from certain areas. Lawns in particular must be kept unplanted and obviously any external vista used in the design needs to be kept clear of trees.

In a large garden, town park or city park, the plantings of trees should never be haphazard. They fall into the two main categories of framework and individual features, both of which will be discussed in the following pages.

Background or Framework Plantings

Every park and garden is an entity and needs to define itself from what lies beyond. Its very existence as a park or garden assumes an inherent difference in land use from that adjacent. In all cases there will be a need for visual emphasis towards the boundary to some extent. Town and city parks are intended to be as different as possible from the urban scene and the world outside should obtrude as little as can be arranged. Hyde Park and Kensington Gardens, in London, are large enough to overcome this problem successfully and they are mainly planted around the perimeter with avenues and lines of large trees. These isolate the interiors as rural scenes, from some parts of which no building or other signs of the city can be seen. From most parts, however, and increasingly of late, nearby and even some more distant buildings are tall enough to be seen over the tree screen. This is not as disastrous as it might be, for it serves to emphasise the fact that the parks are in a city and thus to enhance the value of the sylvan landscape within. In a town garden this is less acceptable, but being so much smaller, the boundary trees are closer to the viewpoints and so are more likely to hide even very tall buildings.

Even in a city, there can be vistas towards buildings which enhance rather then detract from the scene. This is particularly true in small parks, for the eye does not like to be boxed in all round, even by trees, if the plantings are obviously screens. It likes to roam outwards at some point to a long sweeping view. St. James's Park, in London, is a good example. Ringed by trees in all but two directions, the view from the bridge to Horseguards Parade and the extraordinary cupolas of Whitehall buildings, and the smaller views of Buckingham Palace at the other end of the park, are triumphs of design in a city park. In a country garden any reasonably pleasant outward prospect will be seized upon and no boundary-marking planting should obtrude to spoil the sense of space it gives. The more closed, short-vista, internally designed the garden, the more one appreciates the long external vista, however unspectacular it may be. Even in the 48-hectare arboretum at Westonbirt, which has no real external vistas and is designed around broad and narrow rides, two of considerable length and width, one can feel very enclosed. Hence, the northern end of Holford Ride is left quite open, looking out over very ordinary fields to a skyline a mile distant, a view of little merit but like a breath of fresh air to those who come upon it from the close plantings nearby. It also serves to emphasise that these groves and glades are in open agricultural land and were pasture before they were planted.

Boundary plantings are thus of vital importance in the layout and concept of parks and gardens, especially when these are in surroundings of very different land-use, but their absence in well-chosen parts can be equally important. Sometimes a large garden may be laid out in a well-wooded area and intended to be an extension of, rather than a contrast to, its surroundings. In such cases, there is not only no point in defining the boundary but it is positively undesirable to do so except perhaps at points of entrance to the garden. The design of such a garden is an interesting exercise because there has to be a gradual change in the kind of tree planted in order to blend the ordinary countryside tree of the outlying parts harmoniously with the more highly coloured foliages and flowers of the exotics and cultivars generally required in the part of the garden nearer the house. Very useful in this context are the fastigiate and weeping forms of the common trees, for whilst they share the foliage and the seasonal colouring of the wild trees, their shapes show that the change to decorative planting has begun. For example, in a beechwood area, a pair of Dawyck beech, one each side of a path, gate or approach to a bridge, blends perfectly with the beechwoods but has a formal, flame-like shape which makes a point of emphasis. The Hornbeam 'Fastigiata' and the Cypress oak, in their appropriate settings, are other examples. The weeping beech, 'Pendula', should be a little nearer the house, for it is more at home in gardens and amongst those trees which are, properly speaking, exotics, like the Norway and Oregon maples, the

Italian alder, Sweet chestnut and Hungarian oak, but which blend well with the true natives. The Red oak and Horse chestnut belong more in the truly decorative garden area nearest the house, where all variegated, golden, silver, and, if they must be included, purple-leafed trees should be strictly confined.

The framework includes not only the boundary but the main blocks of internal planting such as clumps, roundels and woods, which are essential in a big park or garden to avoid having a well planted boundary surrounding a field-like interior spotted with single trees. Part of the land can, of course, be 'Old English Parkland' planting, the essence of which is widely separated trees of the largest ultimate size for the main planting, with a few of moderate size for variety, all needing to be spaced so that when fully grown there is nearly everywhere more space between the crowns than their width. In strictly rural surroundings, these parkland trees will be Oak, Beech, Ash, Lime or (formerly) Elm, but elsewhere many exotic species are used to great effect. Surprisingly, rural parkland quite often features cedars and Giant Sequoias as well as more homely-looking deciduous exotics like Sweet chestnut, Sycamore, Larch and Walnut. For the best development of parkland planting there need to be cattle grazing, keeping the crowns of the trees trimmed (if inelegantly) at about 2 m up, and making mowing unnecessary. If, in addition, all selective weedkiller sprays can be banned from the area, the grazing cattle, unlike the mower, will create or preserve a sward rich in wildflowers which further contributes to the parkland scene.

Apart from areas of parkland planting, every large space requires some true woodland, partly as a delightful form of landscape in which to walk, partly for the wildlife it can support, and partly as a contrast to the wide areas of open grassland necessary for vistas and also, in parks, for recreation. These woodlands and clumps are the main landscape features made by the trees and their siting is very important. Different species will be needed for different sites, and their choice will also depend upon the sort of countryside nearby or, in towns, on the soil. Low, rounded hills look well crowned with a wood, but only in beech country, and sparingly there, should this be a neat roundel. Normally the wood should sweep down the steepest slope as well. Banks and ridges are also places for woods, some ridges planted all over but others with the woodland stopping at the crest on one side. Valleys, too, should have woods as these will be much richer in wildflowers and hence all forms of wildlife, especially if there is a stream. Paths should, in this case, be kept away from and above the stream as much as possible, mainly in order to keep the valley bottom as an untrodden sanctuary, but also because they will become muddy and thus gradually broader as people pick a less trodden way.

When planting woodland in a flat, open area, the main point to remember is that this must have a definite minimum size in order to look like woodland and not just a mass of trees. The edge effects of light and wind penetrate 50 or 60 metres into most woodlands and only in areas beyond this are the conditions truly woodland. In such open-crowned species as Birch and Ash, there is little difference between edge and centre. For most purposes woods need to be planted in fairly solid blocks of at least 1 hectare. Another point to bear in mind is that glades are the most attractive parts of woodland to wildlife and humans, and therefore winding, or at least curved, fairly wide grassy paths and a few broader glades should be planned in even the smallest wood. It is too seldom realised that trees alone are of minor importance to the songbirds that we wish to encourage. Nearly all of these are birds of woodland edge or scrub and nest in long grass, brambles and thickets, even if they feed partly in the crowns of trees. It is therefore necessary to have some areas as sanctuaries in the open land adjacent to woods in the breeding season.

Since framework trees are features in large-scale landscapes, as distinct from ornamental gardens, they need to be in conformity with their surroundings if rural, or to create an appearance of natural countryside if urban. This means that they must either be native trees, or trees that so resemble natives that they are acceptable as such, or trees so long introduced and so widely planted in the countryside that they are regarded as part of the rural scene. No fancy-coloured

leaves or spectacular flowers, then, in the background trees. For the same reason, plantings will be bold – large numbers of a single species should be the rule, but mixtures, fairly uniform in composition, can suit certain soils and districts. The notable example is in areas on, or marginal to, chalklands where Beech grows with Whitebeam and Gean at the edges, whereas Ash keeps largely to richer, damper soils and is best not mixed with Beech although also a chalkland tree.

The ban on overt exotics can also be breached to advantage in some circumstances. In Perthshire, Argyll and Inverness-shire especially, the dominance of conifers often looks right and large numbers of western American and some Himalayan conifers grow as well here as in any part of the world. They grow remarkably rapidly and remain shapely and dense and are thus of great value in garden design. By the mischances of geological history, this supreme area for the growth of spruces, hemlocks and Silver firs, has only one native conifer of stature, the Scots pine, which can hardly be put to the same uses. Although conifers in general are not well adapted to towns, parks and gardens in small towns or even cities grow some excellent specimens. Both here and, even more, in large rural gardens the framework trees can include generous plantings of Western hemlock, thuja, Silver fir, Sequoias, Douglas fir and others.

Large-scale Features

In planning an extensive prospect it is important that the main features, or framework, should be on a proportionately bold scale. A single tree of the largest size may sometimes be required, such as for a skyline feature, the crown of a bare knoll, the end of a lake, the centre of a glade or at a large cross-rides. To carry off such a solitary position, a tree must not only be capable of reaching a large size, and that as soon as possible, but it must have durability and good health and, very important in the circumstances mentioned, it must have character. Big trees are also necessary in lining or defining a long glade and particularly in narrowing a glade with false-perspective, for the effect is greatest at the most distant point and will be lost unless the trees are prominent. The trees chosen for a long avenue must be of the largest ultimate stature too, as should those of background plantings. If the species chosen for clumps and roundels are, like the larches, of only moderately large growth, the area of each should be increased to avoid a spotty effect and, in the case of a roundel on a knoll, to clothe the upper slopes and prevent it being a mere tuft on the top.

Screens and Eye-catchers

Where a distant prospect is of countryside or sea it will of course be preserved except where it is necessary to keep out strong winds, and the more enclosed the garden or park, the more valuable is the occasional distant view. Where, however, the nearer parts of the outer world include too many pylons or too much industry or housing to be acceptable as a prospect, some planting to lessen its impact will be needed.

Old estates and gardens secluded themselves with broad belts of beech, larch, Austrian pine and Turkey oak – fast-growing, cheap and reliable trees – and on the largest scale this approach, with variation in the species, is sound. The belts are broad enough to absorb the occasional loss of trees which will inevitably be blown down when a solid belt is athwart strong winds. On a less grand scale, the tendency today is to plant a narrow belt of evergreen conifers, usually Thuja or a cypress, but this has much to be said against it.

In the first place, a solid wall of foliage creates strong eddies of wind around its edges and over the top, and actually increases locally the speed of the wind. Secondly, a narrow belt will suffer damage and random losses when gusts cannot penetrate the dense foliage and so exert sudden high pressures. Thirdly, a uniform line of cypress or thuja foliage is dull and monotonous and not what one would choose for an end to a vista. And this leads to the last demerit of such a screen; it baulks the eye, and having no visual interest itself, invites curiosity as to what is hidden beyond the screen.

A filter rather than a barrier has none of these drawbacks. However unsightly the scene may be to open viewing, when broken into segments by a series of attractive features in the middle ground it is reduced to an unobtrusive back-cloth. The eye can range beyond the features at will and use the background for distancing, but it is continually drawn back to the decorative plantings. The wind filters through the gaps without building up damaging speeds or pressures, and each group of trees can be varied and attractive in shape and colour. Some industrial objects seen from a distance framed by trees make interesting features, adding to the character of the garden and emphasizing its contrasting form and purpose. A group of cooling towers or the silver-painted labyrinthine pipework and towers of a refinery do not have to be hidden completely, but can be used as distant features, so long as the eye is drawn preferentially to the nearer garden scenery.

An effective eye-catcher is created by contrasting colours and forms. With the general aspect of trees being one of greens and of rounded shapes, the necessary contrasts come from golden, blue, erect, spire-form and weeping trees. They will be in groups which at maturity fill about half the prospect. However, this will take time and during the early years a greater coverage may be required. The final groups can be augmented either by intermediate groups of fast-growing trees, to be removed before they merge with those intended to remain, or by enlarging the final groups with temporary plantings that are removed before they affect the crowns of the desired trees.

Where a large building is too close and too big to be effectively screened it is much better not to attempt to obscure the lower parts by a line of trees, as is often seen. Groups of decorative trees are needed, to draw the eye away from the building and to create different planes of interest to give varying depths in front.

Since the prospects considered unpleasing and requiring diversion of the eye are inevitably not rural ones, there is no restriction to countryside trees for the planting. This is as well for the most effective trees will be exotic evergreens and of columnar, conic or other distinct shape and of the tallest growth.

Wind-breaks

It has been noted above that a solid line of evergreen trees is not an effective method of giving shelter from wind. Experiments have proved that the effect of the wind-break in reducing the speed of the wind extends furthest from the planting when the shelter-belt is about half-permeable; the gaps being equal to the barriers. Wind-breaks can thus be treated in the same way as is recommended for screens, but they may also be needed more for their practical effect than for beauty. If that is the case, the structure will be the same – spaced groups in limited areas, and broad belts where space is no problem – but the species will be different. There will be no reason to avoid more uniform plantings and they can be entirely of species which give rapid and effective shelter. In exposure to sea-winds these are Monterey and Bishop pines for early effect and Holm oak for long-term. Monterey cypress tends to be vulnerable to windthrow when grown in groups but is more stable on its own when it makes a hugely broad tree in western areas. Leyland cypress is also liable to be unstable but usually only where the soil is shallow or where it has been planted in a line. Its foliage is thicker and creates more of a barrier than that of the Monterey cypress or the two pines mentioned, so it must be planted in small groups.

Deciduous trees give adequate shelter to crops and other plants which are dormant in winter. Hop-gardens are often surrounded by poplars and alders which provide shelter when it is most needed, in the growing season. Even when bare, deciduous trees break the force of the wind significantly and a broad belt of Beech, Larch or Birch has a beneficial effect over a great distance. In a new and exposed garden, deciduous trees are invaluable for early and temporary shelter. Vigorous and rugged pioneer species like Larch, Birch and Sallow are cheap and easily found and give early shelter with minimum summer shade, allowing main plantings to be made reasonably close to them and so not interfering with the final plan. They will be removed when the permanent shelter trees have grown enough to be effective.

An evergreen plant is at a disadvantage in the winter, when it has to withstand freezing and drying winds, making a number of desirable trees tender as garden subjects. The areas in which such trees as *Michelea*, *Drimys* and *Pittosporum* can be grown is much extended by providing them with shelter against winds from the north and east, and this shelter also has to be evergreen since it is needed in winter and, even more, in spring. Abbotsbury Garden in Dorset relies on old-established belts and woods of Holm oak. Westonbirt, at 120 m altitude in Gloucestershire, was from the beginning given a northern edge of Yew, Holly and Cherry-laurel to which were added later Lawson and Leyland cypresses. The problems arise where space does not permit the generous widths of shelter plantings which are available in such large gardens.

The commonly seen single line of trees, with all its disadvantages, is presumably kept to this minimum width in order to allow as much room as possible for the decorative plantings for which the shelter is grown. This is treating the wind-break as a practical feature only and not as an adornment in itself. If, on the other hand, it is made into a decorative feature and viewed as an integral part of the garden scheme, there will rarely be any need to reduce it to a single line. Where space is severely limited, broadleafed trees, deciduous or evergreen, are unsuitable because of their normally spreading crowns. Any deciduous tree needed for variety has to be a larch or Metasequoia. The line, as explained, must be broken up so that about one half is open space and the other half foliage. Fortunately, the best trees for this purpose have conic crowns and this allows the desired ratio to be achieved with the tapering tops forming less than half of the wind-break while the bases occupy more than half, providing shelter where it is most needed. By using such conic trees as the Golden-barred thuja and many of the best coloured forms of Lawson cypress, three-quarters of the boundary can be planted yet never grow to present more than half a solid barrier to the wind. It will also make a more effective feature when young if planted in this way than if only half the line had been planted. In any but the shortest belts the planted lengths should be varied and the spacing between them irregular; again, the use of conic trees allows more scope as a larger number can be planted than with trees of a less compact shape.

Where space can be made, at least in parts, for more than a single row of trees, it is very much easier to plan an effective and attractive wind-break. The ideal is to have varied clumps. A clump is able to withstand a degree of failure and loss without becoming ineffective whereas a line of trees can be ruined by the loss of a single one. A clump allows great variety in shape, texture and colour, and helps to create a wind-break that is less of a utilitarian necessity of no interest and more of an arboretum and a major feature. The more strikingly-coloured conifers which are so useful for eye-catching and shelter plantings are, on the whole, not among the fastest growers, but early rapid growth is of value in shelter and screen plantings. Each clump should therefore include one or more specimens of very rapid growth on the outer or windward side of the colour feature. Unless the clump be large, the need to avoid shading or crowding the other trees will rule out the use of Monterey pine and most of the poplars, but some eucalypts, the 'TT' hybrid Balsam poplars and Grand fir will be less spreading. Because rapid growth is important in shelter plantings generally, the best trees with this ability are given in the following section.

Trees of Very Rapid Growth

The fastest growths recorded for a number of trees in Britain and Ireland may be useful to those who wish to see quick results. Nearly all trees grow much faster than is commonly realised and some examples are given to show the extraordinary rates attained by a few of the fastest at their best.

The eucalypts as a group lead the field. Blue gum has grown 12 m in four years on the Isle of Man and 14·5 m in five years in County Kerry. On the Isle of Wight it was 19·5 m × 48 cm when nine years from seed and in County Down it was 21·5 in 14 years. Shining gum is much hardier and nearly as fast; in Cornwall one grew 13 m in

five years and in Argyll one was 20 m in nine years. Even the common, hardy Cider gum has grown 17 m in seven years at Kew and 22 m in 12 years in Cornwall. The 'Robusta' poplar is not far behind, with one 16 years old and 24 m tall in Kent and one 31 m in 23 years in Hereford, where a hybrid Balsam poplar is 21 m in 13 years. Cricket-bat willow must be grown fast to be of use as timber and may start at 9 m in five years and be 21 m in 16 years.

Some of the Chilean Southern beeches grow rapidly. A Rauli in the Isle of Man was 7 m after three years and two trees in Devon were 15 m after nine years from seed. An annual shoot of 2 m is seen on some young specimens. A Roblé beech in Windsor Park was 21 m when planted 14 years and 26 m in 22 years. The Hybrid wing-nut is remarkable for the size of the bole as well as for height; one in Gloucestershire was 11 m in 12 years, and another is nearly 20 m × 70 cm in 30 years. At Kew, when planted 23 years, the Hybrid wing-nut was 19 m × 67 cm and when 36 years old was 25 m × 85 cm. A Chestnut-leafed oak nearby, planted in 1953, is 21 m × 1 m and one at Westonbirt, 24 years planted, is 20 m × 40 cm.

Conifers excel in rapid growth to 30, 40 or 50 m because their pattern of growth often relies on a persistent central stem, a habit soon lost by most broadleafed trees well before such heights, except in the eucalypts. In early growth few conifers are outstanding. A Coast redwood in the New Forest is 37 m × 92 cm 35 years after planting. A Monterey pine in Kent grew to 17 m in 15 years and one in Surrey was 28 m in 34 years, but they often start with 9 m in ten years before slowing down. The Dawn redwood usually grows 1 m a year on a damp sheltered site. Leyland cypress is well-known for its 1 m a year growth for many years; one at Westonbirt is 11 m after nine years and one at Windsor was 15 m in 14 years and 23 m in 26 years. In Kent it has reached almost 30 m in 45 years and the tallest Leyland cypress, in Devon, is 34 m high at 61 years old.

For reasonably rapid growth continued well above 40 m, there are none to compare with the three forestry species, Grand fir, Douglas fir and

Sitka spruce. Grand firs often have leading shoots of 1·3 m and reach 20 m in 20 years. One in Powys was 31 m after 38 years; one in Perth is 44 m in 50 years, and in Inverness-shire a Grand fir 56 m tall is 98 years old. Douglas fir have exceeded 31 m in 29 years. In Perthshire one 67 years old was 50 m tall and in Moniac Glen, Inverness-shire, a grove of 98 years old is mostly of trees 55–58 m tall. A Sitka spruce in north Wales was 21 m tall in 23 years while one in Somerset was 33 m at 31 years and grew on to be 42 m when 47 years old. A giant Sitka in Inverness-shire is 50 m tall when 103 years old, and typical of several in northern Scotland.

The Bishop pine, in the blue form from its more northerly stands in California, has made exceptional growth on very poor, silty soils here for some years but does not in the end become a very tall tree. Trees three and four years old were growing 2 m in a year but when 20 years old they were only 20 m tall. Western hemlock, on a damp site in some shade either on sand or clay, can add 1·3 m a year for many years and also attain 20 m in 20 years but, unlike the Bishop and Monterey pines which seldom exceed 30 m at maturity here, this hemlock is still growing fast when 40–45 m tall in parts of Scotland. In exposed, wet western areas on peat, the Shore pine is for some years as fast as any tree, sometimes adding 1·5 m in a year, and invaluable for early shelter in those parts.

The three common larch species make shoots of 1–1·4 m in good conditions, but again only for a few years. A European larch in Powys is exceptional in growing 16 m in 14 years, as are a Hybrid larch of 12 m in nine years in Surrey and of 19 m in 20 years in Kent. The Monterey cypress starts off with great speed in western parts and slows down when about 25 m tall. One in Devon was 32 m in 41 years.

A few broadleafed trees also grow very rapidly in their early years but then increase very slowly and remain of but moderate size. These are obviously useful in a small garden or in limited space. Several snake-bark maples, notably *Acer davidii* and *A. hersii*, soon make shoots 1·3 m long but within a few years these arch over and the tree may be only 9 m tall when 30 years old. The

Violet willow and the Bowles's Hybrid willow will grow 2–3 m shoots from a cut-back shoot in one year. Left to itself this grows only 20–30 cm in succeeding years, but cut to base it will again grow up to 3 m. The same effect can be produced by cutting back two- or three-year-old plants of Paulownia and Tree of Heaven, and should certainly be applied to any specimen of these trees which has made poor growth. The new shoots will be 2–2·5 m long, very stout and bearing huge leaves. All the Black poplar hybrids will grow from stumped-back plants and make new shoots over 2 m long but numerous shoots arise and, unless required for shelter rather than as trees, only one should be allowed to grow on.

Lines

Single lines of trees are often loosely referred to as avenues, and whilst sharing most of the same needs as to species there is one difference which makes it worth discussing lines as separate forms of planting. Whilst an avenue should be planted with consideration of the path or road between the trees, the same does not apply to a line where lightness need not be the main factor in determining the choice of tree and the spacing.

The hedgerow approach with trees of mixed stature, form and spacing is the best way of planting a belt of trees when an avenue is desired but only one side of the thoroughfare can be planted. A line can also be a good feature in the case of a hillside of beechwoods or other high forest ending at the base to fringe fields. If the wood is liable to be felled, a permanent line along the base softens the sudden clearance and strengthens the line of the contour and division between field and wood or scrub. In the lowlands broadleafed trees would be preferable, with Small-leafed lime, Beech and Oak among the first choices, while in the hills, Western hemlock or Giant Sequoia are probably best, although Douglas fir is often a good choice and Silver fir, Norway spruce and Thuja may be seen.

Large-scale lines, that is, anything more than about 200 m long, should be uniform in species. Alternating two species looks fussy on a large scale and a change of species every 20 trees or so is disruptive to the line as a feature. Also, it is easy to thin a uniform line by removing alternate trees and impossible to do this to an alternating one while retaining both species.

Unlike avenues, lines can be regenerated, although not easily, requiring little additional space. This calls for the removal of alternate trees or better, two trees out of every three, and replanting in their spaces. Only if the trees were planted close and cast heavy shade will the new planting need to be moved a few metres out of line in order to have more light. With broadleafed trees, however, this course is undesirable as the new trees will lean away from the line. The trees recommended for planting in lines are detailed on page 44 ff.

Avenues

These may be twin lines of trees, or trees planted in four, five, or even six rows. The largest avenue planted in recent years, that from Windsor Castle to the Bronze Horse statue nearly three miles away, is made up of individual, spaced trees. Really large avenues, certainly those of conifers, can be planted using spaced clumps of trees to great advantage. Firstly, clumps are accident-proof, the loss or partial failure of a tree here and there having no real effect on the planting as a whole, whereas long lines of individual trees depend on 100 per cent success and good growth; the loss, or even stunted growth, of a single tree can spoil a whole avenue. Secondly, the effect on the road can be regulated more easily with clumps, as the spacing between them controls the amount of light and sunshine let in – a particularly important consideration with conifers (except Yew – and a half-mile tunnel through yews is difficult to imagine) which make wall-sides to the road instead.

It should be appreciated that avenues, like the beech roundels on hilltops, cannot be regenerated. They must be started again. If at least one avenue is desired to be always in good order, a new one should be planted at about the half-life of the old. The fact that an old avenue cannot be restored or repaired, short of clear felling and replanting, is not generally realised by the public and this causes

problems in the management of the Royal Parks. It was recently felt that the avenue in Hyde Park should not have the middle section felled, yet some of the elms were dead and others dying. Replacements in the form of Cornish elm were planted but could not be put under the canopy of the old trees, so had to be placed near its edge; even so, they need constant freeing from the shade cast by the old trees and many of them are leaning. In Greenwich Park the Sweet chestnut avenues give the same problem, whilst it has been decided that at Osborne House, Isle of Wight, no attempt will be made to rejuvenate the Lucombe oak avenue but another shall be planted elsewhere to replace it, in time.

Large avenues can be uniform in species or mixed. In a rural landscape, where the large features are required to conform and not to obtrude, the avenue could be of regularly spaced trees of one of the dominant local species, or a tree resembling them, but such an arrangement would, by its very regularity, sometimes be intrusive. In that case, the avenue could either be of the same species but with the trees set in groups, or of a mixture of species in two rows, preferably arranged at random, or in clumps, each one a mixture of species or uniform. Alternating or regular changes of species should be avoided rigorously.

In a more formal or garden context, where conformity with the countryside trees is of no importance, regular spacing is part of the design. However, avenues of half a mile or longer would look better if arranged in clumps, as would a winding drive where there is no view of the length to show the cathedral-nave effect which can be so impressive. The continued lines of single trees, persisting at every turn, can become quite aggravating.

Avenues of conifers of dark aspect and narrow crowns, like the Lawson and Italian cypress, are not normally planned for a large scale, but if they are, the trees at final size must have open space between them equal to the width of their crowns. This gives the maximum aisle effect whilst avoiding the gloomy alley which could so easily be created. Giant Sequoias, however, have sufficiently tapering crowns to be grown so that they are almost touching at the base – which means a spacing of 15 m – and still let in plenty of light.

Broadleafed trees and conifers can be mixed in an avenue, either where a long, informal avenue of mixed species includes a few trees of Scots pine or Atlas cedar, or in a clumped avenue where some of the clumps can be made up of a number of conifers of a stature similar to the other trees.

It is worth repeating that these large-scale avenues should use only trees of large stature. A mile-long avenue of Kanzan cherry would be grossly out of proportion.

Roundels

These are clumps of trees roughly circular in outline and usually crowning a knoll. The traditional roundel is of beech on chalk downlands but in other parts there is an equally old tradition of planting Scots pines on tumps, or Oak, Larch or Birch and, very occasionally, Monkey-puzzle. Beech on top of chalk cannot grow by itself at first, and must have a nurse species to start it off. The famous Chanctonbury Ring in Sussex was started with Scots pine, ash and sycamore nurses and some remain still. The Ministry of Defence plants roundels on Salisbury Plain and finds Lawson cypress the best nurse.

Roundels, like avenues, cannot be regenerated. A clearing large enough to give the light needed by new trees makes the old ones around it highly vulnerable to breakage and blow. The trees suitable need to be windfirm, to reach good stature in sharply drained soil and to make good boles. Beech and Larch are two of the best but in coniferous areas the Giant Sequoia can be most commanding, and the Monkey-puzzle the most unusual.

Lawns and Trees

A lawn is in effect a clearing in the woods, a glade surrounded by trees. It is emphatically not a place for central trees, only peripheral. It must be kept largely open and free from trees to remain a lawn as a feature rather than just an area of mown grass, which is not the same thing. Too many lawns of no great size have a Blue Atlas cedar right in the centre and this will grow to be a very big tree filling much of the air-space and thus obliterate the prime purpose of the lawn. Small lawns are often seen with a central clump of pampas-grass or a small Cherry; these will not grow to undo the effect of the lawn but look just as wrongly placed. The lawns of some mansions have huge Cedars of Lebanon and these only look right if they are isolated from other trees or if they are grouped on either side of a broad open lawn.

It may be that the only site available for a tree is the lawn and in this case the lawn must be encroached upon from its sides. Ideally the surroundings will be big trees outside smaller trees (both in scale with the area of grass) with one or two big trees forward among the smaller, to prevent too much of an arena effect, and the edges should be in generously sweeping bays. The front positions are the sites for trees selected for their good foliage, bark or year-round appearance. A very large lawn can afford a promontory or two of trees with spectacular but short seasons, but of indifferent appearance at other times, like most of the Japanese cherries, but around a small lawn these should be behind low trees or big shrubs good to look at all the summer.

Watersides

A garden lucky enough to have a lake, pool, stream or river needs to make the best use of it. There may be pools or streams already deep in woods and these can be preserved in that state without further attention, but in general watersides do not want to be crowded and hidden. They should be part of the garden or prospect and part of a larger clearing or glade. There is often a natural fringe of alders, which are valuable for attracting redpolls and siskins and for the protection their roots give against erosion of the bank. Alders are not, however, often well-shaped or attractive trees; they never provide any autumn colour other than their customary dark green, and a single waterside line is usually ragged. It is better that such a line straggling across a vista be removed, allowing the prospect to continue over the water; alternatively, a broad opening can be made, with a more decorative tree or group of trees planted on each side of the gap.

A small lake should ideally be set into, or run alongside, a lawn and trees should be kept well clear of it except for one or two specimens towards the distant end. Part of their function is to be seen in reflection, and weeping trees are especially effective in this respect. Autumn colour is also a great advantage. The scheme for a garden confined to one bank of a (usually) broad river must depend considerably on what is on the other side, but however, unprepossessing the outlook it is still better to filter it and allow visual access to the river in places rather than attempt a riverside screen.

The traditional tree for a waterside setting is the Weeping willow and in places none is better. It will weep well over water but surprisingly, in view of how commonly it does so, there is said to be a danger to fish from toxins released by rotting willow leaves. Leaves of any kind are a nuisance, if unavoidable, especially in standing water, and a Weeping willow set back from the edge will weep just as well. The White willow and, especially good for winter colour, its cultivar, the Coral-bark willow, and for speed of growth and upright, light crown, the Cricket-bat willow, all have their places. The Crack willow adds large glossy leaves but tends to an untidy, broad crown. Where the labour is available, the Crack and White willows can be pollarded, that is, cut to about 2·5 m either annually or every few years to create the old riverside scene as in a Bewick woodcut.

A more recent tradition, much observed in town parks, is to plant the Swamp cypress. It is completely at home by the wettest waterside and where flooding is frequent it will often, once 40 years old, produce the familiar wooden 'knees' over quite a distance. It is distinctive although twiggy in winter and it takes a very long winter rest, but it makes up for it by the fresh green delicate foliage after June and late autumn rich foxy red-brown colours.

More recent still is the planting of the related and not dissimilar Dawn redwood by water. It grows best in wet soils, 1 m a year for ten years or more, and has two months or more longer in leaf than the Swamp cypress. In autumn it is coppery-brown, pinkish or deep red.

Poplars are well-known waterside trees but the Lombardy poplar needs to be planted with discretion. Growing rapidly as it does to 30 m tall, one on its own will soon make a small pool look ridiculous. A group on a lawn behind a lake or a single one where a stream enters a fairly large pool are very effective. The Poplar 'Robusta' makes a good alternative although broad-conic and not columnar. It grows even faster than the Lombardy, has large handsome leaves which emerge bright orange-red to brown, and before that it is liberally hung with big dark red catkins.

The Caucasian wing-nut is a splendid tree for a lakeside, but unless kept in check it will need some 50 m of bank to itself for it throws up strong suckers to make a thicket. Its merits are very rapid growth, big compound bright green leaves and bright yellow autumn colour. The Hybrid wing-nut is much the same for this purpose but grows even faster and is eventually taller.

The Sweet gum looks exceptionally well on a lakeside lawn and grows its best there. Given full light it should be a blaze of scarlet or deep red in autumn. Another weeping tree, but much smaller than the willow, is Young's weeping birch, which lends itself to a place beside a small pool to be seen in reflection.

The Golden alder is rare and rather slow but makes a useful change of colour at a lakeside, and the golden form of the Grey alder (*Alnus incana* 'Ramulis Coccineis') although probably more at home where rarely flooded, has the advantages of scarlet winter buds and catkins and less slow growth. The Red maple is a tree of swampy bottoms in North America and while the crown of mature trees is a little untidy and dull in winter, the summer foliage is good and in autumn, given sunshine, it is a fine blaze of yellow, orange and scarlet.

Trees for Special Conditions

Chalk and Limestone

Chalk is a special type of limestone, the youngest and most active one, so if a tree can cope with a chalky soil it will be happy enough on any other limestone. Broadly speaking, the older a limestone is geologically, the less harmful it is to plants which do not thrive on alkaline soils. The Oolitic limestones cropping out as a belt from Dorset to east Yorkshire are some 40 million years older than the chalk of the Cretaceous times and are much less limiting. The Carboniferous limestones of Devon, the Pennines and Ireland are 200 million years older again. In the western Highlands there are bands of limestone nearly twice as old as that and in the prevailing very acid soils in those parts the limestones stand out as oases for plant growth. Alkaline soil also occurs independently of bedrock limestone where soils are currently forming among sand-dunes and have formed recently behind them. The lime here is derived from fragments of shells which make up a small proportion of the sand. Slightly older but still very recent, post-Ice Age limy soils occur when fen-peat has formed in a hollow, even if, as is the case with raised bogs, they were subsequently overlain by acid peats. In Irish 'cut-away' bogs, with the top peats removed for fuel, the remaining basal peat grows good vegetables without needing the addition of any lime. This lime derives from the first waters draining into the hollow having come from and through soils which until then had not had the base salts, including lime, leached from them.

The limiting effects on plant growth of alkaline soils are due to the free lime, which is the calcium ions, making iron less available to plants. Iron is an essential element to plants as it is an ingredient in the vital chlorophyll, the major and distinguishing feature of green plants. When a plant is prevented by too much calcium from obtaining enough iron for the chlorophyll it needs it turns yellow. This is 'lime-induced chlorosis' and is seen where some rhododendrons and certain conifers are grown on shallow soils over chalk. Chlorosis, or yellowing, in general can have other causes, such as bad drainage.

There is great variation among plants in the ability to mobilize and use iron in the presence of calcium. Chalk and limestones have floras of their own. These assemblages of plants can be a mixture of three categories as defined by their attitude to lime in the soil. Some will have a long history of evolving on chalky soils and be so adapted to them that they cannot grow freely on any other. Travellers' joy and even more so, Field scabious, are sure indicators in eastern England of pure chalk close to the surface. They need free lime in the soil and are called 'obligatory calcicoles'. Another group, including the Common ash, needs a base-rich soil for proper development – one where the nutrients either gather or have not yet been leached out – but they will grow for a while, if not very well, in the absence of free lime; these are called 'calcicoles'. The last group, the 'facultative calcicoles', can grow on chalk but they grow equally well in the absence of lime or on acid sands. The Beech and the Lawson cypress are good examples, and there are numerous other trees which are tolerant of a wide range from alkaline to acid soil.

Limestones and chalk are calcium carbonate and this is soluble in very weak acid. Rainfall in pollution-free air becomes faintly acid from the carbon dioxide and from traces of oxides of nitrogen made by lightning, while near cities or in industrial areas it is acidified by sulphur dioxide. Hence the run-off in rivers carries away the lime salts, and other base salts which have been dissolved by the rain, and top-soils become leached, or acidified, by their continued removal. Plant remains breaking down in the litter on top of woodland and field soils produce weak acids which speed this process. Hence all soils have their bases continually removed and will become acid unless they are being derived from a base-rich rock, either a limestone or some ancient schists which contain calcium salts. The process is obviously enhanced by rapid drainage, as in sands, and by high rainfall.

It is important to appreciate that it follows from the above that the surface layers will be rendered acid even when the underlying rock and subsoil are limestone if there is a sufficient depth of freely draining sand above it or of rotting plant remains. There are even small areas of acid, heather-bearing sands on top of the chalk downs. It is also important to realize that the feeding roots of even the biggest trees are confined to within 20–30 cm of the surface. Thus there are many places on chalk or limestone where excellent growth of trees regarded as 'calcifuge' – those plants which cannot grow in limy soils – is possible. A prime example is the St. Clere pinetum at 230 m on the chalk ridge near Wrotham in Kent. In a faint hollow of clay-loam a wide selection of conifers including calcifuge species has made normal and often excellent growth for seventy years. Another is Roche's Arboretum at West Dean on the South Downs where there are Douglas firs to 45 m tall and, just beneath their root-run, chalk that could be used for writing on a blackboard. Extreme calcifuge rhododendrons and other shrubs can, however, run into trouble when grown in artificial peaty acid soil immediately over chalk. During times of drought, the movement of water can be upward and the lime can be brought up to their roots.

A less extreme example is Westonbirt, a vast collection of trees and shrubs established on soils over Oolitic limestone in Gloucestershire. Here the soils vary from almost none, the limestone cropping out in one small area of Silk Wood, to clay-loams and sands to well over 1 m thick. The rhododendrons and more susceptible conifers were planted on the deepest soils but some of the latter were also included in mixed collections in all parts. None has suffered chlorosis and most have grown very well. Now that the tallest-growing conifers, 90–120 years old, have been 40 m and more tall for many years, their tops are dying and many are going back seriously. It is traditional to say that their roots have reached 'something they do not like', in this case the underlying limestone, but this is completely unconvincing. It is unlikely that the roots of a tree of that age will have increased their depth of penetration at all in the last eighty years. They will have extended laterally near the surface all the time, but their sinkers will have been grown in early years. A more likely explanation is that for the last forty years or so their tops have been clear of any surrounding shelter from the general level of tree crowns. They have been projecting into exposure from all quarters on a plateau in an area of but moderate rainfall, and Silver firs and Douglas firs can withstand such conditions for a limited time only. In a high rainfall area like Argyll or with cool, damp summers as in Perthshire, or in shelter, they could remain healthy and grow to much greater heights than can be expected where drying winds are frequent.

The occurrence of calcicoles and calcifuges is very broadly by family or genus. Amongst the conifers there are many genera in which all the species grow well on chalk. The dwarf conifer addict is fortunate here since the calcicole or tolerant genera include most of those with a large array of dwarfs. These are *Cedrus*, *Chamaecyparis*, *Juniperus*, *Taxus* and *Thuja*, to which may be added *Larix* and many species from *Pinus*. The Black pine group, *Pinus nigra* forms and *P. leucodermis*, are particularly good above chalk. Among the Silver firs, the American and Asiatic species are rather calcifuge as is the European *Abies alba* and only the southerly species, Spanish, Algerian and Grecian firs, thrive for long in chalky soils. However, the American Low's fir in particular, and also the Grand fir and the Japanese Nikko fir, all achieve large stature in a very moderate depth of loam or sand over the chalk. Forrest's and allied Chinese firs and Noble fir are best regarded as calcifuge.

Among the spruces the position is similar to that of Silver firs. In general the American species are calcifuge, especially the Sitka spruce, but excepting notably the Colorado spruce and its blue forms. Brewer spruce is thriving in one garden over chalk but cannot be guaranteed to do this. Few of the Asiatic spruces relish a limy soil, the Morinda spruce and the Likiang spruce being perhaps the most tolerant and certainly doing well if there is 30 cm or so of less alkaline soil on top. The Norway spruce has similar needs, but Serbian spruce is native to limestone hills and grows well on anything from chalk to highly acid sand.

The Giant Sequoia or Sierra redwood is scarcely deflected by any type of soil from its normal vigorous growth although it soon becomes thin on shallow soil over chalk if growing on an exposed ridge. The Coast redwood tolerates old limestones much better than it does chalk but needs a damp site even then.

The Swamp cypress and, to a slightly lesser extent, the Dawn redwood are often grown beside water where in any case they grow best. Damp sites in chalk and limestone areas are usually those by a river or lake, and fine specimens of both are seen beside chalk streams, so neither can be called calcifuge. The Monkey-puzzle is fairly tolerant but not of very shallow soil over chalk. With the minor, but delightful, exception of the Mountain hemlock, the genus *Tsuga* is distinctly calcifuge.

The cypresses are generally able to grow well on any soil. The Arizona cypress is equally at home on very alkaline and very acid soils and the Monterey cypress grows better on soils with chalk beneath than on acid peats. Only bad drainage or shade can slow down the Leyland cypress. Incense cedar starts well in alkaline soils but it needs a good depth if it is to reach a large size without having a thin, moth-eaten crown. The Ginkgo prefers lime soils to poor acid sands.

There are several extensive genera and families amongst the broadleafed trees and these tend to some uniformity in their reactions to lime soils. All the important genera and their species in the family *Rosaceae* – the thorns, crabs, cherries, pears, whitebeams and rowans – either tolerate or positively need lime. It also seems that all the *Fagaceae*, that huge assemblage of oaks, the beeches and Sweet chestnuts, are lime-tolerant as are *Salicaceae*, the willows and poplars, and *Juglandaceae*, the wing-nuts, walnuts and hickories. In fact it is simpler to seek out for mention only those broadleafed trees which do *not* like lime soils. The family *Ericaceae* is well-known for its tendency to harbour true calcifuges amongst its heaths and rhododendrons – the Sourgum, or Sorrel-tree, is one of the most calcifuge of all trees (although it is 10 m tall at Westonbirt, where the limestone is beneath 1 m or so of loam); there are also a few calcicoles in *Ericaceae*, such as the Strawberry trees – both *Arbutus menziesii* and the native. *A unedo* at least tolerate some lime. The magnolias include some better not attempted on lime soils but the common bushy Saucer magnolia hybrids can be seen in many a chalk garden doing well. Their reputation as calcifuges probably arose from the splendid tree-magnolias of the Himalayas and China, for *Magnolias campbellii*, *sprengeri* and *dawsoniana*, although thriving at Westonbirt, would probably fail on chalk. The American tree-magnolias, *MM. fraseri*, *tripetala* and *macrophylla*, probably dislike lime although the biggest-growing, *M. acuminata*, seems tolerant of it.

The maples are all allowed to be in the single genus, *Acer*, and their great diversity in form and leaf is paralleled by their reactions to soils. Presence or absence of lime is not crucial to any maple, but chalk soils are limiting and those that grow best on chalk are Sycamore, Field maple, Cappadocian, Nikko, Italian, Lobel's, Zoeschen and Paperbark maples. The Japanese maples, *palmatum* and *japonicum* and their numerous forms, tolerate lime too but may not colour as well in the autumn as when growing in more acid soils. The same is probably true of the American Red and Silver maples.

Heavy Soils

As with chalk, so with heavy clays the surface layers are modified by weathering and are less restricting than the solid rock. The trouble for a tree may be a lens or belt of heavy clay beneath a top soil of sand. This remains unweathered and can prove impenetrable to some root-systems. The tree roots widely in the surface layers but has no deep anchorage and is liable to be blown down. The New Forest has areas of this kind and beech growing on them are frequently tipped over, raising huge root-plates.

Heavy clays have their fine particles spread uniformly and closely. In loams and worked clays the fine particles are flocculated, cohering in small lumps, leaving passages for water and air among them. In this kind of soil, aeration is therefore poor and insufficient for deep root-growth; its density also makes it difficult for roots to penetrate. Hence clays restrict rooting and, although they retain moisture well, if they do dry out the plants on top, with their shallow rooting, will suffer from drought, which is made worse by the clay shrinking so that large cracks open out and more moisture is lost.

In their favour, clays retain their base salts since water can scarcely move through and leach them. This means that any tree able to grow on clay should seldom lack nutrients and, with water readily available as it usually is, an extensive root-system is not as necessary to good growth as it is on other types of soil.

Conifers in general need open well-drained soils, but a few will do well on heavy clays. The one best able to grow in the stickiest sites is not in the front rank of useful trees – the White cedar or eastern American thuja is short-lived and remains a fresh green dense little tree for insufficient time before it becomes thin. The splendidly healthy and vigorous Western red cedar, however, is almost as tolerant, with perhaps a little more reliance on better aeration at planting. The Tamarack, which ranges across Canada, is at home on very ill-drained soil and the Swamp cypress, native to much-flooded creeks and river-bottoms, can also cope with clays. Even among the pines, which are mainly trees of sandy soils and dry rocky hillsides, there are a few which will grow well, at least if there is a shallow layer of better draining soil above the clay. The Corsican pine is the one most planted over clay and it grows rapidly to 35 m or more. Ponderosa pine is probably at least as adaptable and the Bhutan pine thrives for many years. Douglas fir, if planted into light soil above clay, will mostly grow very well although on some Wealden clay it will not make a good stand of timber of more than large-pole size yet individual trees grow on to big specimens. Western hemlock is another good conifer on these soils and grows very fast. Many silver firs, especially Grand and Low's firs, make big tall trees rapidly on clay, but preferably planted with some lighter soil to start them away. The Ginkgo thrives on clay.

The broadleafed tree best known for growing on the stickiest clay is the Hornbeam, but the Common oak is the dominant native tree on most stretches of clay still under woodland. Several poplars which are forms of, or hybrids of, the Black poplar grow very fast. The Lombardy poplar, the wild Black or Manchester poplar and the hybrids 'Serotina', 'Robusta' and 'Regenerata' are the most common. The Balsam poplars and their hybrids are similarly adapted. Most willows do well on clays. Given a loamy surface layer such foliage-trees as the Tulip-tree, Sweet gum, Katsura tree, wing-nuts, zelkovas and hickories thrive, as will magnolias, crabs, cherries, Horse chestnuts and the London and Oriental planes. The Midland hawthorn is a tree of clayland woods and the common Red hawthorns are derived from it so they too do well. The Common ash and the preferable Manna ash and euodias are also useful on clays, as are all the limes.

Acid Sands

These soils drain rapidly so are poor in nutrients but being well aerated and open they allow roots to penetrate deep and wide. They are thus not always more severe sites in drought than are clays as the quality most needed in a tree in order to grow well is the ability to grow at low levels of bases and nutrients. The natural or semi-natural growth (after early clearance or fires) on acid sands is heathland plants. Here the Heather, *Calluna*, may get a hold, its very acid litter and its competition keeping out plants which would improve the soil. Scrub oak originally grew on the lowland heaths and persists where fires are few, and Common oak can make a fine tree on some very acid soils but remains a low bushy plant on heaths. The Silver birch is the chief heathland tree, colonizing rapidly and densely after fires. In 1976 it surprisingly died of drought in many areas – normally the driest periods do not affect its deepest roots. The sallows will grow on acid sands and so will the Rowan. On the less severely acid sands many fine trees thrive, like the Red, Pin and Sessile oaks, and the Sweet chestnut; the Sour gum must have acid soil.

Among the conifers, the pines include specialists at growth on very poor sands. The Maritime, Aleppo and Stone pines need nothing else while the Scots pine ramps across the poorest heaths and the Corsican pine makes fine stands. The Lodgepole and Shore pines, the scruffy Scrub pine and Jack pine grow well, but so does the elegant Western hemlock. A highly useful decorative conifer which can grow as happily on a heath as on chalk is the Smooth Arizona cypress while the numerous forms of Lawson cypress are nearly as tolerant. The Bishop pine can make 2 m leaders on exceedingly poor soil and its fellow Californian, the Monterey pine, is nearly as fast-growing, while the Sierra redwood hardly cares at all about soil.

Industrial Areas

The bad effects on plant growth come from both solid matter and gases in the air. The solids can be various dusts in the surroundings of lime, concrete and mineral works, but the main particulate matter is soot. In this way inner cities and large towns were as polluted as purely industrial areas until recent clean-air legislation made striking improvements. Again, although various noxious gases were and sometimes still are damaging around chemical works, the chief offender is usually sulphur dioxide, also prevalent in towns where the source is the burning of either coal products or oil. This pollution has not been lessened to the same extent as that arising from soot.

Soot in the air has three ways of affecting plant growth adversely. The particles screen out some of the necessary radiations from sunlight and shorten the effective day; they are deposited and clog the vital gas-exchange apparatuses of plants, that is, their leaves and bark; and soot acidifies rain and soil, causing more rapid leaching of plant foods and base salts.

Some trees are pre-adapted to cope with these effects to a certain extent. Smooth, shiny leaves collect less soot and are washed clean by rain. Trees which normally leaf out late and shed early have their foliage active only for a short time and that in the hottest period when least fuel is burned. Bark that is shed readily starts clean again once a year, and bark that is craggy clogs more slowly and resists soot in the deepest crevices. Many trees are indifferent to the soil becoming acid and poor.

The London plane leafs out rather late and the down on the new leaves is soon shed and they become shiny. The bark too is shed, often in inconvenient quantities and large hard plates, early every autumn. The native Black poplar, or 'Manchester poplar', is much planted in the industrial north and manages well. It has smooth shiny foliage, is not late into leaf but has somewhat craggy bark. The Sycamore is one of the very best trees in bad air, largely because of its sheer toughness but it also sheds its bark freely in scales and has glossy leaves and smooth shoots. Another inherently tough tree is the Locust which leafs out late and sheds early, has craggy bark and smooth foliage. Yet another is Hodgins's holly which, like the Sycamore, is also excellent in exposure to sea-winds; the high polish of the leaves offsets their being held for three or four years as they wash clean in every shower of rain.

The Ginkgo is outstanding for its growth amongst skyscrapers in the downtown areas of

American cities, even in Upper Manhattan. Its leathery smooth leaves unfold fairly late. The Indian bean tree has downy foliage but thrives in Inner London because, like the Locust and other trees to be mentioned, it comes from a region of very hot summers so in England is scarcely fully in leaf until mid-June and loses its leaves early in autumn. Its scaly bark sheds freely. The Swamp cypress, also used to the hot summers of the south-eastern USA, cannot be in leaf much before midsummer and, being deciduous, it has an advantage over most conifers and thrives in Inner London. Similarly the Honey locust, seen downtown in every city in the USA, leafs out late with shiny leaves.

The Tree of Heaven is very late to unfold its smooth, glossy leaves and grows with great vigour in London. From its behaviour in Washington, Atlanta and other large American cities it seems London is only saved by its relative coolness from being engulfed by seedlings and suckers.

Although still rare and tried in only a few places, the euodias grow exceptionally well in city parks. *Euodia hupehensis* is the best known and its handsome glossy leaves are late to unfold. The Chinese privet is evergreen but is like the Euodia in having glossy, leathery leaves and copious white flowers in autumn. It makes a splendid city street tree in London and is found in almost every hot city from Tangier to Texas.

Maritime Exposure

The adverse aspects of a seashore site arise from salt and wind. Salt is carried inland by gales in damaging quantities for many miles so a tree does not have to be on the shore or cliff-top to suffer maritime exposure. Both aspects, wind and salt, are nearly always combined so resistance to both is a necessary condition for good growth. Resistance to wind is largely a matter of having evolved in an area exposed to it and so is most likely to be found in trees native to mountain ridges and coastlines. Beyond a tendency towards hard leaves and away from big leaves, there are

no evident features common to such trees, although resistance to salt is also associated with leaves that are glossy and wash clean easily. The soils in maritime areas are liable to contain some common salt after gales and there are some trees to which this is fatal and which are unable to grow near the sea.

Conifers tend to have very small, hard, waxed or resined leaves so some of the trees best able to stand up to sea-winds can be expected to be conifers from coasts or mountains. All the west coast of Britain is warm enough to grow three of the most resistant trees, which come from California. The Bishop pine has never yet been seen to be scorched by any gale; from its northern outposts around Mendocino, seeds grow into narrowly conic, blue-needled trees, sometimes at 2 m a year, whilst from the little colonies of Bishop pine scattered further to the south of California it grows broad, dark, yellow-green and densely crowned. The Monterey pine is common here as a wind-break by the sea except on the east coast where it is less rapid in growth and suffers foliage scorch in east winds. The Monterey cypress is common all round our coasts although it too scorches in severe winters and is occasionally killed by them. The golden form 'Lutea' is usually a little more resistant.

Another pine for the front line is the Austrian pine, *Pinus nigra nigra*, which although dark and not elegant is a useful tree in areas of extreme exposure. The Japanese equivalent, *P. thunbergii*, is a shoreline tree in its home and useful here although rarely tried. The Sitka spruce grows fast by western seaboards but not in the lower rainfalls of the east coast.

Conifers more suitable for the second line, that is, reasonably resistant to maritime influences but not reliably stable or salt-proof where these are extreme, include the hybrid Leyland cypress, Lawson cypress and all its innumerable and indispensable forms, Corsican pine, Maritime pine and, on west coasts only, Cryptomeria. Shore pine, good near the west coast, has an interior form, the Lodgepole pine, more suited to the east.

Pre-eminent among the broadleafed trees used around the coasts for shelter from wind and salt is the Holm oak. The deciduous oaks cannot be as effective against winter gales but the plants to be protected have no leaves either in winter and will not often come to harm. Both the native oaks, *Quercus robur* and *Q. petraea*, can be found growing along or very near a shoreline. They will be short trees but they are upright. Some elms are good in exposure, none better than the true Cornish elm, even now (1981) surviving Dutch Elm Disease, or not yet reached by it, and standing tall on ridges above the Atlantic shore. The Wheatley elm, the Huntingdon elm and the native Wych elm resist exposure well, and on south and east coasts so does the English elm.

In many places on the coasts of north-west Scotland, villages and crofts rely for their shelter on Sycamore and Ash. The Sycamore is far superior as a tree anywhere round our coasts and in north-western areas it is the only broadleafed tree that can maintain a good height and shape. The Ash survives but makes a poor tree. The White poplar makes a bushy low tree, but can do this by rampant suckering on blown sand even where the dunes still encroach. The much sturdier and taller Grey poplar will make a big tree in considerable exposure to the sea. The Strawberry tree grows wild on some low cliffs in County Cork; it is a shrub on those rocky soils but can become a small tree in a garden. The Phillyrea has similar evergreen, hard, dark leaves and is a low, domed tree in south coast villages. Hodgins's holly, one of the toughest of all evergreens, is much used in seaside parks, putting-greens and promenade gardens.

Framework Trees; Avenue Trees

The **Beech** (*Fagus sylvatica*) is the most widely used and one of the best trees for boundary planting, clumps and roundels. Most of the big gardens in Devon and Cornwall rely greatly on beech and this reflects its ability to withstand exposure to sea-winds, and to do so at some height in the hills, as well as to grow taller there than other possible trees. It also gives good shelter with its dense leafage and the leaf-fall makes a great contribution to the soil for quite a distance around. Being a native tree, it accords well with the countryside and adds a rural aspect to a city park, growing well either on acid and sandy soil or on chalk and limestone. Unfortunately, there are drawbacks to set against the long list of the Beech's valuable qualities, all connected with its relatively short life and the manner in which senility assails it. With so much landscaping and garden creation in the middle of the eighteenth century, the beech plantings so important in the laying out of parkland are nearing the end of their life. Beech is difficult to replace piecemeal because of the dense shade from surviving trees, and these break up disastrously and without warning. The public should therefore be discouraged or prevented from walking among old clumps of beech or sitting under a veteran tree. (See p. 88.)

The **Common oak** (*Quercus robur*) is frequent as a framework-tree mostly in lowland clay areas unsuited to the growth of beech. It does not become so tall and a wider belt is needed to provide the same amount of shelter as beech would give. The leaf-fall is just as beneficial as that of beech and the autumn colour is later and nearly as good. The Common and Sessile oak have the great advantage over beech of an expected life twice as long and a protracted and obvious senility. The **Sessile oak** (*Quercus petraea*) has rarely been a framework-tree but given the same or somewhat lighter soils as the Common oak enjoys, it makes a much more handsome tree and ought to be more used. The leaves are regularly spaced, unlike those of the Common oak, and cast a more even shade. A group or copse will have a grass floor with few shrubs – a condition which attracts pied flycatchers and redstarts. (See p. 128.)

For urban parks, where many trees may not flourish, the **London plane** (*Platanus × acerifolia*) is of utmost value and is much used. It has as great a stature as any tree and can thrive in the most difficult conditions. It has come to look urban from its very success in cities, and is therefore desirable in country parks only if mixed in the framework and clumps with other trees. (See p. 113.)

The **Grey poplar** (*Populus canescens*) has great possibilities in this role. It has the rapid growth and final stature required and makes a fine, imposing tree of character. The early spring purple cast from expanding catkins is marked and unusual while the emergence of silvery foliage is a striking feature. It has, for a poplar, a dense crown effective as a screen and it turns quite a good gold in autumn. A clump or a belt soon becomes effective and it has a reasonably long life. (See p. 114.)

The **Black Italian poplar** (*Populus* × '*Serotina*') has been much used around the edges of city parks and as a single tree. It has in its favour remarkably rapid growth and it achieves an enormous size, often over 40 m tall and 2 m in diameter. Its attractions should, however, be resisted. It has a very open crown, of minimal effect as a screen; it is short-lived and unsafe with big, heavy branches; it is very late into leaf and fairly early to shed, and without autumn colour. (See p. 115.)

The **Golden black poplar** (*Populus* 'Serotina Aurea') is altogether different from the type in these respects. It can be 30 m tall but it is not nearly so rapid in growth nor so heavy in the branches. It has a dense crown of bright yellow leaves and may have a rather longer life. It is very much a city-park or a garden tree, but a group in the right place is highly attractive. (See p. 115.)

The **Ash** (*Fraxinus excelsior*) has a limited role here. It grows well in cities, given a retentive soil, and in exposure and on chalk. It can have a fine straight bole and be 25 m tall even under some adversity, making a good clump if thinned judiciously. It is not long-lived – about 230 years, like the Beech – and is somewhat ungainly as a single tree. It is late into leaf and any autumn golds will be brief. (See p. 90.)

The **Sweet chestnut** (*Castanea sativa*) is a good tree for this purpose and can be seen in avenues and clumps of considerable age. It is long-lived, if not nearly as long as is often claimed, 400–500 years being as much as any old specimen really indicates, for it grows fast even when apparently

very venerable. It decays slowly and when heavy branches have been lost the stump makes sprouts and survives as a picturesque relic. Although best on light soils many old trees have grown well in city parks on gravels and clay. It makes a good screen, has prominent flower-catkins and fruit and turns fine yellows and browns in autumn (See p. 78.)

The **Horse chestnut** (*Aesculus hippocastanum*) is often a framework-tree around and in the interior of town and city parks and in old parkland. It has a good tolerance of soils and can achieve the necessary size and be an effective screen. Its flowers and fruit are great favourites with the public. Nonetheless it is not a wise choice for widespread planting on public land. Its branches tend to crash down if suddenly weighted by a summer shower. Many trees are senile when not much more than 100 years old and still in reasonable shape. (See p. 67.)

The **Sycamore** (*Acer pseudoplatanus*) may be a dull tree but it is of immense value in severe conditions because it is so extraordinarily tough. Neither strong sea-winds nor badly polluted air seem to affect it and it makes the biggest tree in many city parks. It has a very dense crown, is good as a screen and will grow well as a crowded clump that, if thinned, will contain some splendid boles. It is safer than most trees with its branches, is very long-lived and almost never blows down. (See p. 62.)

The **Norway maple** (*Acer platanoides*) is a good tree for clumps and short avenues but has not quite the stature for the biggest scale features and in a boundary planting it needs to be mixed among others. Its merits are fast early growth, whether on acid or chalky soils, a good densely domed crown of light green leaves (a foil for the dark Sycamore) and splendid autumn colours, a scarlet tree here and there but mostly gold and orange. However, its best point may be its abundant bunches of bright yellow flowers before it or most other trees have any leaves. (See p. 62.)

The **Silver maple** (*Acer saccharinum*) has, foremost of its merits, an abundant vigour of upward growth so that it soon has long, erect and arched slender branches and a stout bole. The prettily lobed and toothed leaves are light green above and silvery beneath giving the fully foliaged tree an ethereal aspect, and they turn soft yellow with some pink, or sometimes red, in autumn. It is, however, somewhat fragile and short-lived and will lose branches in an exposed position. (See p. 64.)

For avenues on the largest scale the **Sierra redwood** or **Giant Sequoia** (*Sequoiadendron giganteum*) has no rival. It is also excellent for small roundels and clumps but is quite unsuited as a perimeter-belt tree and too thin in smoky air to be advisable in a city park. (See p. 177.)

The **Coast redwood** (*Sequoia sempervirens*) has not been seen planted as a grand avenue and this may be for the best since there is quite a wide variation in the habit of growth, making an uneven avenue likely; the crown does not taper like that of the Sierra redwood so would give less light, and to avoid a gloomy atmosphere the trees would need to be more widely spaced. However, in good redwood country the huge red boles are impressive and in small groups, widely spaced or among other trees, it can be the major feature of an informal avenue, as in the drive to Coollattin in County Wicklow, planted in 1851, where the redwoods are now 38 × 2 m. They are excellent in clumps or roundels but are much too thin in large urban areas. (See p. 177.)

In the regions where conifers flourish, mainly in the wet western hill country, the **Douglas fir** (*Pseudotsuga menziesii*) will make an imposing avenue but it needs to be widely spaced, about 20 m between trees since the trees can lose shape with age and the avenue becomes informal. Glenlee Park in Kirkcudbright has Douglas fir each side of the drive for about 250 m; there is considerable variation in size but several are immense trees over 50 m tall and 1·5 m in diameter with a spire top, making a remarkably impressive approach to the house. In a park or garden in a valley among mountains, Douglas fir can be a perimeter and general framework-tree, provided it is not planted in heavy, dull, solid belts which would hide the mountains. It is not suitable in lowland areas. (See p. 176.)

Unfortunately the larches, especially the **European larch** (*Larix decidua*) will not flourish in large towns, but in more rural areas this is a first-

class perimeter tree, ideal for roundels, clumps and irregular copses. It grows fast, is attractive to many birds, can support a dense growth of bluebells and is bright in early spring and late autumn. (See p. 163.)

The **Common lime** (*Tilai × europaea*) is widely planted in urban parks, lines, avenues and old parkland. As a screen it does well for height but the narrow upper crowns allow regular gaps if the trees are in a line rather than a belt. The poor shape of the middle and lower crowns and the vigorous sprouting around the base render this lime too untidy to make a pleasing single tree despite the great size it can attain. It is very long-lived and rarely sheds any but well-decayed light branches. (See p. 140.)

The **Broad-leafed lime** (*Tilia platyphyllos*) is inferior to the Common lime in stature only. It clearly surpasses it in its fine hemispheric crown, clean growth and fewer aphids. (See p. 142.)

The **Small-leafed lime** (*Tilia cordata*) would make a splendid tree for framework plantings but has rarely been used. It can exceed 30 m in height and its foliage is small, prettily heart-shaped and slightly silvered beneath. The starry little flowers spray out at all angles which makes it unlike the other big limes when in flower. As a single tree its clean straight main branches and big stature add to the good foliage and it has been omitted from the selection of 'single specimen' trees only because the crown is a little shapeless and shares some of the defects of the Common lime. (See p. 139.)

The **Turkey oak** (*Quercus cerris*) resists city air very well. There are some fine trees in London parks and it makes an imposing avenue in Central Park, New York. It has rapid growth and usually a good bole in its favour but the foliage is a little dull and dark for it to be planted in large belts pure. As a roundel tree it is excellent. (See p. 124).

The **Elms** can no longer be recommended for the reasons given on pages 143–5, but in the past many city parks depended on Wheatley and English elms for parts of their main plantings.

Many other trees have the stature and ease of growth to qualify, but they are of too striking or special an aspect to be used in the framework, which should not compete with or subdue the smaller decorative plantings. The trees omitted for this reason are treated in the section on Single Specimen Trees.

Single Specimen Trees

Monumental Size

To end a long, broad vista, a single tree may be chosen instead of a clump. In the traditional parkland landscape specimen trees are planted to become enormous, widely spaced single trees, or occasionally a garden will call for a tree of the largest size as its major feature. In any situation a single huge tree should meet the following requirements:

Imposing stature. Ultimate size of at least 30–40 m tall and reliability in attaining it.

Longevity. The chosen tree is not going to do its job properly if it has to be replaced every 150 years.

Character. This includes individuality of shape, formal or striking, foliage, flowers, fruit and autumn colour. Winter aspect is important.

General robustness; firmness against windthrow.

Other features which are desirable rather than necessary are a tolerance of varying soil types and rapid early growth. No single species earns top marks in every feature. Conifers will tend to rate highly because they are mostly evergreen, they grow fast with a spire form from the persistent bole, making them tall, and they are mostly undemanding of soils.

The list below is a selection of the trees that can be recommended, with their merits, limitations and failings:

Giant Sequoia (*Sequoiadendron giganteum*) This is the top scorer in almost every feature. It is, and

was remarkably soon after being introduced, the biggest tree in every county and is growing fast still; many are 45–50 m tall and 2·5 m in diameter; in 50 years it can be 30 m × 1·5 m. Growth is much the same in all parts and on all soils (except on shallow soil over chalk or on peat). It is virtually windfirm. The crown is shapely, and misshapen, stunted or forked trees, while known, are rare. The potential life-span is about 4000 years, which is enough for most purposes, although there is no guarantee that this will be achieved in Europe where some trees fall victim to honey-fungus when only 100 years old. This tree has character – from its majestic form, strong, tapered bole, dark red bark, elegantly upswept branch-ends – and it is evergreen.

It has only one big failing: in the south and east where big thunderstorms arise, it is singularly liable to be struck by lightning, no doubt partly because the older trees project from all surrounding trees. Usually the damage is confined to the top 2–3 m which dies back and eventually bushes out in a broader apex than the natural slender tapering tip, but occasionally the whole tree explodes and only a shattered stump is left. (See p. 177.)

London plane (*Platanus* × *acerifolia*) Few broadleafed trees can equal this for sheer size. Many are more than 35 m × 2 m and a few are over 40 m. Even the oldest and biggest are still adding rapidly to the size of their huge boles. Growth is fast even in the difficult conditions of city streets and parks and on poor, rubbly soils. Apart from the Anthracnose fungus which can kill back the new shoot after a sudden warm spell in a cold spring, this plane is singularly healthy and robust and the oldest trees are in full vigour when about 300 years old. It has only very rarely been known to blow down and then in unusual circumstances, and rarely sheds a branch. It has character from its imposing size and shape, with big twisting branches clad in variegated bark – straight branches and whiter bark in the scarce form 'Augustine Henry'. The leaves are large, firm, often glossy and interestingly shaped, while the fruit, a short string of globes, remain for most of the time that the tree is bare of leaves.

The limitations are that growth to giant size is restricted to the south and east of England; the Plane does not make a good specimen tree in the north or in Wales, Scotland or Ireland. This tree also lacks autumn colour of note and is somewhat late into leaf. Although tolerant of most soils including some difficult ones like stiff clays, it does not thrive on dry sands. The fruit break up in spring and tiny spicules become windborne and can irritate the eyes of susceptible people. (See p. 113.)

Western hemlock (*Tsuga heterophylla*) Few trees are more uniform and reliable in shape and, in the right areas, in reaching good size rapidly. It is conspicuously elegant, with regular branching, each branch ascending at the same angle, and has a long spire with a drooping leader at the tip. The foliage is small, neat and dense. On clays or sands it can soon be growing annual shoots 1·3 m long and may attain 30 m in 50 years. It is very healthy, failing only sometimes in plantations from butt-rot (*Fomes annosus*) and, as a single tree, is very resistant to wind-throw. The earliest trees here date from 1855 and are in full health and vigour. Some not as old as this are well over 40 m tall. The limitation of this hemlock is that it thrives and makes a splendid specimen only in the cool, damp coniferous areas, but is thin and slower in the east of England except in sheltered damp hollows. It will not do well on thin soils on exposed ridges or on chalk or near towns. (See p. 182.)

Cedar of Lebanon (*Cedrus libani*) This is an outstanding tree for single planting growing rapidly to a great size, and achieving a unique shape.

An original tree, planted in 1643, is still thriving, so a long life can be expected although some have died younger. Limy or sandy soils are no deterrent to good growth but an unexplained falling-off of vigour and early shedding of needles, usually associated with the presence of an aphid, can occur here and there.

The only other drawback is that wet snow can cause serious breakage of the long, level branches (See p. 155.)

Hungarian oak (*Quercus frainetto*) A good big specimen of this tree is the finest of all the oaks and among the best of all broadleafed trees. It grows rapidly and steadily and has great character. The pale-barked sturdy bole holds a great umbrella crown of straight branches, splendid in winter and crowded in summer with big leaves more lobed and toothed than those of any other oak. The earliest trees are now 130 years old, keeping up their rapid growth and in complete good health. One of the finest specimens is in Cumbria and others are in East Anglia and Angus, so climate is unlikely to be crucial, but it probably does need a deep soil. (See p. 124.)

Blue gum (*Eucalyptus globulus*) In Ireland and the Isle of Man this Tasmanian tree must be a contender. Growing at 2–3 m a year and soon 30 m tall, it is capable of reaching twice this size although so far few are over 40 m here. Its evergreen crown and cream and grey shedding bark are so distinctive that some people do not think they should be planted here at all. In the right sort of garden, but only in the areas stated, it can be valuable. (See. p. 86.)

Silver pendent lime (*Tilia* 'Petiolaris') This is consistently high in the ratings. Every plant is a graft from the same source so it is reliably constant in form and in moderate shelter it can attain over 30 m and grows fast. It is completely healthy and like most limes, very long-lived. It has character in abundance, with its long-pendulous outer crown showing the silver undersides of some of the hanging leaves and its scented flowers. It also turns soft yellow-browns in autumn. The winter aspect is graceful.

A disadvantage often claimed about the Silver pendent and the two limes below, is that bees are killed by their toxic pollen. This is now being studied and it seems that it is bumble-bees rather than hive-bees which are affected, and then not often. (The fact that the Sycamore can also be highly lethal to bumble-bees when in flower does not seem to arouse comment.) (See p. 141.)

Common lime (*Tilia* × *europaea*) With all its demerits, this tree can be a good specimen in parkland, if not in a garden. It has the stature – no other broadleafed tree is so frequently 40 m or more tall. It is very long-lived and windfirm. It is also very healthy despite attracting greenfly in spring and autumn and abundant nail-galls. It has a distinctive crown, a long rather narrow top composed of several vertical branches with short side-branches arching out level. And it has fragrant flowers. In a grazed parkland the cattle keep the basal sprouts down and give the canopy a good 'cattle-line' as well as providing ideal hunting ground for spotted flycatchers. (See p. 140.)

Small-leafed lime (*Tilia cordata*) This really rates above the Common lime but it is smaller in stature and so is slightly less imposing in a vital situation. It has, however, achieved 37 m and is often 30 m tall. It has a similar crown but with more character, in that the leaves are very neatly heart-shaped, slightly silvered beneath and much less coarse, and the bright, starry flowers are not in hanging clusters but in bunches that may be erect or sideways spreading, making the aspect of a tree in flower quite distinctive. (See p. 139.)

Horse chestnut (*Aesculus hippocastanum*) No other tree here bearing an unvarying abundance of conspicuous flowers has the stature of the Horse chestnut. The general run of older trees may be around 27 m tall but there are a number well over 35 m. A good specimen will have a splendid bole for 3–6 m and it may be nearly 2 m in diameter. Some trees give early bright red colours in autumn and others turn bright yellow, then orange-brown. The flowers, fruit and unusual leaf-shape add to its character. A few are known to be over 300 years old.

    One serious disadvantage is that the wood is brittle and weak. In full leaf in summer, the sudden added weight of water from a thunderstorm will sometimes tear out a branch with no warning, and this can be a huge limb. (See p. 67.)

Jeffrey pine (*Pinus jeffreyi*) Away from its natural range above 1800 m in the mountains of Oregon and California, this tree rather surprisingly grows in a wide variety of conditions to become a superbly shapely specimen. It makes a rapid start with a stout leading shoot to build up a sturdy trunk with blackish bark, its short branches forming a narrowly conic crown and bearing long blue-grey needles. After some thirty years, it may bear the big cones which start purple and ripen pale brown (See p. 170.)

Grand fir (*Abies grandis*) This is one of the fastest-growing of all conifers and has become the tallest of all trees in Britain. It can be 40 m in 50 years and 55 m in 100 years. At these sizes it has a fine bole, running right through the crown to the tip in many cases. In the open it may have some heavy low branches. Grand fir grows best in sheltered hollows and valleys with cool damp summers and cannot be relied upon for a massive presence on thin soils in exposed places or in hot dry places. (See p. 149.)

Tulip-tree (*Liriodendron tulipifera*) In the southern parts of England only, the Tulip-tree grows rapidly as a densely leafy conic tree until it matures into a hugely domed specimen bearing uniquely lobed leaves which turn bright yellow and orange in the autumn. It needs a deep rich soil and it is not very attractive in winter. (See p. 102.)

Beech (*Fagus sylvatica*) This makes a superb single specimen tree provided that the bole is kept clean of shoots and branches from the early years to ensure the massive, smooth grey cylindrical column that is needed. It will grow reasonably rapidly on almost any well-drained soil, even on acid sands, and is often 35 m tall. It loses the higher ranking its form and foliage merit because it is liable to sudden death when 150–200 years old and if it has big branches it becomes dangerous. (See p. 88.)

Black walnut (*Juglans nigra*) If this tree were more often 30 m in height it would be near the top of the list, with its massive, rugged-barked bole and lofty dome of big, glossy, bright green compound leaves. Alas, nearly all the many fine trees are confined to good soils in the south-east of England because summers are warmer there than in the west or north where it grows but slowly. (See p. 96.)

Turkey oak (*Quercus cerris*) This oak grows very rapidly to make a huge domed crown on an impressive bole. It should have low branches cleaned off the bole from an early age, or it will develop a heavily branched crown and have far less character. It is tolerant of any well-drained soil and withstands a good deal of exposure but it is a little gaunt without foliage. (See p. 124.)

Sessile oak (*Quercus petraea*) Far more handsome in foliage than the Common oak and with a more shapely crown, the Sessile oak also grows faster. It likes a high rainfall but sharp drainage and must, for the purpose of a single specimen, be kept to a long clean bole. (See p. 128.)

Western yellow pine (*Pinus ponderosa*) Ranging as it does over the vast area of all the Rocky Mountain system southwards from southern British Columbia, different imports of the seed of this pine will be expected to give varying results. Nonetheless, it is nearly always shapely and vigorous here in all areas except the far west of Ireland. It makes a splendid conic crown with bunches of long needles, similar to Jeffrey pine but dark green and with the bark pale orange or red-brown, breaking sometimes into curiously curved flakes shed in quantity. (See p. 172.)

Caucasian zelkova (*Zelkova carpinifolia*) This depends for its remarkable character on growing into the peculiar form usually, although not always, seen here but which seems unknown in the wild; the bole breaks at 1–2 m into a hundred or so upright branches which can reach a height of over 30 m. In this form it is a superb feature. After a slow start of slender shoots, growth becomes quite rapid. Autumn colour is old gold and russet. It grows on any reasonably good soil and stiff clays but the biggest are all in the south of England so a warm site is needed. (See p. 145.)

Of many other possible trees, the **Douglas fir** (*Pseudotsuga menziesii*) has the growth and size but except in some wet northern and western areas it

loses shape at height and becomes untidy. The **Coast redwood** (*Sequoia sempervirens*) is superb with a fine red bole and very rapid growth but needs shelter, cool damp summers and a deep soil, and the foliage is dull. The **Common silver fir** (*Abies alba*) has made monumental trees even in East Anglia but pests trouble its early years now and big trees away from the western and northern hills tend to become thin and broken. The **Noble fir** (*Abies procera*) rapidly grows a smooth silver-barked bole and has bright blue-grey foliage, but for an important focus it is unreliable except in north Wales, eastern Ireland and most of Scotland. The **Blue Atlas cedar** (*Cedrus atlantica* var. *glauca*) is frequently used for individual planting but is better where the very biggest tree is not required as it rarely has a massive presence. The **Sitka spruce** (*Picea sitchensis*) has that, in good measure, and very rapid growth but only in the wet areas mentioned above; elsewhere there is a risk of it being thin and unimposing. The **Western red cedar** (*Thuja plicata*) has the growth and stature in wet regions but needs its bole cleaned up for 5–6 m or it is obscured by a branchy, not very interesting crown.

The **Chestnut-leafed oak** (*Quercus castaneifolia*) very rapidly becomes a huge and imposing tree with handsome leaves but it is seldom obtainable and, despite their good shape, the leaves make a dark, rather dull crown.

Until ten years ago the **Wheatley elm** (*Ulmus* 'Sarniensis') would have been one of the first trees on this list, with its splendidly shapely conic crown of fine shoots. There are, at the time of writing (1981), still some fine trees in the Midlands and northwards, but it can no longer be planted in expectation of a fine specimen 50 years hence and must therefore be omitted.

Medium-Size Trees

This category includes trees which rarely achieve 30 m in height but can be expected to culminate at around 25 m. They are therefore suitable for planting in an important position, as a focal point or where there is room for only one tree of moderate size. These trees are also big enough to be used in parkland where massive specimens are not required, although not all are scenically suitable for this purpose. The list that follows is a short selection of the more choice, medium-sized trees, arranged roughly in order of importance. Since many of these are described elsewhere, only a few details relevant to their usefulness as medium-size trees are given.

Ginkgo (*Ginkgo biloba*) Every garden in which there is space should have this unique tree. It usually needs very little room, having few branches and those ascending. It goes well with most buildings. (See p. 146.)

Dawn redwood (*Metasequoia glyptostroboides*) Every garden should have one of these, also. In time to come it may need to be promoted to the 'monumental' category as it is probably able to grow 32 m tall, but being grown here only 33 years (1981) its final size cannot be known. Trees already 22 m tall may round off soon, but it makes a splendid feature and grows fast. (See p. 164.)

Swamp cypress (*Taxodium distichum*) Almost a monumental tree but seldom above 30 m, this has great character. The densely twigged conic crown is bare for a very long season but is a positive feature even then. (See p. 178.)

Monkey-puzzle (*Araucaria araucana*) A tree of great character, with a bold uncompromising, resulutely straight single stem, the Monkey-puzzle demands to stand in a prominent place on its own, or in a well-spaced group. There are people who cannot enjoy Monkey-puzzles at all, but they are probably secret admirers of 'copper' beeches anyway. (See p. 153.)

Brewer spruce (*Picea brewerana*) Attracting attention wherever it is, Brewer spruce would come nearer the top of the list were it to take 15 years less in getting started. As a single tree or in a small group at 5–6 m spacing, it is superb once 5–6 m tall but seedling trees, the only good source, are thin and do not have long weeping

shoots for at least ten years, often more. Once away, growth is fairly steady and not so slow but it does need full light all round to keep a dense crown. Several Brewer spruce now about 60 years old are around 18 m tall. (See p. 165.)

Golden larch (*Pseudolarix amabilis*) This Chinese oddity has great character but it is very slow and difficult to start. In summer a leafy fresh green with pale grey thickly plated bark, it becomes in the autumn a golden then fiery orange-brown spectacle, often bushy, or a broad conic tree. (See p. 175.)

Golden-barred thuja (*Thuja plicata* 'Zebrina') Varying considerably in the amount of gold, only the brightest should be selected for a focal point where it will grow steadily to a broad conic tree of great substance. (See p. 181.)

Dawyck beech (*Fagus sylvatica* 'Dawyck') As a tolerant, reliable tree of quite rapid growth to a column of foliage, fresh green in early summer and russet and orange in autumn, this beech is outstanding as a single mark of emphasis or as a tight group at 4 m spacing. (See p. 89.)

Cypress oak (*Quercus robur* 'Fastigiata') This has slightly more character than the Dawyck beech and grows only a little less rapidly. Seedlings vary in shape so a grafted plant is needed. (See p. 88.)

Katsura tree (*Cercidiphyllum japonicum*) This is a tree of great elegance and mixed but splendid autumn colours. It has a tendency, easily checked from the start, to grow several main stems or to branch low, and it is susceptible to drought and, although only briefly disfiguring, to late frosts. A site which is damp but not a frost hollow is called for, and growth will be rapid. (See p. 81.)

Italian alder (*Alnus cordata*) This grows rapidly and steadily to 25 m and maintains a loosely conic crown. The catkins are early, large and bright and the leaves neatly heart-shaped and shiny. It grows on almost any soil and although, being an alder, it lacks any change of colour in the autumn, it is a really fine tree. (See p. 69.)

Incense cedar (*Calocedrus decurrens*) As a single exclamation mark, this good, tightly columnar tree cannot be bettered, on a fairly large scale. It will not achieve gigantic size and there is no tree of this shape that will (although Leyland cypress can be nearly as columnar). For the largest-scale feature, particularly as an eye-catcher stopping an unsuitable prospect, a group of five, seven or more at 4 m spacing is arresting. (See p. 153.)

Leyland cypress (× *Cupressocyparis leylandii*) Currently still in the 'medium-size' group, it is evident that enormous specimens of this tree will soon be seen. Even so, it would remain here for it is not ideal as a single vast tree as a focus, being rather dull. It is, however, excellent for rapid effect on a more modest scale, making a fine focal pillar 20 m tall in 20 years as in the Savill Garden, Windsor, where it is now 24 m. By the turn of the century it will be about 40 m tall and becoming out of scale, and could be replaced. (See p. 159.)

Smooth Arizona cypress (*Cupressus glabra*) This tree scores all along the line. It grows at rather moderate speeds on any soil from fiercely acid sands to thin loam over chalk; it has never been noted as suffering from frosts or drought; it has a characterful bark, and a neat and shapely blue crown. Best as a single tree, it can also be used in a group but needs plenty of room, about 6 m spacing, and takes some years to create an effect. (See p. 160.)

Serbian spruce (*Picea omorika*) For spot effect this is hard to beat as a single tree but it is not always good in a group as its form is uneven and a large group can be ragged. On any well-drained soil from peat and sand to limestone it makes a slender tower of dark blue to 20 m in about 35 years. (See p. 166.)

Wissel cypress (*Chamaecyparis lawsoniana* 'Wisselii') This bizarre form of Lawson cypress grows on any soil and makes a turreted tower of dark blue. It can be thin and inadequate so it is worth observing locally before deciding whether to plant one or a group as a feature. (See p. 157.)

Bosnian pine (*Pinus leucodermis*) One of the very few pines with the shape and character to stand as a focal plant of medium-scale. The crown is neatly ovoid, the bark pale grey or whitish and the cones are blue in summer. It also grows steadily on any well-drained soil from chalky to very acid. (See p. 170.)

Macedonian pine (*Pinus peuce*) A singularly healthy tree, this grows at a steady moderate rate wherever it is planted and has a dark blue, neat columnar crown. Some specimens need strong lower branches removed in their early years to make a fine clean bole. (See p. 172.)

Turkish hazel (*Corylus colurna*) The regularly conic crown of large glossy leaves and singularly sturdy growth make this a valuable focal tree, even without the large catkins and the bright, glossy fruit with long-pointed lobes and green spines. It is tolerant of any but the most acid or driest sands. (See p. 82.)

Monarch birch (*Betula maximowicziana*) Foliage and bark are the features of this tree. On young trees the leaves emerge covered in orange down, big, broad and elegantly toothed. On older trees they are glossy bright green. The bole should be cleaned up early to develop and show the white then pink bark. (See p. 74.)

Lombardy poplar (*Populus niga* 'Italica') When well grown, in a damp hollow, these make fine spot trees on a fairly large scale. They also make imposing groups, as at Canizzaro Park, Wimbledon, where most of those in a glade are 30–31 m tall. The Lombardy poplar does not qualify as a 'Monumental' tree, because of its fragility in the open as a single tree, its relatively short life and lack of sheer bulk. But in shelter to some degree and on a less grand scale, it can be highly effective. (See p. 115.)

Weeping willow (*Salix* × *chrysocoma*) Any reasonably damp soil, however sandy, will suit this tree whose roots set out for and acquire all the water it needs. Very much a tree for an open clearing, it will not thrive and weep well where at all shaded, and no other tree can live where the roots of this one run. It is an obvious choice for watersides but can be a good feature elsewhere. (See p. 131.)

Sweet gum (*Liquidambar styraciflua*) is a striking foliage-tree during the summer to make up for its occasional waywardness in autumn colouring. Seedling trees usually seem to make better, more vigorous and shapely trees than those raised from root-suckers, which often start with a thick corky bark. A good deep and damp soil suits this best but it will grow, and often colour well, on a wide variety of soils. (See p. 101.)

Chinese sweet gum (*Liquidambar formosana*) This is a very choice variation from the commonly seen American species. Its hard, dark leaves, spikily toothed, turn to fiery oranges and crimson in autumn. (See p. 101.)

Fastigiate or Pyramidal hornbeam (*Carpinus betulus* 'Fastigiata') This is often used as a focal tree in fairly small-scale landscaping and it well merits such use. Growth is quite fast to 15 m and after starting as a thin column it soon broadens to an upright ovoid; it is equally striking whether in leaf or quite bare. (See p. 76.)

Tupelo (*Nyssa sylvatica*) This tree falls down only because it is rather demanding of site and soil to do its best and unless it can thrive it is too slow and thin to be impressive. Even on good trees the autumn colours in some years are no more than a pleasant yellow and pale orange. However, a well-grown tree is worth having for its shapely glossy foliage and the good chance of rich orange, scarlet and deep red leaves in autumn. (p. 109.)

Rauli (*Nothofagus procera*) This Chilean tree is about the best foliage-tree for rapid effect. It can grow 2 m a year and 20 m in 15 years while the growth of a stout bole is equally remarkable speedy. The handsome, hornbeam-like foliage with 18–25 pairs of parallel veins is at first tinged orange and in autumn turns orange with some dark red. (See p. 109.) The crown is quite narrowly conic for many years and a small group

of trees looks well either bringing an edge of woodland on to a lawn or as a group on its own. They can be planted at 5 m spacing for early effect and thinned after 20 to 30 years to give them the space to develop their big, domed crowns. Kept clean of lower branches, the boles become smooth, silvery-grey and attractive. (See p. 109.)

Oliver's lime (*Tilia oliveri*) A tree of such high quality foliage can well stand on its own in an important position. The big, very flat pale green leaves with silver undersides are held out level by a twist of the petiole from hanging shoots, and the bark is good. (See p. 141.)

Pin oak (*Quercus palustris*) This is a good medium-sized specimen tree found in a number of gardens. The clean bole of silvery bark holds up a down-sweeping skirt of fine shoots bearing pretty leaves which turn crimson-red in autumn. (See p. 128.)

Yellow buck-eye (*Aesculus flava*) This is a tree of class. It has elegant, glossy bright green leaves, good flowers of a colour unusual in its group and displays brilliant autumn colour. It is also completely hardy and undemanding of soil. Its only weak point is its rather poor crown in winter. (See p. 67.)

Small-Scale Features

A semi-miniature avenue can be planted along a short length of path joining two areas. An avenue wider than 6 m will be more apparent if it is at least 20 m long unless closely spaced formal trees are used. Widely spaced informal planting only suits an avenue on this scale if the trees are the same species, and preferably one that is very distinct. It provides a good opportunity to plant one of the small weeping trees which is not of much account on its own, such as Young's weeping birch, 'Cheals weeping' and Rose-bud 'Pendula Rubra' cherries, which weep asymmetrically anyway. A small avenue is most easily planned using conifers since formal shapes can be selected, regular in size and to the desired height, and of almost any colour.

If the avenue is very short, say five or six trees, it can be of mixed or alternating colours, either as a colourful corridor linking two decorative areas or as a sudden contrast between two sober, shady green areas. An avenue perhaps twice this length would be effective if planted uniformly with one of the very strong colours found in the cultivars of the *Chamaecyparis* cypresses, but it would not want to be more than 50 m long; one entirely of the brightest gold would be quite a sight. The ideal trees for these formal, small avenues are the numerous cultivars of Lawson cypress and a few of Monterey cypress. Lawson forms can be tightly columnar, green ('Kilmacurragh', 'Green Spire', 'Green Pillar', 'Masoni'), grey ('Columnaris', 'Ellwoodii') or narrowly conic, blue ('Allumii', 'Fraseri') or gold ('Lutea', 'Lanei', 'Hillieri', 'Winston Churchill') or fluffy and columnar ('Fletcheri', 'Pottenii', 'New Silver'). The best Monterey cypresses are 'Goldcrest', 'Golden Pillar' and 'Golden Spire'.

These fairly small or slow, strikingly coloured or shaped trees, together with the two bright gold Hinoki cypresses 'Tetragona Aurea' and 'Crippsii', have numerous other roles in small features. Mixed blue and gold narrow trees in a small clump make the most arresting eye-catcher or lighten up the dullest (but not shadiest, for they need good light) corner and make it shine in winter sun. Similarly, the above species can be used in single lines which make quite striking small garden features.

Alphabetical List of Garden Trees

Broadleafed Trees

Acacia dealbata Mimosa; Silver wattle

Cut to the ground in the most severe winters in all but a few favoured spots, this tree makes good use of a run of less extreme winters and within three or four years it is back on the house roof. Coming from south-east Australia, it really needs a south-facing wall unless close to the south and south-west coasts of England and Wales or in southern Ireland; it is in every other garden on the Isle of Wight, and common in the south of Devon and Cornwall and in Ireland, where it makes a free-standing tree. The first few days of 1979 were colder in Cornwall than elsewhere in England, and all the plants there were cut to the ground except those in the tiny area west and south of Penzance. As a tree on its own it will make a 12 m plant on a sinuous warm brown bole, liable to lean and be blown down. The long snaking budless shoots of a young or regrowing plant are silvery blue-green with narrow ridges below each leaf. The leaves are feathery, doubly compound with about a dozen pairs of pinnae, each bearing about 30 pairs of oblong, narrow leaflets, many pairs scarcely parted, bright blue-green. The yellow flowers are 3 mm globules, 20–30 on a head, opening in January in Torquay or Penzance and in April in Surrey.

The uses of mimosa are severely limited by the climate so it is not in the first rank as a tree. Its best place is against a wall where it can be grown in all the southernmost counties and will sow itself freely in adjacent flower-beds.

Acer buergeranum Trident maple

The Trident maple is rare but it is so attractive that this ought to be rectified. Native to China, it was first sent here in 1896 and even the oldest trees are scarcely 13 m tall so it is suited to quite small plantings. The crown is domed and carries a markedly dense mass of leaves on a usually rather short, slightly sinuous bole with a flaky, pale orange and brown bark. The leaf tapers evenly to a slender petiole which is as long as the blade and at its outer end it has three forward-pointing triangular lobes. Occasional leaves are unlobed. Three prominent veins spring from the base and

Trident maple

the leaf is often slightly cupped showing the pale or bluish underside contrasting with the fresh bright green upper side. In autumn the leaves turn crimson and dark red. The flowers open with the leaves and, like them, at that time are pale yellow. They are small and numerous on a hairy-stemmed domed head.

From seed this tree makes rapid growth at first, but the long, slender dark red stems tend to be too many, and too similar in length, leading to a bush, unless steps be taken to make it a tree. Growth seems equally good on acid sandy soils as on neutral clay and probably also in limy soil.

Acer campestre Field maple

The native maple is a tree of the hedgerows and spinneys in chalk downlands and on limestones. It also grows on quite acid soils and in clay and is healthy in cities. It is a little dark in the crown in summer but this is relieved by crimson on the wings of the clustered fruit. The leaves, small and prettily lobed, turn yellow, old gold, russet or even purple in autumn. It is therefore very valuable as a background tree in city parks and on alkaline soils. Trees left to grow in hedges at wide intervals develop good boles and broad, domed crowns about 16 m tall. In the wooded parts of a few gardens from Sussex to Angus there are trees to 25 m tall. As a specimen or group in a woodland garden it may need relieving of suckers around and on the bole, and this should not be neglected.

Acer capillipes Red snake-bark maple

This is the most attractive of the many snake-bark maples in several ways. It is the only one with such shiny leaves and regular rows of parallel veins. The bark is clearly and brightly striped white on grey-green and the shoots are dark red. The petioles are scarlet and stand out among the bright glossy green leaves. Unlike the somewhat similar grey-budded snake-bark (p. 64), the leaves are longer than they are broad by a good margin since the central lobe is long-acuminate and dominant, the two lateral lobes being short. The underside of the leaf is pale, slightly glaucous, and has little red or green pegs in the axils of the main

veins. The flowers are borne from an early age at almost every node, pairs of arched catkins of yellow flowers ripening to tiny winged fruit which are, in summer, pink and yellow and quite a feature. In the autumn the foliage turns yellow, orange, bright red and crimson.

Introduced from Japan via the Arnold Arboretum in 1894 this maple grows rapidly when young but the branches arch over and it has not exceeded 15 m in height. A few of the oldest have boles 40 cm in diameter and these retain areas of stripes and are highly impressive.

Another of this tree's good features is its tolerance of any garden soil, but it also has a failing. The larger trees nearly all have patches of dead bark around the base and are liable to die. Sometimes the cause is apparently careless use of gang mowers, sometimes it appears to be hungry voles, but sometimes there is no obvious reason and it must be accepted that the Red snake-bark is short-lived for one reason or another.

Red snake-bark maple

Acer cappadocicum Cappadocian maple

This tree has a unique breadth of range since no other grows both sides of the Hindu Kush massif; it ranges from the Caucasus Mountains, along the Elburz Mountains south of the Caspian Sea,

Cappadocian maple

through Afghanistan to the Himalayas and beyond into China and even Japan. It was introduced in 1838 from Asia Minor and is uncommon here even though found in most of the largest gardens and many smaller ones and parks. The entire margin of the long-acuminate lobed leaf is unusual but the most marked feature of the tree is its propensity to sucker. A few other maples do this but none with such abandon. In the absence of cattle, mowers or gardeners, each tree becomes enclosed in a thicket. It has even reached the point where the tallest Cappadocian maple, 25 m high, is a sucker from a tree which itself achieved only 23 m before dying.

The value of this tree, where there is room for it, lies in its soft grey smoothly crinkled bark, and particularly in the reliable bright butter-yellow autumn colour of its shapely foliage. It grows notably well in western gardens with high rainfall and cool damp summers but is equally at home in the north-east and in dry areas like East Anglia. It also grows in chalky soils.

'Aureum' is delightful in spring, and as a young tree at least, throughout the summer. The leaves emerge bright yellow and to some extent turn green with time, but young trees continue to make new growth through much of the summer so their outer crowns remain bright yellow; some old trees remain bright throughout. Like the type, this grows rapidly.

Acer carpinifolium Hornbeam maple

This is really more of a large bush than a tree as usually seen but it is technically a tree, being on a single stem and exceeding 6 m in height. It is

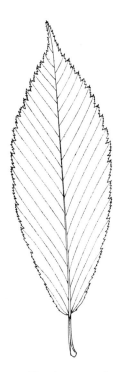

Hornbeam maple

Japanese and its handsome leaves suggest that it is a relation of the hornbeam until it is noticed that they are in opposite pairs. They are a good fresh green and 8–10 cm long, unlobed but sharply toothed, and have 20 or more pairs of parallel veins. The leaves are lanceolate to a slender acuminate tip and somewhat sparsely placed along the shoots. The flowers are green, star-shaped on slender catkins, and most plants here seem to be male.

The merits of the Hornbeam maple are, apart from its apparent disguise, the fine foliage and good soft yellow autumn colour.

Acer cissifolium Vine-leaf maple

This little Japanese tree is one of the trifoliate maples and has broad, boldly toothed leaflets on wire-thin stalks. It flowers profusely and the pairs

Vine-leafed maple

of arched catkins with their tiny winged fruit dominate the foliage until autumn when the leaves turn pale yellow then brown. It has a short bole, usually less than 1 m, holding widely spreading level branches that make a flattened dome. It is of unusual aspect but in a small planting it takes up more room than it justifies ornamentally and its best role is as a group on a broad bank.

Acer crataegifolium Hawthorn maple

Although one of the snake-bark maples from Japan, this makes such a slender stem that the bark is of little note. Indeed the tree looks better arising from behind shrubs which hide its spindly lower parts. The foliage is carried on short, twiggy, spur-like shoots close above each slender branch which curves to the horizontal. The finely pointed leaf is only 6 × 3 cm and is faintly lobed and finely toothed. It is borne on a scarlet stalk and is tinged red from the time it unfolds. The thinness of the foliage is reduced by numerous catkins of level-winged fruit which are red soon after they appear. This tree takes up very little room and its layers of red fruit and reddish leaves add colour to a mixed foliage planting.

Hawthorn maple

Acer ginnala Amur maple

Whether a small tree on a pale grey-barked bole or more of a bush, this very hardy plant from northern China and Mongolia is highly desirable for small gardens and for a shrubbery or the edge of a wood. It comes into leaf yellowish with numerous erect rounded heads of pale yellow scented flowers, and by the time the leaves are dark green the bunches of fruit are tinged red. The leaves, 6–8 cm long, have a long, slender, pointed central lobe and a small triangular lobe each side near the base, all of them deeply and irregularly toothed. In autumn this is among the first trees to show colour, the leaves turning deep red.

Much planted where winters are really cold, as in Winnipeg and Quebec, often in tubs, the Amur maple has a crown of rather dense, twisting branches on which the bark is smooth silvery-grey. The fruit turn dull brown and are conspicuous before leaf-fall and that is about the only point which may be held against it.

Amur maple

Acer hersii Hers's maple

This tree is named from the French collector who found it in China and introduced it in 1927. It is one of the best of the snake-barks and very distinctive. The bright white stripes are on a smooth green background which is retained until the bole is some 30 cm in diameter, after which corky patches of brown and grey appear and angular pits become prominent.

The crown develops long arching branches well clothed with leaves but with few or no lateral shoots and they sweep down as a fine fountain of green, a feature shared only by one form of David's maple and a very rare snake-bark, Forrest's maple. The singular character of Hers's maple among the snake-barks is its devotion to olive green. It leafs out olive green, not red like David's maple, and its shoots and leaf-stalks,

flowers and fruit all remain this colour. The leaves are rather densely held and grow to 12×9 cm, with a broad central lobe and a small acute triangular lobe each side, or are unlobed. It is entirely glabrous and in the basal vein axils beneath there is a purple spot. The abundant flowers on paired, arched catkins (strictly racemes – they have tiny side-branches, as in all the maples with 'catkins') ripen to big broad-winged fruit 5 cm across, yellow-green until tinged pink, then brown.

Hers's maple grows strongly in any reasonable soil and is known so far to 17 m tall. Its value lies in its splendid shape, bark and foliage, and very much in its autumn colours. The leaves turn yellow, then bright orange, then some turn crimson. With its shapely crown this tree is spectacular in autumn.

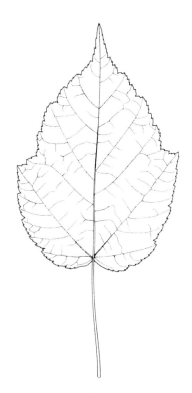

Hers's maple

Acer japonicum Downy Japanese maple

The type here is a bush, which, however splendid, belongs in a book of shrubs. Of the numerous forms cultivated the one below is the only true tree.

'Vitifolium'   This old selection in Japan was sent here in about 1863 but is still uncommon despite a well placed group up to 15 m tall at Westonbirt Arboretum, attracting such crowds for its wonderful autumn display that it should be known as 'Kodak's Benefit'. This form has a very short bole before breaking into two or three sinuous stout upright main branches with pale grey bark. Like the type it has bunches of flowers with quite big dark red petals and a leaf with 7–9 acute triangular finely toothed lobes. It differs from the type in its superior stature, in the leaf being larger, often twice the size, about 10×15 cm (on a few trees even 22×24 cm) and in the variety and brilliance of its autumn colours. The outer leaves which receive sunshine turn scarlet and deep red while those a little inside the crown turn pink, lilac and yellow and those further in are green, then yellow.

Acer lobelii Lobel's maple

As a young tree, Lobel's maple from southern Italy is strictly upright with rather few branches and even fewer side-shoots. It is therefore highly suitable for restricted sites despite the fact that it grows 1–1·3 m a year. Later it grows more slowly and its branches begin to spread. The biggest are 25 m tall with a spread of less than 10 m. The shoots are bloomed lilac in the first year and the leaves, which are held level from little spurs on the erect branches, resemble those of Norway maple except that the five lobes are entire but for an occasional tooth, and the whiskers into which the lobe-tips are drawn curve upwards or sideways. The leaves are light green in summer and show some yellows in autumn, but nothing brilliant.

Any well-drained soil, whether alkaline or acid, will grow this tree well but on a dry site it will need watering for a few years to establish

strongly. Lobel's maple is recommended where a tall tree is wanted in limited space; it is not neat or formal enough to be effective as a group.

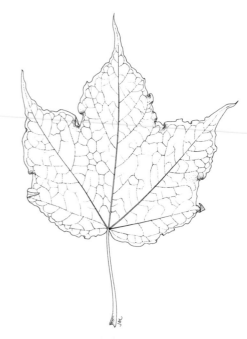

Lobel's maple

Acer macrophyllum Oregon maple

Conic, with a strong leader as a young tree, the Oregon maple matures with a hugely domed crown on radiating and arched branches. The stout shoots bear very big but thinly textured leaves, divided almost to the base into five lobes, the central and two outer ones tapering much towards their bases with a large acute tooth each side at their broadest part and a few smaller ones from there to the leaf-tips. They can be more than 25×30 cm on petioles of 30 cm which expand at the base to enfold the shoot and hide the bud. In May the large expanding buds bear among the leaves an erect, substantial inflorescence which bends over and hangs 25 cm bearing yellow-green flowers, the basal ones maturing into a bunch of large green fruit covered in hard white hairs and with 5 cm green wings. In autumn the leaves turn brown briefly before falling although in Oregon especially, they are a blaze of orange for weeks.

As an open-grown specimen, this vigorous tree needs much space. Although a little dark in summer, the big leaf makes it interesting and the fruit are conspicuous. Leafing out and in flower, it is striking. It can be grown to mature among a group of other trees when its foliage will still show and its fine bole with orange-brown square plates can be well displayed.

Acer negundo Ash-leafed maple; Box-elder

This is one of the trees received by Bishop Henry Compton at Fulham Palace where it arrived in 1688. Its native range is remarkable – from Northern Alberta to California, where it becomes a thickly pubescent variety, and from Quebec to Florida. In the Allegheny Mountains and New England the leaves are handsome, a rich shiny green, but in Britain this is a dull, shapeless and short-lived tree not worth planting.

'Auratum' is, however, a choice tree, and the bright feature of some colour-plantings at Kew. With upswept upper crown and level-branched lower crown, it covers itself in leaves of a rich bright yellow fading to greenish in the late autumn.

'Variegatum' is about the most conspicuously white-variegated tree grown. It is entirely a female tree and carries masses of small fruit of which the wings are mainly white and tinged pink. Sprouts of normal green foliage will keep emerging, and having all their leaf surface green and active in photosynthesis these are much stronger than the variegated shoots and will shade them out unless the secateurs are kept busy.

'Violaceum' is a very vigorous and handsome form which occurs scattered in the wild. It has lilac-bloomed shoots, deep green leaves with red petioles, and soon makes a stout bole and a good tree.

Acer nikoense Nikko maple

One of the trifoliate maples, this Japanese tree has rarely reached 15 m in height and is an excellent medium-small tree. One of its merits is that it colours bright deep reds in autumn even when growing on chalky soils, which it is beyond some Japanese maples to do. The leaves emerge yellow then turn very dark green above, while beneath the leaflets are blue-white and densely hairy, like the dark red, stout petiole. The flowers are cup-shaped and yellow, hanging in threes below the opened leaves. The fruit are 5 cm across with broad pubescent wings obtusely spreading, dark green tinged dark red with white hairs over the big nutlets. The bark is smooth, tight and dark grey.

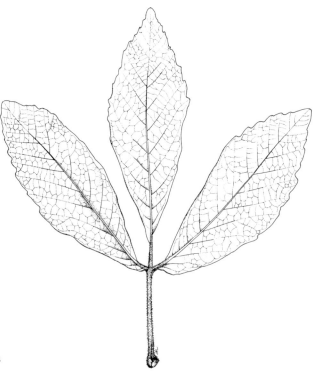

Nikko maple

Acer platanoides Norway maple

This species has several features which combine to
make it one of the amenity trees of greatest value.
For a start, it will thrive equally on thin soils over
chalk and on acid sands. It grows well on clays
and tolerates a largely paved root-run. It
transplants well as a big tree 2–4 m tall and even
then it can grow rapidly. It is easily pruned to give
a clean, smooth bole in a few years. Then the tree
itself has many merits. It approaches the
spectacular when thickly covered in bunches of
bright acid-yellow-green flowers towards the end
of March when few trees are flowering and before
the leaves emerge. The flowers turn to green as
the leaves unfold and darken with them but even
in midsummer the dense crown is a fresher green
than the sycamore, without that tree's blackish
cast. In the early autumn a few trees turn bright
orange while the majority are reliably butter-
yellow all over during most of October. The broad
leaves are thin in texture and the five lobes of each
have a few large teeth which, like the lobes, are
tipped by a finely drawn-out whisker.

The Norway maple ranges west from the
Caucasus Mountains across much of Europe north
to southern Sweden and just into Norway. It was
being grown in Edinburgh before 1683 and has
long been planted around the edges of estate parks
and in large gardens. In Scotland it tends to be
mostly on large estates but in south-east England
especially it is more widespread and on some
sandy soils it sows itself freely. It is common on
the chalklands. Although it can grow 2 m a year
when young it soon culminates in height at or
below 25 m and it is not very long-lived. Boles
more than 1 m in diameter are rare and only seen
in trees aged around 100 years; few seem to live
much longer although some may reach 150 years.

The cultivars of Norway maple are numerous
and of highly varying value.

'Columnare', 'Erectum' and 'Pyramidale' are in
effect all the same tree, which arose in France and
was marketed under the first name. Slender and
very erect, this valuable form is almost unknown
here but is seen in some cities and many
collections in the USA.

'Globosum' similarly is planted in the USA and in
Europe but its tightly spherical dense crown is
scarcely seen in Britain.

'Schwedleri' has deep red buds in winter and
opens its flowers two weeks later than the type;
they are on red pedicels and have red calyces and
yellow petals, giving a strange brownish
appearance among unfolding red leaves. In
autumn the foliage turns early to orange and then
to crimson. This is quite a good tree but it has
given rise to the over-planted forms below.

'Goldsworth Purple' has large leaves of that deep
dull blackish-red known in trees as 'purple'. Often
used in plantings of mixed colours it takes all the
light and life out of them.

'Faasen's Black' is even duller than 'Goldsworth
Purple', with even bigger, blacker leaves, tinged
brown.

'Drummondii' remains of very moderate size, with
a neat dense crown, brightening everything
around with its small leaves thickly margined and
spotted pale cream or white.

Acer pseudoplatanus Sycamore

The Sycamore or Great maple ranges from the
Caucasus Mountains to central and southern
Europe near to Paris and may have been brought
here by the Romans. It is remarkably resistant to
maritime exposure, polluted air and high altitude.
It yields hard, white first-class timber, neither
giving nor receiving taint from foods, dyeing well
and taking a fine finish. It can be invasive in
fertile woodland soils, seeding abundantly. In
many areas it is of poor form but there are
majestic trees with fine boles in Kent, much of
Yorkshire, and lowland Scotland. In these areas
it is known to 35 m in height and 200 cm in
diameter. From periodic measurements since
1880, the biggest tree in diameter, near the
River Tay at Birnam, Perthshire, must be
about 380 years old while the Corstorphine

sycamore, the original tree of a form which leafs out rich gold then fades to green, is 375 years old now, quite healthy and only 117 cm in diameter, in a tiny suburban front garden in Edinburgh.

Although not naturally found near the sea, the Sycamore is the best hardwood tree for the extreme maritime winds and cool summers of the Western Isles and in smoky cities. It cannot be said to be ornamental, and its only contribution to wildlife is to provide a perch for town pigeons and house sparrows, but it will grow and make smooth, reasonably good boles on limestones as well as on acidic city soils, gravels or clay, so it has a great value in the least favourable places.

The heavily leafed, domed crown of the Sycamore makes it suitable for screens and for clumps and roundels. Although a small clump can be pure sycamore, it will have a poor sward beneath as the big, leathery leaves can form mats very slow to break down; woods or lengths of peripheral belts should be small-sized if pure. If used more extensively it should be mixed with trees with lighter crowns, like birch or larch. Thinning Sycamore is a lengthy procedure as cut trees sprout strongly and, if left, the sprouts deaden the wood by shading out all other plants and are of no interest to birds; they therefore need cutting back several times early in the year.

'Brilliantissimum'. No garden should be without this remarkable cultivar as it is among the most spectacular of foliage-trees for nearly two months in late spring. Grafted on a 2 m stem of ordinary Sycamore, it forms a small, tight, bun-shaped crown on a leg for some years, gradually becoming less odd-looking and making a shapely, if bushy tree nearly 12 m tall in 60 years. The buds open with leaves expanding bright pink. These become red and pink for a few days then begin to change through orange to yellow, a fine spectacle which lasts two weeks; they remain a clear yellow for up to three weeks then fade to white for about a week before turning a rather poor dull green. A similar form, 'Prinz Handjery', is a little more open and bears numerous 'catkins' of yellow flowers when the leaves are at their reddest. It has more sharply-lobed leaves, often purple beneath.

Both these trees are invaluable for brightening up a corner of a shrubbery or as one among several small trees on a small lawn. As a single specimen they suffer from very dull foliage after July so despite their long period of glory they are better when not prominently solitary. They are quite undemanding of soil and will tolerate light shade.

Acer rubrum Red maple

First brought here by John Tradescant in 1656, this tree ranges throughout eastern North America. The name is due to the red flowers which wreathe the shoots in spring before the leaves unfold. Autumn colours are, in most young trees, spectacular, with scarlet outer foliage and orange and yellow interior, until it is briefly deep red all over. The leaves are pale orange when unfolding after which they are dark green above and silvered beneath. They have three main large but shallow lobes, coarsely toothed, and may have two smaller basal lobes. The petiole is slender and red. The crown is somewhat narrow with long,

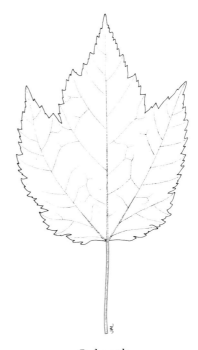

Red maple

slender and often curved, whip-like shoots, and
the bark is pale, dull grey, smooth at first but
becoming fissured and flaking in strips.

A tree of rapid early growth and with the
above features should be very popular, but the Red
maple is little known and so seldom planted. It has
a reputation for not succeeding on chalky soils but
will in fact grow well on them although it may
colour less riotously in autumn. It can achieve
22 m without spreading far, but the autumn
display of old trees is more limited, the outer tips of
foliage turning early to crimson-red and the
interior a less reliable, dull yellow which may fall
before also turning red. A good tree, nonetheless,
to have in a group of specimens, or above shrubs,
as it casts little shade until old. In a park, a drift of
these along a bank would form a notable feature.

Acer rufinerve Grey-budded snake-bark maple

This Japanese tree is somewhat variable, or
perhaps there are two forms. One has pink stripes
on very pale grey bark, large firm leaves and a
good constitution. The other, which is rather more
usual, has green stripes on dull grey bark, smaller
darker leaves and a bad tendency for the upper
branches to die back. Both forms make a fine show
of orange and scarlet autumn colours. This tree is
known from the other similar snake-barks by its
leaf being broader than it is long; by the shoot and
buds bloomed pale grey, quite blue on buds of old
wood; and by the rusty down at the base of the
underside of the leaf, reduced by midsummer to
rust-brown patches between the basal veins. The
fruit, usually copiously borne in dense bunches,
are very small, up to 2 cm across the widely
angled wings.

Grey-budded snakebark maple

Acer saccharinum Silver maple
(*A. dasycarpum*)

This close relative of the Red maple (p. 63) has the
leaf underside much more strongly silvered and
a gust of wind can make a tree seem suddenly white
with frost. It is a far bigger and more vigorous
tree, 27–30 m tall and 1 m in diameter, and when
young will often make shoots 2 m long. The
flowers are dark red, showing some green,
clustered on short spurs at the nodes of the shoots
before the leaves unfold, as early as February in
some years. The leaves emerge reddish-orange
before assuming the pale green upper surface of
summer, then in autumn they become mostly pale
yellow and brown, although a few are scarlet. The
broadly-winged fruit are rare in this country.

The deep lobing and toothing of the leaf,
together with the distinctly silvered underside,
cannot help but make the Silver maple a good
foliage-tree, and its great vigour is a useful asset,
but it also has some less desirable features. The tall
crown of upright arched branches is often too thin
to be a good screen and is liable to breakage in

gales. The stout bole is often sprouty and looks better if kept clean, and the tree is unlikely to live more than 150 years. However, a tree which grows so well on clays or sands and in city air has its uses.

'Laciniatum' is a variant frequent in the wild, but the extreme form 'Weirii' found in Rochester, New York, is the one grown, very vigorous with brown, pendulous shoots, red petioles and deeply incised leaves. In this named selection they are not only cut to near the base, but have red petioles and the crown is long-pendulous. It is just as vigorous as the type and will, no doubt, reach the same sort of size.

Acer saccharum Sugar maple

Few trees are more underrated and overlooked, although quite often present, than the Sugar maple from the eastern United States. Many gardens and estates grow a fine specimen or two unknown to the owner. Although many gardeners think of this tree as a failure here, it grows quite fast for many years and there are trees 20–25 m tall from Hampshire to central Scotland, many in Perthshire and in Ireland, while Westonbirt has a dozen or more. The finest specimen in the country was, until recently, labelled 'Norway maple' and, although it resembles this tree (p. 62), the bark is very distinct with long open fissures and dark grey shaggy plates. The leaves have fewer teeth than the Norway and all are minutely round, not whisker-tipped. It is a fine foliage-tree of moderate size and some trees show bright scarlet autumn colour briefly. However, none here achieves the flame-orange scarlet which is perhaps the most brilliant of all the New England fall colours. The Sugar maple is tolerant of any reasonable garden soil.

Silver maple

Sugar maple

Acer trautvetteri Trautvetter's maple

This Caucasian tree resembles a Sycamore but it has two good features which that tree lacks. Its leaves are deeply divided into five lobes, making the summer crown less heavy and more interesting visually, and it has most decorative fruit with broad wings, each 5 × 2 cm, at an acute angle and turning in early summer bright rosy pink. A heavily fruiting tree appears to be covered in pink flowers. It is not, in fact, a close relative of the Sycamore as is shown by the flowers being in erect, loose panicles and by the sharply acute dark brown buds. It also has smooth grey bark. This makes a good parkland tree, growing well in any ordinary soil and needing, to show at its best, to be isolated from or well in front of other trees and where the full light on its crown encourages flowering.

Trautvetter's maple

Acer × zoeschense Zoeschen maple

This hybrid was raised in a German nursery from a Field maple crossing with either Lobel's maple or, more likely, the Cappadocian maple. It has a tendency to sucker but its broad crown largely suppresses these growths. The leaves are 5-lobed, blackish-green and glossy, held level on 10 cm ruby-red stalks. Zoeschen maple grows quite strongly but has not exceeded 20 m in height, adding a dark but shiny, handsome foliage to a large mixed group.

Zoeschen maple

Aesculus flava Yellow or Sweet buck-eye (*A. octandra*)

This splendid American tree has been here for some 240 years and although seen in city parks, like Battersea Park, London, and in some large gardens well into Scotland, it is much less common than it should be. It would be of immense benefit visually if every one of all those dull Red chestnuts had been a Yellow buck-eye. Frequently

grafted on to Horse chestnut, because of the difficulty in importing fresh seed which cannot be stored, it makes a somewhat narrow-crowned tree to 20 m. The five leaflets are elegantly lanceolate and taper evenly to a fine point; they have slender stalks of 1–2 cm, very fine toothing, are a bright glossy green in summer and turn orange and crimson in autumn. The flowers are not spectacular but are highly attractive as pale yellow spikes among the bright green leaves. The conkers are small and few germinate when sown from trees here.

Aesculus hippocastanum Horse chestnut

So familiar is this tree that it was made one of the four 'British Trees' in a set of postage stamps. It grows freely into a big tree in every part of these islands and most English village greens and rectory gardens would look strange without it. Yet it is native only to mountains in northern Greece, was unknown to Northern European botanists until described in 1596 and did not grow in England until about 1616. At its best, on deep, damp soils in a warm, sheltered site it can be a very fine specimen, to 35 m × 2 m or more, but it will achieve 25 m × 1 m almost anywhere not too exposed and can seed itself around in woodlands. Young plants grow straight, sturdy 60 cm shoots but old trees grow very slowly. The life-span is unusually variable. A few trees known to date back to 1662 are in full health whereas many trees shed branches and break up when probably no more than 120 years old. The weak wood renders a tree in full leaf liable to shed a branch when it is weighted with water from a sudden storm.

The oppositely placed leaves have seven leaflets with broad tips narrowing abruptly to a small point, and radiating directly from the centre without any stalks. They colour well in autumn but vary with the individual tree, a few turning scarlet early but the majority turning yellow then orange from mid-September to early November. The 30 cm panicles of flowers never fail to be prolific on old trees but some years are much better for the resulting 'conkers' than others. The occasional tree in every district comes into leaf and flower as much as a month ahead of the rest. The sticky, resinous dark red-brown buds are not found on any of the numerous relatives of this tree in America, the buck-eyes, nor are they so well developed in the Indian or Japanese horse chestnuts. The bark on old trees is pinkish-brown with hard scales. This is unlike the bark of the Red chestnut or the Yellow buck-eye which are both often grafted on to the Horse chestnut at 1–2 m, when the change to smoother dark red-brown bark is prominent.

'Baumannii' is the form with double flowers and hence without conkers and is planted for that reason in some residential roads where missiles to dislodge conkers can be a hazard. One at Westonbirt, Gloucestershire, is 30 m × 120 cm but no other has been seen of this size and it is not yet a common tree.

'Hampton Court' has leaves variegated with pale yellow or even entirely this colour and is rare. It is named from the tree in the Wilderness at Hampton Court Palace.

Aesculus indica Indian horse chestnut

Brought here from the Himalayas in 1856 this tree is popular with those planting city and resort parks because it flowers nearly two months later than the common Horse chestnut, in late June when parks are having their fullest use. It also has the advantage of coming into leaf a good orange-brown colour, but is nothing special in the autumn except that the conkers can be shining black. The leaflets have stalks, slender and usually red; they are lanceolate and often dark and hanging, with a slightly silvered underside. Some trees bush out with strong low branches and need

Indian horse chestnut

early attention to give them shape. The flowers are on narrow, 30 cm panicles and often so flecked pink that it seems a pink-flowered tree. It grows fairly vigorously in any normal soil.

'Sidney Pearce' is a very sturdy form selected at Kew in 1928. It differs from the type in its larger heads of whiter flowers and broader, lighter leaflets on stout green stalks, less pale beneath.

Aesculus turbinata Japanese horse chestnut

In most respects this can be regarded as a rather superior common Horse chestnut with huge leaves and rich orange autumn colour. It differs in having a smooth grey or grey-pink bark and narrower flower panicles, and the leaflet-tips taper gradually to a long acute, not an abrupt point, but it shares the sessile leaflets. The conkers are smaller than in the common tree, with a bigger white circular patch which covers more than a third of the seed.

The leaf can be 40 cm across on a 42 cm petiole and the underside of the leaflets has small tufts of orange hair at the base of the veins. This tree seems to grow on any normal soil with considerable vigour and is well worth planting for its vast leaves and as a change from the common tree.

Ailanthus altissima Tree of Heaven

Liking a hot summer, this tree from northern China makes little growth in the north or west and is a big tree only from Devon to East Anglia. It is common and grows very rapidly in London, fortunately not as fast as in the cities in the hottest parts of the USA. In the run-down streets of suburban Washington, Atlanta and elsewhere it ramps around by suckers and seeds, breaking up the side-walks, erupting in the medians and filling the gardens and unused plots. The bole is smoothly circular in section and long, with a few stout branches, and the bark is pewter-grey with shallow fissures marked with streaks of white. The leaves emerge very late and dark red and expand to 30–40 cm, bearing 11 to over 40 unequally cordate leaflets to 15 cm long, each with a

distinctive minutely swollen large tooth or two near the base; they fall without colouring, fairly early. Male trees have dense clusters of small white flowers on spikes and female trees have greenish flowers which ripen to fruit with 1–5 wings in big bunches, turning scarlet in the summer and dull brown from autumn to winter.

To have luxuriant foliage at shrub height, a Tree of Heaven can be stumped back annually and the rods will bear huge leaves. As a tree it is suitable only in large spacious places in the south and is in leaf for too short a time to be a good screen.

Alnus cordata Italian alder

The tallest and most shapely of the alders, this tree also has the most distinctive and decorative foliage, and among the best catkins. The leaves are small, 5–8 cm, and heart-shaped; late leaves unfold pale orange, and all mature a smooth, glossy, usually dark green. The catkins are out early and lengthen to 8–10 cm, thick and bright yellow. The fruit are big, glossy dark green, 2·5 cm long, nearly black when woody and old, with numerous separated scales. The bark is dark grey, or brownish-grey, smooth between the few, broad dark fissures. The crown is conic or narrowly domed, sometimes until over 25 m tall.

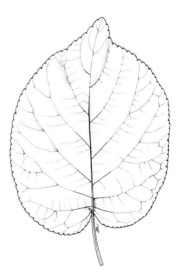

Italian alder

The Italian alder is a remarkably useful tree. It grows very fast when young, to 15 m in 15 years, and beyond this slows much less than other alders. It is not dependent on a wet site, growing best in normally drained but fairly retentive soil and about as well on thin loams over chalk. It is completely hardy and apparently windfirm, early into leaf and late to shed.

Alnus firma Japanese alder

This is a rare tree here and none so far is known as a big tree, but none is yet very old. It is well worth growing for the numerous catkins, neither very long (to 8 cm) nor stout but the brightest gold of any alder, or perhaps any catkins. The leaves are remarkably decorative having numerous prominent parallel veins. It requires only a normally retentive soil. It is one of the few alders grown here which has the bud unstalked.

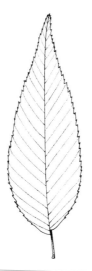

Japanese alder

Alnus glutinosa Common alder

For normal planting this is not a good tree, lacking grace and any positive feature as well as autumn colour. It has one useful purpose and that is holding the banks of lakes and rivers firm against erosion. It will also grow in much-flooded water-margins or hollows, but so will a few preferable trees. The native Alder is usually 15–20 m tall and the crown either one-sided or thin in large patches, not always due to crowding or leaning out over the water although such conditions do not help. But occasionally one sees a sturdy straight tree with a trunk and bark like a prime oak. They grow very strongly for a few years, especially as sprouts from a cut tree, and have a good conic crown but this flattens with age. The bole should be cleaned of all branches as high as can be reached. The male flowers, on catkins, open brownish-yellow over a long period, from February on some trees to April on others. Female flowers are tiny dark red globules on short, branched stalks. The broadly-rounded and indented end to the leaf distinguishes this from all other alders grown here.

'Laciniata' Cut-leaf alder This grows very like the type, and to the same sort of size, but is much more attractive as the heavy dull foliage is transformed by the regular triangular lobes cut halfway to the midrib, giving a light and interesting effect.

'Imperialis'. This is altogether different as it is a slender, rather graceful little tree, often leaning out at the top, with light branches bending to become level. The leaves are light green, on 4 cm petioles and cut deeply, sometimes to the midrib, into five acuminate lobes each side.

'Aurea' Golden alder. Rare, slow and small, this is a good foliage-tree with rich golden leaves.

Alnus incana Grey alder

Although of little merit itself in the garden, and included largely for its cultivars, the Grey alder from Europe is unusually tough and grows vigorously on the inhospitable soils of mine-tips and rubble. The young branches are a good smooth silvery-grey and the acute, well-lobed leaves are pleasant but they are held loosely and from a distance the crown is dull. The grey pubescence on the shoots and underside of the leaves, especially on the veins, is an unusual feature in an alder. The male catkins are variably early and quite attractive. This is a tree for fast growth on a really difficult site – 9 m in nine years is known.

'Aurea' and 'Ramulis Coccineis' are almost identical, the latter having more prominent, brighter catkins in bud when they are scarlet. Both have winter shoots bright orange-red, leaf-buds scarlet and leaves bright yellow. Neither is anything like as vigorous as the type and both make rather bushy small trees.

'Pendula' is an untidy, irregular and very pendulous weeping tree of no great size or attraction.

Alnus rubra Oregon alder; Red alder

The Oregon alder starts in great style with shoots to 1·5 m long (one at Westonbirt is 18 m after 12 years) and huge leaves, sometimes 15 × 12 cm, even on poor wet peats or clay over chalk, but it rarely keeps its promise. It was introduced in 1880 but the oldest at present on record dates from 1930 and is only 19 m tall. Many fail when younger. The leaf is like that of the Grey alder but broader, with bigger lobes and – a useful spot character – the margin is minutely but sharply curved under, all round the lobes and their teeth. In its native damp wooded valleys along the Coast Range and Cascade Mountains, south from Washington and especially through Oregon, the bark of even young trees is silvery-white but here it is always leaden grey.

　　The value of this tree is to raise rapid shelter in wet, peaty hollows, and few trees are better for the purpose if mixed with longer-term species like Sitka spruce or Shore pine. These grow much the better for having the Alder amongst them as alders fix nitrogen in nodules on their roots and their leaf-litter acts as a nitrogenous fertilizer.

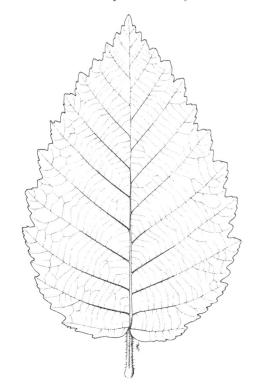

Red alder

Alnus subcordata Caucasian alder

This alder is little known as yet and the four trees at Kew, 50–60 years old, are almost the only indication that it does, to some extent, retain its great early vigour of growth. They vary much in the shape of their big leaves; some broad and floppy, others narrow and willow-like, others in between. This is an interesting tree to try in an unimportant position, for its rapid early growth; one in Surrey in its third year from seed had grown a leading shoot 2 m long with leaves to 25 cm long and now 14 years old is 15 m × 40 cm.

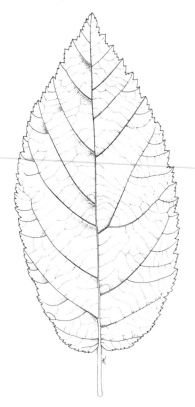

Caucasian alder

Arbutus andrachne Cyprus strawberry tree

This little tree is ideal for warm dry south-eastern gardens. The main attraction is the bright rufous-orange bark peeling or flaking away each year to show whitish or pale lemon smooth patches. When halfway through this moult the stem is remarkably beautiful. The bark of branches in the crown is yellow-green, in contrast to the only other Strawberry tree with entire leaves, the Madrona, where the branches are orange-red. The Cyprus species has small white urn-shaped flowers in nodding heads in mid-spring and 1 cm smooth red berries in autumn.

With the glossy dark green foliage as well, this is a tree of abundant attraction. Its rarity here is only partly due to its climatic needs, and there should be more in gardens near the south coast of England.

Arbutus × andrachnoides Hybrid strawberry tree

This hybrid occurs in the wild in Greece where the Cyprus and the Common strawberry trees both grow. It is much more robust than either parent, can be 15 m tall and grows in gardens northwards into Scotland. It has rich dark red, slightly purplish, ridged and scaly bark only flaking here and there to leave bald smooth orange-brown. It has a sinuous bole and branches, the latter stout, dark red and often from low down making a broad crown. The flowers are similar to those of both parents and may open at the times appropriate to either, that is, in spring or in late autumn. The mat, pale leaf is serrated. This is good as a substitute for the Madrona or the Cyprus tree where neither can be grown.

Arbutus menziesii Madrona; Pacific strawberry tree

The Madrona is uncommon in the south and rare in the north although there is a fine tree in Morayshire. It grows quite fast into a tree of 20 m and great distinction. Short as we are of reasonably hardy, large, decorative evergreen broadleaf trees, this should be planted more often, in the south-east at least. The bark is pinkish-orange or orange-red and sheds big flakes to leave large irregular bald yellow-pink areas, and on branches within the crown it is rich orange. Seedlings have serrated leaves but after a few years they grow into adult entire leaves which can be over 12 cm long and 7 cm across. They are evergreen and crowd rather towards the tip of the shoot, deep shiny green above but yellower and paler, often blotched black, before being shed and glaucous blue-grey beneath. The flowers are prominent in spring, numerous and small, crowded on and spreading from an erect panicle which is 20 × 15 cm. The fruit are small and globose dark green, ripening orange-red in August in some years and in others remaining green until October, both here and in America.

The striking bark, good evergreen foliage, plentiful flowers and fruit, the vigour and stature make the Madrona an undoubtedly first-class tree for town parks and general planting except in great exposure to the north, and it is not fussy about soil. The only difficulty is the minor one that for three or four years from seed it can be killed by frost if it is growing in tall grass.

Arbutus unedo Strawberry tree

Native to the south-west of Ireland in Counties Kerry and Cork, and further north in Sligo, this has become very much a village tree in England, more often found in old gardens and churchyards than in larger gardens. It does not give the good display of coloured bark that is often associated with Strawberry trees as the bole is soon grey-brown scaly ridges or largely dark grey, but it does present a unique and cheerful aspect in late autumn. At that time its nearly black foliage is decorated both with nodding heads of white flowers and with the fruit of the previous year's flowers turning yellow, orange and scarlet.

'Unedo' means 'I eat one', an academic joke implying 'one only' since the fruit tempt but are unacceptably insipid with a not very pleasant after-flavour. On low rocky cliffs in County Cork this is growing as a tangle of low shrubs, and in gardens it rarely achieves 9 m in height or a bole of 2 m in length, but is usually broad, low-boled and bushy. Grown cleaned up on a 'leg' of 2 m or more it would make a far better single specimen than is usually seen, but it is an interesting tree to have and admirable in late autumn. It should have a sheltered corner for, notwithstanding its coastal home in an area noted for strong winds and its very hard close-grained pink wood, the Strawberry tree can have branches blown out of it or be upturned by gales.

Betula ermanii Erman's birch

Erman's birch grows over wide areas of Manchuria and Korea as well as Japan which is where the first seed came from. It therefore tends to be variable in gardens but retains several distinctive features. The leaves are cuneate, tapering to the stalk in varying widths; they have prominent impressed parallel veins in 7–11 pairs and they are densely borne with many spreading out level. The fruit, compact cylinders 4 cm long, are usually abundant and persist through the winter during which, from a distance, they are a good indicator of the species. The bark of the branches and bole of young trees is clear white and in somewhat older trees the branches remain white while the bole becomes dull pink and beribboned with loose, fine horizontal papery strips. When the lower branches are stout with age they also have strips hanging in fringes.

This tree is grown more for its very white bark in youth than for the attractive foliage. It has ascending branches and grows vigorously on any well-drained soil including poor sands. It is not among the best birches for autumn colours but it is a good tree in leaf and when bare.

Betula jacquemontii Jacquemont's birch; Kashmir birch
Betula utilis Himalayan birch

These two are not easily distinguishable and the form of Kashmir birch often supplied is botanically the Himalayan birch. The latter has a strikingly white smooth bark and good leaves marked by 10–12 pairs of impressed parallel veins. The true Kashmir birch has seven pairs of veins and similar bark although some may, like those in the native stands, be cream or pale orange and shed big papery sheets. The Himalayan birch has strong, steeply rising branches and firm, shiny leaves on stout, grooved and often dark red stalks covered, like the shoot, in long hairs. In autumn the leaves turn pale then bright yellow. Bark is remarkably variable. Apart from the Kashmir form, the usual Himalayan birch has the clearest white bark of any birch, but some have smooth tan-brown bark and others olive-brown, while a few are marbled in red-brown, pale brown and black and look like a python skin.

In any form these are excellent trees as single specimens with winter interest and autumn colour, or as small clumps. They are also one of the very best trees for the edges of glades or for fringing woodland where it grows near a lawn.

Betula lenta Cherry birch

This has much in common with the Yellow birch (below) including a similar range in eastern North America and the strong scent of oil of wintergreen when shoots are skinned or crushed. In the wild woods, the two are easily distinguishable by the bigger, broader leaves of the Yellow birch but in cultivation there is less difference in the leaf. The barks are reliably different although both are partly dull grey and roll horizontally into papery strips; that of the Cherry birch has a purple shade or dark red patches while that of the Yellow birch has a yellow-grey, silvery cast or pale pinkish patches. The Cherry birch has a broad crown of level branches at the base and ascending ones above, with large, remote leaf-spurs. The fruit are erect, often numerous, ovoid-oblong 3·5 m long with spreading tips to the scales. Briefly in autumn the foliage is moderately bright yellow. The leaves are narrow-ovate-acuminate, slightly cordate, regularly double-toothed with 9–12 pairs of parallel veins. This is a pleasant little tree, growing on any fairly normal soil to 16 m.

Betula lutea Yellow birch (*B. alleghaniensis*)

This is very like the Cherry birch (above) where the main differences are outlined. The leaf is noticeably flat with 12–15 pairs of parallel veins, rounded at base and irregularly double-toothed, ovate and acute rather than acuminate. Autumn colour is earlier than in Cherry birch, as fleeting but brighter gold. This also grows to 16 m but seldom more, in any reasonable soils.

Betula maximowicziana Monarch birch

A good specimen of this Japanese tree is indeed the king of the birches with big, substantial broad leaves like the Lime, to 15 × 12 cm, glossy rich green and elegantly toothed. Each of the 10–12 veins on either side ends in a fine bristle of a tooth projecting beyond the several sharp teeth between. An added attraction is that in young trees the leaves emerge covered in pale orange hairs. The male catkins are 10–12 cm long when open and yellow, among freshly unfolded leaves. The crown

is more strongly branched than in other birches, the branches rising at a fairly wide angle. Growth is quite rapid and although decidedly uncommon, with few trees to be found more than twenty years old, some of these are over 20 m tall. The bark is at first dark red-brown but soon becomes smooth, white striped horizontally with grey-brown, and later it is in parts orange and pink.

This makes a handsome and unusual lawn-tree, tolerant of most soils and perfectly hardy.

Monarch birch

Betula medwediewii Transcaucasian birch

This tree from the mountains around the south of the Caspian Sea makes a short-stemmed, broad, upright bushy tree to 12 m. It has a dull silvery-grey bark flaking in ridges and large dark green leaves, to 14 × 11 cm, ovate to nearly round, deeply set with about 12 parallel veins each side.

It is slow and in view of its shape is best planted where a large shrub is needed, one with character and giving beautiful golden autumn colour.

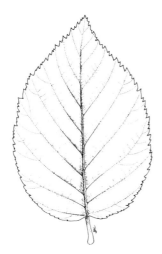

Transcaucasian birch

Betula nigra Black or River birch

Although ranging across the eastern USA as far north as Vermont, this tree has, everywhere in its range, hotter summers than it finds here, and grows better down in Tennessee and Georgia than in the northern states. Hence it is rarely seen away from south-eastern England, where it is still scarce and only a few mature trees are known. It prefers a damp soil and sheltered site but must be more adaptable than is commonly thought for a few have grown quite well in the pavement of a

Black birch

road near Woking. It grows a broad crown with pendulous outer shoots on a few stout up-curved branches. The characteristics for which the tree might be planted are its bark and foliage. Young trees have pale orange to brown bark with blackish scales. When around 30 years old the bark is deep red-brown with papery rolls and strips which hang from the branches in translucent tatters. The leaves are unusual in being rather diamond-shaped, lobulate and often silvered beneath.

Betula papyrifera Paper-bark birch

Almost the whole of Canada from coast to coast is the home of this birch, as well as the northernmost fringe of the USA and its north-eastern corner. In most of this range, the tree has a chalky-white bark and in the New England states the bark is bright white, banded by black rings and grey-stippled faint ridged rings, with black moustaches over branch-scars, as it is in northern Alberta. In gardens here, however, the bark is seldom white for long but has orange tones, pink or pale brown areas, or is largely dark purple. The Paper-bark birch is known by its large, few-veined leaves with relatively stout, sparsely long, silky-haired petioles and the rough, warty shoots. It is occasionally 23 m tall but is probably short-lived; remarkably few trees are seen approaching maturity, yet it is a well-known and long introduced plant.

Betula pendula Silver birch (*B. verrucosa*)

The two native birch trees are found growing together on many heaths and in mountain valleys, with the Downy birch, *B. pubescens*, in the wet patches and the Silver birch on the dry. The adjective 'pendula' is then seen to be usefully apt, for from a distance the twiggy bunchy crown of the Downy birch distinguishes that tree from the gracefully pendulous shoots of the Silver birch. Further distinctions are the black diamonds on the bark of the Silver, as against grey bands on the Downy, and warty as opposed to softly pubescent shoots.

Of the two only the Silver birch is of garden

and landscape value except where trees are needed in a boggy patch of sandy soil. The Silver birch grows rapidly, at 1 m a year when young, to 23–25 m on almost any soils including chalks and clays as well as acid light sands; where these dried out to a depth in the 1976 drought, birches were killed, but this very rarely happens. In a garden on fairly good soil, the light shade cast allows good growth of bulbs and herbs under the trees as well as azaleas and other shrubs; on hungry sands, however, the tree's strong root-system gathers wherever good soil is placed, so shrubs planted in leaf-mould are soon sitting on a mass of birch roots and suffer accordingly. This is a good tree for extending planting into the edges of a lawn or for framing a vista, as a natural edge to thicker woods. It also makes a good medium-scale roundel or clump. As a lawn specimen it responds to early cleaning of all growth from the lower bole not only by looking better for losing shaded-out twiggy shoots but also in producing cleaner and whiter bark which is enhanced by exposure to winds, and makes the Silver birch more visible. In late autumn the leaves turn yellow and remain longer than on most birches.

'Dalecarlica' Swedish birch; Cut-leaf birch In Sweden the ordinary birch has a smooth, cylindrical straight bole whereas in Britain most boles are fluted, often sprouty and not straight for very far. The Cut-leaf was found as an individual at Ornäs, north of Stockholm, in 1767 and in 1810 grafts were raised at Stockholm. Hence this tree, even grown here as a graft or seedling, has not only the pretty deeply-cut leaf but a smoothly rounded, white-barked long bole. It makes a remarkably decorative specimen, very pendulous and adaptable, needing only full light for its proper growth. Being so light and airy, it makes more impact in a large garden planted in groups of three at some 7–8 m spacing.

Betula platyphylla var. **szechuanica**
Szechuan birch

This tree was sent from China in 1908 and is decidedly rare. Although not a great grower nor a very shapely tree it has good points in its very

pure white bark, unmarked over large areas, and solid, leathery, dark, nearly round leaves.

Carpinus betulus Hornbeam

This native tree was one of the last to enter England before the land-bridge was eroded and is wild only in the south-east and perhaps west to Somerset and north to Hereford. It is of great value, although little planted until recently, in liking to grow on heavy clay. It is the typical tree of the fragments of the old forest on London Clay in Hainault and Epping where there was a long history of lopping – cutting back periodically at 2·5 m from the ground. The old trees in those forests are thus pollards, with branches springing from that height. The wood is among the hardest known and immensely strong. It was used for cogwheels in mills and for the centres of cartwheels, which need holes for the spokes but must retain great strength. It is still used for the hammers in pianos and in butchers' chopping-blocks, where the hornbeam centre is set in beech; the beech-wood is softer and wears away to leave the raised centre required for chopping meat.

The Hornbeam is an attractive tree in winter, with its leaden grey bark patterned with dark streaks and broadly domed crown of fine, straight shoots. In early spring the small, brownish catkins open in profusion. The female flowers are slender, down-curved green catkins and ripen into the dark green Chinese lanterns which adorn the crown. The leaves have fine, sharp teeth and prominent parallel veins. In autumn the leaves turn yellow, then orange-brown.

This tree grows quite well to a moderate size in town parks, it is a little dull for planting in numbers but a useful background tree, especially on heavy soil.

'Fastigiata' Pyramidal hornbeam. This splendid form is deservedly now very popular for streets, parks and gardens and makes a fine specimen tree of moderate size but great distinction. Left to itself as a cutting, it makes a huge, upright, dense bush but it is far better, as is normally seen, grown on a clean stem of 2 m, from which the very shapely crown grows as a tall ovoid. It has all the good features of the type and a strikingly dense, formal shape, ideally suiting it to short avenues and groups. Young trees are strictly columnar, which is confusing, for the form 'Columnaris' makes a shrubby and untidy small tree quite unlike 'Fastigiata'.

Hornbeam

Carpinus japonica Japanese hornbeam

Unfortunately this little tree is both rare and slow-growing. One can have nearly the same effect with much more vigour by planting a Hop-hornbeam instead (p. 110), but the Japanese hornbeam has better leaves. They are oblong-lanceolate, to 10 cm long, and have 20 or more pairs of parallel veins, each vein running to a longer tooth than the two between, and the ends curl above the surface of the leaf. The bark is smooth, dark grey or dark green marked by pink wavy stripes. The fruit are broad cylindric bunches, 3 cm long, of in-curved, bright green coarsely toothed bracts flushed crimson after midsummer. Like the similar Chinese species, *C. cordata*, which has the leaves twice as broad and deeply cordate, this is better regarded as a shrub than as a tree in isolation.

Carya cordiformis Bitternut

This hickory from the eastern United States is easily distinguished from all others likely to be seen in Britain by its slender bright yellow buds, and by usually having nine leaflets, the terminal leaflet cuneate down its stalk to the base. The bark also is distinct, being grey-brown to brown shallow ridges in a network. It is an elegant tree with long slender branches raised at a steep angle and arching out at the top. Hence, although conic when immature, it later becomes vase-shaped, broadest near the top. It has achieved 25 m and more in several gardens in the south and 15–20 m further north but it really needs hotter summers than it finds here and is rather slow-growing even though planted on the good, well-drained soils on which it does best, and in some side-shelter. The male flowers are greenish on three-pronged catkins; the females grow 2–3 together close to the shoot near the tip, swelling and ripening to pear-shaped, yellow-green 4 cm fruit with four flanges on the outer half. It is the rather elegant form and bright clear golden yellow of the autumn foliage which make this a desirable tree. Hickory seeds do not store, nor keep long, and the plants resent being moved when more than a few years old and still very small. Hickories are therefore not easy trees to acquire and if plants more than two years' old are bought they should be in containers unless they can be planted at once on their final site.

Carya ovata Shagbark hickory

From an early age the grey bark accords with the tree's name and when fairly old, dark grey surfboards seem to be growing on the bole. The only other hickory – in fact, the only tree – in Britain with similar bark is the Big shell-bark hickory (below). The Shagbark hickory from eastern North America has big five-parted leaves 45–65 cm long which are either smooth, faintly oily and thick or, less commonly, thin, hard, parchment-like and dark. The oily leaves are yellow-green. There are minute tufts of hair between the teeth of the leaf and often rings of pale brown hair near the node on the stout green young shoot. The crown is distinctively broad with stout level branches and gaunt in winter. The big leaves turning bright yellow in autumn make this a foliage-tree of some worth, hardy, but best in a sheltered spot on good, preferably deep loam.

Carya laciniosa Big Shell-bark hickory

This is one of the two hickories from the eastern United States with very big seven-parted leaves, the other being the Mockernut (below). The Big shell-bark has dark grey shaggy bark like the Shagbark and when young it is pale grey with adhering slender curving strips. The leaves can be 75 cm long and are rather thin; the rachis and petiole are densely but softly pubescent and the terminal leaflet has a stalk 1 cm long or less. The crown is like the Bitternut, with ascending and arching slender branches, and although a scarce tree several are over 20 m tall. It is handsome in leaf, bright pale green, and turns a good yellow in the autumn.

Carya tomentosa Mockernut

The feature separating this at once from the other hickories is the smooth dark grey bark which is unfissured or ridged or plated even when the tree is 50 years old. Only very old trees in their native woods in eastern North America acquire shallow ridges. The leaf is no longer than 50 cm and its rachis and stalk, like the shoot, are covered in dense and hard pubescence. The leaves are hard, thin and dark and pleasantly aromatic when crushed. The crown tends to be tall-conic and in autumn it becomes a tower of brilliant gold. The terminal leaflet has a slender, 2–4 cm stalk. Although slow to reach a good size and rarely seen over 20 m tall, the Mockernut is a good-looking tree at any time it is in leaf and spectacular in autumn. It has the same needs and problems as are recounted under Bitternut (p. 77).

Castanea sativa Sweet chestnut; Spanish chestnut

The Sweet chestnut is a member of the Beech and Oak Family native to Southern Europe but thriving in our mild northern climate. Probably introduced by the Romans, it is a common woodland tree over most of these islands and grows very fast in the south but less rapidly in the north. The oldest known tree of any sort in Britain with a documented planting date is a Sweet chestnut at Castle Leod in Easter Ross, north of Dingwall. Planted in 1550 it was 2·47 m in diameter in 1980. In England and Ireland some trees scarcely half as old are 2·7–2·8 m in diameter. This is evidently a long-lived tree but the age of over 1000 years credited to one tree must be mythical as the bole is not nearly big enough to indicate such an age at the rates of growth observed.

The Sweet chestnut makes a very good background tree, being fast-growing, exceedingly robust and capable of making a fine clean bole when grown in a group. It also has a broad crown of quite dense and very handsome foliage and is ornamented each June with sprays of whitish male catkins. In late autumn the leaves turn a good yellow, then pale brown or sometimes orange. As a single specimen, this tree is not in the first rank; open-grown, it seldom makes great height growth but spreads far on big, low branches and it is nondescript in winter. The oldest trees have become picturesque in their senility but this is a long time to have to wait. By then the bark is in spiralled grooves at a small angle from the ground. These grooves start as vertical fissures in the smooth grey bark of the tree when it is about 40 years old and 60 cm in diameter. Gradually the bark turns brown and the ridges and fissures begin to lean into a spiral which may be at about 45° when the bole is 1·5 m through but is ever nearer the horizontal with increasing age.

The Sweet chestnut grows best on light soils and gravels and is not good on heavy clay, but it is fairly tolerant and will grow in city parks. It coppices freely and chestnut coppice is an optimum habitat for bluebells and nightingales if some oak standards are also grown. The hop-pole market has almost disappeared but chestnut-paling fencing is still in demand.

The arrangement of the flowers is unusual. The prominent long catkins seen first are strung with male flowers. Female flowers are white stigmata from bright green bracts – on shorter catkins nearer the tip of the shoot. The outer parts of these catkins bear closed buds at that time but weeks later these may open as white male flowers on erect spikes.

Catalpa bignonioides Southern catalpa; Indian bean tree

Coming as it does from the American Deep South with long, very hot summers, it is not surprising that the best trees here, with plenty of flowers, are in the cities and sheltered gardens of the southern counties of England and in East Anglia where it grows very fast but rarely lives long. It also branches low unless pruned to one strong bud every year, for although a young plant will grow a single rod 2 m long, it grows on too late in the season to harden off the last 15 cm or so. Consequently there is never a terminal bud active in the spring and two or three shoots emerge from lower whorls. These have to be sorted out before any one has dominated and become strong. This can be done for only a few years before even a singled shoot makes but weak growth and the crown inevitably starts to bush out. It is soon broader than it is tall and old trees are usually very spreading. Since catalpas require all the sun they can have in order to bear a worth-while crop of flowers, they do need space. They are also only summer trees if grown for foliage, as they are late into leaf and early to shed. The Catalpa is gaunt and often shapeless in winter, and it rarely has time to show any autumn colour. After leaf-fall it has only fruit to ornament it – these are bunches of slender pods 20–40 cm long, green and then brown.

In its season this is an excellent tree because its large ovate leaves, to 25 cm long, are fresh yellow-green and a change from the general run of foliages in a garden. The frilled white late summer flowers, spotted yellow and purple, on panicles 20 cm high, are an added bonus.

The Catalpa ought to be planted in position as a one-year seedling so that it can make its second-year big growth of shoot and root without further disturbance. Unfortunately the market is geared towards selling big trees rather than seedlings, and new plants thus have big tops but have been shorn of the feeding roots to support them, and there is a check while new roots are grown. North of the English Midlands the Catalpa is a short-season foliage tree only, as it will not flower freely; nor is growth fast there so, unless a slow, small, bushy tree of unusual foliage is much needed, this is not a tree to consider in cool areas.

'Aurea' Golden catalpa. As an effective tree this is even more restricted to the south and east with warm summers than is the green, type tree. The best trees are in the warmer cities like Bath and London and it is seen in Surrey nurseries but not much elsewhere. The leaf is the same size as in the type but expands pale then firms up a bright butter-yellow, greening a little during the summer. It is a fine feature in early summer but gaunt for a long bare season, and no asset if it flowers, white among yellow leaves. The leaves sometimes scorch in hot sunshine; to prevent this, a little shade from the midday sun is a help but it will decrease the gold colour. It tends to have a lower and proportionately broader crown than the type.

Both Golden and the type Catalpa grow well on light sandy soils, also on gravelly or clay soils, and tolerate lime.

Catalpa speciosa Northern catalpa

We received the wrong Catalpa first when the Southern species was sent in 1726 for, by the time the Northern arrived in 1880, the southern tree was firmly entrenched. The Northern catalpa comes from Missouri and Illinois, a region with hotter summers than ours but not as hot, steamy and long as those of Louisiana where the Southern species flourishes. The winters in which the Northern trees live are much more severe than in Britain, so this type should be hardier in general. But it remains decidedly scarce. There is a huge one in a Twickenham park; some collections grow it and there are a few in front gardens and streets in Reading, Aldershot, and Banstead, for example, but the catalpas in most London squares are the Southern species, despite a good planting of the Northern at Southwark Cathedral.

The Northern catalpa foliage is very like the other except that the leaf-tip is longer-drawn-out, more acuminate and the base more often deeply cordate while the petiole, at first at least, is pubescent, and the leaves become yellowish late in the summer and bright pale yellow in autumn. The bark is a much more positive point of difference between these two trees. The Southern has pink-brown or grey-brown thin scaly bark whereas the Northern has dark grey willow-like bark with deep spiral ridges. Its flowers open a month before those of the Southern, in mid-summer, and at 6 cm across are a little bigger, on a slightly smaller, more open panicle which thus does not carry so many.

Catalpa × erubescens Hybrid catalpa
(*C. × hybrida*)

Where space is available, this is the Catalpa to choose. It has decidedly larger leaves than either of the foregoing, flowers earlier in life although later in the year, and grows more vigorously into a big tree. It may either be tall, to over 20 m, or hugely spreading, rarely both. The leaves are mostly shallowly five-lobed and broader than long, to 35 × 30 cm. They emerge from the bud dark purple and turn pale green until they fall. The flower panicles are 30 × 20 cm, open and rather sparsely bearing highly fragrant flowers much like the others. The bark is dull grey and deeply ridged. This is a cross between the Southern and the Chinese yellow catalpas which arose in 1879 in Indiana. The lobed leaf is the only feature that shows the influence of the Chinese parent; the Hybrid was thought for some time to be a cross between the Southern and Northern.

Catalpa ovata Yellow catalpa

This tree is scarce even in the south, although one is the central tree in Leatherhead, Surrey. It has noticeably dark leaves and dark reddish petioles while the flowers appear to be pale yellow but are whitish with yellow spots. In southern counties it is a useful change from the other catalpas.

Cedrela (Syn. *Toona sinensis*) Chinese cedar

The reason for a tree with very large pinnate leaves being given the name 'cedar' is that in new-found countries any tree with scented timber was called a cedar and the first of the *Cedrelas* was found in Cuba; its timber being good for cigar-boxes, it was called Cigar-cedar. When others of this genus were found elsewhere the 'cedar' part of the name was retained. The Chinese cedar is a rare tree with very handsome leaves to 70 cm long, and 20–30 leaflets to 12 cm long, usually lacking a terminal one. The bark breaks early into smooth grey plates tinged copper or purple then becomes rough and shaggy. It is hardier than it looks and there is a good tree in the Royal Botanic Garden at Edinburgh. The winter aspect is gaunt as there are singularly few branches, stout, level then up-turned towards the tips.

Cercidiphyllum japonicum Katsura tree

In garden design, this is an important tree imparting an air of elegance and adding a distinctively different kind of foliage as well as a great display of autumn colours. It looks delicate, but apart from a tendency to wilt in bad droughts and for late frosts to kill the flushing leaves, it is remarkably robust and grows very fast. The bark is dull grey and stripping and the crown varies from being a superb spire on a single bole right to the tip to a tall bush on many nearly equal stems or from big low branches. It therefore needs to be watched at first, with the secateurs at the ready. The leaves are small, nearly round and borne in opposite pairs all down the shoots and on spurs along the branches, making a deep, dense crown but with a light, dainty look. It flushes coral pink or deep red, spends the summer a fresh green, and the autumn colour varies from tree to tree and year to year. Young trees usually turn bright deep red but older trees may turn yellow, or yellow followed by pink and red, or yellow and pink, while some with many yellow leaves remain green until late in the season when they turn lilac or purple. Dry autumns can make the leaves shrivel before colouring, and a damp soil solves this problem as well as being best for growth. Many of the finest Katsuras are beside open water or in moist hollows. Given such a soil, this tree is not fussy about lime or strongly acid sands. Several are now 22–24 m tall, and the tree is scarce at this size only because few were planted more than 50 years ago; by now almost every large garden has one (Westonbirt in Gloucestershire has at least 30 over 15 m tall) and in time big trees will become quite common.

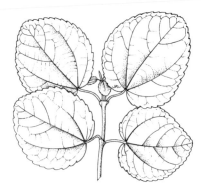

Katsura tree

The Katsura tree grows in China and Japan and was sent here first from Japan in about 1864 but in larger quantity in 1881. It is botanically a primitive kind of tree and, as with many but by no means all such trees, has the female and male flowers on different trees. They open with or just before the leaves, dark red bunches of stamens with grey anthers, or dark red slender up-curved styles, 5–6 mm long. The fruit are little claw-like pods, 4–6 per bunch, blue-grey tinged crimson during summer, close along the shoot in pairs, ripening shiny green and persisting after the leaves, then turning brown. If there is a flowering male tree in the vicinity, seed collected here is fertile.

In winter the Katsura takes the eye with its tracery of numerous up-curved slender long shoots – whether it is a fine spire on one bole or broader on several stems – made the more unusual by the regularly spaced prominent paired buds like knots along a cord.

Cercis siliquastrum Judas tree

This is a small tree, excellent in the summer warmth of a courtyard or on a south-facing bank. In places like these it should ripen enough new shoots each summer to flower well in the following spring and to be densely floriferous after a warm summer. Then it will bear flowers not just on the outer, new shoots but back on to the branches as well, and down these on to the bole. Bunches of short-stalked typical Pea-Family flowers, bright pink, bursting from the bark,

makes this an unusual-looking tree from root to tip, at its best before the leaves unfold. The foliage is pleasant – rather greyish-green, nearly round leaves about 10×10 cm, arranged alternately on dark red-brown shoots. This is a broad bushy low tree which lies down with age and has broad pods which are rich purple in the summer and hang in bunches, some from the bole after good flowering. Autumn colours are pale yellow and brown. The Judas tree comes from South-West Asia and needs warmth to flourish. It will not flower or grow much in cold areas.

Cornus controversa Table dogwood

Coming as it does from Japan, China and the Himalayas, there should be some very hardy forms of this fine tree but although occasionally seen as far north as Edinburgh, it remains that the only large trees, to 15 m tall, are in Sussex, Gloucestershire and the south-west. The bole, with grey bark in broad smooth ridges, bears from about 3 m up, long, level, well-spaced branches

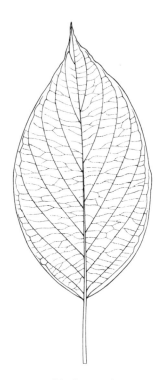

Table dogwood

with short, dark red shoots proliferating on their upper sides, from which in season hang alternate broad, oval, abruptly pointed shiny bright green leaves. It is thus attractive in winter and summer, but it is at its best in mid-June when white flowers are massed in flat heads strung along the branches above the foliage. These turn into blue-black berries which do not remain long but by then the leaves are turning soft yellow, pink and sometimes purple. This tree likes a good, deep soil with or without lime; it is best with some shelter from trees around but must be open to the sun or it will not flower fully.

'Variegata' is a very special little tree. It is slow-growing and is much prized by the time it is 2–3 m tall. It is not often seen much bigger but there was one in County Kerry over 10 m tall with a clear bole 2 m long and 30 cm through. The level layers of foliage are striking because the leaves, only 4–5 cm long and often twisted, are broadly margined clear white or pale cream.

Corylus colurna Turkish hazel

This tree has been grown here since 1580 or so but only now is it being properly appreciated and planted in urban areas, both here and in the USA, for its splendid shape, vigour and foliage. It rapidly makes a medium-conic crown of sturdy level branches hung in summer with dense foliage of shining dark green big leaves, cordate, 12 cm each way on reddish petioles densely hairy like the shoot. Male catkins early in spring are 6 cm long and the bunches of fruit have brilliant shiny green involucres with long slender lobes and prickles. Several trees are over 20 m tall and one is 25 m. Shoots of over 1 m can be grown in a season on sands or clays, acid or alkaline. The pinkish-grey or brown bark scales coarsely but attractively and altogether this is a tree in the front rank for a specimen of moderate dimensions.

Crataegus 'coccinea' Scarlet haw

Some similar North American trees grown under this name are *C. mollis*, *C. submollis*, *C. coccinioides* or *C. pedicellata*. All have big broad leaves 8 × 6 cm, with large lobes and hanging bunches of very big bright red berries. All have broad, branchy crowns to 12 m tall and dark brown fissured and scaly bark. All are tough, dependable and worth while, and may be seen occasionally in small urban parks. *C. pedicellata* has the best fruit as they are glossy scarlet.

Crataegus crus-galli Cockspur thorn

This tree, widespread in its American range, is quite rare here and one of its presumed hybrids is usually planted instead, understandably, as the parent tree has no great merit. It grows taller than either of the hybrids planted, to 12 m with an open bushy crown. The small long-cuneate leaves have a few teeth towards the tip and are a mat dull pale green, broadest near the blunt tip. The hybrids are plainly distinct from this and from each other, and neither has the rows of parallel long curved thorns seen on some of the type trees, but the spot feature separating Cockspur thorn from any of its hybrids is its glabrous flower- and fruit-stalks.

Crataegus × lavallei Carrière's hybrid thorn

Frequent beside arterial and suburban roads and formerly named *C. × carrierei*, this fuzzy-topped little tree is distinctive in winter as well as in leaf. The bark is light grey with dark, scaly vertical fissures and the branches are level with their upper sides lined with congested short spur shoots. Long shoots are dull green and sparsely long-pubescent. Thorns are few, 5 cm long, brown. The obovate leaves are dark glossy green above, pale pubescent beneath. The flowers are abundant in heads of about 20 each, white with anthers pink when fresh and a prominent red disc. They ripen to orange-red fruit speckled brown, remaining darker red through the winter. The leaves stay green until late autumn then turn dark bronzy red, often rather briefly.

Carrière's hybrid thorn

Splendid in flower and with good foliage, some late colour and fruit, and with a curious rather than beautiful winter aspect, Carrière's thorn is a useful tree in restricted sites, the more so because like other thorns it is exceedingly tough and little concerned with niceties of soil. It is normally disease-free but could be attacked by Fire-blight, when the flower-heads and the leaves nearest to them are killed in early summer and persist on the tree withered and brown.

Crataegus phaenopyrum Washington thorn

This tough little tree has the daintiest foliage of any thorn and although much planted in many cities around its native range in the eastern USA, it is seldom seen in Britain. The biggest so far found is in Victoria Park, Bethnal Green in east London. A short bole with pale orange-grey cracked bark bears a low, open crown of red-brown shoots with numerous purple thorns 5–7 cm long. The leaves are 6 × 5 cm with 3–5 deeply cut lobes, each lobuled or toothed, and are smooth pale green, becoming dark and shiny. In autumn they turn orange and red. Numerous flowers open 30–40 on each erect head, pale greenish-white with pink anthers. They ripen into hanging bunches of 6 mm glossy scarlet fruit which remain on the tree through the winter. As a small tree well able to cope with a paved root-run in a city and with good foliage, autumn

colour and long-lasting brilliant fruit, this has such obvious merits that it is likely to be more commonly planted in the future.

Crataegus × prunifolia Broad-leafed hybrid cockspur

Very often grown as a bush, this can be a broad, flat-crowned tree on a 2 m bole with dark brown bark. It is, unlike Carrière's hybrid, not at all distinctive in winter although it can be identified easily enough at close quarters by its shiny purple glabrous shoot and dark purple, equally sparse thorns. In leaf it is quite distinct as its rich dark green leaves are broad-ovate and glossy, plane and smooth, not folded along the midrib, nor puckered by deep side-veins. It is less showy in flower, more leafy, but in autumn it is outstanding, turning rapidly from yellow to orange, then a striking colour of burnished copper until it is crimson. The large dark red fruit add to the effect and are then shed.

Although out of leaf this is a twiggy, tangled, broad bushy plant, it is so good in leaf and so spectacular in autumn that it is of great value in an informal planting and in sites where conditions are difficult.

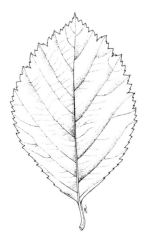

Broadleafed cockspur thorn

Davidia involucrata Dove tree

Père David found the Dove tree in 1867 in
Szechuan, China, with soft white down on the
underside of the leaf. Ernest Wilson also found this
form which, being the first described, is entitled to
the Latin name given above, and sent it in 1903,
but Père Farges had already sent to France in
1897 another form with the leaf underside shiny
and smooth. This second form, var. *vilmoriniana*, is
much the commoner and usually of greater vigour
than the type. They are otherwise very similar and
share the unfortunate name of Handkerchief tree
in some quarters but are known as Dove tree here.

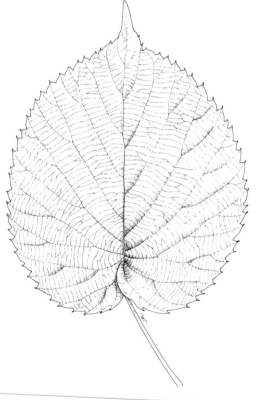

Dove tree

The somewhat gaunt winter aspect of sparse
branching and spiky shoots is offset by dark purple
bark flaking and crumbling to pale brown. The
large leaves have coarse triangular teeth and are
broad-ovate drawn out to the tip, leathery dark
green with scarcely any autumn colouring. The

true flowers are tiny and purple in bud, opening
yellow, clustered in a globular head on a long
stalk hanging between two bracts. These bracts
open yellow then soon turn clear white, making
the tree a unique picture as one bract is the same
size and shape as a big leaf and the other is about
half this size.

The Dove tree, so fine in flower for two or three
weeks in May, is also quite handsome in foliage
and seems to have no pests at all. It is, however,
among the first to show signs of severe stress
during a long drought and should be found a
damp site. It grows best anyway in a rich, moist
soil although it manages well on lighter and sandy
soils if they do not dry out readily, and seems
tolerant of some lime. Older trees, where they are
in some shelter, are 18–20 m tall but less if much
exposed. The tendency to heavy low branching or
even forking must be watched, for it can and
should be made to grow into a shapely tree with a
good bole. On lighter soils a mixed or nitrogenous
fertilizer is of benefit for some years in spring.

Drimys winteri Winter's bark

The name originates from one of Drake's captains,
William Winter, who found in 1578 that the
natives around the Straits of Magellan used the
bark of this tree as a tonic with strong
antiscorbutic properties which made it valuable on
board ship, and as a spice for meats. It ranges in
four forms all the way along the Andes into
Mexico. The older trees, 15 m tall in Irish and
south-western gardens, are attractive when the
large evergreen leaves are relieved by masses of
loose heads of small white flowers with 5–7 de-
curved narrow petals and yellow stamens, but at
other times they are just tall, tapering evergreen
bushes. The form more usually planted now is a
different matter; with no flowers at all it is very
decorative, with whorls of level then upswept
branches making a regular, conic crown and the
light green leaves bright silver-blue beneath,
veinless and smooth. Away from the areas of
notably mild winters this should be grown against
a wall, but where it can stand as a tree it shows its
shape and worth fully. It takes about 15 years to
start flowering and may be irregular for some

1. Mixed coloured conifers giving form and variation to a planting of shrubs. Lawson Cypress 'Winston Churchill' (gold, left), White Cedar 'Rheingold' (yellow, right). Wakehurst Place, Sussex.

2. Ornamental planting contrasting with background of neutral countryside and largely screened from it. Mixed Maples. Scarlet foliage is Smooth Japanese Maple, 'Osakazuki'. Winkworth Arboretum, Surrey.

3. Water enforces open vistas and is best edged mainly by lawn. Sycamore 'Brilliantissimum' prominent in spring. Thorp Perrow, Yorkshire.

4. A broad glade or lawn may be encroached by one or two trees. A tulip-tree adds to the prospect from the House at Batsford Park. Gloucestershire.

5. A wide vista shows off the trees, while some encroachment on the space removes any wall-sided effect. David's Maple, 'Ernest Wilson', centre. East end of Mitchell Drive, Westonbirt, Gloucestershire.

6. Golden conifers at focal points in middleground and background give this scene its rich quality. Lawson Cypress 'Lutea', middle distance; Chinese Juniper 'Aurea' in distance. Sheffield Park, Sussex.

7. A screen of great variety of forms and stature, in depth closes a vista across a stream. Western Red Cedars, Lawson Cypresses and Douglas Firs behind the New Zealand Cabbage-tree. Annesgrove, County Cork.

8. The glimpse of the clear, open glade beyond gives depth to this scene of soft greens and prevents it seeming a dull, shaded corner. Weeping Willow and Lawson Cypresses. Cowdray Park, Sussex.

9. Narrowing a vista and making a focal point near its end. Lawson Cypress 'Lutea' far left; Monterey Cypress 'Lutea' mid-left; Incense Cedar, centre. East end of Mitchell Drive, Westonbirt, Gloucestershire.

10. Small eye-catcher for summer and winter. Paperbark maple; Lawson Cypress 'Lutea' in front of Lawson Cypress 'Wisselii'. Dunloe Castle, County Kerry.

years after that, but the flowers are not important among its merits. It grows at moderate speed with or without lime in the soil but does prefer a damp sheltered site. In some specimens the shoot and petiole are bright red.

Eucalyptus Eucalypts or Gum trees

This huge genus of the Myrtle Family is the hallmark of the Australasian flora, almost defining the Wallace Line, but is not native to New Zealand. In many parts of the Australian desert interior, eucalypts have ribbon-like ranges as they are confined to the river-banks and this makes the populations particularly liable to split into numerous closely related species. By most reckonings there are more than 600 species and identifying them is a problem in the field. It is a worse problem to sort out some of those in cultivation, with perhaps only a single tree in widely separated plantings and with the readiness of the genus to hybridize. So the eucalypts can be botanically difficult to handle. They are also difficult to place in a landscape, and some people do not like to see them at all. At all times their evergreen and distinctive crowns and their strange bark are conspicuous and they should not be scattered about. In a large garden a eucalyptus grove can be a fine feature; in a smaller garden a single specimen can be impressive, or it can look quite out of place.

Yet another difficulty is hardiness. In Ireland this is no problem with any of the 40 or so species growing there; even the Blue gums as far north as Belfast were unaffected by the hard winter of 1979. In other parts, even in Cornwall, it is a necessary consideration. The gums as a whole being much the fastest-growing of any trees and undeterred by poor or dry sites, there is a great interest in growing them. The winters of 1947 and 1962 had killed most of the more tender species, like the Blue gum, in Cornwall and many others elsewhere but Cider gum survived unscathed and became the standard fully hardy Eucalypt. But in 1979 Cider gums were killed in several places and other new hopes which had grown well up to then, for instance the Shining gum, also showed a few losses. It is not the low temperature that is lethal, but a sudden drop, as when it fell from above freezing to −19°C early on the first day of 1979, on the south coast of Cornwall where the more tender trees were concentrated.

While the eucalypt enthusiast who needs to see his trees achieve great size must move to Ireland, it is surely still very much worth while to persist with these trees elsewhere. After all, killing winters seem to be fifteen years or so apart, and eucalypts can make such enormous growth and give such pleasure in the run of mild winters that can be expected in between.

Eucalyptus dalrympleana Broadleafed kindling-bark

This can be regarded as a poor man's Blue gum, and grows nearly as fast for some years with equally big, 20–25 cm falcate leaves leathery blue-green and similar but more yellow-pink bark. The spot difference after juvenility is the tiny flower-buds and seed capsules in threes; during juvenile growth it has much smaller, more tapered yellowish and pinkish-green leaves. It is also much hardier but is variable in this, probably from the altitude of the parent stand; in 1979 a completely unharmed tree could be in the same garden as another scorched right back to the bole or killed.

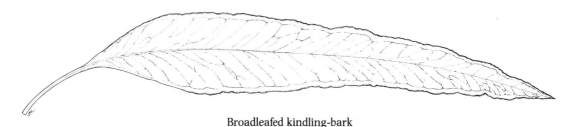

Broadleafed kindling-bark

Eucalyptus globulus Blue gum

In its native Tasmania this is no record-breaker but in tropical and sub-tropical or Mediterranean climates it is in many parts of the world the fastest tree to 30 m and one of the very few to be 60 m tall. In Ireland and the Isle of Man, this is the gum to plant for an enormous specimen; anywhere else it is unlikely to survive more than four or five winters so it will scarcely achieve 12 m. Juvenile plants are well-known as annual spot-plants in bedding schemes, with big floppy broad silver-blue leaves joined around the square, flanged stem in pairs. Adult foliage is hard, leathery dark blue-green, often over 20 cm long and curved. The flower-buds are usually solitary on a stout short stalk and are 2–3 cm long, opening by extruding bunches of white stamens at almost any time of year. The seed capsules become black intensely bloomed blue-white, and are twice the size of any other eucalypt capsules grown here.

Eucalyptus gunnii Cider gum

This Tasmanian gum is the standard eucalypt of suburban and other gardens throughout Britain and is perfectly hardy in normally severe winters but may occasionally be caught by freak falls in temperature; some were killed in 1979. Juvenile foliage is in opposite pairs, nearly round and blue-grey or bright blue-green, and soon yields to alternate, elliptic leaves on slender yellow petioles. Young trees have a conic acute crown and become rounded with age. Growth is variably rapid, some trees making shoots of 2 m but others about 1 m each year for some years, and a number of specimens are 30 m tall. In one form derived from a tree at Whittingehame, East Lothian, with narrow leaves, the branches are distinctively warm brown.

Eucalyptus johnstoni

Another gum safe only in Ireland, where it should be grown with the Blue gum for its superior shape. It keeps a slender conic crown until about 40 m tall and the bole is so smoothly cylindric that it appears to be a machined pole. The foliage is unusual in being bright deep green and glossy. Growth is often more than 2 m a year. Juvenile trees are narrowly erect with rough deep red shoots and stalkless dark green leaves. This Tasmanian gum has survived some hard winters in south Devon and in Cornwall but the worst winters exact a heavy toll and it is unlikely to last long in other parts.

Eucalyptus mitchelliana Weeping Sally

Found only on Mount Buffalo in Victoria State, this is turning out to be very hardy. It has slender red shoots hanging from arched branches and a long drooping leading shoot, with slender 15 cm pale greyish-green leaves, and is very attractive.

Eucalyptus nicholii Pepper gum

Although in most areas this is likely to be killed by any winter less than mild, the Pepper gum is so attractive when juvenile or as a small bushy tree that it is worth replacing when necessary. It has very slender little ribbony leaves to 5×0.5 cm, grey-green bloomed red-purple on red-purple shoots.

Eucalyptus niphophila Snow gum

This Australian tree raised from seed collected at the highest parts of its range, at nearly 2000 m, has come through the winter of 1979 quite unscathed. It is the only gum for which no death or damage has been reported. It has no distinct juvenile foliage and new leaves on young plants emerge rich orange-brown on glossy red-brown shoots. The leaves are soon grey-green with a fine margin of dark red; elliptic, falcate, to 14×5 cm. The shoot, however, soon becomes brilliantly blue-white and the bole and branches are also this colour and the main attraction of the tree. The flowers are large, in bunches and pure white. The Snow gum takes a few years to grow fast and is variable but can make shoots of 1.3–1.5 m for a few years before rounding into a broadly domed tree.

Eucalyptus nitens Shining gum

This is the fastest gum grown in Britain in its early years and has grown to 20 m in nine years. Until 1979 it had proved hardy everywhere but almost all the trees were badly scorched in that year and are resprouting along the boles. It has very broad large juvenile leaves, blue-grey on square stems, and makes a broad columnar crown with regular ascending, rather big branches from which the big, very dark adult leaves hang.

Eucalyptus deBeauzevillei is of recent introduction and of promise, being unharmed in a Devon garden when 12 m tall in 1979. It is rather similar to Snow gum with darker leaves and orange where flakes come off the bark, and has a more shapely columnar crown. It is the most attractive of all the gums.

Eucommia ulmoides Gutta-percha tree

This is a good and unusual foliage-tree from central China, growing into a broad dome with deep glossy green leaves. The leaves are lanceolate-elliptic, to 18×10 cm, with an elegantly tapered apex and shallowly toothed. They have a party trick, which is as well for otherwise they are hard to place when received as a detached specimen; when torn gently across the middle, latex from the veins hardens in the air and one half of the leaf can hang 5 cm below the other on the threads. Only Table dogwood (p. 81) can also do this. The bark is dull dark grey and coarsely fissured. The trees are either male with little tufts of brown stamens for flowers or female with a single pistil and then winged fruit. It is perfectly hardy and amenable to most soils but better in a sheltered position.

Euodia hupehensis Chinese euodia

Perhaps from observing the splendid big tree which has flourished in the era of smoky air in Greenwich Park, London, the Royal Parks have planted a few more and this tree should become a more frequent feature of city plantings. It was sent from central China in 1908 and ranges northward into Korea in the form known as Daniell's euodia, *E. daniellii*, which is seen mainly in collections, and differs only in the leaflets having shorter stalks and the fruit ripening purple. These trees have some unusual features which help to identify the group. They have no bud-scales but spend the winter with the leaf folded tightly and covered in red-brown hairs. The compound leaves are in opposite pairs and the petioles do not cover the side-bud as in the related cork-trees. The flowers are in flat heads sorted as to sex but male and female heads are rather randomly placed over the tree. The flowers open in the autumn. The bark is grey and very smooth, but not shiny.

The late flowering, which is profuse and handsome, and valuable when so few other trees are in flower, and the very vigorous, sturdy growth on soils which are far from good, make this an important tree to consider when planting, but it has other good points. The 5–9 leaflets are a glossy dark green and often cupped which enhances the effects of light, and their petioles and rachises are dark pink. The fruit ripen from mid-autumn despite the late flowering and, in the Hupeh form, are bright orange-red then dark red.

Evidently this tree has great potential for more frequent use. It is absolutely hardy and one of the biggest and fastest to grow is in a garden in eastern Perthshire.

Euodia velutina Downy euodia

This comes from further west in China than the Hupeh tree and was sent at the same time. It remains rare but comes easily and very vigorously from seed. It has soft down on the shoots and leaves and has more slender, lanceolate leaflets as well as flowers tinged yellow, about a month earlier, to distinguish it.

Euonymus lucidus (*E. fimbriatus*)

This tree is seen only in Cornish gardens and while known to be too tender for London, it should be tried more widely in the west and should certainly be safe in Ireland. In Cornwall it makes quite a shapely tree to 14 m and in spring it is one of the most colourful trees, like a tall *Pieris forrestii*, for the old leaves, dark, glossy green, set off the rich scarlet new growth. The leaves become hard, ovate-lanceolate, slender-pointed and regularly toothed. As a brilliant variation among the numerous dark evergreens in those parts, it has great value, and when the new shoots are at their brightest it carries masses of heads of little greenish-white flowers as a further variation.

Fagus englerana Chinese beech

This is an elegant, small version of the Common beech, highly desirable for its foliage in summer and autumn. It has a tendency, which should be checked, to fork at the base or very low, but can make a shapely tree, so far to 15 m, but none is yet 70 years old and most of the few seen are much younger. The bud is very slender, almost needle-like, and the leaves taper at each end. They are fresh light green above, slightly silvered

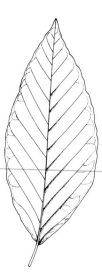

Chinese beech

beneath and have a somewhat crinkled margin. In autumn they turn gold, then the outer ones turn orange and russet-brown.

With the well-known ability of beeches to grow equally on acid sand or chalky loam – almost anywhere that is not poorly drained – this is amenable as well as decorative, a first-class tree of moderate size.

Fagus orientalis Oriental beech

This very uncommon tree from the Balkans and Asia Minor is a shade more vigorous than the Common beech and is similar except that the leaves are further apart, have seven to ten parallel veins each side instead of up to seven, are more slender-cuneate and entire with a less marked wavy margin and are larger, to 14 × 7 cm but usually 10 × 4 cm. The autumn colour is a rich orange-brown; the bole fluted and the crown an upswept ovoid. It is an interesting change from the Common beech and makes a good specimen but is not so effective as a group, since it lacks the smooth bole.

Fagus sylvatica Common beech

The manifold uses in landscaping of this, one of the most valuable and widely useful of all the big trees, are detailed on p. 44 and in many landscapes, roundels, clumps and fine woods would not be possible without it. One of its advantages for wide-scale amenity use is that it is native to England. Its one major defect, and that less of a drawback in large plantings, is the dangerous way in which it decays at senility after not a very long life, for a large tree. In the open, or grown at wide spacing, few beech live much more than 200 years, Grown in early years at close spacing, however, about 1·5 m and gradually thinned to the best boles, beech make long clean boles which are supremely attractive and are also prevented from growing heavy branches at a wide angle, making their crowns far less vulnerable to breakage and decay and prolonging their life as well as their period as safe trees. Some fine examples of beech wood remain in the Cotswolds, but the best on the South Downs were blown over in 1987. One at Slindon near Arundel dating from about 1830 had many trees to 40 m clean-boled for 20 m, and with all inferior trees removed in 1950, it had been a source of top quality seed.

Never less than pleasing at any time of year, the best time for beech is when the leaves are freshly out. They are then of a brilliant shiny green which is most effective with the silvery grey bark. Being native trees with a vast population from seed, beech vary considerably more than most of the exotics, which have been raised from samples of a few hundred seed in the original imports, each from only a few trees of the entire range. Some beech are thus well in leaf when others are still bare and autumn colour varies much in time and shade. Beech grow well in city parks.

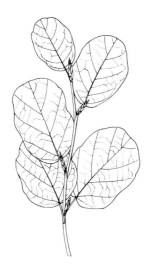

(Common beech 'Rotundifolia')

'Dawyck' Fastigiate beech. The parent tree from which all the erect beeches are raised as grafts, stands by a gate at Dawyck, a fine garden and enormous tree collection in Peebles-shire. Shaped very like a Lombardy poplar, this has greater presence with its more solid crown and heavier foliage, and it colours much better in autumn. It is a splendid tree as a mark of emphasis on a fairly

large scale, marking an entrance (one on each side), or a cross-rides or path junction, or planted as a tight group. Five to ten trees at 4–5 m spacing, five for a close feature and larger numbers only for distant prospects, will add character to the end of a vista.

'Asplenifolia' Fern or Cut-leafed beech. Previously named 'Heterophylla' and 'Laciniata', the usual form of this tree is now considered the one first named 'Asplenifolia'. It is identifiable in winter, even were every one of the half million or so leaves of a big tree to be swept away, by the fine shoots sprouting from branches and bole and by its generally finer and more dense crown. It is a good tree as a lawn specimen, makes less impact in a group and is wasted in a wood.

The majority of the leaves have a slender central lobe making a long apex beyond 4–5 deeply cut, acuminate, forward-pointing lobes and are only 4–5 cm long; some late season leaves at the tip of the shoot are linear or strap-shaped. These are all grafted trees and each shoot has a chimaeral structure, that is, it is made of tissues from two different forms. The interior tissues are of the type beech. Shoots regrowing from breakages in the crown come mainly from this interior tissue and bear normal beech leaves while some sprouts are variably modified by the fern-leafed tissues outside and bear leaves with varying degrees of lobing.

'Laciniata' Oak-leafed beech ('Quercifolia'). This was found in a beech hedge in Saxony in 1792 and is rather rare but two estates in southern Scotland have big trees beside their drives, one 25 m × 1 m. The leaves are the same size as those of the type, a little darker and edged by regular triangular lobes. Similar leaves are found here and there in the crowns of 'Asplenifolia' but in 'Laciniata' the entire crown is of this form of leaf. It is a pleasant variant on Common beech.

'Pendula' Weeping beech. This is one of the best of all weeping trees, rapidly growing a stout silvery-grey bole from which two or three rather sinuous erect branches arise at about 2 m and tower to 20–25 m with small branches arching out and weeping to the ground. In the earliest form here, growing at Knaphill Nurseries in Surrey, when the shoots reach the ground they rest on it and send up a vertical shoot or two, eventually rooting, and the layers become a ring of big trees around the old stem. Branches from the layers repeat the process and now, 166 years after the planting, each original tree is a large grove of remarkable boles and connecting branches. Unlike some weeping trees this beech can look after itself and needs no splinted leading shoot. A big broad tree will send up verticals 5–6 m above the crown in succession, which bend gradually with the weight of hanging foliage to swell the main cascade of crown. The layering form needs room, a great deal of room if it is to be allowed to spread, but either there is another form or this same form reacts to a limited space, for many weeping beech are slender, to 29 m tall and without any layers.

This is a fine specimen from a moderate distance, so it needs to be on an extensive lawn or down a vista, for it is rather overwhelming at close quarters and casts a wide area of shade. Some specimens are grossly misshapen, lack central stems and send snaking branches far out on each side, in some cases evidently where the graft was made 2 m high on the stock and suffered early breakage; young trees should always be watched for signs of this sort of misbehaviour.

'Purpurea' Purple and Copper beeches. The pigment which masks the green in the leaves of these trees has little effect on the growth and they are about as fast as the green form and become nearly as big. One is 20 m × 85 cm in 50 years, one is 38 m × 1·6 m, and a few are around 2 m in diameter. Although very popular for the purpose, no Purple beech should ever be planted in clumps, lines or avenues. For six months of the year when the garden is most admired these would be heavy, dark masses, garish without being bright, blending with nothing, contrasting pleasantly with nothing, absorbing light uselessly. A single specimen has the same failings and has but one ideal position – on someone else's lawn half a mile away with the top just visible.

The paler, browner form 'Cupraea' flushes a curious pinkish colour for a day or two, an interesting hue hardly suited to a garden. 'Riversii' or 'Rivers's Purple', which must be a graft to be true, is a much deeper red than the usual muddy blackish-brown and is quite presentable at a distance.

'Rotundifolia'. Among the variant foliage-forms of the Beech, the Fern-leaf is often seen but this round-leafed one is scarce. It grows into a broad-crowned tree 20 m tall and so needs a large space but it is well worth it for its unusual foliage. The neat, small leaves are nearly round, 1–3 cm across; in the form 'Cockleshell' they are only 1 cm across.

'Zlatia' Golden beech. If any of the beech cultivars has not been planted as much as it deserves to be, it is the Golden beech. Like the purple ones, its growth is not retarded by the colour and it is very vigorous and grows anywhere that the type will. Found in Serbia, it has been available only since 1890 and the older trees are confined to botanic gardens and a few collections, but it has been used more widely lately. It comes into leaf soft yellow and just about achieves a good gold before midsummer when it turns green very like the type, but usually paler at the shoot-tips, and sometimes new growth keeps the outer crown golden. It is a refreshing variation on the Common Beech and the countryside would be vastly improved if for the next 150 years every intended planting of purple beech were required by law to be 'Zlatia' instead.

Fraxinus excelsior Common ash

Although useful in places as a framework-tree, good in city parks, on chalky soils and in exposure, this native tree is a coarse one for a garden. It is late into leaf and sheds early with a minimum of autumn colour. It is prone to being misshapen and having canker. Altogether it is best left in the countryside where it has its place.

'Diversifolia' One-leafed ash. This variant has simple, long-stalked ovate-acuminate, irregularly toothed leaves to 20×12 cm and a good straight bole with rather remote branching so that it has an open, shapely crown and can be $27 \times 1 \cdot 3$ m. A handsome, unusual specimen.

'Jaspidea' Golden ash. This is the tall-growing ash with yellow to orange shoots and leaves golden in spring and autumn. 'Aurea' has golden leaves all the time but is a rare dwarf. 'Jaspidea' is seen to 20 m $\times 1$ m and is conspicuous in winter and autumn. It might suit the edge of a prospect but is not a specimen for a prominent position.

'Pendula' Weeping ash. Too often seen on or around small lawns, this is a sad-looking tree. Grafted usually at 2 m the head makes a mass of contorted branches and hangs shoots straight to the ground. There are better weeping trees.

Fraxinus ornus Manna or Flowering ash

Ash trees are in the Olive Family, the more familiar members of which are lilacs, privets, forsythia and jasmines, plants with tubular flowers, often fragrant. The Common ash has dispensed with insects as pollinating agents and uses the wind, so has no need for petals or scent. A small group of Asiatic ashes does, however, have flowers with petals and scent to attract insects. The only one frequently seen is the Manna ash. It can be raised from seed but is slow and nearly all the trees seen are grafted on to Common ash. Since this rootstock has a ridged bark and the Manna ash has a smooth grey one, the union is evident even when the graft was made at ground level, for then there is a sprouty boss.

The Manna ash makes a broadly domed tree distinguished from Common ash in winter by the shape, the smooth bark and by the buds not being jet black but two shades of brown and covered in grey pubescence. In early summer it is well covered in bright green shiny panicles of narrowly petalled creamy-white flowers with a strong sweet scent. It is then quite pretty but for the rest of the season it is dull and, being broad, it does not repay the room it takes up and is no specimen tree.

Fraxinus oxycarpa Caucasian ash

Now regarded as a form of the Narrow-leafed ash, *F. angustifolia*, which is seen most in London parks and has a knobbly bark, the Caucasian ash is a smooth-barked, more shapely smaller tree. It is scarce but highly attractive, for an ash, and one of the few mature trees has a broadly domed crown. The attraction is the light grey branches against the decorative bright glossy green foliage of 5–9 slender lanceolate leaflets. Although basically opposite-leafed, as are the entire family, this tree has some leaves in threes.

'Raywood' is a very vigorous form received from Australia in 1925 and becoming popular. It grows narrow and tall for some years, with the same pretty foliage as the type, but in autumn this turns a rich purple, although not reliably everywhere.

Gleditsia triacanthos Honey locust

This tree from the central USA is so tough that it alone can compete with the Ginkgo in the downtown parts of American cities and is widely used in all of them (except in the far south-west) north as far as Toronto. In Britain it is seen only occasionally, mostly in Cambridge and London, two of the warmest places in good summers; there is one in a street in Chichester but there are few in gardens, even in the south-east where it grows well.

Any tree that can grow in Paley's Garden and Park Avenue, New York, and in the Peach Street buildings in Atlanta is welcome there without needing to be unusually beautiful, but its ability to grow in those places does not necessarily recommend it for planting in a garden. It has an open, none too shapely crown and too thin a foliage to make a feature, but its narrow compound leaves of tiny leaflets have a good bright green colour and provide a brief flash of gold in the autumn. For interest in a position not close to a path, the type tree with ferocious bunches of sharp, branched thorns – the newer growth on them green – is possible, but for street and town planting the thornless form 'Inermis' is advisable. It has a dark red-brown bark with wide, scaly flanges and is known here to 23 m tall. The fat pods 30 cm long, often curved and bent, are seen here only much smaller and rarely, but they are a nuisance on paths anyway. For a hot dusty, dry corner with rubbly soil or paving around, this tree has obvious value.

'Sunburst' is a thornless form recently planted in many suburban and larger gardens. It comes into leaf bright yellow and stays that colour as long as growth continues while the early, interior leaves turn bright green – a most effective contrast. Even where an older tree makes no late growth and all its leaves are green, the colour is bright and tinged yellow so it is still a good tree. From its wide use in the towns of the American Mid-west and in Denver City, it must be almost or quite as tough as the type, and as hardy, because some are seen as far north.

Gymnocladus dioicus Kentucky coffee tree

In the south-east of England this peculiar tree grows, if slowly, to a reasonable size. In winter it is an ungainly, gaunt tree with dark grey bark in big scales, but it has stout shoots well bloomed lilac-blue. Late in spring the leaves unfold pink, then pale yellow, nearly white, then expand fully a good fresh green above, silvery beneath. They are hugely and doubly compound, about the biggest leaves of any except the Japanese banana. Over 90 cm long, they branch and branch again before bearing the entire, ovate leaflets. Rather oddly, the domed crown seems from a little distance to be covered in single leaves and in the autumn, with the leaflets and minor leaf-stems all shed, the central leaf-stems remain radiating from the branch ends.

The flowers, male and female on separate trees, are pretty at close quarters but far from spectacular, small and white with a green stripe on the petal, in loose heads.

Too stark in winter to occupy an important position, this scarce tree deserves to be grown more, amongst other trees but not crowded by them as it needs full light.

Halesia monticola Snowdrop tree

This tree from the high woods deep in the Great Smoky Mountains of Tennessee and 27–30 m tall there, was not introduced until 1897 but is quite widely planted. It is a vigorous young three making a sinuous bole with a grey, fissured bark and a crown broad near the base and tapered to the top. The foliage is, like the growth, coarse and dull, oblong-ovate dull yellowish-green leaves about 20 cm long, but for its two or three weeks in flower it is worthy of a place in a mixed planting. In late spring, slender pink buds hanging in threes from every joint open to white 3 cm bell-shaped flowers. They are not brilliantly white but they are in such profusion and of such a pleasing shape and carriage that the tree is then a fine sight. The fruit hang in green bunches during the summer, four-winged, each 1 cm wide. The tree likes a damp acid soil, but well-drained, and grows well on sands if they are not dry.

'Rosea' is a pale rosy-pink flowered form of the var. *vestita* which ranges to the west of the type and has soft white pubescence on the shoot and leaves. All forms need attention in early life to keep a good dominant single stem. They should not be allowed to degenerate into bushes. The smaller *H. carolina* is available if a shrubby form is required.

Idesia polycarpa

If it were not for much the finest specimen being very public in Bute Park, Cardiff, this attractive tree could not be included. Resembling a bright, shiny Catalpa, it nonetheless remains too rarely seen. It is a little more frequent in parks and big gardens in the eastern USA but there the hot summers enable the female trees to produce the red berry-like fruit in conspicuous bunches and it is not just a foliage-tree, which is the only way to regard it here. As such, it ranks high with glossy yellowish dark green, hook-toothed, cordate, ovate leaves 20 × 20 cm on scarlet perioles 12–30 cm long, and smooth bark.

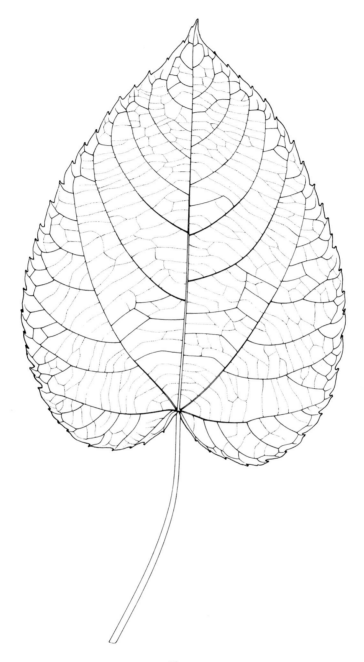

Idesia

Ilex × altaclerensis Highclere hybrid hollies

A popular plant for red berries in the winter in conservatories about 200 years ago was the Madeira holly, *Ilex perado*. In order that it should bear berries, the flowers had to be pollinated and for that purpose, as well as to clear the building for the summer plants, the hollies were grown in big tubs which were trundled out on to the terrace in spring to be visited by bees. But the bees had often been on the common native holly first, so when the Madeiran holly berries were sown to raise more plants, some of these were hybrids. This happened in many places and several nurseries began to raise and select different forms, especially in Derbyshire and Northern Ireland, but the first hybrid to be named arose at Highclere House on the Berkshire-Hampshire border and hence all become forms of *Ilex × altaclarensis*.

They are mostly very sturdy, exceptionally tough and rather tall hollies with big, thick, broad and flat leaves, spined, unspined or with one or very few spines and often with purple stems. The following is a small selection of the best for general planting:

'Hodginsii' Hodgins's holly. A very robust form often 15–17 m tall with a good bole 40–50 cm in diameter and clear for 3 m, this is known by the dull sheen on the broad, 9 × 8 cm leaves which on each tree vary from entire to many-spined, usually asymmetrically, and the large bunches of male flowers, dark purple in winter (and lack of berries). It is singularly resistant to sea-winds and industrial atmosphere so is seen in promenade gardens and inner city parks and churchyards. It is a handsome tree, even though it has no berries, throughout the year and gives substance to a group of small trees or tall shrubs, on any soil.

'Heterophylla'. This is peculiarly attractive near to as it has broad, few-spined leaves on the early season growth, tipped by later narrow, spiny, smaller leaves. Holding four or five year's foliage, it shows the changes of leaf-form all along the stems.

'Camelliifolia'. This makes a splendid isolated specimen because it has excellent shape and foliage as well as being female, with large darkish red berries in good clusters. It grows as a shapely cone with regular branches, light and level, and the leaves are glossy green, elliptical and entire or with a few teeth. The relatively big flowers have the white petals prominently marked violet at the base.

Holly 'Camelliifolia'

'Lawsoniana' is broad and may be bushy and makes a fine splash of colour as the 10 × 6 cm leaves are marbled two shades of green with most

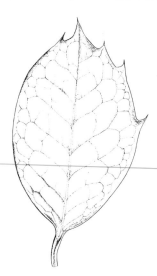

Hodgins's holly

of the centre bright and pale yellow. It has a tendency to throw green-leafed shoots which must be cut out to the base, for it is worth trouble to preserve the coloured form. It is a sport from the female 'Hendersonii' so it bears berries, but that is a very dull-foliaged tree to which to revert.

Lawson's holly

'Wilsonii' is a broadly conic bush or tree to 12 m and has glorious foliage. The new shoots unfold purple and the leaves open out to as much as 14 × 9 cm, bright glossy green and very flat, with 4–10 forward 5 mm spines, yellow or white, each side. It should be near a path where its foliage can be admired.

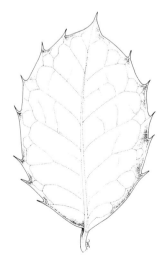

Wilson's holly

'Nobilis' is almost 'Hodginsii' and as sturdy and tall but with even more purple on the shoots and more varied toothing, many of the smaller leaves having none; the big leaves have more spines, more symmetrically placed.

'Golden King' is a female tree with large leaves, often de-curved at the margin, mainly entire and broadly margined or wholly deep yellow.

Ilex aquifolium Common holly

Native throughout these islands except in the extreme north, this is common in shady oak- or beechwoods but makes there a straggly tree flowering and fruiting little if at all. It needs to be grown in the open where it makes a tall, spired crown to 20 m and fruits heavily, if female. Both sexes are in some years so thickly wreathed in flowers along the shoots that this holly qualifies as a flowering tree. Its tolerance of exposure and any moderately-drained soil gives it great value for shelter. As a single specimen, one of the Highclere hybrids is preferred (p. 94), but in a group the Common holly is better.

There are innumerable cultivars; at least 20 variegated with yellow, cream or white margins, alone. The commonest is the male 'Golden Queen' but several with whiter margins are frequent to 15 m tall and 'Perry's Weeping' is a tall, long-pendulous mound with leaves broadly margined nearly white, which always catches the attention. 'Handsworth New Silver' is the cleanest and brightest of these, the dark purple shoots setting off the dark-centred and clear white margined spiny leaves.

The best of the other kinds of variant for garden use are:

'Bacciflava' Yellow-berried holly. Growing similarly to the normal form but tending to be broader, this is a lovely sight when the shiny black leaves are the background to long clusters of bright lemon yellow berries.

'Laurifolia'. This form can be grown where a tall, neat spire of a crown is wanted. Old plants are usually 18–20 m tall and still taper to a long point, or perhaps to two or three. The foliage is good, dark and glossy, 6–8 cm, nearly all entire ellipses with sharp pointed apices, but it is male, so no berries.

Laurel-leaf holly

'Pendula' Weeping holly. This makes a bower to the ground, 8–9 m tall, the long hanging shoots attractively lined with very spiny, fairly buckled leaves and plenty of bright red berries. A splendid specimen small tree which may need a little shaping at first as there are some untidy ones around, but these may be partly shaded and it does need full light.

'Pyramidalis'. A desirable form as a specimen, with lighter, bright green leaves, rather crowded, often curled, and almost all entire and broad. It grows in a shapely, conic form and is prolific with big, bright berries, so it has much to recommend it.

Juglans ailantifolia Japanese walnut

This is a splendid, hardy foliage-tree, much more planted as such in the northern USA and southern Canada than it is here. It makes broad, dense, very leafy domes of dark green huge leaves and can be 18 m tall. The shoot and the leaf rachis are densely covered in tacky dark red short pubescence. The leaf can be 1 m long with 17 abruptly tapered oblong leaflets, bright shiny green but in the mass appearing darker. Some are only 80 cm long with 11–15 leaflets. The female flowers are remarkably attractive, in 10 cm erect heads, showing bright deep red stigmas and ripening to globose 5 cm fruit covered in sticky pubescence.

Juglans cinerea Butternut

This American white walnut is undeservedly scarce but where grown it is vigorous and handsome. None is known bigger or better than one at Cliveden, Buckinghamshire, which is 25 m × 81 cm. The bark is similar to the Common walnut but the crown is more open, less spreading, with straighter branches. The leaves are the best feature, to 60 cm long with 15–17 widely spaced oblong-lanceolate leaflets, finely toothed and stalkless on a slender densely pubescent central stalk. The buds are white or pink and the female flowers, showing red styles, and the fruit, are on 15 cm spreading catkins. It likes a deep, moist, fairly rich soil and some shelter from strong winds. The pubescent leaf-axis and the remote leaflets, which decrease in size very markedly towards the base of the leaf, distinguish this well from the Black walnut as does the bark.

Juglans microcarpa Texan walnut (*J. rupestris*)

Very scarce and apt to be bushy, this has made a splendidly decorative tree at Cambridge Botanic Garden in 56 years, 11·5 m × 46 cm. The bark is very dark brown fissured deeply into rectangular plates. The foliage is the best feature, delicate, drooping and bright glossy green. Each leaf has 15–25 obliquely based slender lanceolate leaflets closely set, with fine, mucronate teeth, and is 30–40 cm long. No doubt the relatively warm summers of East Anglia are needed for good growth.

Juglans nigra Black walnut

In an area with warm summers and on a good deep soil, this native of the eastern USA is one of the most stately and handsome trees we can grow.

It does not grow well in the equable climate of the south-west nor in the cool summers of the north-west, but in the Midlands and south-east it grows rapidly and many are 25 m tall with splendid straight stout boles. One in Battersea Park, London, is 32 m tall and the larger of two in Mote Park, Maidstone, has a fine bole nearly 2 m in diameter. The bark is dark brown on young trees, deeply ridged and fissured and becoming black on old trees, with deep holes among the crossing ridges. The leaves have about 15 ovate-lanceolate, shallowly toothed, rich shiny green leaflets, longest in the middle length of the leaf and there about 9 × 3 cm. This luxuriant foliage is well spaced all over the crown and hangs somewhat on the outside. It turns bright yellow, sometimes rather briefly, in the autumn.

To raise the Black walnut, it is best to have fresh nuts imported from the USA in damp peat and sown early in spring, or even, being woody and slow to germinate, on arrival in autumn. The first-year shoot is around 1 m long and this should be cut back to ground level – hard though it may seem – when the tree is then put in its final position.

Juglans regia Common walnut

If more Common walnuts could grow like a remarkable specimen near Newport Pagnell on the Northamptonshire border, it would be worth planting more often. This tree is like a prime Oak in shape, 25 m × 2 m, and by a long way the biggest and finest in these islands. Most specimens, however, have a short, sinuous bole and a low, spreading crown. This is the only walnut with entire leaflets but sometimes a shaded leaf will have a few small-toothed ones. As a specimen of very moderate size, the Common walnut has a picturesque, Chinese aspect with twisted branches and soft grey platy bark. When coming into leaf, which is very late in spring, the foliage is orange-brown then pale brown. Crushing a leaf gives rise to a strong scent like polish and it is said to be a repellent to flies, even from a sprig placed in a jar on the window-sill. Its origin is thought to be South-West Asia.

Walnut

'Laciniata' is a rare and attractive form with dark purple rachis bearing leaflets which are deeply and very irregularly lobed with slender, often curved points. It remains a small tree, growing slowly.

Kalopanax pictus Castor Aralia
(*Acanthopanax ricinifolius*)

For a tree which looks, in leaf, to be a tender foliage-plant and yet must be very hardy indeed to thrive at 200 m in Peebles-shire and near Aberdeen, there must be wide uses. Although in winter strangely gaunt with few branches and few stout, spiky shoots, it is luxuriant in leaf and curious in flower and fruit. The bark is thickly ridged dull grey on the bole and on big branches well into the crown. It has nearly level spreading lower branches and short upper ones, and a leaning spire-top. The bole has many short but sharp, broadly based spines, most prominent when it is young.

There are two extreme forms of foliage, and many trees are somewhere between them. The type has maple-like leaves with three broad, shallow, finely pointed lobes and two small ones at the base, on a slender 12–15 cm petiole which is green and glabrous. The var. *maximowiczii* has 5–7 deeply cut elliptic-acute lobes, a red-brown pubescent and rough petiole 10–20 cm long, and the leaf-blade may be 20 × 20 cm. The margins of

Prickly castor-oil tree (var. maximowiczii)

both forms have hard, thick but fine toothing, very sharp. The flowers open in late summer, small and white in umbels of about 25 on thin white stalks 8 cm long, about 30 such stalks radiating from the tip of the shoot. In late autumn each umbel is a cluster of 5 mm black berries.

The variety is Japanese and the type ranges to China, Korea and Manchuria. Trees of 15 m are sometimes seen but there are few old enough to have grown as big and it is still scarce. It deserves to be seen more and adds splendid foliage effects to any planting, especially valuable where more tender trees cannot be grown.

Prickly castor-oil tree (typical)

Koelreuteria paniculata Golden rain tree; Pride of India

Since this tree is not Indian but Chinese, and several other trees are called 'Pride of India', the name more often used in America – 'Golden rain tree' – is preferred. Gaunt and dark red-brown-barked in winter, late into leaf and early to shed, this is nevertheless worth a place in southern plantings. The leaves, dark red from the bud, are up to 45 cm long, pinnate and often doubly so at base, with leaflets to 8 cm long, broad and lobed or doubly toothed on a red, flanged and grooved rachis. They turn briefly yellow and pale orange in autumn. The crown becomes a broad dome of short-jointed shoots on a few twisting raised branches. The late summer flowering is the tree's best point and it is freely produced only where summers are warm – notably in Cambridge and Chichester, where there seem to be more Golden rain trees than in other parts. Great open panicles, 30–40 cm long, grow out beyond the foliage and bear 1 cm bright yellow four-petalled flowers; these ripen into conic bladder-like fruit 4–5 cm long which are bright pink in autumn. This late flowering, of an unusual colour in any tree after spring earns the Golden rain tree a place, if not a prominent one because it has a long season being undistinguished. It is best on a good garden soil but is not very demanding although it must have full light.

+Laburnocytisus adamii Adam's laburnum

Not many trees are first-rate conversation pieces and tenth-rate trees but Adam's laburnum can claim to be, without doubt. For 50 weeks of the year it stands shapeless, the meagre shoots apparently afflicted by a witch's broom, the foliage, when present, dark, dull and scanty. Single-handed it could ruin any group or prospect. During those remaining two weeks it is an eye-catching harlequin of a tree. The 'witches' brooms' become 25 cm bunches of little 4 cm racemes of soft rosy-purple flowers, spread randomly through a crown which is mostly hung densely with 15 cm racemes of pale pinkish-purple or coppery-pink flowers but also at random bears normal bright yellow laburnum racemes.

Monsieur Adam had grafted the Dwarf Purple broom, *Cytisus purpureus*, on a leg of Common laburnum at his nursery near Paris in 1825 and one branch grew out with the pinkish laburnum flowers, which are yellow-based with purple overlay. When this was propagated by grafting, the new plants began to produce the flowers of each parent tree here and there. A shoot from any part of the tree will do the same if grafted. The shoot was evidently a 'chimaera' with the two parent tissues remaining unaltered, and some of the flowers derive from both together.

A place has to be found somewhere for such an interesting tree, but preferably where it is not obtrusive when out of flower, like the interior of a large well-spaced group or as a single tree in a planting of large shrubs attractive all through the year, and where it can be ignored as a minor part until it flowers.

Laburnum × watereri 'Vossii' Voss's hybrid laburnum

This hybrid is so much superior to either parent or to other forms of the cross that it is the only one which needs to be considered. The flower racemes are usually 45 cm long and can be 60 cm and do not shorten as the tree ages to the extent that occurs on the Common laburnum. They are densely strung with big flowers and last well, while few seed-pods disfigure the tree, brown and dull in autumn. It has superior foliage densely along the branches with 10 cm leaflets, not thinning noticeably with age, but still a poor tree when not in flower and thus difficult to place.

Ligustrum lucidum Glossy privet; Chinese privet

There are many other privets wild in China but this one can claim the name not only because it is the finest of them but was the first one here, brought in 1794 and widespread in central areas of that country. It is one of the choicest and most continuously attractive trees we have, as well as being one able to thrive in cities. It probably needs warm summers to do well, for it is little seen in northern countries but grows well in the main

street of Tangier, runs riot in Georgia and Alabama and yields big fruits in Jackson Square, New Orleans, which it does not do in England. The relatively cool summers of Devon, however, are adequate, for the tallest – over 20 m – is in a garden above an estuary in the far south-western corner of the county.

The points on which this tree scores so well, apart from being very amenable to soil and site, are its good crown, foliage and flower, strong scent and long season. The crown is a high dome, leafy and evergreen, but not dense, open inside with straight ascending branches; it provides shade without gloom, and appears to be flowering all the season with the light glinting on the leaves. These, in opposite pairs, are ovate-acuminate, entire, about 10 cm long and glossy dark green. The flowers begin their display as pale green conic panicles in early spring, continue as ivory white buds through the summer and open in autumn, whiter and intensely sweet-scented. Fruit not developing here, the panicles remain, tinged dark red until early spring when more buds appear.

Three forms are in a few parks and gardens with leaves variegated yellow or white. The whitest is handsome and can be 14 m tall but is not improved by its flowers, which make it look too fussy and ill-defined in colouring.

Liquidambar formosana Chinese sweet gum: Chinese liquidambar

This is a really choice tree but is rarely seen as few seed-lots have been received since the first from Hankow in 1884 and the next from Ernest Wilson in Hupeh in 1907. Young trees are quite vigorous, narrowly crowned and conic. The leaves unfold glossy red-brown then have a crimson cast before turning blackish-green, the veins remaining deep purple and the petiole deep red. The leaf is hard and very three-lobed, the margin finely cut into sharp, hard teeth. This makes a distinguishable foliage in any group, if not very exciting, but in autumn it stands out with a unique mixture of orange, deep red and bright purple colours. It seems amenable to different soils but benefits from shelter, especially from the north and east. A tree at Killerton is now 20 × 0.5 m.

Chinese sweet gum

Liquidambar styraciflua Sweet gum

For summer foliage and autumn colours the Sweet gum has few equals. It never grows particularly fast but it keeps on upwards for 100 years or more. Fairly mature trees of 20–25 m are in many gardens and the oldest trees are 28–29 m tall and magnificent with their heavy crowns of rich green, shiny, big star-like leaves. Each leaf can be 15 × 15 cm, deeply 5–7 lobed on some trees, notably so when growing wild in the Allegheny woods or on the shallow rocky low hills of Arkansas and Texas, hanging with a long central lobe. The lobes are obovate, narrowing to their base, with minute in-curved teeth. The bark is from an early age deeply furrowed dull grey. The crown is conic, fairly broad at base, and with age the top broadens to a big dome but a strong branch may carry a conic tip out to one side. Small branches and shoots on some trees, and suckers from most trees have corky wings, probably because the trees with them were raised from suckers, but these can also occur on seedlings.

Male flowers are little globes on 5–10 cm erect stalks and are soon shed. Females are more prominent, yellow-green dense clusters, each globe 1 cm across, on a 5 cm stalk, ripening to a woody, spiky hanging globe, dark brown in late autumn. Autumn colouring is notoriously variable but rarely fails altogether. It is best on trees in full light in a damp, rich soil. Some trees turn early, scarlet then deeper red. Others turn later, soon deep red, others again turn later still, a grand marbling of pale orange, red and purple, while a few as late as mid-November are mixed green, pale yellow and plum purple. This amounts to two months of varied colours spread over different trees, and a group will rarely colour together.

Liriodendron chinense Chinese tulip-tree

This was introduced from central China in 1901 and until seed is more freely available it will remain scarce, but it is as good a tree or marginally better than the common American species. It is just as vigorous and will evidently make a tree in this country about as big; two in Sussex being 27 m (Wakehurst Place) and 24 m × 75 cm (Ashford Chase). Some of the best trees are in Ireland. The foliage unfolds rich brown and the petioles become red. The leaf is truncated with a central lobe narrowing sharply to make a pair of lobes at the base, and the underside well silvered; it colours pure bright gold in autumn. The flowers are pale orange without the blue-green band (see below).

This is an excellent specimen tree but preferably in some sheltered position as it may suffer breakage.

Liriodendron tulipifera Tulip-tree

The American name 'tulip poplar' is apt for the way the tree grows in its native area, for until 30 m tall it has an open, conic, lightly branched crown like the poplar 'Robusta', then it makes a more dense dome to 50 m height on a clear bole of 30 m. Here it is broad-conic and dense from the start and old trees have broad crowns on branches often arching to the ground. It can grow fast to 25 m in the south but progressively more slowly towards the north and is a low tree, little planted north of Edinburgh. The bark is grey and well-ridged until on very old trees (and some are 300 years old although many break up before that) it is warm brown and may have deep fissures.

This is no flowering tree, despite its name, but a superb foliage-tree. Not only will it be shy to flower in northern and cooler areas, but it needs to be about 25 years old before it starts; it then flowers when in full, dense leaf and although often very numerous the flowers are not seen as a blaze of colour, but provide a splash here and there. They have a broad blue-green band across the petals which also helps to conceal them. The leaf has a broad truncated central lobe with parallel sides to small basal lobes; on some trees there are

sprouts bearing leaves with the same shape as those of the Chinese tulip-tree, described above. Growing best on deep, moist, rich soils the Tulip-tree will also thrive with some lime and on sands if moisture is available, a not too distant pond or stream being a great help.

Although lacking in presence in winter, this is among the best of the largest specimen trees in a suitable, warm site.

Tulip-trees do not move well, having brittle roots, and need to be well established in a container when planted, for small seedling trees are slow and need careful nursing for a few years. Grass must be kept well away from the bole, even of the biggest trees, for damage round the base from voles and mowers rarely heals and rots set in. Old trees become vulnerable to breakage and

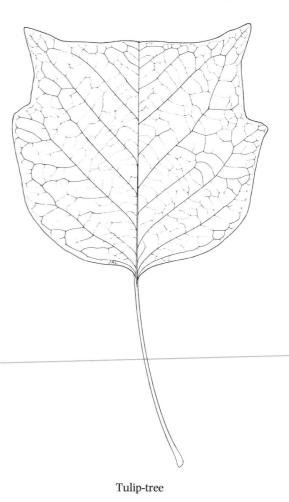

Tulip-tree

are likely to die back but are reasonably windfirm. Several of the once big old trees are now headed back to little more than stumps. They would be better replaced by three young ones each.

'Aureomarginatum' is a much less vigorous, narrow-crowned tree with leaves broadly margined rather dull yellow. Despite this, a well placed tree can be very effective.

'Fastigiatum'. This is very erect, usually broadening at a narrow angle straight from the base with strong branches arising there. It is too ill-defined at the top, where it begins to splay a little, to be a good formal erect tree but a group of three at some distance from the viewpoint makes a good feature with bright foliage, particularly when gold in autumn.

Magnolia acuminata Cucumber tree

Like the tulip-tree, and also in the Magnolia Family – a name conjuring up visions of huge flowers – this is strictly a good foliage-tree. The flowers are hidden in the leaves, as in all American magnolias, and are smallish, brownish-yellow and seldom numerous. Growing quite rapidly at first, even in Scotland, this settles to rather slow progress to become a tree 25 m tall with a straight bole 2–4 m long and with a well-furrowed dark brown bark. In leaf it is a pleasant tree with dark yellowish-green 20 cm elliptic leaves, but without leaves it is on the sparse and spiky side.

Magnolia campbellii Campbell's magnolia

In the Himalayas this is the biggest of the Asiatic magnolias and can be well over 30 m tall; some say 45 m. From the Thames Valley south and westward and in Southern Ireland it makes a large tree branching low from a very stout, smooth, elephant-grey bole. The flowers open in January in some years and places but usually a month or two later. The buds protect the flowers through the hardest winter frosts but once they begin to open, the flowers are vulnerable. In a frost-free spell they

open to 25 cm across, like great rose-pink water-lilies, at the end of each still leafless shoot. Then the outer tepals (sepals and petals are not distinguishable in this family) droop, showing the inner ones standing in a cone shape. Neither the crown nor the heavy dull foliage has much to recommend it, and with 15–25 years to wait for the first flower, these are all the tree offers for nearly a generation. It would be preferable to plant *M. sprengeri* var. *diva* instead (p. 104), or the following form:

'Charles Raffill'. Raised at Kew about 1945, this is a cross between Campbell's magnolia and its smaller flowered Chinese form, var. *mollicomata*. When 10 or 12 years old this should bear some flowers, not quite as big as in Campbell's, described as deep purple outside, pink-purple and white inside, but usually seen the same bright rosy pink and on a vigorous, shapely crown.

Magnolia delavayi Chinese evergreen magnolia

This is grown in the south of England and Ireland in the same way as the Southern Magnolia, against a wall, and only in the far south-west as a lawn specimen. Judging from the way it will grow on above the shelter of a garden-wall, it could more often be free-grown than it is. It makes a very stout bole with a thick, corky, cream or white bark and heavy low branches. The leaves are much bigger and very different from those of the common species, being broad ellipses 25 × 18 cm, silvery grey-green, unfolding coppery-brown. The cream flowers are 25 cm across, regular but not prolific, and it is as a superb foliage-plant that this magnolia is desirable. On alkaline soils it should replace the common evergreen Southern Magnolia.

Magnolia denudata Yulan; Yulan lily

Opening its fine pure white flowers two or three weeks before the common bush, Saucer magnolia (*M.* × *soulangiana*), this broad, much-branched, domed Chinese tree has a gracefulness absent from the other, so is possibly more attractive when not in flower. The leaves are 8–15 cm long, obovate, broader than those of the Saucer magnolia and abruptly acute, more grey-green. It thrives in the gardens of cities in the south.

Magnolia × loebneri 'Leonard Messel'

A small, so far, and rather bushy tree of the highest class when in flower, arose at Nymans when a pink-flowered form of *Magnolia stellata*, v. *rosea* crossed with a *magnolia kobus* which had a crimson patch at the base of the petals. The hybrid opens fairly early its rich rose-pink buds to expand soft pink petals which spread pale pink shading to white. For two or three weeks, the variation in the stages of opening of the prolific blossoming present a charming spectacle. The leaves unfolding later are 10–12 cm long, obovate with bluntly rounded tips and broad-cuneate bases, on stout, curved petioles 1 cm long. It thrives in any garden soil not too dry, even in limestone areas.

Magnolia sprengeri var. diva

This is the best of the big-flowered tree magnolias in many respects. It grows fast and flowers relatively young. At Westonbirt when planted 15 years it was 17 m tall and bore five flowers. The next year it had 550. It is a shapely, conic open-crowned tree with broad obovate leaves 17 × 12 cm but the flowers open on the bare shoots; they are a little smaller than those of Campbell's magnolia but tidier and a purer bright rose-pink. It is only by a quirk of its taxonomic history that this tree has to be named as a variety. It is the only pink-flowered *M. sprengeri* and derives from a single tree at Caerhays Castle raised from the batch of seed sent by Ernest Wilson from near the Ichang gorge in western China in 1900. All the others chanced to be white-flowered and much inferior and are called var. *elongata*.

Malus floribunda Japanese crab apple

This tree cannot be omitted despite its formless twiggy crown which is no adornment to any planting in winter or summer, for nothing else can quite replace its foaming mass of pink buds and white flowers in spring. Very early in the season, it unfolds bright green little lanceolate leaves, some with lobes, and it seems impossible that any abundance of flower could hide them. But it does, always. The problem is, as in the laburnums, how to hide the tree when it is not in flower. Nothing must crowd or shade it or it becomes thin, straggling and poor in flower and hence only bonfire-worthy. A bed in front of it planted with tall annual or biennial herbaceous plants like *Verbascum* or *Macleya*, or tall shrubs which are cut to base every spring, like *Buddleia*, is one possible solution.

Malus hupehensis Hupeh crab

A number of strange crabs can be found growing under this name in British and – far more – in American collections, but the one intended here, at least when in flower, is unmistakable. Ernest Wilson, who discovered it, regarded it as the finest of all the flowering trees he sent from China and in the summer of 1979 many must have agreed with him. From a broad, level-branched crown a profusion of large pink, globular buds radiate on slender, 4 cm stalks and open to pure white cup-shaped flowers spraying out from long sectors of shoot, then opening further to broad-petalled 6 cm stars with golden anthers at the centre. They are well spread among bright green leaves with enough flowers beyond them to turn the whole crown into a dense cloud of white.

This superb tree has other merits, too. It is a triploid and will not cross with other species within bee-flight, so it is true to seed. Seedlings grow straight and fast, about 1 m a year for a few years, and soon make a sturdy, well-boled tree over 10 m tall. The bark is good in winter, orange-brown fissured into big plates. Like all apples, this will grow on limy soils, compacted soil or ones of suspect drainage. A few trees have pink flowers, a frequent form in the wild, and are grown as var. *rosea*, but the white form is preferable.

Malus 'John Downie'

The starry white, rather small flowers of 'John Downie' are attractive but would not on their own earn this tree a place here. It is the great bonus of the fruit that qualifies it as a specimen tree. Strung along the ascending branches of a young tree in long-stalked bunches, they are conic-ovoid and ripen yellow, orange and scarlet with a high gloss. Among the green leaves they are spectacular and can put growers in a quandary, for these fruit make the most delicious and beautifully coloured apple-jelly jam. The best idea is to plant several trees. Being narrow when young, they stand well as a group. The name 'Cherry-apple' is sometimes heard for this tree and although bigger than any cherry the long-stalked bunches of the fruit do give the two some similarity.

Malus × magdeburgensis Magdeburg apple

This broad, low and rather pendulous apple tree bears large clusters of big, semi-double rosy pink flowers with paler interiors, amongst soft grey-green leaves. It is beautiful in flower but not good at other times and seems to be seen more in village gardens than in bigger gardens or parks.

Malus × purpurea Purple crab

With the exception, perhaps, of the one mentioned below, these are so unsightly, badly shaped and miserably foliaged that they have no place in a well ordered garden. For the brief and uncertain period in which they are presentable, enough of them can be seen in streets, parks and other people's gardens. They are exceedingly resistant to harsh conditions and a big array of them has been raised in the Prairie States of Canada and the USA. Few of those purple crabs will reach here, but 'Royal Red' is good and might be welcome.

'Profusion'. Bred partly for improved foliage, this cultivar is also superior in its dark red flowers spraying out and wreathing long sectors of shoot around the deep red opening leaves.

'Liset' has been raised from 'Profusion' and promises well, the flowers fading less readily to a poor purplish colour.

Malus trilobata

This eastern Mediterranean apple is scarce and highly distinctive. It is easily mistaken for a Wild service tree, *Sorbus torminalis*. The bark is closely cracked into small squares, light and dark brown, and the crown is open and conic to 12 m tall, growing quite fast. The leaf is on a 6 cm petiole and is cordate and deeply three-lobed, cut to 1 cm of the base of a leaf 7 × 6 cm, the central lobe has 3–5 lobules, and the spreading basal lobes have one lobule each side; all have a few small triangular teeth and are grey-green. The flowers are 5 cm across, white and bunched in terminal heads. In autumn the leaves turn blackish with the veins bright deep red.

This unusual and attractive tree is robust and undemanding as to soil. It will be a pity if it should remain so rare.

Malus tschonoskii Pillar apple

This Japanese tree is almost tailor-made for street and courtyard, precinct and small garden planting. It makes a very vigorous young plant, moving easily when quite big and able to thrive in very poor or compacted soils and withstanding

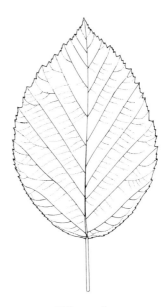

Pillar apple

cold and drought. It is as nearly vandal-proof as any tree, for planted when 3–4 m tall its branches are high, upright and so difficult to reach, and very tough. Its neat, strictly but not too tightly upright crown keeps its foliage away from lamp-posts and fits it into small spaces. Its buds open silvery with hairs and produce firm, substantial leaves but not big enough to be a nuisance in gutters and drains. Its flowers are pleasant and yield small 2 cm glossy yellow and red fruit but not in quantities to litter the paving. Above all, the leaves turn in autumn to bright yellow then scarlet and deep red, making it one of the very best trees for an autumn display, the better for being unusual in a fastigiate tree. It is formal enough in shape to make a good line among buildings while groups of three are also suitable there or as a feature in formal gardens, with bigger groups for a large scale. It is now much planted but there are few mature trees; these have become broader and less formal and achieve 16–17 m in height.

Malus 'Van Eseltine'

This is like a small, columnar *M. floribunda* but with bigger, 5 cm, double, rosy pink flowers. It is exceedingly attractive in flower and being so narrow and small it is unobtrusive for the rest of the year but can add a vertical motif of value in a group of shrubs.

Michelia doltsopa Michelia

Michelias are a genus of magnolias which bear their flowers in the leaf-axils instead of terminally. This grand evergreen is reliably hardy only in the far south-west of England and in Ireland, where it grows very fast, making a shapely tree to 17 m, so far, with upswept medium-conic crown; it is nevertheless worth risking in favoured sites in the south for its handsome foliage and fragrant flowers. The bark is smooth and grey, the shoot is bright green, and the long conic buds are purple-brown. The glossy deep green leaves are 15 × 6 cm, oblong lanceolate and entire, with a glaucous underside where the veins are orange-pubescent. The flowers are pale yellow or white, 10 cm across with about 15 petals. The flower-

buds are prominent through the winter, 5 cm long with orange-rusty hairs on pale green scales. *M. doltsopa* was sent from western China in 1918 and was in flower by 1933.

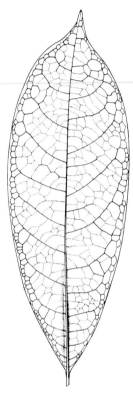

Michelia

Morus nigra Black mulberry

With a dense crown of large leaves it would be odd if this tree from South-West Asia were to be as slow-growing as is popularly believed. Trees with boles only 50 cm through are cheerfully credited to James I and the silkworm industry he encouraged. One of the largest trees is in a Suffolk garden where the owner was amused to have it assessed as about 300 years old since he knew it was planted on the day he was born, 64 years before. Many mulberries look venerable before their time because they were raised by the curious method used for this tree alone, the planting of truncheons. These are big branches from an old tree, cut into lengths of 1·5 m and set with about

0·5 m in the ground. They sprout copiously and make a tree but the bole is short and 40–50 years older than the crown; consequently rot may invade the cut top and the new branches may break out. To stop this some trees were mounded up to the spring of the branches and the bole can no longer be seen. In general, well-shaped trees, either seedlings after a long slow start, or long truncheons pruned to one or a few shoots, are about 40 cm through when 40–50 years old. Few are more than 10 m tall.

The dull orange scaly bark is attractive and so is the broad dense crown when bearing its heavy rich green foliage, or pale then bright yellow in autumn. The fruit, copiously borne after some 20 years, would be more effective if all the same bright red but a proportion is deep red then black when it falls, over a long period. Delicious to eat when fully ripe black, the fruit attract birds and the ground beneath becomes messy if a mown lawn or a hard surface. This detracts somewhat from the value of the tree in a courtyard but it is a fine foliage subject in long grass or a shrub bed.

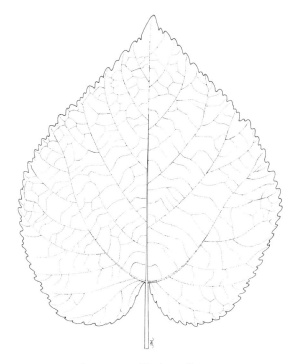

Common or Black mulberry

(The White mulberry, *Morus alba* from China, has glossy, quite smooth leaves more given to fancy lobing but not so hardy and exceptionally liable to damage so cannot be recommended. This is the Mulberry preferred by silkworms.)

Myrtus luma

This tree from South America runs wild in the gardens of Counties Cork and Kerry and makes a tree to 15 m in Devon, Cornwall and Argyll, but further east and even along the south coast, it is progressively smaller and struggling until only a bush in Kent and not reliably hardy east of Dorset. Well grown it is splendid as a background with its neat black evergreen foliage setting off the bright orange boles which strip in patches to leave white areas. The shoot is densely pubescent and dark pink above, and bears opposite pairs of oval 2·5 cm entire leaves from every axil of which a single, slender-stalked red and green bud projects and opens pure white in late summer. The black crown then becomes mixed with a starry white cloud and, held on the orange branches, it makes an arresting sight.

Nothofagus antarctica Antarctic beech

As befits a tree which ranges south into Tierra del Fuego, this is absolutely hardy anywhere, although it has a delicate look about it. This comes from the sparse branching carrying-systems of short fine shoots and tiny leaves and the crown often bending out to one side. In the second year from planting there will often be shoots 1 m or more long but this does not last and few trees exceed 15 m in height. In most trees the bark is very soon rough and fissured into grey-brown flaking plates but in a few it remains dark red with shiny smooth areas between bands of lenticels. In winter, therefore, although very bare-looking and wandering rather than of positive decisive shape, there is an attractive look about this tree. It is even better as the leaves unfold, shiny bright green. They are crinkled by four pairs of veins and are only 3 cm long, becoming deep green, still shiny, then yellow and pale brown in autumn. They have irregular shallow toothing.

Nothofagus dombeyi Coigue; Dombey's southern beech

This Chilean tree is the best hardy evergreen *Nothofagus* and remarkably vigorous particularly in the west. In County Wicklow two trees less than 50 years old were 25 m × 1 m and even in Kent one of the same age is 17 m × 47 cm. Young trees are sometimes cut back badly by severe frost but in the very hard winter of 1979 trees in Kent were not even scorched at all. The bark of young trees is smooth but horizontally wrinkled dark grey. Older trees have rich brown and red-brown plates and strips. The slender shoots bear irregularly toothed, oval, 3–4 cm, hard shiny blackish-green leaves, smooth, mat and veinless beneath.

This is unusual among our evergreen trees in having such small foliage and reaching such a size. The smallness of the leaves prevents the big blackish crown from being oppressive and makes the Coigue a grand specimen tree although in numbers it would be too dark.

Dombey's southern beech

Nothofagus fusca Red beech

This semi-evergreen New Zealand tree is remarkably hardy and grows in Edinburgh, while at Mt Usher a fine specimen is 22 × 0.9 m. For much of the year it has some of its leaves colouring yellow and dark red preparatory to being shed, livening up the rather sparse crown of dull pale green younger leaves. The leaves are thin and papery, 4 × 2 cm with a few big in-curved teeth each side, and unlike those of any other tree grown here.

Nothofagus moorei Moore's southern beech

This Australian tree has by far the most handsome foliage of the evergreen Southern beeches but it is not hardy outside Cornwall and Ireland. The leaves are a deep glossy green, 8 × 3 cm, hard, edged by small forward teeth, ovate-lanceolate with 12 veins each side of the whitish-green midrib. It is a fine tree to 16 m at Caerhays and Trengwainton in Cornwall and in several Irish gardens.

Nothofagus obliqua Roblé

The Spanish name used here means 'oak' so until this tree is more widely known it may be useful to call it 'Roblé beech' although it makes little sense in translation. The Roblé was introduced from Chile in 1902 but it ranges widely into Argentina and now some of these origins are being tried. It is a tree of remarkable vigour even on poor sandy soils. Leading shoots of 1·3 m are seen and 26 m has been reached in 22 years. Specimens over 30 m tall are rare, largely because the branches are usually weak and tall trees are liable to breakage high in the crown, but one in County Cork is 30 × 1.1 m. There are few trees older than 40 years but there has been much planting since 1950 and some in small forest plantations, mainly experimentally. One original tree has a bole over 1 m in diameter. Slender shoots spray out at a sharp downward angle from the upper crown, tapering regularly in outline as the straight laterals, close and parallel, decrease in length towards the tip. The leaves are oblong-elliptic,

Roblé beech

5–8 cm long with 7–11 pairs of impressed parallel veins and sharp irregular toothing. Dark green in summer, they turn yellow, orange and crimson before falling.

Nothofagus procera Rauli

The Rauli is a deciduous Southern beech from Chile and Argentina, like the Roblé, but is superior to that species as a specimen tree in several ways, except on soils of extreme reaction, acid or alkaline, and in some exposed, cold places. It was introduced in 1914, but the biggest known may not be quite so old. It is a superb tree 30 × 1.3 m at Brodick Castle on Arran. Many young trees add shoots 1.5–2 m long and one was 15 m in nine years from seed. Its form is very

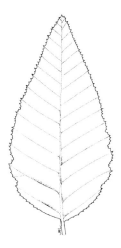

Rauli

different from that of the Roblé, as it grows a stout bole rapidly with strong upswept branches and stout spreading shoots. The leaves are the best of the deciduous Southern beeches, being prominently marked by 15–22 parallel straight veins each side of the midrib. They vary in size since every tree has some very small leaves 4 cm long but others are 8–10 cm, oblong-elliptic and shallowly toothed, orange-brown from the bud, then fresh light green; they become darker and grey-green in late summer. In the autumn the leaves turn yellow, pale orange and some dark red.

On any loamy or not too dry sandy soil in a little shelter this makes an imposing specimen more quickly than any but a few eucalypts and willows, and in a damp, sheltered site it will go on to be a very big tree, some 25 m × 80 cm in 40 years. The leaves begin to unfold early in spring and are held back if a cold spell occurs but are rarely damaged more than having scorched edges. Trees one or two years old can be killed to the ground but then sprout with several stems, which need to be singled.

Nothofagus solandri Black beech

This evergreen tree from New Zealand is, together with the Mountain beech, the only evergreen Southern beech with entire leaves. The Mountain Beech, var. *cliffortioides*, differs only in the leaves – equally small, 1 cm – being buckled, and it is hardy almost anywhere. Both are strange trees with small, slender branches arching out maybe 1 m apart, with a shallow layer of dense twiglets and tiny leaves above each, and a bole with smooth blackish ribs. Very vigorous in the west but less so in the east, the biggest being 20 × 0.8 m at Benmore, Argyll.

Nyssa sylvatica Tupelo; Black gum

The Tupelo ranges over eastern North America south of a line from Chicago to the coast of Maine, scattered in woodlands which are a grand Persian carpet of a hundred fine tree species; a forest structure quite unknown in Europe. It enjoys hot summers throughout the region, where the inhabitants pronounce its name 'tooperlow'. There is one at Holker, Cumbria, 12 × 0.4 m but this is an outlier from its general planted range here, which is more southern. It is infrequent even in the south and mainly confined to sheltered sites on rich, deep soil in the largest gardens. An informal line of some twenty is a fine feature at Winkworth Arboretum, Surrey, along the bottom of a big bank planted with a diversity of trees almost like a hillside in the Allegheny Mountains, beside a path above the lake. Around 40 years old, these are about 12 m tall. The major planting of Tupelo in Europe is that at Sheffield Park in Sussex where 400 were planted in 1909 and some 150 are good trees now, the best 23 m × 60 cm. These figures show that growth here is at best moderate and the slowness and rather thin appearance of young plants may be one reason for it not being planted more often. The early years should be borne with for the tree has a long, healthy life and in sunny autumns it will be the most spectacular plant in the garden. The glossy leaves, 5–18 cm long and equally variable in width from lanceolate to broad elliptic, retain the high gloss as they turn gold, then the outer leaves turn through orange to scarlet. It is then at its most distinctive best, but later the whole crown

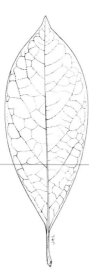

Tupelo

is scarlet and dark red. On some trees and in some autumns, shades of orange are as far as the leaves will go but they are still a fine sight.

Ostrya carpinifolia European Hop-hornbeam

The Hop-hornbeam is included entirely for its unusual appearance in summer when the crown of dark, quite handsome foliage is varied by the white fruit, 5 cm broad-cylindric bunches of bladders like a big hop fruit. Otherwise it is rather a dull tree with a broad crown from level branches low on the fissured and flaky brown bole, although the leaves are good at close quarters. They are 10 × 5 cm ovate with about 15 mostly parallel pairs of veins to very sharp teeth with smaller teeth between those at the vein-ends.

Oxydendrum arboreum Sourwood; Sorrel-tree

As a member of the great Rhododendron-Heath Family, *Ericaceae*, it is not unexpected that the Sorrel-tree, unlike most of the trees we grow, really does need an acid soil and cannot tolerate any lime. This limits its use somewhat but few of the great gardens of the west are thus restricted and many of them grow a specimen or two. The Sorrel-tree from the eastern United States, would prefer eastern districts with hotter summers so the larger specimens tend to be in Sussex gardens on acid soils; even here it is only 15–17 m tall and grows very slowly. Luckily it may flower well when only a few years old and with its good autumn colours it is worth a place where a small tree is required. The bark soon fissures into dull grey ridges and the crown becomes an open dome on ascending, twisting branches, so the tree is somewhat sparse in winter. The leaves are oblong-elliptic, acute and finely serrated, deep glossy green above and smooth, greyish-green beneath with only the midrib showing white. In autumn they turn scarlet then deep red but, like the Tupelo, they need full sun for this to happen here, although in their native woods they colour brilliantly beneath quite a dense canopy.

The flowers are a feature, spraying down at a slight angle from the branch-ends on slender

25 cm panicles with about six branches. Each flower is a tiny pendulous white urn and they open over a long period from midsummer. Since the fruit is almost the same colour, ivory-white until it goes woody, the tree seems to be, and probably partly is, in flower when in full autumn colour.

In a small planting, the Sorrel-tree warrants a fairly prominent position and must be unshaded. On a larger scale, it needs to be planted in groups to have much effect, particularly as it grows slowly. If the soil is acid, it makes little difference how poor it is but it should not dry out too rapidly.

Parrotia persica Persian ironwood

This is often no more than a tall, wide-spreading bush but there are specimens on boles 2–3 m long showing the mottled brown flaking London plane bark well. As a garden tree the Persian ironwood is planted for autumn colour but it would make more of a show if the upper crown of long, shallowly arched branches did not colour and shed before the rest of the crown has properly started. It needs a very big garden to accommodate groups of this tree, particularly as they are far from exciting in summer and can be only a part of a larger scheme, but it is as a group that they are most effective. The obovate, wavy-edged leaves broaden from the base to near the tip and are thick and dark green until some turn yellow in early autumn. By mid-autumn they have changed through orange to crimson and dark red and the top branches are bare. The flowers are little bunches of dark red stamens which often open in January but the value of this early flowering is diminished by the flowers being so small and inconspicuous. Winter flowers are most appreciated near a much used path or near buildings, but these are not usually the best places for this plant at other times of the year.

Paulownia tomentosa Paulownia; Empress tree

The Paulownia needs the warmest summers it can have both in order to grow well here and to flower abundantly, so it is largely restricted to the south-east of England. The tallest tree, 27 m high, was at Westonbirt in Gloucestershire sheltered in the narrow Specimen Avenue. This tree came from seed sent in 1907 from China by Ernest Wilson while most of the earlier trees are of Japanese origin, having come via France. The Paulownia needs shelter in order to grow tall since its branches are brittle, but it also needs full sun to flower well. The flowers are on terminal panicles which are prominent in winter, and are in orange-pubescent buds which survive cold winters but can be killed in spring if a sharp frost follows a mild spell in which they begin to open. The panicles are 20–30 cm long and carry 15–20 flowers each but in hotter countries they are 40 cm with far more flowers and are much more numerous.

The flowers open in late spring before the leaves emerge, trumpet-shaped, 6 cm long, violet blue or pale purple, and ripen to shiny green globular, beaked and horribly sticky 3 cm fruit.

The spectacular flowers, being terminal, are mostly above the crown, so it is not easy to see them from beneath the tree. The Paulownia is therefore a tree to plant on the lower slopes of a bank with a prospect from above. It is also well placed sheltered beneath the walls of a castle or below ramparts with a walk along the top, or a sea-wall, for it grows well near the coast but not in full exposure to sea-winds.

The leaves of an adult tree are hugely long-triangular, entire, cordate and to 40 cm long. The petiole is 10–15 cm long, pinkish and densely pubescent, and the leaves are softly white pubescent all over. With the smooth grey or purple-grey bark and a good cylindric bole, this makes an attractive foliage-tree. It is raised from seed and should be planted out at the end of the first year when it may be 50 cm tall, and cut back late in spring, to a basal bud. It should then grow a rod to 2·5 m long, carrying great broad leaves 45–50 cm each way with several shallow triangular lobes. This stumping-back should be

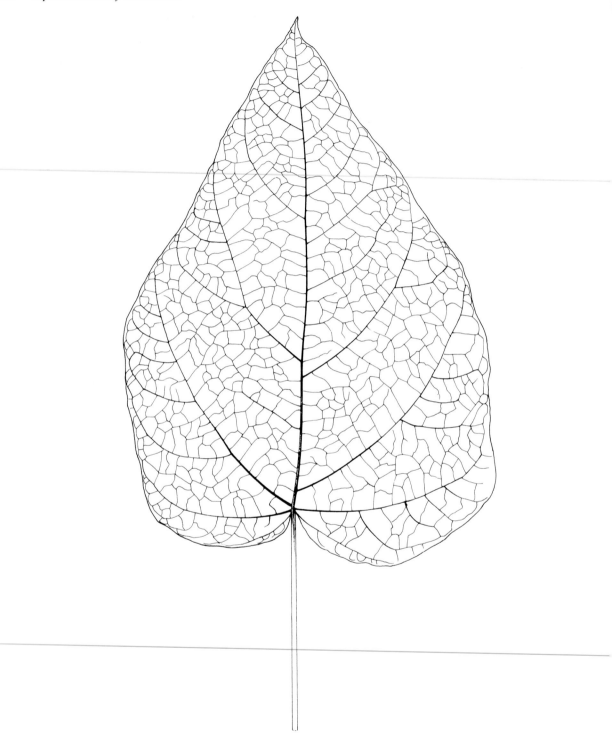

Empress tree

done, if omitted before, on trees planted out two, three or many years previously since they will not have made strong straight growth if left uncut. Because Paulownias grow on through the summer nearly into October, the tip of the shoot cannot be hardened against winter frosts and always dies back. New growth starts from one or two whorls of paired buds some way below the tip, and to ensure a longer bole the strongest must be selected and the others cut out. The foliage on the one-year shoot after cutting back is so luxuriant that it can be the purpose of the tree, especially in cooler areas where it cannot be expected to be a good flowering tree. In this case, two or three rods can be left, and cut down each spring.

Picrasma quassioides Quassia tree

A rare little tree from China and Japan, this adds distinction to a planting with its foliage, fruit and, particularly, its autumn colours. The leaf is rather like that of an Ash with 11 broad-ovate leaflets but glossy rich green on a crimson central stalk. It turns yellow and bright red in autumn when there may also be numerous flattish heads of tiny berries, orange-red turning black. These arise from little yellow-green four-petalled flowers. Winter interest is added by the dark purple-brown shoots with scarlet buds.

Pittosporum tenuifolium Pittosporum

This is much the hardiest of a number of New Zealand plants seen in Cornish and Irish gardens, and grows as far east as London and northwards along the west coast to Argyll. In the mildest parts it is a tree to 16 m with a smooth dull grey bole and upright dense ovoid crown. Elsewhere it is an upright ovoid bush valuable for foliage of a different colour and texture from all others, and a useful evergreen low screen. The slender dark purple shoots bear rather remote groups of leaves which are bright pale green and deeply crinkled and waved, hard oblong-elliptic and 5 cm long. Dark purple cup-shaped flowers open in late spring, not conspicuous but highly fragrant, and ripen to black 1·5 cm berries.

Platanus × acerifolia London plane

This cross between the Buttonwood or American plane and the Oriental plane has hybrid vigour combined with near indestructibility and a great life-span. The oldest are nearly 300 years of age, immense and still growing fast. It is almost unknown for one to blow down, or even to die, so there will be gigantic trees all through our cities one day. This ability to grow fast in almost any conditions, together with its ease of propagation from stool-beds, cuttings or seed, makes the London plane nearly irresistible to those who have to plant in cities. No tree should be planted unless it has about a quarter of a hectare to expand over without causing trouble. Planes tolerate pruning very well, but it does not make them look anything but grievously wounded and truncated afterwards. These considerations apply only in the southern third of England for, liking hot summers, the Plane does not grow so fast nor reach great sizes in other parts. It is in the southern gardens like Mottisfont Abbey in Hampshire and Pusey House, Oxfordshire and in towns around London such as Carshalton and Richmond that the giant trees are found, to 40 m tall and 2·4 m in diameter. In southern Scotland it is a very modest-sized tree.

To some, the large, much-lobed shiny leaves of London plane are out of place in a rural setting and bring the air of a city park with them. The first may be true but there is nothing of a city park about a vast Plane or two on a mansion lawn where they can be monumental specimens worth going far to see. Trees of great size no longer have the well-known mottled bark on the bole, but only high on the branches. The boles are warm red-brown, finely fissured, ridged or folded in patches.

There are many different forms of London plane grown. The aristocrat among them is 'Augustine Henry' which has a long clean bole and straight, sparse branches both with prominent pale yellow or white patches on the bark, and sparse deep green hooded leaves. This is scarce, with trees at Kew and one in the Mall in London and at Tortworth Court in Gloucestershire but few others. The form 'Pyramidalis' is very common in London and has a sprouty, burry dark bark and usually only a single large ball of fruit on each catkin, like the American plane. The leaf is smaller than in other forms, bright and shiny and tending to have three lobes. The huge old trees have big leaves, about 20×30 cm with five large, toothed lobes and 3–6 smaller fruit-balls on the catkin.

The uses of London plane are discussed more fully on pp. 44–5 and 47–8.

'Suttneri' is a very rare and striking Plane strongly variegated white or very pale yellow, which is now being planted a little more than it was, limited perhaps by availability.

Platanus orientalis Oriental plane

In the Levant this is one of the world's biggest and longest-living trees. There are a few very big and relatively old ones in British gardens and parks in the south of England. It has the advantage over London plane of much more attractive foliage with deeply cut slender pointed lobes and bronzy autumn tints, but it is not a good specimen tree since it sprawls widely and rarely has a tall crown. Old trees are picturesque when they lean huge branches on the ground but few plantings have room for this, unless in the middle of a big park or the side of an extensive prospect in a garden.

'Digitata', which may be a form of London plane rather than of the Oriental, is a delightful foliage-tree of reasonably narrow crown and rapid growth when young. The leaves are deeply divided into five widely parted long slender lobes with lobulate margins.

Populus alba White poplar; Abele

The type tree from central Europe has no place here except to be recommended as a temporary shelter tree on sea-blown sands. It makes a poor specimen, slender and leaning, although pretty when first coming into leaf bright silver, and suckers widely, ruining a lawn. It is this suckering that gives it value for seaward shelter as it is profuse in the poorest soils and grows rapidly to a useful 5–6 m.

'Richardii'. Perhaps it is because of the excessive suckering of this form that it is exceptionally rare although often mentioned. Its crown of pale grey-green, strikingly white-backed leaves is partly of leaves with a bright gold upper surface, which is very unusual and attractive.

'Pyramidalis'. This is a distinctly short-term tree since at no great age, but at considerable size, it tends to open out and disintegrate. However it can give 60–80 years of good white-backed foliage on a narrow vase-shaped crown. In the Prairie States of Canada and the USA it has a pure white bark and narrowly tapered crown, greatly superior to the trees seen here and perhaps a different form. The European tree is also known as Bolle's poplar.

Populus × candicans 'Aurora'

This tree is prone to bacterial canker and may be short-lived, but by cutting branches back to the trunk every year it can be a striking, if odd sight seen often in Irish villages. It grows fast until cut, into a conic-crowned dark-leafed poplar early in the season until new leaves grow at the tips of the shoots often looking like pure white waterlily flowers. As the shoot continues the leaves unfold broadly splashed with creamy-white, some with a pink tinge. It looks and grows well in the damp soil near the edge of a pool but will also grow on poorer soils.

Populus canescens Grey poplar

Although rapidly growing too big for smaller gardens or spaces this is the tree to grow as a specimen rather than the White poplar. It does not sucker so intensively and the leaf undersides are not quite such a clear white, but it is a splendid, robust tree brought from Southern Europe by early colonists. In the limy alluvial soils of lowland valleys in southern England and central Ireland it reaches its perfection but it makes a very big tree even in Easter Ross north of Inverness. The biggest trees are around $36 \times 1 \cdot 3$ m with long boles and few strong upswept branches which arch out to a high-domed crown; they are a feature in very early spring as almost all are male trees and the catkins swell and turn purple. Later, coming into leaf the big crowns are silvery, greying as the leaves unfold. On young trees the strong shoots bear ovate leaves 8–10 cm long but the crowns of mature trees are entirely of nearly round leaves with hooked teeth.

Populus lasiocarpa Chinese necklace poplar

Although a gaunt, shaggily grey-barked tree in winter, this is a fine foliage-tree during the summer. Sent first from central China in 1900 it has been at times in short supply and some trees are grafted but have not grown well. Seedling trees are not fast either, except for a superb and shapely tree in the Botanic Garden at Bath, which is now 25 m × 70 cm. The leaves are broadly ovate-acuminate to over 30 × 20 cm and bright shining green with red veins towards the base, on 20 cm pink petioles. The flowers are conspicuous and numerous, thick yellow 25 cm catkins of male flowers, often with 5–6 females at the base, or on female trees 25 cm with sparse green flowers and later globose green fruit sprouting long pale brown wool.

Populus nigra 'Italica'

This very well-known tree was brought to Essex from Turin in 1758 and is highly adaptable to site and soil. It is no ornament to the countryside in lines because some trees will always be broken or stunted, but it is superb as a group for a large-scale feature and many of these are now passing 30 m in height and are highly impressive.

All trees deriving from the true form are males with dark red catkins opening in March. After a long sunny autumn the leaves turn bright gold. A form scarcely half as broad in the crown as the common one is over 30 m in many gardens, almost too thin to be more than a curiosity. A female form quite often seen has a crown of ascending big branches, broadest at its top. It is known as P. × 'Gigantea' but its origin is obscure.

Populus 'Robusta' Robusta poplar

Of the many hybrids between the European black poplar and the American Cottonwood, *P. deltoides*, this is the best for general planting. It is most like the Cottonwood, with its very luxuriant, heavy foliage of broad ovate deep glossy green leaves, and is exceptionally vigorous, young trees usually growing shoots of 1·5–2 m and sometimes more. The bole should be pruned clean of shoots by the third year for 2 m and later for as high as can be reached. 'Robusta' is often seen in southern England by roads in town or country, in small plantations in the latter, making broad conic-columnar crowns with regular branching in whorls. Its great merits in landscaping are the rapid growth, the shapely crown, the abundance of deep bright red 10 cm male catkins in early spring, the bright orange of the unfolding leaves and the dense handsome foliage; also, being male, the absence of clouds of cottonwool in summer. The limitations on planting this tree, apart from those common to poplars near buildings on heavy clays, are that it does best in regions with warm summers and needs base-rich moist soils. There are few old trees yet but those up to 70 years of age are 32–38 m tall, so this is not a tree for small plantings. It makes a superb specimen by a lake or river and a group can be an important feature in an extensive landscape.

Populus 'Serotina Aurea' Golden Black poplar

The Black Italian poplar itself, P. × 'Serotina', is altogether too coarse, fragile, short-lived and late into leaf to appear here. 'Robusta' (above) excels it in every way. The Golden form, however, is a good tree, with a denser and more tidy crown, slower growth and good foliage. The leaves are bright lemon yellow to butter-yellow and a crown 30 m high seen across a town, in sunshine but against a dark cloud, is spectacularly beautiful. Rate of growth being slower in the Golden form, and not always important, this can be grown on less fertile or damp soils than 'Serotina' itself. Two tall trees in Aldershot have partially reverted green crowns but this can happen only rarely.

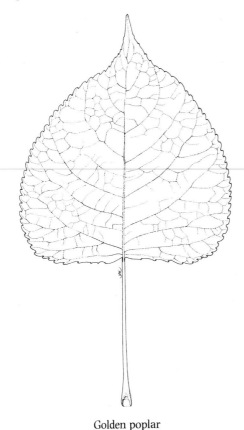

Golden poplar

Prunus 'Accolade'

A hybrid from Sargent cherry, this wide-spreading little tree is outstanding for early season abundance of rosy-pink, semi-double, fringed flowers. Its thin straggly crown and sparse slender leaves are rather a let-down for the rest of the year until it turns pale orange red in autumn.

Prunus avium Gean; Wild cherry

The native Gean is a tree of great and varied amenity values. It grows best on chalky loams but does very well on neutral clays or sands and adequately on fairly acid sands. It grows rapidly with a conic crown of whorled branches unusual in a broadleaf tree and has the proper cherry bark of mahogany red-brown in smooth shiny bands. Flowering is prolific in mid-cherry-season and remarkable when seen on a forest tree 25 m tall, and the fruit feed birds. The foliage is dreary until

it turns yellow, dull orange and dark red in autumn. As a specimen this has a place in a spring or autumn planting but not one which is mainly used in summer. On a large scale it makes a good clump. A 'witch's broom' often bends quite large branches down, and should be cut out at first sighting.

'Plena'. Double wild cherry. This flowers later than the single form, more or less with 'Kanzan', and is a good foil and diluter for it. Globular flowers hang in dense lines beneath bright green new leaves and last well. Although not quite so lavish a spectacle as a double white 'Sato' cherry (p. 117) it has an elegance that the others lack and likewise a central stem which can take the crown up to over 20 m.

Prunus cerasus 'Rhexii' Double-flowered sour cherry

Something of a Cinderella, this has been in the country nearly 400 years and although not scarce, and seen around most towns, people can rarely identify it. It has a poor, flattish, untidy crown and dull-looking foliage but at the end of the cherry season it bears among the leaves pale pink long-stalked buds opening to white, very double, rather button-like flowers, and then has considerable charm.

Prunus maackii Manchurian cherry

The bark of a young Manchurian cherry is a unique glistening honey colour, soon darkening with age to pale orange-brown then dark orange with wide grey fissures. It grows too fast for its own good; the vigour-cracks soon detract from the bark for which it is grown. Little erect spikes of fragrant flowers emerge late in the cherry season amongst the minutely peg-toothed dark green leaves. The bole can be 80 cm through in 40 years.

Prunus padus Bird cherry

Native mainly in the north and common as a shrubby tree along becks in the Craven limestone hills of the Pennines, this little tree has much to recommend it. When young it has a conic crown of slender branches with shining dark brown shoots. It flowers late in the cherry season, the leafy 12 cm clear white spikes spreading abundantly from pale green new leaves. In early autumn the leaves turn pale yellow, then the outer crown is tinged with red. This tree will grow amongst pavings, on limy or poor soils but not on dry sands. It will not be more than 12 m tall.

'Colorata'. A dark-crowned little tree with blackish-purple leaves with red petioles, this is worth a place for its curious foliage colour and is lovely when the dark red-purple flower spikes open with pink and white insides to the petals.

'Watereri'. This is a coarse-growing vigorous tree to 18 m with large dark leaves remotely set on long whippy shoots, redeemed only when the numerous long, 20 cm spikes of white flowers spray out in all directions.

Prunus sargentii Sargent cherry

This Japanese tree is commonly planted around towns because it grows strongly, is easily propagated by grafting on to Gean, gives a reliable early display – a soft pink cloud of flowers – and then leads the autumn colour show, scarlet and deep red. Hence its lack-lustre, hanging, abruptly tipped summer foliage is a price worth paying, and the dark red bark in smooth bands tides it through the winter. Seedlings spread wide branches from the base, as do grafts made at ground level, so roadside trees are worked at 1·5 or 2 m and have a stout bole of Gean bark. Although unsuited to a fully rural landscape, this is a splendid tree for an extensive park planting where generous groups, 8–10 trees at 8 m spacing, make spectacular features in early spring and early autumn. A single specimen needs much space and will attain 12 m in time, with a widely spread crown. Bullfinches rarely strip any flowers from this, unlike the other early single-flowered trees, but its small bright red cherries are soon eaten by birds, or shed, so are little noticed.

Prunus serrula Tibetan cherry

Sent from Western China in 1908 and 1913, this tree is scarce as an old plant but has recently been used much more and has the most attractive bark of any tree. Young trees have deep mahogany red or sometimes orange-brown, satiny-surfaced, shining peeling bands between lines of lenticels. The boles expand rapidly and although the branch bark looks after itself, the bole can become hidden in blackish scales and numerous sprouts unless it is frequently smoothed and the papery rolls removed without tearing. Hence this tree is best planted by a well-used path where it will incite passers-by to stroke and smooth it. When the bole is some 40 cm through, the lenticel bands have usually narrowed the shiny strips and made it less attractive, but nothing can be done about this except perhaps to graft the tree on a less vigorous rootstock than the usual Gean and to grow it more slowly.

The flowers are never the reason for planting this tree, just a minor bonus; but they are prolific, in bunches of 2–3 amongst the open green leaves, slender-stalked, white and 2 cm across. The tibetan cherry has been used as the stem for grafted trees of 'Shimidsu' and other 'Sato' cherries. These are marketed as 'Sheraton cherries' but although it seems a brilliant idea to combine such striking bark with spectacular flowers they somehow look odd when in flower – perhaps there is just too much to admire – although they make a more presentable tree than the 'Sato' when not in flower.

The Tibetan cherry has a twiggy, broad crown and slender, lanceolate leaves, sharply toothed and dark green. Despite its crown, and since the bark is always prominent and the tree never becomes big (or can be replaced when it does), this is a good single specimen for an enclosed, much frequented area like a courtyard.

Prunus serrulata
The 'Sato' cherries

The opulent-flowered Japanese cherries often called *P. serrulata* are of hybrid origin and much selected so better called by the cultivar name directly after '*Prunus*'. They all flower in the latter half of the cherry season, beginning with 'Shirotae', and all are from Japan except for the strange case of 'Pink Perfection' which is a hybrid between two of them and occurred at Bagshot, Surrey.

Only the salient features for landscaping purposes, and the most distinct and attractive types of Japanese cherries will be mentioned here since this is an immense subject better covered in books devoted to it like *Flowering Cherries* by Geoffrey Chadbund (Collins, 1972). These trees are all grafted on Gean and will grow on any fairly good soil including chalky soils and surrounded by pavings, but not well on light sands.

'Amanogawa'. This cherry which is strictly erect and columnar when young, but opens with age, is ideal for very restricted spaces among buildings. In a garden it is better as a group than singly. The pale pink, large, frilled, semi-double fragrant flowers open medium-late among slightly bronzed leaves which in autumn turn pale yellow and pinkish-red.

'Fugenzo'. A useful change from 'Kanzan', flowering two weeks later on a lower, more spreading crown, with short-stalked bunches of similar flowers but redder buds and leaves.

'Hokusai'. A sturdy tree, frequent but little known to the public; it is probably regarded as an early 'Kanzan' as it flowers earlier but with more bunched, much paler flowers, opening to show a red eye, among pale brown leaves which in autumn are orange and fiery red.

'Kanzan'. The universal double pink 'Japanese cherry' of suburbia. Strong upright branches later bend out, heavy with long-stalked bunches of very pink flowers from red buds amongst slightly brownish-red leaves. The heavy criticism this tree attracts is perhaps due less to the over-planting seen than to the unvaried pink of the flowers. It cannot be faulted for reliability or sheer abundance of flower.

'Okiku'. The most beautiful of all in some ways, but still very scarce. Strong upright growth is wreathed in great clusters of frilled semi-double, green-eyed, pale pink flowers in mid-season.

'Pink Perfection'. The only 'Sato' cherry not of Japanese origin, this is a cross between 'Shimidsu' and 'Kanzan' raised in 1935 and quite frequent around its county of origin, Surrey, but less so elsewhere. It comes into flower towards the end of the 'Kanzan' period and has a few sprays opening sometimes around midsummer. It improves upon 'Kanzan' in that the bright red buds amongst pale bronzy-green leaves open rich pink and fade gradually to white, avoiding any uniform and unvarying colour. The flowers are in big hanging bunches and in good years it is as laden with them as is either parent. The one drawback is that not every year is a good year for 'Pink Perfection'. At its best it is the most opulent of all, the big, tightly packed clusters having some flowers bright pink and others all shades to white.

'Shimidsu'. This makes only a low-crowned, flat-topped spreading tree of slow growth but it is unsurpassed when in flower, and is among the last in the season. Copious big bunches of buds hang with a lilac tint beneath similarly coloured leaves which become bright green as the flowers open, large, 6 cm, very double purest white, long-stemmed in bunches.

'Shirofugen'. This is a glorious variation on 'Shimidsu', flowering at the same time but lasting much longer and with occasional sprays until July. It is a stronger tree, taller and equally spreading and it has a three-colour trick. The buds are a good pink and beneath deep red leaves they open pink for a few days then turn shining pure white, superb against the dark leaves for a week or more. Then as the leaves green, the flowers turn pale pink again for another week or two.

'Shirotae'. The first 'Sato' cherry in flower, this is similar to an early flowering 'Shimidsu' but wider in the crown and with shining bright green leaves above the prolifically produced pure white flowers which are mixed single and semi-double. In summer it can be identified by the still shiny bright leaves.

'Tai Haku' Great white cherry. Lost in Japan around 1700, a single tree of 'Tai Haku' was found in 1923 growing from a job lot of plants from Japan planted in 1900 in a Sussex garden, by which time it was nearly dead. Collingwood Ingram, who discovered it, raised grafts and every 'Tai Haku' in the world, including Japan, is derived from this plant. Young plants have strong, raised branches and long shoots wreathed by mid-early season in big, wide, 7 cm, single white flowers among deep red leaves. On rather older trees the crown spreads and the flowers are in huge globular clusters. The leaves, like those of all 'Sato' cherries, have abrupt long tips and sharp, whisker-ended teeth and differ from others in the group except 'Ukon' in being very dark, well spaced, leathery, and to 20 cm long. On occasional trees they turn bright red in autumn.

'Ukon'. This is the only Cherry generally planted which has, for the first week of its flowering, pale buff-yellow flowers. They are semi-double, long-stalked and below pale brown or khaki leaves, in mid-season. They mature pure white with a red eye and then resemble the flowers of 'Tai Haku' although smaller and with more petals. The leaves are large and dark, like 'Tai Haku' in size and appearance but predominantly oblong.

Prunus subhirtella Rose-bud cherry

The type species is not known in cultivation, but the following are some of the forms that are grown.

'Autumnalis' Winter cherry. Despite the twiggy, shapeless crown and dull slender leaves, a place must be found for one of these Japanese cultivars. In October the tiny white flowers begin to open, on very short stalks, among leaves that are by then turning yellow. They continue to open, a fresh set after each hard frost or continually if mild, and on longer stalks, with a last burst in April. The buds are pink and the contrast with the flowers makes this preferable to the pink-flowered 'Autumnalis rosea'.

'Pendula'. A wonderful hummock submerged in white single flowers in April, best planted high on a rock-garden or on a tiny island in a pool. (It ought not to be in a book of trees.)

'Rosea'. This seems to be the name of a superbly floriferous, rather upright tree densely, if rather briefly, a rich uniform pink all over with starry single flowers, but not often seen.

Prunus 'Hally Jolivette'

This has Rose-bud and Yoshino cherries in its parentage and is, in flower, of exceptional elegance. The delicate little flowers spray out like snowdrops, faintly pink then white, with a purple calyx on a slender purple stalk, before the leaves, in mid-season. It makes only a small tree, slender when young and rounded with age.

Prunus 'Kursar'

This was raised by Collingwood Ingram and named when the parentage was assumed to be *P. nipponica* var. *kurilensis* × *P. sargentii*. Ingram now finds that the second parent was in fact *P. campanulata* but the name cannot be changed (and 'Kuricamp' is hardly euphonious.) This is a first-class tree with an early and long display of unusually bright pink single flowers with dark red calyces. It looks purplish-pink from a distance and makes an upright tree of good growth. A sister seedling, Okame, is inferior, with bunched darker flowers with narrow petals making a bushier tree.

Pterocarya fraxinifolia Caucasian wing-nut

To accommodate this immensely vigorous, superb foliage-tree one needs either a large clear area or to be vigilant and severe with suckers. Left to itself each tree disappears in a thicket which soon becomes high woodland. It can grow as a close group of a score or more big trees, as in Cambridge Botanic Garden. It makes a broad crown on level branches and a dense shade from the big compound leaves, which are bright shiny green with around 21 leaflets crowded and overlapping, narrowly oblong, slender-pointed and sharply toothed. The buds are peculiar; they have no scales but are two small, richly brown pubescent leaves held together, and lateral buds are stalked and may sprout not quite within the axils. In spring the male catkins are thick, yellow and soon shed and the females on the same tree, to 15 cm long, hang with the flowers showing pink scattered on the basal part, closer towards the tip. In summer these catkins are 50 cm long and hang prominently strung with circular winged green fruit. In autumn the leaves turn bright yellow. Only in the winter is this not a very remarkable tree. Old ones are rare but huge in southern gardens and at Melbury and Abbotsbury in Dorset there are specimens 35 m tall; that at Melbury has a single straight bole nearly 1·9 m in diameter.

Growing best in wet fertile soil, this wing-nut is handily planted on a waterside bank, which halves the area under siege by suckers, but it should be a wide, open bank as the view to water should be framed but not obstructed. It grows more slowly in the north and is hardy.

Pterocarya × rehderana Hybrid wing-nut

The Caucasian wing-nut crosses with one of the several Chinese species, *P. stenoptera*, if grown near it. The latter does nothing here that the Caucasian does not do better, so is not mentioned again, but the hybrid does. It grows even faster, in fact few trees grow more vigorously. It also keeps to one bole for longer as the suckering is less strong. At 10 years it should be 10 m × 25 cm; at 23 years at Kew on a poor gravel, a Hybrid wing-nut was 19 m × 64 cm; cuttings inserted in July rapidly make strong plants, better than lifted root suckers. The main distinction is the channel or flanged groove along the rachis, but for general effect of foliage and fruit it is just an extra vigorous wing-nut.

Pyrus calleryana 'Bradford' Bradford pear

Although hardly seen, if at all, in Britain, this splendid tree has been widely planted in the USA for years. It is the backbone of the plantings in Chestnut Street, Philadelphia, in the Commons precinct in Ithaca, New York, and in similar sites further west and south, and is obviously very

tough indeed. In shape it is like the Fastigiate hornbeam, with a neat, broad-ovoid-conic, dense upright crown. The broad-ovate leaf, 9 × 5 cm, is pale, becoming darker grey-green and turning orange and red in the autumn. Selected in Maryland from seedlings grown from Chinese seed after 1918, this ought to become widely known and much planted, as a variant on the Fastigiate hornbeam as well as in its own right as a fine tree.

'Chanticleer'. Another seedling from the Chinese pear, this was selected by that great connoisseur of town and street trees, Ed Scanlon of Ohio, and regarded by him as among the very best that he found. Luckily it is now being planted in England. It makes a tall, conic tree and has the following remarkable combination of star points: it is robust in any soil; it bears masses of heads of white flowers before the leaves unfold; the leaf-buds expand bright silver-white; the leaves are a soft green and through the summer some often turn yellow, orange and red; autumn colours are bright yellow, orange and red, and it may open some heads of flowers at the same time.

Pyrus elaeagrifolia

At first sight this may be taken for the more familiar Willow-leafed pear (below) but it grows taller, is not weeping and has broader, 8 × 3 cm entire leaves, greener above. It is a good foliage-tree for silvery-grey and green where a bigger tree with the Willow-leaf and non-weeping, is required. It has spines on the shoot, and comes from South-east Europe.

Pyrus salicifolia ['Pendula'] Willow-leafed pear

It is debatable whether this is a form entitled to a cultivar name or whether the type tree is pendulous. Usually below 9 m high, this tree from South-east Europe is sometimes as much as 12 m and its rather shapeless crown is not ornamental in winter. Covered in the slender 7 × 1.5 cm silver-haired leaves, however, and enhanced in late spring by the heads of pure white 2 cm flowers tipped scarlet in the bud, it is a good lawn-side tree.

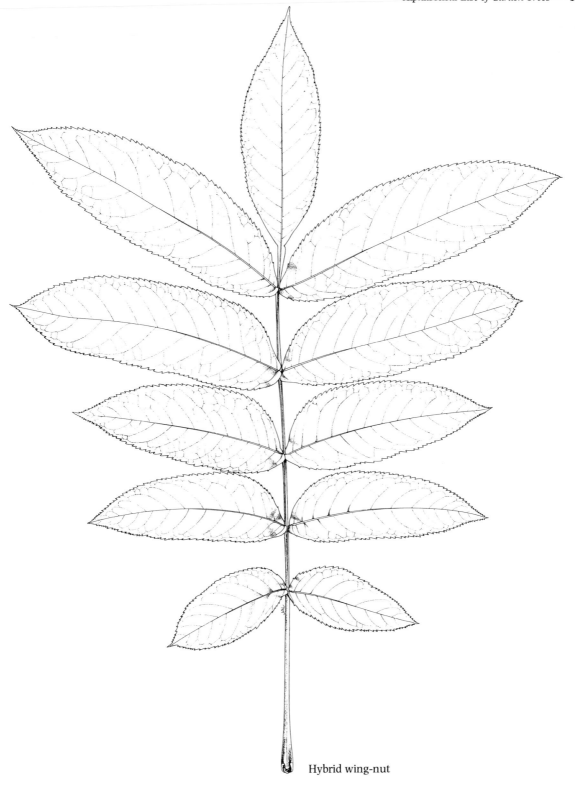

Hybrid wing-nut

Quercus acuta Japanese evergreen oak

This tree looks more like a leafy rhododendron
shrub than an Oak until it bears spikes of big
orange-brown acorns. It is fully hardy, at least in
the Midlands and in Edinburgh, although it has
made a well-boled tree to 15 m only in the far
south, from Surrey to Cornwall. The crowded,
evergreen, narrow elliptic, abruptly-tipped leaves
unfold covered in soft orange wool which rolls off
gradually by autumn, and are dark shiny green.
This is an unusual but not particularly exciting
foliage-plant of very modest size, often more of a
spreading bush.

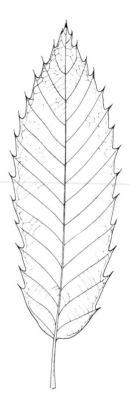

Sawtooth oak

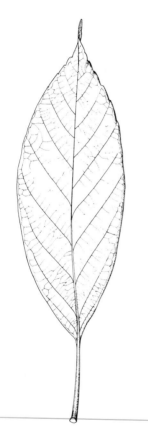

Japanese evergreen oak

Quercus acutissima Sawtooth oak; Japanese chestnut oak

In America this is known by the first name above
and since more are grown in many north-eastern
states than we ever see here, it should be adopted.
Very hardy, it is also highly attractive when in
leaf, although in winter it is a fairly narrow tree
and somewhat stark with an open few-branched
crown and coarsely ridged dull grey bark. The pale
green smooth shoots bear big, handsome glossy
leaves, 20 cm long, oblong-lanceolate, rich
darkish-green with some 15 pairs of prominent,
parallel veins each going straight to a sharp,
triangular, spine-tipped tooth. Ranging as it does
through Korea, China and Japan, this tree could
well have provenances which grow faster than the
slow progress shown by those we have, probably
all Japanese.

Quercus alba White oak

Although this tree has rarely justified more than occasional planting for interest, some source of seed between Ontario and Texas should yield more successful plants, although they will still find our summers too cool for full growth. The merits of the tree are the elegant lobing, deeply cut by curved sinuses on the leaves in full light, with the long-cuneate base seen in so many American oaks, and the autumn colours. The brilliant reds and oranges natural within the native woods cannot be expected but some trees here do show splendid orange and purple colours not seen in other oaks. The bark is dark grey, shaggy with lifting flakes or plates.

Quercus canariensis Algerian oak; Mirbeck's oak

This is one of the few really first-class oaks for a highly distinctive, vigorous and shapely specimen on a large scale. The bark is dark grey, rough and fissured from an early age and the crown is then a fine regular ovoid with upright branches, and spreads only a little when the tree is very big. This is a semi-evergreen oak so in autumn about half the leaves turn yellow and fall while the rest remain green through the winter. Since the leaves are 12–20 cm long, of considerable substance and obovate with a dozen or more lobes each side decreasing in size regularly from base to tip, this is always a tree of great presence and stands out in a group. Some specimens are now more than 27 m tall and still growing, and all promise to be very impressive trees. One of the best specimens is in Cumbria, another in Northumberland, and there seems to be no ordinary kind of soil on which the Algerian oak does not thrive, making it an exceptionally valuable tree. The native range is in North Africa and southern Spain – no longer in the Canary Islands – and it was introduced here in 1845 or perhaps a few years earlier.

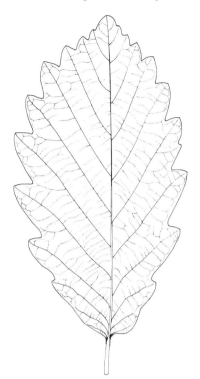

Mirbeck's oak

Chestnut-leafed oak

Quercus castaneifolia Chestnut-leafed oak

The original tree of this Caucasian oak was planted in Kew Gardens in 1846, has always been by far the biggest specimen known and is one of the finest trees of any kind in Britain. In 1956 it was 25 m × 1·70 m and by 1979 it had grown to 32 m × 2.00 m. A plant raised from it and put out in 1956 is now, in 1981, 16 m × 58 cm, so this is a very vigorous oak. The bark of young trees is smooth and black but it breaks with age into small square plates of dark grey on big ridges. The foliage is handsome, each leaf being about 20 cm long, narrow-elliptic, acute and with a dozen or so pairs of parallel veins ending in obtuse triangular teeth; the underside pale glaucous and pubescent. Clearly this makes a monumental tree in a relatively short time, with splendidly shaped leaves, but it has a dark crown in summer and is not remarkable when bare.

Quercus cerris Turkey oak

The Turkey oak is useful as a fast-growing framework-tree thriving on poor light soils and in the parks of big cities. It is not in the top rank for beauty; big branches leave the bole from unattractive swellings, the foliage is a dull dark green and dead male catkins remain in the crown for months. However, these flowers are first visible as crimson buds on bunches of catkins, the leaves are cut variably deeply into many lobes and it can be a sturdy and tall tree. The bark is dark, rough and knobbly and the straight shoots coppery-grey, densely pubescent. Most of the very big trees are in Devon or the south of England where some are 35 m × 2 m. Although they grow faster where summers are warm, the biggest are around Exeter, where the early trees were most planted. In some years the leaves turn a pleasing orange-brown but mostly they are dull brown before they fall.

Quercus coccinea Scarlet oak

Although first grown here as long ago as 1688 there are no very big Scarlet oaks in Britain, where they are seldom seen more than 25 m × 85 cm. This is partly because the tree is not long-lived – none here is much above 100 years old – and partly because even in its native Appalachian Mountains area it is seldom very much bigger. The crown is open with a few big branches at wide angles from the sinuous bole, each with its own canopy. The red-brown slender shoots bear leaves glossy on both sides, widely and deeply cut into three lobes on each side, each with a few big-spined teeth, and have a slender 3 cm petiole. In autumn they are fairly reliable in turning from bright scarlet to deep wine-red, and from leaf-shedding until the New Year can be recognised by the way they hold much of the foliage of the lowest branches, dark red-brown. As a somewhat wispy tree, the Scarlet oak is most effective planted in groups of at least five in parkland or flanking a long vista. It grows on any normal soil but best on rather light ones.

'Splendens'. Raised at Knaphill, Surrey, where the original tree is now 24 × 0.9 m, this is noted for even better autumn colours. It also has larger leaves, to 18 × 13 cm as against 12 × 10 cm in the type, and has small tufts of whitish hairs in the vein axils on the underside.

Quercus dentata Daimyo oak

This Japanese oak must be mentioned for its giant leaves. In shape very like those of the Common oak but more tapered to the base and with a stout, densely pubescent petiole, they can be 40 × 20 cm, and cause some interest for their absurd size. There are some reasonably shaped trees to 15 m and it grows in Edinburgh, but often, like certain other Japanese trees, it is unhappy and has stout branches bearing little whiskery sprays of shoots which die back annually. Nevertheless, it is still worth having for the gigantic leaves.

Quercus frainetto Hungarian oak

One of the most vigorous and handsome of all the trees we can grow, the Hungarian oak is an outstanding specimen tree hardy enough to grow near Aberdeen. It has a stout bole with pale grey bark, finely and evenly divided into small ridges, from which the big straight branches begin to

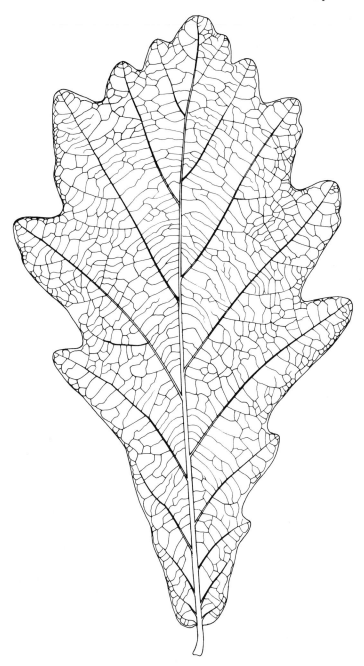

Daimyo oak

radiate at 2–4 m to form a huge, high-domed crown. The rich green leaves emerge crimson-tipped from the bud and covered in grey hairs which are soon shed. They are deeply and closely lobed, about 12 a side, and even from a distance the tree can be recognized by the jagged edges of its big, 22 × 10 cm leaves. Growth is very rapid on any well-drained soil and a new tree is very soon a fine ornament. All it needs is space in which to develop its big crown.

Quercus × hispanica 'Lucombeana' Lucombe oak

This series of forms of a hybrid which occurs in Iberia, where Turkey and Cork oaks grow adjacent, was raised at Lucombe's Nursery at Exeter in 1765. Grafts were made of the first cross and planted on several estates in the area. In 1785, Mr Lucombe had the original seedling felled for his coffin, and then one of the first grafts, after the first boards had decayed, and was buried in these when he was 102. Acorns collected from early grafts yielded more trees in 1792 and 1830. These were not second generation hybrids, because there was only the single clone, but backcrosses to Cork Oak, and they show this in their corky bark and small, very dark leaves, bluish-white beneath. One of these from 1792 is the common form outside Devon. All these are evergreen except in very hard winters, while the original clone is a semi-evergreen tree and keeps a fringe of dark yellowish-green leaves around the outside of the crown.

Lucombe oak

None is a first-class tree for planting in numbers – a belt or avenue of Lucombe oak is gloomy – but the tree has value as one of the few completely hardy evergreen broadleaves to reach a great size. There are specimens over 32 m tall and others more than 2 m in diameter. The Lucombe oak is good in sea-winds, it can be a fine specimen on its own, and it can show excellent boles when grown as a clump, which should be small, or when amongst other trees.

Quercus ilex Holm oak

This Mediterranean tree has been with us some 400 years and is common everywhere in parks, gardens and churchyards, although few people seem yet to know that any oak can be evergreen. It has been planted in long belts and avenues on estates all round the coast as good shelter from sea-winds, but it makes a rather dreary landscape. It has black bark and foliage, the felted white underside of the leaf hardly showing. Only in June is it other than black and then it is silvery-white with new leaves at its periphery and gold with dense bunches of male catkins. This sounds as decorative as it is, but only briefly. As a young plant the tree is bushy-crowned and slow. There may be a place for the Holm oak in maritime exposure but mostly the Lucombe oak would be preferable if available.

Quercus libani Lebanon oak

This is similar to the Sawtooth oak (p. 122) but more suited than that tree to dry soils and hot summers. The leaves are smaller, 10–12 cm, with 10–12 pairs of veins in triangular, whisker-tipped teeth. They are dark glossy green above and pale beneath with hairy veins, and have a short, slender stalk. The acorn is on a short, very stout stalk and hardly emerges from the deep cup, but now and again will mature into a big 4 cm seed. This scarce tree has an open, shapely crown and is very attractive when in leaf.

Lebanon oak

Quercus × ludoviciana Louisiana oak

This is unfortunately very rare both in gardens and in the wild, where it was described from a single tree in Louisiana, a natural hybrid between the Willow oak and the Cherry-bark oak (*Q. falcata* var. *pagodaefolia*). One at Kew is singularly beautiful and vigorous with a long-spired crown. The leaves have one main, big, triangular forward lobe on the outer third of each side and a smaller one or two on either side of it. They open bright copper-brown, turning gold then dark shiny green until in autumn they are bright orange. They are about 20 × 8 cm. The bark is smooth, dark grey with fine pink stripes. Ludwig's oak is obviously a tree to acquire, however difficult this may be.

Quercus macranthera Caucasian oak

This robust tree has a slightly shaggy silvery and dark grey bark and upswept branching. Its shoots are stout and densely orange-pubescent and bear firm, handsome, often hooded leaves 20 × 12 cm with shallow ovate lobes decreasing in size regularly towards the tip. They are very like those of the Algerian oak (p. 123) but have persistent grey pubescence on the underside. Although there are few old trees and none more than 102 years, these are 25 m tall. It makes a shapely foliage-tree on any fairly good soil and is very hardy.

Quercus myrsinifolia Bamboo oak

This graceful small tree from southern China and Japan is evergreen but with a light, airy crown, seldom 12 m high. The distant, slender lanceolate leaves, 10 × 2·5 cm, unfold reddish-purple and mature to hard pale fresh green on the upper surface and silvery-green beneath, entire or with a few tiny sharp teeth. It is hardy, very ornamental and interesting, being, like the Japanese evergreen oak (p. 122), one of the Asiatic group of oaks which bear their acorns on spikes, although these are seldom seen here.

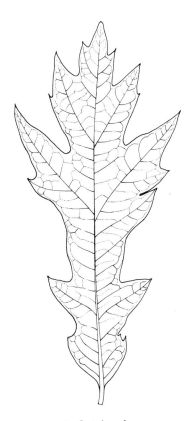

Ludwig's oak

Quercus palustris Pin oak

This oak is suited only to the eastern and southern regions with the chance of hot summers. It thrives in city streets throughout the eastern USA, especially in the hottest parts, but also in Pittsburgh and New York and in parts of the west. In England it grows fast as a young slender tree but becomes much slower with age, reaching around 25 m. The crown has a feature shared by no other tree here; it has a good clean bole for 2–4 m, then bears a dense crowd of shoots which spray at a downward angle, straight for 2–3 m, as a sort of high skirt. The leaves are prettily and deeply cut into seven lobes, very like the Scarlet oak (p. 124) but usually smaller and always with the vein-axils underneath prominently tufted with pale brown hairs. In autumn the tips of the shoots start first to colour scarlet, then the whole crown follows, finally turning dark red, but not reliably every year. This oak is suited to very damp soils and makes a splendid group in a wet corner as well as being a good single specimen tree.

Quercus petraea Sessile oak; Durmast oak

This was the earlier colonist of the two British oaks and is in general the Oak of mountains, high rainfall, the north and the west. Nonetheless it grows better on light sands than does the Common oak. A small outlier from its main range is on the sandy hills south of Leith Hill summit in Surrey, and the biggest outlier is Enfield Chase on gravelly hills above the River Lee in Middlesex. This is a far finer tree than the Common oak in growth, form and foliage. The bole is straight and clean without burs and the branches radiate mainly straight to make a high dome. One in Herefordshire is 43 m tall and much above any Common oak. The acorns are sessile, or nearly so, but the leaves have a good, bright yellow smooth stalk 2·5 cm long and taper from it, having small auricles only where there is some hybridity with Common oak. They taper also to the tip, have regular symmetrical lobing and are firm, thick and healthy, usually free of the assortment of galls which disfigure the foliage of Common oak. The leaves are held evenly spread, not bunched, with

an ecological significance mentioned on p. 50.

Except on the stiffest clays and in wildlife refuges, the Sessile oak is the one to plant for landscaping, groups and specimens. It is an uncommonly handsome tree.

'Columna' is very narrowly erect with the same good foliage but too strict for any but very formal plantings.

Quercus pontica Armenian oak

Coming from the Caucasus mountains, this occasionally qualifies as a tree and even were it always strictly a shrub, the rules would be bent shamelessly in order to include it. The shoots stand up, green, stout and ribbed, holding out positively noble leaves, big smoothly plane broad ellipses 15 × 10 cm, bright fresh green above with some 15 straight parallel yellow veins each side running out to little hooked and spined teeth. The underside is soft blue-grey or glaucous green and in autumn the upper side turns yellow, then yellow mixed with brown, and finally all brown. Male catkins can be 20 cm long and acorns 4 cm, deep mahogany red.

Quercus robur Common oak; English oak
(Q. pedunculata)

This is the oak of the clay lowlands of south-east England and the Midlands and extends to Dartmoor, even to the highest oakwood in Britain, Wistman's Wood at 400 m. Most of the famous old oaks are or were of this species except for some in Powys and Herefordshire. With its short, often burred bole, twisting branches, irregular broad-ended and much-galled leaves, it is not so desirable generally as the Sessile oak (above) but on heavy clay soils it is invaluable as the main framework-tree.

'Fastigiata' Cypress oak. Varying from the shape of a Lombardy poplar to that of a huge goblet because these forms arise from seed, the true, narrow tree is grafted. It is splendid amongst buildings or in gardens, especially in groups, and grows quite fast to 24 m or more.

Quercus rubra Red oak

The Red oak may live up to its name in autumn when a young tree, and be bright then dark red, but when older it is more likely to turn yellow and brown. In the wild it ranges from north of Quebec right across to central Texas and has been grown in Europe since about 1730 when the seed will have come from North Carolina, but little or nothing is known of the growth here of different origins. The Red oak grows very vigorously on most soils, and on light sandy soils it will do so where Common oak might be no more than scrub, but the Red oak is not a substitute for Common oak, it is so different in aspect. It does not fit into fully rural scenery but is a good frame-work-tree in city parks and large gardens, in screens, shelter-belts or roundels and clumps. Grown fairly close for 20 years the trees make good long boles whereas grown as a specimen in the open it usually produces a broad crown springing from big branches 1·5–2 m up the bole. The Red oak is also very different in aspect from the Scarlet oak (p. 124) for the short bole is stout and straight and the strong, more regularly placed branches make a single dome of a crown; the leaves are coarser, larger, 20 cm long but varying in vigour of growth and up to 30 cm on sprouts, less deeply or regularly lobed, and mat on both surfaces. As in Scarlet and other 'red' oaks, the acorns take two years to ripen and during the first year they are like brown buds on short stalks along the middle length of the previous year's growth.

Quercus variabilis Chinese cork oak

This all too rare tree should be planted whenever it can be acquired, both for interest and as an exceptionally fine tree for foliage. The bark is deeply cavitied, corky pinkish-grey and more attractive than that of the Cork oak, *Q. suber* (which is a very dreary tree). The crown is tall, to 18 m, open and level-branched. The leaves are elliptic, 20 cm long on a curved yellow 3 cm petiole, and remarkably handsome. The rich glossy green upper surface is marked by a white midrib with 18 pairs of parallel veins running to the margins where each ends in a whisker projecting from the otherwise straight edge. The underside is covered in a fine silvery pubescence. One Cornish garden has six trees loosely grouped and 16 m tall, and in late autumn the ground around is carpeted with these big leaves still silvery beneath.

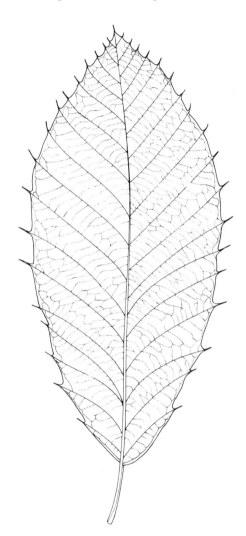

Chinese cork oak

Quercus velutina Black oak; Quercitron oak

This eastern American oak has a nearly black bark, much roughened between orange-brown fissures, and although not common it is in some gardens here and to 30 m tall. It is of more effect as a foliage-tree when young and the leaves are low enough to be seen at close range before they fall. They resemble those of the Red oak (p. 129) but are hard, parchment-like, softly downy on the veins beneath, have a stout yellow 4 cm petiole and are usually bigger. An odd feature is that many of the leaves have a forked midrib splitting the leaf, usually equally.

'Rubrifolia' is a rather remarkable form sometimes seen as a graft from the original seedling found in a Hammersmith nursery, with leaves to 40 cm long.

Rhus verniciflua Varnish tree

Remarkably hardy for such a luxuriantly large-leafed tree, the Varnish tree is around 15 m tall in mid-Wales and Edinburgh and is a beautiful tree in the summer and autumn. In winter it is gaunt but relieved from near to by the stout, pale, lilac-grey shoots thinly freckled orange and the shiny brown buds. The bark is dark grey and fissured, becoming flaky with curved plates. The leaves are alternate, 50–80 cm long, with around 14 big leaflets perpendicularly lateral and a 20 cm terminal one. They are entire, leathery, hanging and rich glossy green, on a scarlet rachis. In autumn they become yellow, red and crimson. Small yellow-green flowers radiate on 50 cm panicles axillary to the leaves near the tips of the branches in midsummer, and some of them bear small glossy cream-brown berries in the autumn.

This tree is found from the Himalayas to Japan. It completes its annual shoot growth in early July so it should rarely be damaged by frost except in late spring, and with a watch kept on too strong lower branches it can be grown with a good long central stem.

Robinia pseudoacacia Locust tree; False acacia

This hardy tree from the eastern USA will tolerate soils too dry, hot, poor or compacted to suit almost any other. It is thus a necessary pioneer tree on hot coal-tips ('bings') and on made-up ground consisting largely of brickbats, and a useful change from London plane. Its feathery light-green foliage is even a good foil to grimy Portland limestone buildings and it sometimes manages to cover itself in fragrant white flowers. In no other circumstances is there any use for this tree. It is graceless, rough and brittle; it is very late into leaf and early to shed without noticeable change of colour; it fails to flower more often than it succeeds, and it sends up spiny suckers at considerable distances.

'Frisia' is so good that the outbreak of it in new suburban gardens is enough to put some people off it as a cliché. Its fresh butter-gold foliage may green a little or not at all until it turns orange in autumn. As tough as the type, and grafted on it, 'Frisia' can be grown anywhere except in the coolest summers of the far north and west. It may sucker and it is no beauty in winter, but it is worth having for that great splash of gold.

Salix alba White willow

A native whose right to that claim is under some suspicion, the White willow is far less common along riversides than the Crack willow. It is taller, with a conic crown until it billows out with age at some 25 m, and distinctively blue-grey. It is a good tree to accept by a waterside but as a specimen elsewhere it is rather thin and the cultivar below is preferred.

'Argentea' Silver willow. This grows much more slowly than the type, but still quite fast and nearly to the same size. It is a fairly broad tree with a silvery-grey, densely leafed crown. It stands out amongst other trees and sets off golden foliages particularly well.

'Britzensis' Coral-bank willow is a fine waterside tree with shoots glowing orange-red in the winter.

Salix caprea Goat willow; Sallow.

This native sallow is the only one of several
similar native species to grow into a genuine tree.
It often exceeds 10 m and can be found 19 m tall
with a good, slightly sinuous trunk and upswept
branches with short-jointed stout twigs. It is quick
to colonize bare ground, especially on damp soils
and is common on the edges of woodland spreading
into wet grassy land in hill country. Both male
and female plants are valuable in giving early
shelter to a new garden with their rapid early
growth, but males with their great display of
golden flowers will be retained and the silvery-
grey flowered females removed in the first
thinning. The males are worth a place for this
early spring flowering, sometimes starting in
December but variably held back until April.
Unfortunately the Goat willow is not one that can
be raised from cuttings, but comes easily from
seed; hence the sex of the plant cannot be chosen
from the start.

Salix × chrysocoma Weeping willow (*S. alba*
'Tristis')

Not the Babylon willow by which name it is often
known, but probably a hybrid between that
Chinese tree and the White willow, this is the
familiar Weeping willow. It grows almost as well
on a sandy soil away from open water as it does
by a pool-side, for its roots go out and find all the
water it needs. In a garden it will often find water
in or leaking from water-mains and sewers. It
soon becomes too big for a small garden; even in a
street it can be 20 m tall and still spreading. Easily
raised from cuttings, the resulting plant can be
reluctant to make a good leading shoot and
splinting up of the best shoot may be called for. If,
however, the cutting is made from a short length
of fairly stout shoot and is cut back to the ground
and the next year's shoots singled early, there
should be no trouble.

Sallow

Salix fragilis Crack willow

The common waterside willow everywhere, this is
sometimes seen growing among other trees and
on a good damp soil it holds its place as a foliage-
tree. The leaves are often 16 × 4 cm and are rich
glossy green. In autumn, many are bright shiny
gold but the crown as a whole does not turn,
many leaves remaining green. It is a very vigorous
tree and with attention from secateurs could be
given a splendid bole, but is all too often allowed
to be bush at the base. The hybrid with White
willow is S. × rubens and is frequent and
intermediate.

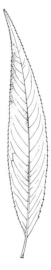

Crack willow

Salix matsudana 'Tortuosa' Dragon's claw willow

This twisting form of the Pekin willow is now very popular, which is a good thing. It grows very rapidly, for a few years at least, on any soil, even rather dry sands, and is one of the first trees into leaf. It flushes bright green which becomes paler during the season and, with very little change except a little yellowing, it holds its leaves as long as any, well into December in some years. The sharp sinuosities of the shoots show in summer as well as in winter and in older wood, branches and bole, they are progressively smoothed out but still visible. This willow may grow as a bush if allowed to. It does not need a long bole and would look top-heavy with one, but it is a better plant with about 1 m clear at the base.

Salix pentandra Bay willow

Native in the northern two-thirds of the British mainland, this lovely tree ought to be planted more in the north as well as the south, for it is seldom seen in gardens. The glossy olive-green shoots bear oblong-lanceolate deep glossy green leaves with yellow midribs and glaucous undersides. Unlike most willows, the Bay willow flowers when it is in leaf and the bright yellow erect catkins look well against the dark shiny foliage, which is an adornment to any group of more usual kinds. This tree is completely hardy and adapts to all soils so there is much scope for planting it.

Sassafras albidum Sassafras

Like so many trees from eastern North America, the Sassafras has a grey, much fissured bark and a need for heat which limits reasonable growth to the south-east of England. A member of the Laurel Family, it is aromatic and crushed leaves yield a scent and taste of vanilla and oranges. The crown here, as in its homeland where it proliferates by suckers and makes long hedges, is bare and open below, with twisting, upright branches holding aloft a shallow dome of very dense leafage. The leaves are unique in their varying shapes on the same tree, from elliptic and entire through one large ovate lobe on one side only (the 'mitten' leaves) to three-lobed with a fairly deeply-cut ovate lobe on each side. The underside is pale blue-grey. In autumn the foliage turns to fine yellows, pinks and then orange, but we do not see the brilliant display of mixed orange, scarlet and crimson which it gives in Pennsylvania.

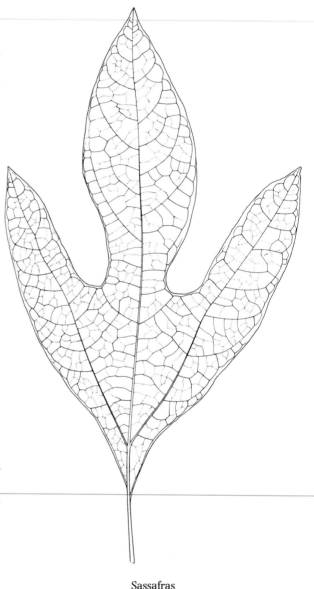

Sassafras

Sophora japonica Pagoda tree; Scholar's tree

In old China there was a strict hierarchy of permitted trees for graves. Only the emperor could have a pine; a princess could have a Paulownia and a scholar or a priest, still fairly high in the order of things, could have a Sophora. The Japanese borrowed the tree long ago and it was first known to botanists as a Japanese tree, hence the specific epithet. The original tree in Britain came from China and was moved to Kew in 1760 where it survives with a horizontal bole. It is far from common yet to see a Pagoda tree here but there was a great vogue for it in the streets and squares of the eastern USA some years ago, from which it can be seen that it survives well in hot cities and poor soils. In southern England it grows rather fast and it flowers freely; in southern Scotland it is slower and less floriferous. It is not a great tree for foliage, nor for shape; in fact, it is very like the Locust tree (p. 130) except that it is thornless, has blue-green shoots and acute leaflets. It scores by never suckering and by flowering in September. The flowers are similar – white, pea-form on panicles – but these are longer, 20 cm and spreading. The fruit are much superior; not dull brown pods but long bright green ones swelling by each seed, like a few large beads on a string, but they seldom develop in Britain.

'Pendula' is a mop-head of violently contorted shoots on a stem of rootstock, with long shoots hanging to the ground all round.

Sorbus alnifolia Alder whitebeam

This Japanese tree has unusual and attractive foliage for a Whitebeam and is a fine sight in autumn as well as during the winter. It has dark or pale grey bark finely striped in buff; acuminate-ovoid dark brown buds on purple-brown shoots, and makes a tree to 15 m tall as far north as Edinburgh. The leaves are ovate to 9×6 cm on red petioles $1 \cdot 5$ cm long with silky hairs, and have prominent parallel veins to sharp double-toothing; they are dark green. The flowers are prolifically borne and mature to bright orange-red berries. The leaves turn bright orange and red around the fruit, which remain a good colour well after the leaves have fallen.

Sorbus aucuparia Rowan

The native 'Mountain Ash' gives the remote north-west its brightest autumn colour, turning reds of a variety and quality of which it seems incapable in a southern street or garden. Every few years, it provides its large orange-red berries in such numbers as to sate and defeat even the suburban blackbirds. It will tolerate very hard conditions and has a place in town parks and streets. Since it is also common in most sorts of countryside there is no need for it in a large garden. Better rowans can be found. It is usually short-lived and the upper crown soon becomes thin and open. Among the superior ones are the two cultivars below.

'Beissneri'. A very choice tree only now becoming known but planted at least 30 years ago in, of all unlikely places, the median of the busy A34 at Begbroke between Oxford and Woodstock where, blasted by road-grit, the boles are pitted and pink-grey. Younger trees, as in Kensington Gardens in London, have a shining dark orange bark. It has a faint bluish wax finish which, when wet, is completely translucent so that in sunshine after rain the stems shine out brilliant clear orange. The leaflets are more prettily serrated than those of the type and in autumn they turn yellow, amber and pink.

'Xanthocarpa'. As well as the big clear yellow berries, this has more domed flower-heads, numerous and late, and is a tall-growing tree.

'Sheerwater Seedling' is one of several similar superior forms, remarkably neatly narrow-conic and upright in crown with good foliage and fruit.

Sorbus commixta Scarlet rowan

This Japanese tree is far less seen than the form 'Embley' below. It has 2 cm shining red conic smooth buds and big 25 cm leaves of 15 leaflets, broad lanceolate, each $8 \times 2 \cdot 5$ cm serrated to within 2 cm of the base.

'Embley', until recently called *Sorbus discolor*, is now regarded as a form of *S. commixta*. It is frequently by roadsides and around public buildings but less seen in big gardens. It is distinguished from the type by its smaller leaves, 15 cm long, and much narrower leaflets, often crinkled. In autumn they assume a rich dark purple border which spreads across them and turns scarlet until the whole crown is a blaze of scarlet before darkening to deep red. In summer it is easily recognized by its crown of slender branches arching out to horizontal, with deeply-toothed leaves in thin layers. Seedlings grow a straight shoot of 50 cm or more in their second year; some old trees are over 16 m tall. Large bunches of big orange-red berries are freely borne.

Sorbus cuspidata Himalayan whitebeam

This makes a vigorous, tall, narrowly conic crown to 20 m with rather few nearly erect branches and stout shoots. It is a very splendid foliage-tree with a distinctive light grey-green overall colour. The leaves are thick and heavy, elliptic, broadly cuneate, acute to 22 × 14 cm, silvery at first, soon somewhat shiny deep green above and white beneath with dense pubescence. It grows well on moist soils, limy or sandy, and has heads of 2 cm fragrant flowers with dull purple anthers.

'John Mitchell' (*S. thibetica*). This is the name by which the tree grown hitherto as *S. mitchellii* should now be known, named after the last curator under the Holford family at Westonbirt. It has massively orbicular leaves to 20 × 18 cm and is a striking tree to 20 m in 40 years. This is now quite widely planted.

Sorbus domestica True service tree

This tree from Southern Europe has been cultivated for a long time. It somewhat resembles the Rowan but is a broader tree with level, lower branches from which hang its larger, rather yellowish leaves. It has a rich brown bark vertically ridged and the buds are glossy green ovoids, but another striking difference from the Rowan is the big,

3–4 cm fruit which are green tinged red-brown.

This is an unusual tree and its stature, to 22 m or more, its bark, bold foliage and fruits earn it a place among specimen trees. The dull colour of the foliage and the open crown render it less useful as groups but it makes a good single specimen where its bark and the large heads of 1·5 cm flowers can be seen. It grows well on any normal soil in some degree of shelter.

Sorbus folgneri Chinese whitebeam

A scarce tree, introduced in 1901, this is an elegant specimen and foliage-tree worthy of more frequent planting. The dark purplish bole with peeling fissures holds a crown of slender branches arching out to the horizontal and which, in the very few old trees known, can be 16 m high. The leaves are lanceolate, slightly obovate, cuneate, to 10 × 5 cm, tapering to a narrow point, very dark green above and variably but, in the best trees, well silvered beneath. It is the late autumn which shows this tree at its best. When most of the autumn colour is past, the leaves turn orange, scarlet and crimson and many fall to lie with the still silver undersides showing. It seems to grow well in slightly acid, moist loams or sands but may be more adaptable than has yet been found.

Sorbus hupehensis Hupeh rowan

A sturdy tree from Western China, transplanting well when it is a big plant, this is finding favour with public authorities as well as with gardeners who want good, rather unusual foliage and very unusual fruit. It has a broad-conic crown of stout rising branches and shoots from which hang 25 cm long leaves with 13 broad-oblong leaflets, entire on their inner halves, very sharply-toothed on the outer, slightly silvered grey-green above and glaucous grey beneath on a pink, grooved rachis. The flowers are on big, open domed heads, white with a yellow centre, and pale purple anthers. The stalks in the flower-head turn bright red as the 6 mm berries turn white with a slight pink stain or, in some trees, bright rose-pink, and hang in bunches 12 cm across. The leaf rachis turns deep red and the leaflets yellow with some

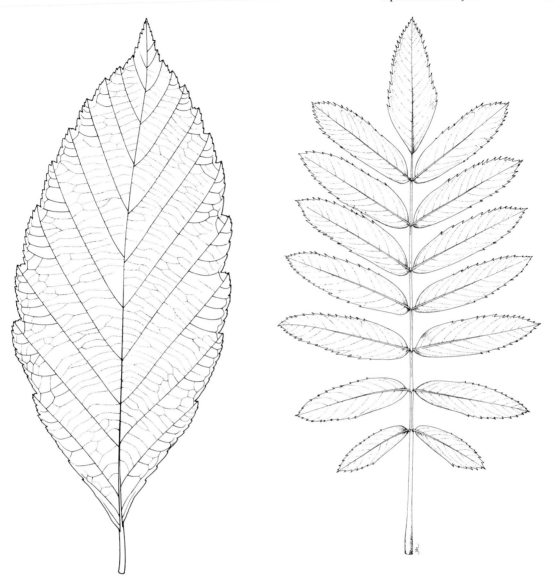

Himalayan whitebeam   True service tree

red, and they fall before the fruit. Birds sometimes eat the fruit but more usually they leave them alone, perhaps thinking they cannot yet be ripe. A well-laden specimen with pink fruits resembles from a distance a tree in full pink flower.

Sorbus 'Joseph Rock'

Quite first-class as a small specimen tree and outstanding in the autumn, 'Joseph Rock' is also ideal in streets as it has a slender crown and very small leaflets which do not block drains. It was sent from China by the American, Joseph Rock, but only one seedling of it appeared in a batch of seeds of another species. Grafts were taken from this tree at Wisley and are being planted now as fast as they can be obtained. The leaves are narrow, 15 × 6 cm, with about 17 small, oblong-lanceolate, rather crowded leaflets on a stalk which is crimson at the base early in the season and increasingly down its length. In summer, a narrow-crowned, dark, somewhat yellowish-green tree, it becomes in autumn a pillar of fire, orange, scarlet and purple. At the same time the little berries are bright lemon yellow so the tree is, to put it mildly, quite a sight. Birds leave the berries to persist after the leaves have fallen. 'Joseph Rock is growing well in gardens on light sandy soils as well as in streets on heavier soil and seems to be adaptable.

Sorbus pohuashanensis

This Chinese species is a vigorous, strong-branched, broad-crowned tree with stout shoots; it has persistent, round, deeply-toothed stipules at the base of each leaf and about 13 leaflets glaucous pubescent beneath and with strongly impressed veins above, on a pubescent pink rachis It is grown less for its good foliage than for the abundance and brilliance of its fruit which are unsurpassed by any *Sorbus*. The tree is closely bedecked with nodding heads 15 cm across, each with some 200 bright scarlet big berries. Cultivated trees seem to be inextricably mixed with, and hybrids of, the similar *S. esserteauiana*.

Sorbus sargentiana Sargent rowan

Ernest Wilson sent this among many other splendid trees from Western China in 1908, during his third collecting trip and the first for the Arnold Arboretum. It is usually seen grafted on to a stem of common Rowan from which its stout shoots spread out and up into a flattened globose crown. It has glossy, deep red big buds exuding clear resin and leaves 35 cm long and nearly as broad, with 11 large acuminate leaflets. The flower-heads are low-domed and to 20 cm across, bearing in autumn some 200–500 bright red but small fruit. These are quite impressive but it is for the autumn foliage that this tree is usually grown. The big leaves turn dull orange then, in good years, uniform bright scarlet; in other years they remain orange, pale and mottled with red, and are nearly as attractive and less usual.

Sorbus scalaris Ladder-leaf rowan

This tree of very distinctive foliage, rare in gardens, was found and introduced in 1904 by Ernest Wilson when he was in West Szechuan. The leaves are well displayed along level branches and tend to hang, dark glossy green with around 30 slender oblong leaflets, each with a deeply impressed midrib. In autumn big domed heads of scarlet fruit stand above the green leaves, highly attractive, before the leaves turn red and purple.

The tree has a tendency to grow long branches from near the ground, but if it is kept to a single clean bole for 2 m before being allowed to spread, it makes a first-class specimen tree of very modest size, at home on a wide range of soils provided that they do not dry out too rapidly. It is good as a group if planted at wide spacing to give the spreading branches room and light so that they can flower. At maturity the spread can be some 10 m, so the trees should not be planted more closely than that.

Sorbus torminalis Wild service tree; Chequers tree

This native tree has many features of interest and others of garden merit. It was formerly grown for its fruit, checkers, from which a drink was made. There were many inns specializing in this drink, most of which have, through an etymological error, a splendid but irrelevant chessboard for their sign. It was a late arrival as a native and is distributed along the woods under the North Downs, at its best, and thinly elsewhere around the Chalk-beds and north on limestones in the Pennines to near Carnforth. The wild occurrence of this tree is of particular interest to ecologists, and carefully mapped, because it is believed to sow itself and grow wild only where the land is primary woodland, that is, has never been cleared or ploughed and is not a plantation.

The leaves have a pair of big triangular lobes and one to three pairs of smaller ones, not unlike some maples but held alternately, not in opposite pairs. They have slender yellow-green stalks and are shiny dark green and hard, turning yellow, dark red and purple in autumn. The bark is dark brown with grey scales.

This elegant tree can be 26 m with a pointed crown bearing open heads of white flowers with yellow anthers and then a few 1 cm, brown speckled fruit. It is a splendid and unsual specimen tree for any garden with the space, growing quite fast from seed and preferring a rather rich soil, damp but well-drained, although it will tolerate lighter, poorer soils.

Sorbus vilmoriniana Vilmorin rowan

This little tree from western China is seen in many of the larger gardens but is not yet widely known to the layman. It is not at all demanding as to soil or climate although it may prefer a damp soil and high rainfall. In one Argyll garden in a wet, rocky glen, it sows itself around freely.

The bole of grey and brown flaking bark is short and often curved. It bears a low wide head of shallowly arching branches with spurs bearing sprays of leaves 12 cm long, each with some 23 2 cm leaflets elegantly placed. The central stalks are scarlet at base, grooved and slightly winged. The leaves emerge brown and become dark grey-green until late autumn when they turn dark crimson. Each spur bears a slender head of small white flowers which ripen into 1 cm ovoid fruit. These are deep red in late summer becoming paler through the autumn, then turning from dark to pale pink, finally being nearly white.

This tree is too small and low to be used as a single specimen except in a very small-scale planting. On a larger scale, a group of three, five or seven makes a feature on a shallow bank, for example, pleasant in summer and moderately spectacular in autumn. Some plants are grafted on to rowan and may sprout at the base; these sprouts should be cut back annually.

Stuartia pseudocamellia Deciduous camellia

This Stuartia is a slender tree from Japan. It has a minor oddity in that its leaves are dull above and glossy underneath which is a reversal of the normal arrangement. Its merits are more obvious; good bark, late flowers, and autumn colour. The bark is mainly dull orange-brown but it grows purplish scales and when these are newly shed they leave patches of bright orange. The open, flimsy crown, sometimes over 15 m tall, bears layers of very dark ovate-lanceolate leaves, round-toothed on the outer half, 3–8 cm long. After midsummer cup-shaped white flowers 5 cm across, numerous but solitary, not in masses, open to show an orange boss of anthers. In the autumn the leaves turn yellow and red, and in good sun, deep bright red all over.

This is an excellent small tree for light woodland, provided it receives plenty of sun and the soil has no lime in it.

Stuartia sinensis Chinese stuartia

A much broader tree usually than the foregoing although with branches upswept towards their ends, this has rather larger leaves and flowers but is grown mainly for its bark. This is flaky from youth and later most of it has shed all the flakes and is smooth, bald and flesh-pink, although some boles are more cream and grey.

Styrax hemsleyana Hemsley's storax

This was among the first trees sent from western China by Ernest Wilson on his first expedition, in 1900. It is infrequent in the more southerly gardens, and although rather shrubby and leggy, it has good leaves and is splendid in flower. Winter-buds are bright orange and produce broad-ovate abruptly acuminate leaves, 15×10 cm, with a few peg-like teeth near the tip, and a spike of flowers arising from the axil, erect and pubescent, with 10–25 flowers mainly to one side. The small flowers open white with a conic yellow centre, in some profusion. This storax can be 12 m tall in some shelter on a good damp non-limy soil.

Styrax obassia Big leaf storax

This Japanese equivalent of the Chinese Hemsley's storax is a sturdier tree with bigger leaves and bigger but less profuse flowers and, again, is seen largely in southern gardens. The winter-buds are enclosed by the swollen base of the stout 2 cm petiole which is densely hairy. The crown, which is upright and open, usually springs low on the grey-barked bole and can be 15 m high. Young plants bear remarkable leaves, 20×15 cm, either truncate across the top or obtuse with three large triangular teeth each side. Adult foliage is orbicular, abruptly acute, 15×15 cm, pale green above, densely glaucous pubescent beneath. The flowers are 20–25 on one side of an erect nodding pale green 15 cm stalk and each is white, 2–3 cm across, fragrant and bell-shaped. The fruit bend

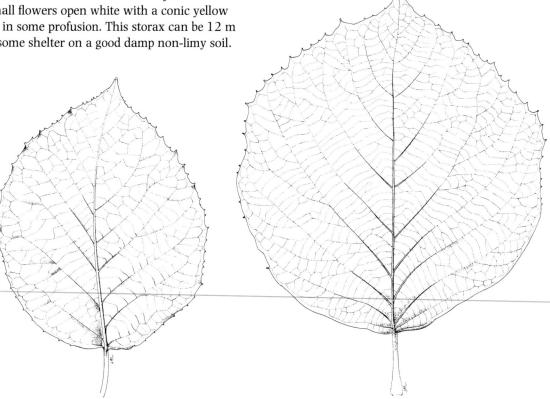

Hemsley's storax   Big-leaf storax

the raceme over further with their weight, 1·5 cm ovoids pale brown densely pubescent, cupped in a broad-lobed calyx. Seeds quite often germinate and grow around the parent tree.

Tetracentron sinense Tetracentron; Spur-leaf

A curiosity from China and the Western Himalayas, this very attractive tree has no close relatives but is near to the magnolias, and has the wood-structure of a primitive conifer. Although apparently completely hardy it is rare, and most of the specimens are in southern and western gardens. It has a slender crown of sparse light branches arching to level, strung with alternate slender buds on long spurs. Unusually, if not uniquely, each spur bears a single leaf, broadly ovate, cordate, 11 × 9 cm, deep green, thick and leathery with very hard jagged fine teeth and sunken veins in a fan layout, on a 3 cm yellow and red petiole. From the base of each leaf a slender catkin emerges in late spring, and hangs 9–15 cm long, green, tinged red with buds which open yellow-green. With each spur and leaf on a long level branch decorated thus, a tree 10–12 m tall makes a splendidly unusual feature. It prefers some shelter and a good damp soil whether acid or alkaline.

Tilia americana American lime; American linden

Americans hardly know our use of the word 'lime', so the second name given is more internationally acceptable. The American linden has been regarded as a non-success here but recent observation suggests this to be far from the case. It is rare, but in Surrey there is a fine healthy tree 26 m tall and some are growing well between a road and a school. Young trees may suffer, as do some other trees with smooth bark, from sap-sucking by great spotted woodpeckers – similar to the work of the Sapsucker in America – which causes dense bands of pits in the bark but does not generally harm the tree. The American linden is worthy of trial here because of the luxuriantly rich green foliage – moderately or very big leaves, shiny and marked by pale, parallel straight veins

and, unlike other lime leaves, the same rich colour beneath. The shoot and bud are apple-green and the big 10 cm bract to the flowers is bright green. No doubt this tree thrives here best where the summers are warmest, but there are a few in Scotland, quite big and healthy.

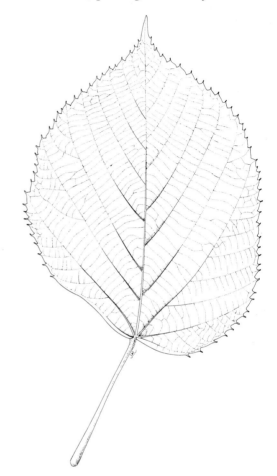

American linden

Tilia cordata Small-leafed lime

This tree, native to limestone cliffs and woods, grows well on any moderately deep and moist soil that is not too acid, and is peculiarly well adapted to city streets. It has hardly been put to the test in Britain, but Small-leafed lime is among the most important city trees throughout the north-eastern USA. As a big old tree it shares one bad feature with the Common lime; it is very sprouty around the base. Until they are old the trees are a good conic shape, but they become irregularly domed and eventually have long branches curving in to be quite erect, making a narrow-topped crown to 37 m tall. Red-brown shoots with red shiny ovoid buds make a distinctive dense tracery of short-jointed systems in winter. The leaves are daintily heart-shaped, around 6 cm long, dark shiny green above, pale, slightly silvered grey-green beneath, with large tufts of pale orange hairs in the vein-axils. The flowers immediately indentify the tree in midsummer since they spray out at all angles in bunches of a dozen, white or ivory, clear and star-like, as fragrant as the Common lime, if less far-carrying. This species is being planted more lately as a replacement for the elms, and few trees could be such a good addition to town and country.

'Green Spire' is a recent form, more seen in America. It has at present a narrow, conic crown and orange shoots.

Tilia euchlora Crimean lime

This tree is becoming something of a disappointment after the high promise it gave. As a young tree, and until it is about 30 years old, it is beautiful. As usually planted it has a smooth, pewter-grey clean bole for 2 m, an ovoid crown of rich, glossy green leaves, obliquely cordate with yellow sharp teeth, yellow 5 cm petioles and the undersides pale with large tufts of pale brown hairs in the vein-axils. It grows excellently in streets and towns and the foliage is free from the aphids which infest the Common lime and to some extent the other common species of Lime. It has a reputation, together with the Silver limes, of poisoning bees with its nectar but this seems to be based on a few observations of bumble-bees rather than hive-bees. Unfortunately the tree has two more substantial troubles. Some trees have a serious die-back of branches with something like a canker, and those remaining healthy develop unsightly crowns with branches arching sharply down like hoops and becoming thickened and misshapen. It is, then, a splendid foliage-tree, with good big yellow flowers, and worth planting, but it may be of less beauty in the long term.

Tilia × europaea Common lime

It is not known whether this tree, which is a hybrid between the Small-leafed and the Broad-leafed limes, arose spontaneously here as well as in Europe, migrated here with the others, or was brought here in the early seventeenth century. It is usually the tallest broadleafed tree in any district with parks or gardens and can be 45 m tall with a narrow upper crown of several vertical stems and light level branches, but the lower crown is broad. Its size and fragrant flowers, its adaptability to various soils, its long life and windfirm nature earn it an assured place as a framework-tree and a parkland specimen, but it is the last tree ever to consider planting in streets or small gardens. In these situations, any other Lime is vastly preferable, and the Common lime is only included because it must be warned against for any use except the two mentioned above.

Tilia × moltkei Von Moltke's lime

This hybrid of German origin, a cross between the American linden and the Silver pendent lime, inherits the big leaf-size of the former and makes a very handsome foliage-tree. The rather pendulous shoots bear sharply-toothed leaves 25 × 15 cm, dark mat green above but silvery with close pubescence beneath. Young trees are very upright and vigorous and may grow a shoot 1·5 m long.

Tilia mongolica Mongolian lime

Until quite recently this decorative tree was scarcely known except for the three original trees, from 1904 seed at Kew. Two 20 m tall specimens were found at Wakehurst Place in Sussex a few years ago, but most of the trees seen are the result of a very recent planting. The bark is at first smooth and grey but with age it becomes fissured and purplish. The shoots are slender and red and bear leaves which are highly distinctive and unlike those of any other Lime. They are 5–8 cm long, orbicular to triangular with big triangular teeth or lobes and an acuminate, coarsely serrated central lobe. They are firm, dark green, on a pink petiole 3 cm long, and are glabrous beneath except for

Mongolian lime

tufts in the vein-axils. With flowers like the Small-leafed lime and pretty foliage, this is a highly desirable tree, hardy and adapted to any normal soil.

Tilia oliveri Oliver's lime

This was another of the earliest trees sent by Ernest Wilson from western China in 1900. None is known of that age but a younger tree is already 28 m tall and small specimens are growing fast so it may well become a big tree. It has exceptionally beautiful leaves, large – to 20 × 18 cm – on a big tree and, oddly, only around 15 cm long on young trees, soft pale green, very flat and smooth above and with white peg-like sharp teeth; the undersides are bright silvery-white. These leaves are well spaced on pendulous shoots and stand out level by a twist in the petiole. As with other limes with stout shoots, young trees growing strongly seem liable to breakage in the first few years and may need help from the secateurs to re-form a good crown. Some side-shelter is beneficial and any fairly damp soil will suffice. In some ways this is the most choice of all limes.

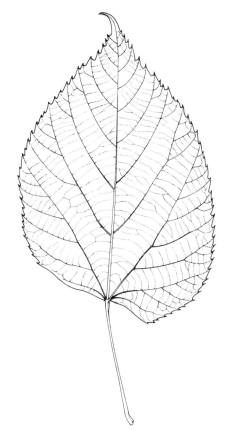

Oliver's lime

Tilia petiolaris Silver pendent lime

This tree is unknown in the wild and is not raised from seed; all the trees are grafted, mostly on to the Broad-leafed lime which suckers less freely than the Common and Small-leafed limes, but sprouts do occur at the base of many grafts, and must be removed relentlessly. Invariably three or four huge branches rise steeply from 2 m on the bole and soon make a pendulous crown often 30 m tall. It is a splendid sight hung with big dark leaves showing their silver undersides and is one of the best large-scale specimen trees, growing well in towns. The leaf is deeply cordate, about 12 × 12 cm on a slender petiole about as long. The flowers are copious, heavily fragrant and short-cylindric with pale yellow petals and bright yellow stamens. The leaves turn pale yellow in autumn then biscuit-brown in some years.

Tilia platyphyllos Broad-leafed lime

This native tree is separable from the other limes by its hairy shoots, densely hairy when fresh, nearly smooth by the end of winter, and hairy petioles. The leaves are no larger than in the Common lime and often smaller. It is distinct too in its crown, which soon becomes a regular hemisphere or at least well domed, and the bole seldom has suckers around its base. It is usually less tall than the other two common limes and few trees are 30 m high. In the early winter a fringe of fruit remains on the crown with the bracts dead and brown, indicating this species clearly. It is not a great specimen tree but it makes splendid clumps and roundels and is good for avenues, where it should always replace Common lime, because of its clean growth and regular crown. It flowers well before other limes, only four or five biggish pale flowers beneath each large pale bract and very fragrant.

'Laciniata', Cut-leaf lime, is of smaller growth, often prolific in flower and attractive in leaf.

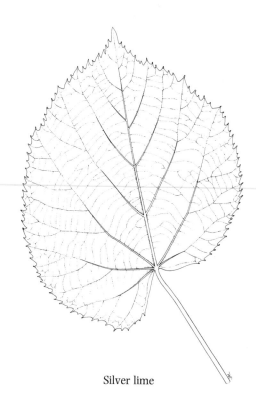

Silver lime

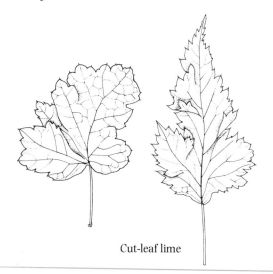

Cut-leaf lime

Tilia tomentosa Silver lime

The Silver lime from the Black Sea region is the best lime in cities and one of the best as a specimen anywhere that has room for a big tree. It grows very vigorously and soon makes a remarkably smoothly hemispheric crown dense with upswept shoots, as attractive in winter as it is in summer when heavily laden with dark leaves, brightly silvered beneath. The tree differs from the Silver pendent lime not only in this crown form but also in the leaf being thick, dark green, crinkled, often with the margin curled up, and on a stouter petiole only half the length of the blade. The flowers are the same as in the other tree. This tree's good growth in cities is utilized more in the USA than here but there are many lines and individual Silver limes of fairly recent planting and a few old trees in the Royal Parks in London, especially in Hyde and Regents Parks.

Trachycarpus fortunei Chusan palm

This is the only true palm which is hardy almost everywhere in Britain; none other can be grown unprotected north-east of Torbay. The Coconut, Date, Canary and Queen palms all have long, 6–8 m, drooping leaves, enormously pinnate with scores or hundreds of linear leaflets, and form our general picture of a palm, but the Chusan palm is not like this at all. Its broad fan-leaves are on a petiole hardly 1 m in length and are divided into 50–60 radiating slender lobes about 1 m long and fraying at the ends. The bole is invested by coconut-fibre around big spiny stubs of petioles, and is cylindric. It does not increase in diameter through the addition of an annual layer of wood as in other trees, but can expand minutely from the pressure of slight thickening of internal bundles of tissues running up the stem to each leaf. The flowers are on 60 cm much-branched panicles, with stout, twisting stems, orange paling to cream, bearing tiny yellow flowers. Several panicles emerge during the summer, mostly either male or female but on the same tree. The fruit are globular and blue-black, and frequent only in the south and west. The tree sows itself freely in many gardens in Ireland and at Borde Hill in Sussex.

This palm is often 7–11 m tall but not more and is stubby and inelegant. It may superficially lend a tropical air to a corner despite being so unlike most of the palms actually grown in warmer climates, but needs to be in groups as a single tree just looks odd. It is better placed away from, rather than beside, a path since spines on the petiole-stubs on the bole will damage a hand painfully if seized on passing.

Ulmus Elms

Until 1970 there were several elms which could be recommended strongly as fine foliage-trees, good in sea-winds, very windfirm and making shapely and huge specimens. There were also several smaller elms of special habit or colour of foliage. In 1981 it is folly to recommend the planting of any elm for a long-term or important feature. Nearly all the big trees in southern England have died except in west Devon and in Cornwall, where a combination of sea-winds unsuitable for big populations of the beetles which carry the disease, and the higher resistance to it of the Cornish elm is, so far, holding the disease at bay. In the north Midlands and in Scotland large areas nearly free of dying trees remain but currently the disease is spreading into them.

Dutch Elm Disease is nothing to do with the Dutch elm in particular, nor with Holland. The English and American elms are in fact the most susceptible and the disease is thought to have an Asiatic origin, since Asiatic elms are the most resistant. The name was applied because Dutch scientists were the pioneers in studies of the disease and breeding trees resistant to it.

There will be but brief mention of the major forms of Elm and no recommendations to plant should be assumed. When all the old trees are dead and removed, the beetles will have nowhere to breed and their population must collapse. Moreover, the suckers arising wherever the elms grew are mostly below the level at which the beetles feed and spread the disease, so these should reach tree-size. Only when the new trees are big and start to die will the disease be important again and by then it may have achieved an equilibrium with the Elm as did the milder form in 1930.

Three species are either very resistant or are hoped to be immune. They are not immense trees and so it is justifiable to plant a few as individual specimens in the hope of their survival. These are:

Ulmus parvifolia Chinese elm

A dainty and attractive tree with tiny 3 cm leaves, fresh green in spring, dark in summer and remaining so until the end of the year. This nearly evergreen crown is a light dome on a bole with remarkable bark. It may be grey or brown at first, with small orange protruding flakes, but with age becomes paler until, in warm climates, it is blue-white with orange flakes and where it is less warm, pale grey, yellow or cream. The equally tiny flowers open in the early autumn.

Ulmus pumila Siberian elm

Quite rare here, this elm must be immensely tough for it is the universal shade tree from the streets of Winnipeg throughout the Prairie States to the deserts of New Mexico and Arizona. It grows very fast when young but soon opens out to an untidy umbrella of a crown with pendulous outer shoots and thin foliage. It has a dark grey, ridged bark, spring flowers, 6 cm narrow leaves that shed early, and can be 20 m tall.

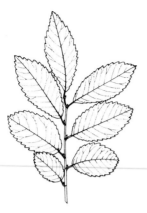

Siberian elm

Ulmus 'Sapporo Autumn Gold'

Now being tested in the Royal Parks in London
and at many institutions as a gift from a Japanese
manufacturer, this hybrid *U. pumila* × *japonica* is
at present known only from a few very young
trees. It is upright and leafy with dark foliage
which should colour well in autumn.

Ulmus carpinifolia Smooth-leafed elm

This was largely confined to East Anglia and the
eastern Midlands and is a hugely domed tree with
numerous rising and arching branches of all sizes,
late into leaf. The leaves are small, leathery, shiny
above with parallel prominent veins.

'Cornubiensis' Cornish elm. Throughout Cornwall
and from there eastwards to Dartmoor, this is the
common elm, completely distinctive in the crown
of rising and arching big branches, each densely
leafed but with daylight showing between. The
bark is dark grey with long parallel deep ridges
and the leaves are bright green. Beyond the range,
it was planted occasionally, usually in groups all
over an estate as at Walsingham, Norfolk, and
Croome, Worcestershire, also in certain areas like
Devizes and the Savernake estates in Wiltshire and
in Regents Park, London, and nearby squares, but
all these trees have now died.

'Sarniensis' Wheatley elm; Jersey elm. Formerly
common in city parks, especially in the Midlands,
in avenues and along ring-roads from Plymouth to
Edinburgh, this was usually called 'Cornish elm'. It
is quite distinct in its narrowly conic, dense crown
on innumerable small branches, and these made it
safer by roads than the elms with big branches.
The leaf is dark, smooth and parallel-veined, and
many are nearly round, while the bark is less
vertically ridged than in other Smooth-leafed elms
and dark brown in blocks like the English elm.

Ulmus glabra Wych elm

The only truly native elm, common in the north
by streams in the mountains and in the south-
west, as a young tree this has smooth dark silvery-
grey bark. Old trees have brown heavily-ridged
bark and a broad, rather drooping crown with
heavy low branches but no suckers. The big
15 cm leaves are harshly hairy and very unequal
at the short, scarcely present but very hairy
petiole.

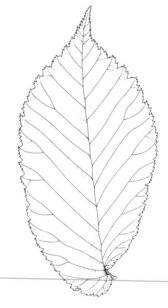

Wych elm

'Camperdown' is the low, domed hummock
weeping to the ground with big 20 cm very harsh
leaves formerly common in parks and city
churchyards.

'Pendula' is the much taller form with sprays of shoots slanting down from the outer crown.

'Lutescens' is the superb bright golden elm with big leaves and smooth bark, uncommon but planted especially by roads and in parks in Devon where some survive at present.

Ulmus × hollandica

These are hybrid elms raised from Smooth-leafed elm crossing with Wych elm. The two below were the only forms seen except a few in the London Royal Parks and some botanic gardens where other forms common in Europe were also growing.

'Hollandica' Dutch elm. This very distinctive tree was frequent in only a few regions, like north Hampshire and Wiltshire where the disease has been rampant for many years, and few survive. It has a sinuous smooth bole with scaly bark and few strong upright sinuous branches holding an open dome of crown to 32 m tall. The leaf is dark, oblique, hard, often buckled, nearly smooth above.

'Vegeta' Huntingdon elm. This was raised in Huntingdonshire in 1760 and was a noble tree in parks and avenues in much of southern England. It has considerable resistance to the disease and is the source of several of the forms selected in Holland for higher resistance. Many fine specimens survived in Gloucestershire especially, when all other elms around had died, but they fell to an unsuspected trick of the beetle. Lacking decaying elm boles in which to breed, the beetles bored into these healthy boles and killed them. The Huntingdon elm has an easily recognized crown: a stout straight bole bearing, from some 2–3 m up, whorls of strong, straight, scarcely tapered branches which radiate upwards to hold a hemispheric dome. The dark red flowers and the green winged fruit are more numerous and conspicuous than those of other elms. The leaves have pink-yellow 2 cm petioles to blades which start one vein lower on one side than on the other and are 12 cm long, leathery, smooth and shiny. This tree is a great loss as a parkland specimen and avenue tree.

Ulmus procera English elm

This was introduced before Roman times to the lower Severn Valley and extended as far as York but not into much of East Anglia, east Kent nor west of Okehampton in Devon. It was the tree of the traditional 'English' lowland agricultural landscape – the major component of hedgerow trees dividing the fields – and was also an important tree in city parks, being resistant to polluted air. The bark is dark brown in small square blocks. The bole is stout and bears a few huge branches arising level then twisting, and often masses of sprouts from burrs, but no small branches. The crown is made up of converging domes, early into leaf and soon very dark green. Autumn colour is late and splendid yellows to russet.

Umbellularia californica Californian laurel; Oregon myrtle

This evergreen is rather dull except in flower when the numerous umbels of small yellow flowers brighten the foliage. It is mostly seen in southern and western gardens but is hardy at least in the Midlands. There was a tree 25 × 1 m, but all the biggest were blown down in 1987 and 15 m × 50 cm is more the usual size at present. It makes a tall, leafy, irregular dome on upright branches which are often lined with rows of slender sprouts. The leaves are held out well from the green shoots and are oblong-lanceolate, entire and about 8 cm long. They are pungently but sweetly aromatic and deep inhalation from a crushed leaf may bring on a sharp headache later.

Zelkova carpinifolia Caucasian zelkova

Zelkovas are in the Elm Family but, while escaping Dutch Elm Disease, they are prone to windblow and many of the biggest have been lost in recent gales. One of the originals of the 1760 seed, the first of any tree from Caucasia, survives at Syon Park, but trees of this origin at Kew were lost. This tree is very hardy and grows in East Lothian although none has been seen yet further north. Old trees are huge and of a unique shape, a stout bole of 1–2 m bearing an immense brush of a hundred or more vertical branches rearing up into a tall ovoid to a height of over 30 m. Many much younger trees are becoming the same shape, but this is apparently not seen in the native areas and some in Britain also are of more normal tree-shape. Specimens of both sorts grow near Hyde Park Corner in London. The leaf is elliptic, short-acute and prettily crenate with round-based minutely pointed teeth, variable in size and particularly in breadth, around 8 × 5 cm and dark green turning yellow, dull orange and brown in autumn. This is an outstanding tree as a single big specimen or mixed among other trees, or in groups. It can sucker and make a long hedge but should be kept clean.

Zelkova serrata Keaki (*Z. acuminata*)

This Japanese zelkova is an elegant yet extremely tough and useful tree which has so far rarely been affected by Dutch Elm Disease and is healthy in badly affected areas often enough to be worth the slight risk. It is seen in a few city parks and squares in southern England but it has been used much more widely from Ontario to Georgia and is the shade tree in the car-park at The Pentagon, Washington DC. The smooth bole is pale grey on young trees, banded pink and orange in fine stripes, and becomes grey and stripping on older trees. It holds up a broad dome of slender straight branches and shoots. The leaves differ from the Caucasian species (above) in having long-acuminate points, bigger teeth, very rounded at base but spine-tipped, and a longer petiole, smooth, pale yellow and 1·5 cm long. They hang very ornamentally each side of long shoots on a young tree and on most trees turn delicate shades of yellow, amber and pink in autumn. It has a tendency as a young seedling plant to grow too many slender shoots with none dominant, so a little help may be needed to make a good crown as it may also with trees bought already on a stem.

The Ginkgo

Ginkgo biloba Ginkgo; Maidenhair tree

Only this single species survives of all the species, genera and Families of Ginkgos in the Order *Ginkgoales*, which dominated tree-life 200 million years ago. It is thus botanically a very isolated plant with no relatives and no other tree resembling it. It is probably still growing wild in China today where monasteries have preserved it from the felling for firewood which devastated woods in long-settled areas. It was introduced into Japan a thousand years ago and was seen first by a European in that country in 1689. The first Ginkgo in Britain was raised in 1754 and moved in 1760 to Kew when part of the Palace grounds was opened as public gardens. It was planted against the wall of a boiler-house which was demolished in 1860 and the tree stands free and in full health today. Although the oldest kind of tree existing, by far, the Ginkgo is almost the only tree able to withstand the peculiarly severe conditions of the most modern kind – the canyons between skyscrapers – and it is a downtown tree in city centres from Montreal to New Orleans. It is now being planted a good deal in the centre of London. It can be almost any shape from a straight flag-pole with one or two side-arms, to a fan like a burst of spray but is usually quite narrow with a good central stem. It is deciduous with thick leathery leaves which evolved before the pinnate branching system of veins, so their shape is determined by a fanwise arrangement of veins spreading from a narrow cuneate base to a broad two-lobed tip. The leaves turn bright gold when and where a warm summer is followed by a sunny, warm autumn.

Every garden with room for a narrow tree or two should have a Ginkgo and they are hardy, if slow in the north, to Ross-shire. The spiky crown and fresh bright green new leaves go remarkably well with buildings whether red brick or grey stone. Some old male trees bear thick yellow catkins and a few females in a number of cities and gardens bear blue-green plumshaped fruit which ripen yellow then orange-brown and decompose with a highly unpleasant smell.

'Fastigiata' Sentinel ginkgo. This is as narrowly and densely crowned as an acute-tipped Lombardy poplar. There are a few in London parks but in Philadelphia, Pittsburgh and New York they are frequent, to 30 m tall.

Conifers

The conifers are in the Class *Gymnospermae* which is relatively primitive and is being replaced globally by the *Angiospermae*, broadleafed or 'flowering' trees and plants That conifers are obsolescent is shown by their distribution. They are herded on to the circumpolar plains and up into the mountains while the warm, long-season areas with rich soils are taken by the newer Angiosperms. The process is far advanced and only in parts of North America do some conifers remain in warm lowland areas, and there on the poorest soils.

It thus happens that in general conifers grow better than other trees on poor soils in cool wet mountainous areas. The vagaries of geological and plant history deprived the mountains of the British Isles of the conifers which are best suited to grow in them. The greatest assemblage of conifers in the world remains along the Pacific slopes of the Rocky Mountain system in North America but many of these grow better in the British and Irish hills than they can in America. Other conifers from the Himalayas, China and Japan also thrive there. In many areas conifers are the most suitable trees for shelter, background and amenity. They look right among mountains, even if many people cannot yet accept this. Along the bottom of steep-sided valleys, the gardens, parks and churchyards of the north and west are verdant summer and winter with subtle mixtures of tones of green. Conifers are here the framework trees in the small-scale village and estate scenery.

Coniferous Areas

The growth of many of the western American and some of the European and Asiatic conifers is sustained and exceptionally vigorous only in certain areas. Rather than have the text peppered with repeated lists of the areas where conifers are desirable and very successful, these will be referred to as the 'Coniferous Areas'. They are:

1 Parts of the south coast from the New Forest westward;
2 Dartmoor, south Devon and south Cornwall – splendid for vigour but continued height growth only possible in sheltered areas;
3 The Welsh mountains, particularly towards the north and west, and the Upper Severn Valley;
4 Cumbria;
5 The Southern Uplands;
6 The Highlands, most notably for continued growth to great heights, Argyll, Perthshire, Inverness-shire, Easter and Wester Ross; also, in shelter, Angus, Aberdeen, Moray etc;
7 The Wicklow Hills;
8 Counties Cork and Kerry, in shelter;
9 Counties Down, Armagh and, in shelter, Tyrone.

All areas except the first enjoy high rainfall and cool, usually damp summers, and these two factors are important to vigorous growth. The conifers in question come from cool damp mountains or coast ranges with the prevailing winds bringing rain at all seasons. None of the tallest-growing conifers achieves great height where at all subjected to hot, dry winds. In eastern England, rapid early growth may be attained in damp sheltered areas but when the tree outgrows its shelter, its top comes under stress from dry winds. Progress thereafter is slow and uncertain. Summers in the west and north are notably cooler and the air remains more humid, particularly in the regions instanced.

A second factor is the high latitude of the British Isles. Day-length in the growing season is proportional to latitude, and Britain, spanning from 50°N to 60°N, is a long way further north than the origin of the exotic conifers we grow. In eastern North America these latitudes run from the north of Newfoundland to the northern tip of Labrador, and in the west from the northern part of Vancouver Island to north of Kodiak Island, Alaska. Trees from Oregon and California cannot be grown at all in Labrador, where it is too cold in winter for them to survive, and too cool in summer for them to grow. A few southern trees range into Alaska but they grow very slowly and those confined to Oregon or southwards cannot survive in Alaska.

In Britain all these trees find a winter so mild that it never upsets them, and an ideal growing season in which every day is an hour or two longer than in their home region, and hence they grow more. In the far north of Scotland, day-length is greatest and winters are among the mildest; only shelter and good soils are not easily found, but where they are, conditions for the growth of many conifers are among the best in the world. Trees native to the Siskiyou Mountains growing in Perthshire are about one thousand miles nearer the North Pole and experience the long days of that latitude, yet are in a climate quite as benign as at home, which in nearly every other part of the world having such long growing days is under tundra or ice.

Abies alba European silver fir; Common silver fir (*A. pectinata*)

This has been grown here longer than any other Silver fir, being first planted in 1603. Around 1770 it was commonly planted in gardens and woods and until the conifers from the American north-west overtook it, it was the biggest and tallest tree everywhere in Britain and Ireland. In the Coniferous Areas some remain, their broken and branchy heads peering out of the tops of broadleaf woods and their huge grey boles standing in gardens, but in the east and south there are none, and very few younger ones. The aphid *Adelges nusslinii* attacks young woods severely so these have ceased to be planted. Although not recommended for planting other than as an occasional group in Coniferous Area parkland, this is so much a feature of parts of

Argyll and Perthshire that it has been included. The foliage is about the dullest of any Silver fir; grey shoots with scattered blackish pubescence, with thin rows of dark green leaves lying nearly flat each side.

Abies amabilis Beautiful fir; Red fir

This is a variably successful tree here, and although the sources of good seed have not yet been ascertained most of the specimens which are remarkably vigorous and shapely are in the areas of high rainfall and cool wet summers. It is native to British Columbia and Washington State where it grows to 70 m tall. British trees have slender, regularly conic crowns to 32 m with whorls of light branches level and very short near the top of the tree. The stout shoots are pale pubescent and bear long spreading glossy dark green leaves brilliantly banded silver beneath and fanning out forward over the shoot. When newly unfolded they are often soft blue-grey. This is a tree for a park or garden amongst the western and northern mountains and needs an acid, damp mineral soil. As a young tree it is one of the most attractive of all silver firs, with a long leader bearing closely in the middle length a few upright side-shoots, and with a crown of luxuriant foliage to the ground.

Beautiful fir

Abies concolor White fir

The type tree grows from Colorado south and westwards and is uncommon in our country. The form Low's fir (below) is a much better tree in any but the most coniferous areas, but the type when growing well has fine long, 5–6 cm upstanding leaves dark blue-green on both sides and is a decorative young tree.

var. **lowiana** Low's fir

This is the form from mid-Oregon south along the Sierra Nevada and was introduced in 1851. It varies with origin, in bark, crown and foliage.

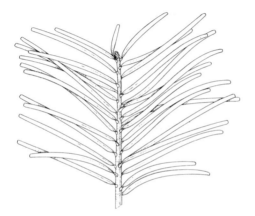

Low's white fir

Those with a black bark have narrowly columnar tall crowns and flat-spreading 5 cm leaves dark green above. This is often the tallest conifer in non-coniferous areas like the Midlands, even in somewhat polluted parts, and may tower out of an estate to 35–38 m before the top thins and dies back. Those with a corky, thick bark, grey with deep brown fissures, are conic to the tip and have grey-blue green leaves curved up each side of the shoot. In the Coniferous Areas this is one of the fastest-growing and biggest Silver firs and remarkably shapely even when 45 m tall. It is at all ages a first-class specimen tree and in groups or amongst other trees it will grow some of the finest boles to be seen.

'Violacea'. A slower form of the type, with the long, upstanding leaves bright blue-grey or silvery. It is remarkably handsome as a young tree but apt to thin before reaching any great size.

Abies bracteata Santa Lucia fir (*A. venusta*)

The wild population of this splendid Silver fir is a relict one of small groups near the heads of damp canyons in the Santa Lucia Mountains of Monterey, California. Hence the tree, although from the generally hot region with dry summers south of San Francisco, grows best in the Coniferous Areas with plenty of summer rain. Elsewhere it flourishes only in moist and sheltered places and is relatively short-lived. It is unique among the Silver firs in the long, narrow, protruding bracts of the cone and in having slender acute buds like a Beech, while the hard leaves with spined points are very unusual in this group.

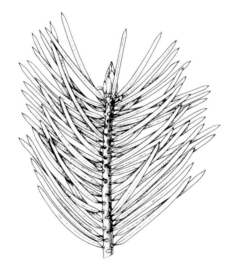

Santa Lucia fir

The bark is smooth and almost black, prominently marked by rings of branch-scars. The crown, after some 30 years, is in two parts. The top is a slender spire with very short, level side-shoots and this rises from a much broader sector of long, downswept branches holding fans of foliage sweeping to the ground. The foliage is on a large scale, the stout shoot – olive-brown then dark red-brown – bearing parted ranks of 5 cm spine-ended leaves, dark green above and with two narrow but bright white bands beneath.

The Santa Lucia fir is slow to start and susceptible to frost damage when it is in long grass, but once established it grows very fast. An original tree achieved 38 m × 1·6 m in Herefordshire before dying from Honey-fungus in 1974.

Abies cephalonica Grecian fir

This grows into a coarse, huge and widely branched tree liable to have high branches broken. It is mentioned for its ability to make a very vigorous tree, quite shapely for years, in dry, warm areas as well as in the Coniferous Areas. It has rigid, acute, dark green leaves radiating all round an orange-brown shoot.

var. *apollinis* has better foliage, thicker and more crowded above the shoot, and makes a better tree.

Abies delavayi var. **forrestii** Forrest's fir
(*A. forrestii*)

In the Coniferous Areas this tree from south-west China grows on to be a fine specimen, so far to over 20 m, while in other parts it fades out, becoming thin and dying back when about 16 m tall. It is worth growing for its best period, however, from 6 to 25 years of age, when it is a sturdy regular cone of whorled, slightly ascending branches bearing orange-red or dark red shoots with densely held deep green, notch-tipped leaves broadly banded beneath with the clearest snow-white. Furthermore, at a surprisingly young age, about ten years, it bears a number of big erect barrel-like cones of deep violet blue-purple derived from cylindric red flowers. It needs a moist acid soil and is best in some shelter.

Abies grandis Grand fir

One of the giant trees of the world, this has been known to be 90 m tall and grows from mid-British Columbia to northern California. It was sent first by David Douglas in 1830. Two very large trees from this seed survive in Ireland but big imports from 1851 to 1890 are responsible for the huge trees common in Scotland. Two of the tallest trees in the British Isles are Grand firs over 60 m tall after 100–120 years' growth, and several are over 40 m in 50 years, so this is one of the fastest-growing trees we have. It is not reliably long-lived partly because of the tendency to tower out of shelter to 50 m tall when the top is liable to breakage and die-back. It is a fine specimen tree amongst other tall trees but it can be rather thin on its own or, conversely, may become hugely branched low down and unapproachable unless pruned. In a small group it is very effective as it grows such a fine bole but is less windfirm. A few splendid trees grow on light sand but the best are mostly on deep mineral soil in woodland and on clays.

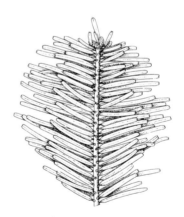

Grand fir

The bright green, grooved leaves stand out each side of slender olive-brown shoots and have two narrow bands of white beneath. They are of mixed lengths, from 3 to 6 cm, and have a strong scent of orange-peel when crushed.

Abies holophylla Manchurian fir

This tree is scarce and little can be said of its limitations, but where seen it is so good that it should be considered among the best smallish conifers for foliage. It is a shapely conic tree with a scaly orange-brown bark. The leaves are bright green above, whitish-green banded beneath, and stand densely and nearly vertically from the smooth shoot, to 4 cm long.

Abies homolepis Nikko fir

This is a very sturdy tree with whorls of parallel raised branches from a bole with a bark crisply scaling in pale pink-orange patches, making a broad conic crown. It comes from Japan but unlike several Japanese conifers it usually remains very healthy, seems to be long-lived and often exceeds 25 m. It is one of the best Silver firs outside the defined Coniferous Areas and even fairly near cities. It has excellent foliage; glabrous, cream, plated stout shoots with two somewhat parted dense rows of dark blue-green leaves brilliantly white-banded beneath. It bears cones sooner and more spread over the crown than many of its relatives, cylindric, domed dark blue-purple.

Abies koreana Korean fir

From the mainland of Korea and Manchuria this grows at some 50–60 cm a year into a slender tree but it is the trees from the offshore Quelpaert Island that are mostly desired. These can be grown in a shrubbery or small bed for their flowers and cones. They begin to flower when scarcely 1 m high and five or more years old and will be only 10 m tall when 60 years old. The female flowers may be red, pink, green or white and are slender cylindric in close lines along the branches. The cones are 6 cm slender barrels, deep blue but much hidden by big de-curved brown bracts. The leaves are slender and rather sparse for a Silver fir, but pure white beneath.

Abies lasiocarpa var. arizonica Arizona fir; Cork fir

This is moderately slow-growing but soon shows a creamy brown thick corky bark and a shapely slender crown. It is the more attractive because the slender up-curved leaves are bright deep blue with white stripes. It grows better in the warmer, drier, south-easterly areas than in the Coniferous Areas. *A. lasiocarpa* itself, the Subalpine fir, neither lives long nor grows well; it is a snow-line tree of incredibly slender crown on all the highest ridges of the Rocky Mountains.

Abies magnifica Red fir

In foliage this serves the same garden purposes as the Noble fir (p. 150) but it differs in the crown which is slender conic to the tip and strongly layered. The leading shoot has at its base a ring of quite level short stubby shoots 1 m or so above a slightly longer ring, and so on. The bole is so stout it can appear to swell or may even be slightly barrelled, and is prominently marked by rings of branch scars. Although there is a slender 23 m specimen on the Bagshot Sands at Wisley, the Red fir from Oregon and California is very much a tree of the Coniferous Areas. In fact almost all the big specimens, now over 30 m tall, are in Perthshire and Northumberland.

Abies mariesii Maries's fir

This is a Japanese version of the Beautiful fir and differs mainly in having browner thicker pubescence on the shoot, shorter leaves and speckled grey bark marked by branch scars. It is less vigorous but it is more reliable for a shapely specimen outside the Coniferous Areas.

Abies nordmanniana Caucasian fir

This is in effect a healthier, less branchy version of the European silver fir with more leathery, glossier leaves across the top of the shoot. A large import of seed in 1854 enabled gardens everywhere to plant it and since then few European silver firs have been planted. In the Coniferous Areas the Caucasian tree is big and richly foliaged and many are now 37 m × 1·4 m. It grows very well elsewhere too, although less heavily foliaged and showing a tendency to culminate at 35 m and for the top to die back. It is a good specimen for any mixed planting of the bigger conifers.

Abies numidica Algerian fir

This bears shoots remarkably densely covered in short, thick, broad leaves with white bands above and broad ones beneath. It usually grows a good clean bole and a regularly conic narrow crown, occasionally to a 30 m even outside the Coniferous Areas, and it is one of the best silver firs in hot, dry areas and near towns. It is very attractive as a small tree.

Abies pindrow Pindrow fir

Although this Himalayan high altitude tree is one strictly for the Coniferous Areas where long life and great size are concerned, the foliage is so handsome that it is worth growing elsewhere in a group as a short-term tree. Big trees have dark grey bark scaling in curves and strictly conic crowns, and even when 30 m tall the leading shoot – straight, stout and short – can be seen to be shaggy with the long, loosely held leaves. These are on very stout, pale pink lower shoots also and are bright shiny green, thick, hard and leathery, springing up and forwards from the shoot in two loose ranks, to 7 cm long.

Abies procera Noble fir (A. nobilis)

This tree was discovered and sent by David Douglas in 1830. It grows from Washington just into California but mainly in Oregon and is known 84 m tall. In Argyll and Perthshire particularly, some are growing past the 50 m mark and it thrives in all but the most southerly Coniferous Areas. It is a distinct blue-grey from a distance as well as close to, so is a valuable tree to vary the coniferous landscape on a large scale. In the cool woods of Aberdeenshire and northwards, seedlings arise in quantity especially beside rotting stumps

and logs of other trees. It grows a stout bole rapidly although height growth is slower than in many conifers and is at best 1 m a year. The bark is smooth silvery-grey with a few dark fissures and the biggest trees have hard square scales or, in the open, often dark purple bark. The slender leaves, blue-grey on both sides, rise sharply from and hide the orange-brown, densely short-pubescent shoot. The leaves are flattened and grooved so will not roll between finger and thumb while those of the similar Red fir (p. 150) are more rounded, with a rib and can be rolled (they also spread widely, revealing the shoot). This makes a very shapely, conic, spired young tree anywhere except on chalky or dry soils and is quite good in exposure, spoiled only if it bears rows of the huge heavy cones when it is still young and the branches bearing them are blown out.

Noble fir

Abies veitchii Veitch's silver fir

This is one of those Japanese conifers with a short life. Few have lived to attain 22 m anywhere. The bole is unsightly with deep ribs and pockets but young trees are attractive and start away fast. The leaves are notched and their undersides are bright white. With the branch ends sweeping up in an elegant curve, this underside shows well with an effect like frost.

Araucaria araucana Monkey-puzzle; Chile Pine

Big Monkey-puzzles can be found in almost every county even though they are much more numerous in the western and northern Coniferous Areas. To rank among the big ones, a Monkey-puzzle has now to be 25 m tall and 90 cm through the bole at 1·5 m. Many in Devon, Wigtownshire, Argyll, Perthshire and County Wicklow especially, but not exclusively, are now bigger than that. The famous avenue to Bicton House in Devon, planted from 1843 seed, contains one 1·2 m through and another 28 m tall.

In very many gardens a single Monkey-puzzle or a pair is a prominent lawn-specimen. Their effect depends less on the unusually broad domed crown than on the rigidly straight, almost cylindrical bole arising from an elephant's foot and encased in tight, finely roughened or horizontally wrinkled bark, smoothly and shallowly fissured on the oldest stems and marked by whorls of branch scars. This therefore needs to be kept clear of ivy which grows strongly in western gardens and has plenty of light on a Monkey-puzzle bole when the lower crown has been shed. Young trees need the bottom 2 m cleared of branches even if they are to be grown with foliage to the ground. No crooked or sinuous Monkey-puzzle bole has yet been seen and only one, by some inexplicable accident, has managed to fork.

Very occasionally a tree is found with both male and female flowers and one is known at present, in Leicestershire. There is no way of telling until it flowers whether a tree is male or female, and some do not flower. Very broad-crowned trees have been noted to be female, but there are males equally broad. In 1967 the mean height and girth of all the trees in the Bicton Avenue were both, by a strange chance, precisely the same for all the males as a group and all the females. Trees of the two sexes need to be growing and flowering within 100 m or so for the seed to be fertile. When the two are adjacent 95 per cent germination may be expected, and up to 200 seeds in a cone.

Any soil suits the Monkey-puzzle and it withstands a good deal of exposure. Big trees are rarely seen blown down and in most cases these were probably dead already. Uniquely amongst conifers here, the Monkey-puzzle can take two years to grow from one whorl of shoots to the next, or it can make two whorls in three years, or the standard one whorl a year, so age cannot be determined by counting the whorls down the stem. A clump is sometimes seen crowning a knoll in open country and is an interesting feature. If the trees are planted fairly closely the interior lower crowns become shaded out and dead. Cleaning them out is quite a problem but it has been found that cattle will do this to 1·5 m or so by pushing around and scratching, and in the absence of cattle, the trees will suddenly clean themselves.

There are several Monkey-puzzle avenues, other than the one at Bicton, such as at Castle Kennedy, County Wigtown, where there is a short narrow one near the old Loch Inch Castle and an enormously broad 'grand avenue' with only a few trees now missing from the original 21 pairs. Many are 26 m tall and some are 95 cm in diameter, but they need to be taller yet to be in proportion as an avenue. The Bicton Avenue has long been very well-proportioned, being only half as wide, but there are patches of uneven growth and some recent losses are spoiling the symmetry.

Calocedrus decurrens Incense cedar (*Libocedrus d.*)

This cypress, related to *Thuja* and not a cedar at all, is the biggest of the erect, narrowly columnar conifers and some of the older trees are 35 m tall and still growing. It is not, however, always very narrow. In its native Oregon and California nearly all trees have open crowns of level branches unlike the tight columns growing in eastern England. In general the further west and north they are in Britain, the more open or loose the crown. In Ireland they are broad columnar and the branches are at a wide angle. In Scotland they tend to grow two or three heavy ascending branches. There are some very narrow ones as far west as Westonbirt, Gloucestershire, and the group there at 4 m spacing, planted in 1910 and now 25–27 m tall, is the classic example of the use of columnar trees in groups. The bright green scale-like foliage emits a strong scent of shoe-polish on the lightest handling. If the bole is cleaned of the dense erect shoots growing on the bottom 2–3 m, it shows rich purplish-brown long plates and is a fine sight although a single lawn-tree may be preferred clothed nearly to the ground. This is a good tree for a mark of emphasis and to vary the crown shapes in a group of conifers. It grows well on almost any soil, but on shallow, dry soils when about 26 m tall the crown begins to thin in patches until only some tufts near the top are green, and the tree finally dies.

'Variegata' may be worth having as a small tree when the blotches on the green foliage are bright yellow but they become dull and sparse, making a big tree look only diseased.

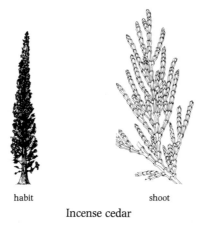

habit   shoot
Incense cedar

Cedrus atlantica var. glauca Blue Atlas cedar

The blue-grey form, found at its best in Algeria by Lord Somers in 1845, is the one to plant and selections have been made that are almost blue-white. The original tree is at Eastnor Castle in Herefordshire and 31 m × 1·4 m, a splendid specimen but some not quite so old are even bigger. It is not a tree to put in the centre bed of the rose-garden, for although the big plants usually sold deceive by growing very slowly for many years, it will eventually shade out the entire garden. This tree grows better in the warm, dry summers of the non-coniferous areas like East

Anglia, which makes it valuable in such places, and in any garden its cool blue foliage is a fine foil to the usual green leaves and the varied colours of flowers.

'Fastigiata' is a slender conic-columnar tree with fine branching, much too seldom planted. It will also grow on chalk and dry thin soils, like the type.

Blue Atlas cedar

'Aurea' is a superb but rarely seen cultivar, growing at less than half the speed of the Blue cedar. It is bright pale yellow or gold on the outer crown and blue-grey on the inner. This is a better tree than the Golden Cedar of Lebanon for general use.

Cedrus deodara Deodar

This tree from north-west Pakistan makes a fine young specimen and an imposing old specimen but is decidedly dull between the two stages. Young trees are attractively pendulous and usually glaucous grey. They grow fast, about 1 m a year, and become dark green, less markedly pendulous and rather twiggy. They are good at maintaining a single bole and a spire top and so make a shapely tree 35 m tall with a good bole, blackish with ashen-grey or silvery broken ridges, sometimes 1·5 m or more through. They grow equally well in the Coniferous Areas and in others, although seldom so tall in the east. A group planted not too closely, at 6 m or more, makes a fine little grove or roundel with good boles. A lawn specimen should have its bole cleared of branches for 1 m by the time it is 4 m tall and for 2·5 m before it is 10 m; the lower branches left will then bend down around a good bole, whereas without pruning the lower bole will be crowded with shaded-out dead twiggy branches and be unsightly, or may grow huge low branches and spoil the specimen.

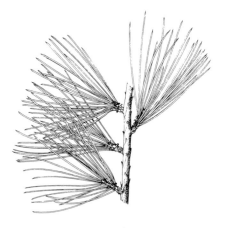

Deodar

Cedrus libani Cedar of Lebanon

The traditional hugely spreading cedar on the mansion lawn started as a slender, conic young tree with a thin open crown. It is not a good tree at that stage and should be planted only where a big open space demands a huge tree. The young tree grows very fast indeed and soon the branches thicken greatly and extend and the bole expands to support them. Most of the vast old trees were planted after 1810 and very few indeed date from before 1760. Growth is much better outside the cool Coniferous Areas and the finest trees are in the Midlands and south in a variety of soils from clay and chalk to light dry sand, but not where drainage is bad. The crown tends to be on five or six vertical boles and this is acceptable, but far too many old cedars are ruined by these boles starting from the ground; they have no true bole and are really giant bushes. Cedars with boles of 3 m or

more, on the other hand, are enormously impressive when this is 2 m through, but the secateurs need to be active in ensuring growth on a single bole. A few Cedars of Lebanon grow in beechwoods or wooded ravines and more should be grown in this way as they can make grand trees with very long boles and a narrow crown more like a larch.

'Aurea' Golden Cedar of Lebanon This is usually very slow and not very brightly coloured but may, on a good damp site, grow fairly fast into a spreading tree little more than tinged with gold except in spring when the new growth is brighter. Unless a big tree is required, the Golden Atlas cedar is to be preferred every time.

Chamaecyparis lawsoniana Lawson cypress

As the commonest and the most gloomy conifer throughout these islands, this would merit no mention were it not also one of the most remarkable of all trees for its unceasing production of irreplaceable cultivars and its almost total adaptability. The species grows wild in now scattered patches in the Siskiyou Mountains each side of the Oregon–California boundary where it is a very tall and rather uniform sea-green tree. It was first sent here in 1854 and by 1855 had thrown up a bright deep green, very erect form, 'Erecta Viridis', never seen in its home woods. Soon after that, more forms began and at an ever-increasing rate the most varied and bizarre forms poured out of British, Dutch and French nurseries. They are all as tough as the type and provide conifers of almost every possible colour, shape, and size, so they are indispensable in garden design. Although few of the western trees in the USA can be grown in the eastern states, Lawson cypress can, and so cultivars of this American tree have been sent back there from Britain and Holland. The 'ordinary' Lawson here is, unlike those in the wild, very dark green, but the seed so prolifically yielded by these trees gives plants of a great mixture of blue-greens and paler greens. None is, normally, sufficiently distinctive to be named, and hedges and lines grown as plain Lawson cypress vary from plant to plant.

The type tree is usually much forked, grows heavy low branches when in the open and is not very windfirm. As a single specimen numerous other conifers are greatly superior. Nor should this ever be planted in an avenue as it makes a gloomy tunnel between irregular, poorly shaped trees.

'Allumii' A common form arising in 1880, this is blue-grey and erect, neatly conic when young, bushing out at the base with age. Good for small formal plantings but in time likely to attain 25 m.

'Columnaris' This arose in Holland in 1950 and makes a slender column, conic at the top, growing 1 m every three years so far and pale blue-grey. Excellent in a formal group or as a spot plant but in view of growth, not on a small scale.

'Ellwoodii'. A common small plant but always growing, and one is 11 m tall after 30 years so caution is advised. It forms a narrow but multiple column, very tight at the base, with adult outer foliage, grey-green.

'Fletcheri'. A common plant to 10 m. medium-narrow multiple column to slender conic tips, this has juvenile fluffy foliage dark grey-blue. A good spot plant in a large rock-garden or in a short line.

Fletcher's cypress

'Green Pillar' and 'Green Spire' are very similar forms with stout silvery boles and tight, stiff, very erect branches so far seen only small; light or bright green foliage; very formal and attractive.

'Intertexta'. Lawson's Nursery found this elegant form among plants raised there from an early import of seed. It forms a slender, tall crown with closely hanging foliage of curiously open, remotely twigged sprays. Although an undistinguished dull green, both the tree and the foliage are attractive, and it is among the best of the tall cypresses to give variety of form in a group. It should, however, be watched for a tendency to divide into two or three stems. This must be dealt with by singling as soon as it is found, or the tree will not only lose much of its spire-like form but become highly vulnerable to breakage in a storm.

Intertexta cypress

'Lane's Golden'. Arising in Berkhamsted in 1938 this is one of the brightest and neatest of the golden forms, free with red male flowers; conic in crown.

'Lutea'. An early gold form, from 1873, and as bright as any. Narrowly columnar and rather pendulous outer crown. Ideal for mixed eye-catcher groups with blue and green forms.

'New Silver'. Unaccountably rare, this is a very tight fusiform plant with nodding shoot-tips bright silvery blue. Outstanding as a single specimen on a small scale.

'Pembury Blue'. Often bushy to start with, this can make a tree and is a unique powdery bright blue-grey, quite distinct from all the other blue-grey cypresses.

'Pottenii'. A nursery in Cranbrook, Kent, raised this seedling in 1900. It has pale green feathery foliage arching out minutely from numerous erect stems; less often from erect branches on a single bole. It makes a fusiform crown useful in small-scale formal plantings like short lines, avenues, false-perspectives and eye-catchers, looking neat and bright. It goes on growing steadily, if rather slowly, and is 12 m tall in several gardens. It therefore outgrows in time a truly small-scale planting. Its upper branches are prone to being bent out by snow, in which case they will not return but must be cut out. A 15 cm mesh net tied round the upper crown makes the foliage bush out and cover the net neatly as if the tree had been clipped.

Potten cypress

'Stewartii'. This is a conic, sturdy golden form peculiarly decorative in the way it holds its fern-like sprays of rich yellow from a bright green interior. Easily recognizable from all the other golds by these layers of long shoots.

'Triumph of Boskoop'. A relatively old form deservedly holding its place for strong, single-stemmed growth and conic crown of bright blue-grey foliage. The most vigorous of the coloured Lawsons and already to 26 m.

'Westermannii'. For some years this grows as an elegantly pendulous broad bush with the hanging new shoots pale lemon and the leaves lemon and

green in a most attractive manner. It goes on to make a broad columnar or conic tree and may grow fast, reaching 17 m in 70 years, with a big bole.

'Wisselii'. A form as remarkable for its growth as for its foliage. It has dense tufts of thickened upright shoots, dark blue much marked with white and covered in spring with pale crimson flowers. Newly struck cuttings look as if they will be dwarf trees for a few years but when put on a small rock-garden they go away at speed and are soon 20 m tall. One in Devon is 73 years old, 29 m tall and 1·2 m through the bole. A good, unusual, columnar, turreted specimen for where there is room for a tall tree.

Wissel's cypress

Chamaecyparis nootkatensis Nootka cypress; Yellow cypress

This sad-looking, dull, dark-foliaged tree has two strong points. It is imperturbably tough and hardy, as it should be, growing north into Alaska from Oregon, and it has at all times and in all places, a crown which is a perfect cone. In the west of Ireland this is enormously broad and obtuse-tipped, and eastwards it is progressively narrower until in East Anglia it is quite slender and very acute. A close group of these dunces' hats is good. Growth is steady but seldom more than moderate in speed and as a single specimen tree it has a place in a garden of moderate size.

'Pendula'. This is for many years a narrowly conic tree with small branches in wide U-shapes dangling the foliage in thin curtains, soon strung with navy-blue 1 cm cones. It is a good plant until it ages into a broad conic open crown with the hanging shoots too thinly spread to look healthy, but some trees age in better shape.

Chamaecyparis obtusa Hinoki cypress

This Japanese tree needs a high rainfall and unless in a damp clay hollow it is happy only in the Coniferous Areas where it makes a broad conic crown to 24 m tall. The bole is straight with furrowed rich red-brown bark and small level branches. The foliage is brilliant shiny rich green, tiny obtuse scales with fine white marks on the underside. In a humid area the good bark and bole with the shapely bright green crown make this an effective foliage-tree of moderate size and growth.

'Crippsii'. This great improvement on the old Japanese form, 'Aurea', was raised in Tunbridge Wells in 1900 and is, when grown in full sun, as bright gold as any conifer. With such a colourful tree there is no great call for rapid growth and this form grows adequately in all parts on an acid or neutral soil. For some years it is loosely conic with nodding shoots, then it grows into a broad cone and old trees are over 15 m tall. A wonderful plant to group in front of a large Blue Atlas cedar.

'Tetragona Aurea'. The green form of this was imported first and cannot now be found. This golden form grown in shade is green but tinged with yellow, and it should be given full light. The shoots are fine, dense and square (strictly, tetragonal) in section and when the outer ones are intense gold the inner are brilliant green. From a loosely columnar growth this ages to a broad, many-topped column of highly distinctive aspect and is a great adornment in the front rank of a group of small conifers.

Chamaecyparis pisifera Sawara cypress

The type tree is much less seen than many of the cultivars and has foliage so unlike them that it is often unrecognized as such. It has flat sprays of tiny bright green sharply-pointed scales, brightly silver beneath in tiny marks, on straight level branches from a bole with long-ridged brown bark. It becomes thin usually before it achieves 20 m but in Coniferous Areas it may be broad-conic and well furnished to 24 m. Except as another species in a collection there is no call to plant it.

'Aurea'. This is far superior to the above and makes an attractive small tree because the new growth is bright yellow and does not fade completely before the next crop is out. Older trees are a little thin but passably attractive.

'Squarrosa'. For those who like fuzzy blue trees none is better than 'Squarrosa' and it is a pleasant variation among other trees. The soft 5 mm leaves are pale green above but broadly banded grey-blue beneath, and standing out at all angles in angular dense sprays they give a very blue fluffy appearance to the crown. The bark is bright red-brown and the crown broad-conic to rounded, sometimes 26 m tall.

Cryptomeria japonica Japanese red cedar

This is really a redwood related to the Sequoias and is the chief timber tree of Japan. It will grow in any district and often very fast when young, but sustained growth to heights over 30 m and huge boles 1·5 m through is restricted to the Coniferous Areas of cool damp summers. The bright, often yellowish-green of the hard, sharp in-curved, long-pointed scale-leaves and the fine chestnut-red stripping bole make this a good single specimen tree where it grows well and an excellent tree for clumps or small groves to show good boles, but elsewhere it is apt to be thin in the crown and not attractive. Young trees are narrow and gaunt. The Chinese form came first, in 1842, and many of the oldest trees are identifiable as Chinese by their loose, hanging foliage while the

Japanese form, planted after 1861, has shorter foliage in denser bunches and the form 'Lobbii' is all dense bunches, even shorter foliage, but equally a tree to 35 m tall.

Japanese red cedar

'Elegans'. This fuzzy pale green foliaged form, dark purplish-red in winter, starts as an upright bush but sprawls around hopelessly or droops great branches everywhere. The bark is bright orange-red but that does not make up for its poor shape. The leaves are 2 cm long and spread, often curved from twisting green shoots.

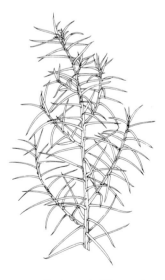

Crytomeria 'Elegans'

Cunninghamia lanceolata Chinese fir

This is a Redwood looking somewhat like a Monkey-puzzle, and is very hardy although little planted except in western gardens. Its very bright green leaves, to 7 cm, tapering to a long sharp point, hard and curved, have two silver bands beneath. The foliage dies red-brown and many are retained on the tree when dead, adding to the crown and stopping it from being thin. It has a good straight, long-ridged bole, warm red-brown, and level branches carrying a columnar crown domed at the top. It may be necessary to clear the crown of competing stems and low branches to make a splendid, unusual specimen.

X Cupressocyparis leylandii Leyland cypress

The first two occurrences of the hybrid between Monterey and Nootka cypresses were separated by 23 years but both were at Leighton Hall, Powys, in 1888 and 1911 respectively. It was another 29 years before the third occured, at Ferndown in Dorest. For some years now this tree has been extensively planted as a hedge, screen, background and specimen, and demand is still insatiable. It is thus unnecessary to recommend it at length for general coniferous evergreenery, on any soil not actually waterlogged, but a few details and particular uses of the several cultivars are justified. As a spot-tree all the cultivars are about of equal value for making a slightly fusiform, variably slender column at 1 m per year for 20 years and 2 m every three years thereafter to, it must be assumed, around 40 m. The usual forms, 'Leighton Green' and 'Haggerston Grey', develop numerous strong vertical branches all stopping 2 m short of the very dominant, if rather wavy, slender leading shoot. For hedges and single specimens, 'Leighton Green' is indistinguishable from the better of the two Stapehill trees, grown as '21', and these two are much the best of all the cultivars with their long fern-like sprays and more vigorous growth in the diameter of bole. 'Naylor's Blue' makes a fine unusual specimen slightly less rapidly. The golden forms are the most vigorous trees of this colour yet available.

'Castlewellan'. Seed parent Golden Monterey cypress, 1970. This has the plumose foliage sprays of the common 'Haggerston Grey' with new growth bright yellow. It may fade to yellow-green which makes the next year's new shoots speckle the crown distinctively, but some trees in some years remain a good yellow through the winter. So far, in the official trial, 'Castlewellan' is keeping pace with the green forms.

'Golconda'. A branch-sport of 'Haggerston Grey' and the brightest gold of any.

'Haggerston Grey'. Seed parent Nootka cypress, 1888. Still easily the most numerous, this has plumose sprays of slender, rather distant finest shoots, dark blue-green or dark green with a grey tinge. It flowers or cones very rarely, unlike 'Leighton Green' and the Stapehill trees.

'Leighton Green'. Seed parent Monterey cypress, 1911. The second most frequent of the earlier plantings and the best for hedges and single specimens, this grows a slightly broader crown in the open than others but in light woodland shade it is remarkably slender. The foliage is in long, flattened sprays of regularly alternate flat systems of thicker, denser, ultimate shoots than in 'Haggerston Grey' and a brighter green. Small golden male flowers are common in some years and most trees bear numerous cones.

'Naylors Blue'. Seed parent Monterey cypress, 1911, same seeds as 'Leighton Green'. This is a more slender tree with plumose foliage, fine and grey-blue.

'Robinson's Gold'. Seedling found among rhododendrons in Belvoir Park near Belfast, 1975. The foliage is of the pinnate 'Leighton Green' form and bright yellow, often appearing brighter and more lasting than in 'Castlewellan' but some trees do fade. It seems to be at least as vigorous as others.

'Stapehill 20'. Seed parent Monterey cypress, 1940. This is easily distinguished by its crown being internally open and holding old brown foliage; also by the very rough foliage in the pinnate layout, the base of each minor spray partly missing as if chewed away. This form suffered much more than others in the 1976 drought and is now largely replaced by '21'.

'Stapehill 21'. Seed parent as for '20', the sister tree. This is awaiting a name to distinguish it better from '20' and is with 'Leighton Green' the most vigorous in a full trial. It can be distinguished from 'Leighton Green' only by the foliage being harsh above. Both flower and cone freely.

The vigour and regular crowns of Leyland cypresses suit them to planting in short avenues; a long one could be dull. As in any avenue of a dark conifer, the trees must be planted or thinned so that the space between the crowns is equal to the width of each crown, to give light and form. No evergreen is better for a really tall hedge than the Leyland cypress, and the only problem is the practical one of ladders or raised platforms from which to clip it.

Cupressus glabra Smooth Arizona cypress
(*C. arizonica* var. *bonita*)

This must be about the most useful of all conifers, other than Lawson cypress, in garden planting. It is utterly hardy; it grows on limestone or extremely acid sand; it is resistant to drought; it always has a neat crown, ovoid-conic, of a lovely smoky blue-grey, and it maintains moderate growth. Male flowers spend the winter decorating the blue-grey foliage with dense patches of golden specks, and the bark is a fine dark purple-red rolling off to leave pale yellow smooth areas. It has no known faults and can be used for a large informal hedge or background of blue.

'Pyramidalis' is even better, with foliage densely speckled white and slightly thicker sprays erect around the crown.

Cupressus macrocarpa Monterey cypress

This is one of the Monterey trees which vastly prefers the damp climate of western Britain to the long dry summers of Monterey, and grows enormously faster and bigger here than on its

American homeland cliffs in California. There are more Monterey cypresses in most Devon parishes than in the two small headlands of native trees put together and it is widely grown throughout the British Isles. It is exceptionally useful in wind-swept coastal areas for rapidly providing high shelter and green background even though the trees are mostly rough, heavily-branched and liable to be broken or blown down in severe exposure. In eastern parts it is much less branchy, narrower in the crown, seldom killed by freezing winds, less often blown down and, as a single specimen, likely to be a shapely tree of moderately rapid growth. In the west, given a large space, it will grow very fast indeed with great branches spreading widely. In western Ireland the shoots on young trees spread at a low angle and the crown is as broad as it is high despite upward growth of well over 1 m a year. Superb specimens are produced if the lower bole is kept clear of branches. If only the enormous tree at Montacute House, Somerset, had been pruned earlier, it would be even better than it is now, with big scars to heal from late pruning of the 2·4 m diameter bole. The Monterey cypress grows best on light sandy but damp soil which is acid, but it will also grow on almost any soil including one with some lime. It will not succeed in or very near towns and cities.

'Lutea'. This cultivar is a broad bun in western Ireland but columnar in England, less vigorous than the type. The foliage is yellow, often bright, and in some places it has been better than the type in resistance to salt-laden winds. It is often too twiggy and untidy below to compete as a specimen with some other golden conifers, and needs watching in youth or it may grow several stems and become a bush.

'Donard Gold' is a recent (1942) improvement on 'Lutea', being a brighter yellow and a shapely tree.

Cupressus sempervirens Italian cypress

The narrowly conic form is the most usual one here, as it is in the Levant, and it comes true from seed. Many people return from Corfu or Israel with a few big cones. While some of these turn out to be from Arizona or Monterey cypresses which are frequently grown in those parts too, seed extracted from others by putting the cones briefly in a warm oven will usually yield fine slender fastigiate plants. Within two years they are 1 m tall and soon grow nearly 1 m a year. Long ago this tree was regarded as tender, but quite big trees in East Lothian and other cold places have been unaffected by very severe winters, and the 20 m trees in some Sussex gardens have shown no signs of frosting. Seedlings can be burned back 30 cm or so in their first few years and will make a new leader, with a little judicious help from secateurs. They make fine trees to place at each end of a group of shrubs or as a tight group. They can also be temporary features among small shrubs or semi-dwarf conifers.

Fitzroya cupressoides Alerce; Fitzroya
(*F. patagonica*)

Named from Admiral Fitzroya who commanded *The Beagle* on which Charles Darwin sailed, this little tree is like a Juniper but has hanging dark blue and white foliage. The little 3 mm leaves curve out their thick blunt tips, dark blue-green with two prominent white stripes on each surface. The crown is vase-shaped, branching low from the bole and arching out. On damp, acid soil in shelter it is a pleasant and unusual foliage-tree of rather slow growth, best in the Coniferous Areas and a little tender when very young.

Juniperus chinensis 'Aurea' Golden Chinese juniper

Few junipers are worth-while trees although there are a host of excellent dwarf forms. The Chinese juniper itself has no merit but this golden form is useful in towns and perhaps elsewhere. It slowly grows into a column, often multiple-topped, on any soil, acid or limy, sandy or clay, and retains its foliage to the base. The gold is added to by copious male flowers, present from autumn until pollinating in early spring. It has mixed juvenile, prickly spreading leaves with adult close smooth scales on the inner parts of each shoot juvenile.

Juniperus deppeana var. pachyphloea
Alligator juniper

One of these delightful trees has survived for over 50 years at the National Pinetum at Bedgebury in Kent. It has reached only 8 m but its bole has the beautiful checkered brown bark that is the tree's outstanding feature together with soft blue fine foliage. Since the Smooth Arizona cypress, which grows alongside it in Oak Creek Canyon south of Flagstaff, Arizona, grows everywhere in Britain, the Alligator juniper may be quite as adaptable. It is worth trying in the warmest and driest places. In a gulch at about 2000 m, above Jerome in Arizona, one with a bole 1·5 m through has just the same rich brown bark, shiny and in little square blocks.

Juniperus drupacea Syrian juniper

This has the best foliage of any juniper and is the only one with sufficient character to make a good single specimen tree. It grows well on any soil and probably prefers limestone. The best, on a Hertfordshire golf-course, is 19 m tall and exceedingly narrow, as are most of the taller trees,

Syrian juniper

although a few are broad-columnar. The leaves are in dense whorls of three on short, twisting shoots from the erect small branches and are 2·5 cm long, rigid, spined, bright fresh green above with two white bands beneath.

Juniperus recurva var. coxii. Cox's juniper:
Coffin juniper

This tree from Upper Burma is more vigorous and attractive than the type, the Drooping juniper. It has orange-brown bark hanging in loose strips as it ages, bright green long-pendulous shoots, and strong low branches arching to make a vase-shaped crown. The leaves, in whorls of three, are well spaced on the slender green shoot, 1 cm long, fresh bright green above, banded greenish-white beneath. Few trees are yet more than 40 years old and some are 14 m tall which, in a juniper, passes for vigour. The interior crown retains dead orange-brown shoots and with the bright green hanging outer shoots this is a good small specimen tree.

Juniperus squamata 'Meyeri' Meyer's juniper

Frank Meyer found this fine plant in a Chinese garden in 1910 and it is one of the bluest of all conifer foliages. It grows unexpectedly fast for a Juniper and is soon 6–8 m tall and a strange shape, with up-curved spires from a crown which spreads low. Young trees are conic and steely-blue and will need replacing in a small feature after some years but as the tree grows easily from cuttings this is readily done. Like other junipers it grows well on any soil, however poor, dry or chalky and is a very tough and useful plant.

Meyer's juniper

Juniperus wallichiana Wallich's juniper

This little Himalayan juniper makes a delightful small specimen tree in any garden. The oldest seen, about 60 years old, are still beautifully narrow, densely branched trees now 13 m tall. Young trees are the same neat shape and the dense foliage is brightened by bunches of juvenile deep green leaves showing mostly their silvered undersides. The adult scale-leaves are dark grey with white edges and the berry-like fruit ripen black.

Larix decidua European larch (*L. europaea*)

No garden tree can have more numerous desirable features, yet neither this larch nor any other is as commonly planted in gardens as many conifers.

European larch

It makes a fine specimen tree with very rapid early growth; it bears pink flowers in quantity at no great age and very early in spring it leafs out before most trees, a striking bright fresh green; it attracts for feeding and nesting many birds especially redpolls, crossbills, goldfinches, blue-, coal- and great-tits, goldcrests and, when older and in groups, birds of prey; it colours gloriously and late in the autumn, and its shade and leaf-fall suit the growth of bluebells and the good oakwood flora as well as other bulbs. It is a fine background tree in any situation and on any soil. It is very windfirm and good in exposure. Even above 600 m altitude in Aberdeenshire it can be 35 m tall. It is very easily cleaned up the bole for 3 m by the time it is ten years old and 10 m tall and then quickly makes a smooth handsome bole. A larch grove is among the most delightful forms of woodland both to walk in and to see from a distance.

To be the fast-growing, shapely tree it should be, a Larch must be planted when two or, at the most, three years old and 1 m tall; better still, provided it is looked after, is to plant a one-year seedling which can be 30 cm tall. On light poor soils larches respond strongly to fertilizer, especially nitrate in the spring, and young trees should not be allowed to be dry.

Larix × eurolepis Hybrid larch

This tree had the misfortune to be named in Latin from its parents, both of whose names have since been changed. In 1919 the European larch was *L. europaea* and the Japanese was *L. leptolepis*, hence 'eurolepis'. As a garden tree it has the same qualities as the European larch except that on the poorest and most difficult sites it is more vigorous, and it usually bears more cones from an even earlier age. Trees when planted as two-year-olds can grow leading shoots 1·3 m long two years later with leaves to 8 cm long. The main differences from the European larch are the variably pale orange shoots, broader leaves with two broad pale grey bands beneath, and tall cones with the edges of the scales curved outwards.

Hybrid larch

Larix kaempferi Japanese larch

This differs from the European in its sturdier, more branched, often broader crown; dark orange or purple shoots; broader leaves of a less bright green, pale-banded beneath; cream and red flowers, and more squat cones with the scales curved out and over. As a garden tree it casts more shade and a heavier leaf-fall so is much less useful as an overstorey of high shade. On poor soils and especially on peats it grows faster and makes a stouter bole. It may never reach the heights of the best European larches, which are over 42 m, but since it has been grown only this century and not many are specimens in good garden soils it is too soon to be sure.

Metasequoia glyptostroboides Metasequoia; Dawn redwood

This deciduous Redwood was a sensational discovery because it is a familiar and very widespread fossil in rocks 200 million years old and there was no reason to assume that it was still with us. It was found in central China in 1941 but not described and published, or generally known, until 1944. With the traditional largesse of the Arnold Arboretum in Boston every major garden could be planting one or more in 1949 from seed received in January 1948. Nearly all the great gardens in Britain did so and in the warmer southerly areas, and also in north Wales, growth has been vigorous and not only sustained – in diameter of bole it has steadily increased. Growth in height was usually at least 1 m a year but has declined with age and the tallest in Britain are 26–31 m when 43 years old, and up to 1 m in diameter, still adding 3 cm a year. On Long Island, New York, one was 1 m in diameter when 25 years old and is now over 1.6 m. In Britain it seems to like warm summers as most of the biggest trees are in Cambridge, Kent, Sussex and Surrey. Ready access to water must also be important because these are all by lake or riversides or in woodlands with springs or wet hollows. In high rainfall areas there is less need for such receiving sites but cooler summers restrict growth and the tree is not always very succesful in Cornwall, and is rarely vigorous in Scotland.

Metasequoia in any but the lightest high shade grows a thin crown although it can be just as tall as in the open. It does need side-shelter however and it is the trees well tucked away that have gone ahead in height whereas those on wide, open lawns slowed markedly once above 9 m or so. Despite the poor appearance in winter, this is a good specimen tree as it is early into leaf and keeps its foliage late into autumn, when it is pink, deep red or red-brown. Through the summer it is fresh green, markedly darker and greyer than the finer, densely-twigged foliage of the Swamp cypress. Metasequoia is the only surviving Redwood with an opposite and decussate arrangement of foliage and branching. A young tree with a long violet-pink leading shoot holds out the level side-shoots in pairs each at right angles to the one above and below.

Metasequoias should always be planted when young and small. It is normal to raise these by cuttings, either softwood in June/July or hardwood in March. The original seed of 1948 was the only seed available until 1980, and between those years metasequoias could be raised only from cuttings. Planted when 20–30 cm tall they need no stake and grow fast. Bigger trees check badly and need to be staked.

Picea abies Norway spruce

Among the first conifers to be introduced, this is very common but not inspiring. In a broad coniferous landscape it can be a background tree used in moderation but it becomes progressively less attractive with age and is not very windfirm. Many are seen grown on from Christmas trees and most of them are absurdly planted in a shady corner or a tiny suburban garden. Properly placed they will grow 1 m a year and are quite a bright green but of coarse growth.

Picea brachytyla Sargent spruce

This spruce was sent from western China in 1901 and three or four times in the next decade. There are several forms from the different seed-lots. The best is a very fine and vigorous tree with an open crown of slender branches on a pale grey bole and perhaps the most beautiful foliage of all the spruces. The leaves are abruptly spine-tipped, hard and pressed forward over the white shoot; they are bright light green above while beneath they are so solidly silver-white that the normally green midrib between the two white bands is silvered right across. The shoots are pendulous from strongly ascending branches on old trees. The Sargent spruce needs an acid soil preferably light but moist, and sheltered woodland surroundings, to make a very good specimen.

Picea brewerana Brewer spruce

Confined in the wild to a few small groves perched at around 2000 m on shelves in the Siskiyou Mountains straddling the Oregon-California boundary, the Brewer spruce is a much sought after lawn-specimen. It is, when well-grown and not in shade (where it is a poor, depressed-looking tree) a remarkable sight, broad-columnar with up-curved branches from which hang long curtains of dark foliage. It does need patience, however. Seedling trees should be grown, and for ten years at least they are thinly foliaged, uninteresting little trees of negligible growth, and maybe 1·5 m tall. By the fifteenth year they may have enough stature to have room to weep. After this, the rate of growth increases and now the trees 60 years old in some gardens are 18–19 m tall and rapidly expanding big boles, whereas in 1950 there was not one more than 14 m tall. Attempts to shorten the period of waiting by grafting already weeping shoots on

seedling Norway spruce are ill-advised. Trees cannot weep effectively when so near the ground, and the growth of grafted shoots does not make a symmetrical head but a leaning, slow, one-sided plant of no beauty. Brewer spruces are superb in some gardens over chalk but do need a damp soil and some side-shelter for their best growth; given this, they thrive anywhere except in a city park where they will grow but are thin and hence ineffective.

Picea jezoensis var. hondoensis Hondo spruce

The Japanese variety of *P. jezoensis* is the hardy sturdy tree grown in many collections and gardens. Although found mainly in the Coniferous Areas this tree is not confined to them and some of the biggest were, before 1987, in Sussex and Kent. Most of the big conifer gardens in Perthshire in particular have a good specimen. It is a broadly conic tree and its outstanding feature is its bold foliage. The stout shoots are white turning cream and the 1.5 cm leaves are densely set each side above the shoot, none below. They are deep or bright shining green above and broadly banded bright slightly bluish-white beneath. This white flashes out as the shoots move to show the close ranks of leaf-undersides.

Picea likiangensis Likiang spruce

This, like the Sargent spruce, was sent from several different areas of western China in differing forms from 1910 to 1930. The best form is the most frequent and many of the major gardens have several specimens. The Likiang spruce is the one on which the masses of crimson male flowers and bright red females among the dark blue-grey foliage surprise the crowds at the National Pinetum at Bedgebury in Kent. A group of trees stands by a stream below the entrance and in mid-May such a floral spectacle excites comment in those who do not expect conifers to be colourful. The crown is very open on strong branches at a low angle, from a bole with pale grey bark with a few black fissures. The foliage is dense on the outside of the crown in a fringe; grey pubescent

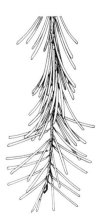

Brewer spruce

shoots with flattened leaves blue-grey above and white-banded beneath. After a slow start as a spindly plant this grows a good bole and several trees are now 23 m × 60 cm. It needs acid, moist soil, but does not mind if limestone is underlying it well below.

Picea omorika Serbian spruce

One of the most useful and decorative of the conifers, this tree grows fast on any soil from limestone to deep peat. It varies somewhat in the degree of slenderness of the crown but is always narrow-spired, and compact. A few are densely short-branched and cylindric thin columns; most are conic and some are fairly open with fine branches, depressed then sweeping up in a curve. The flat leaves are rich deep green above and broadly banded bright blue-white beneath. It is a striking specimen on its own on a moderate scale, as can be seen in the Savill Garden at Windsor, or in a group of three. The tallest are now over 30 m tall yet no more than about 4 m through the crown. It is one of the best conifers in a town, casting little shade and coping with poor soils. The many merits of Serbian spruce make it the more sad that it is often to be seen dead or dying. In many collections, trees that were 20 m tall and rather thin in 1970 are found dead in 1981 or

have already died and been removed. It is known to be highly susceptible to Honey-fungus, which is inevitably present in all woodland areas, but from which there is little risk in long-established gardens in towns. In the country it is a normal hazard, sometimes killing young plants but mostly held at bay until the tree is weakened by old age.

Picea orientalis Oriental spruce

This tree from the Caucasus region is much to be preferred to the Norway spruce even as a Christmas tree. It has more slender shoots arranged most symmetrically in a spire of whorls of decreasing length and the leaves are shorter and held much closer, not snagging the loops when the decorations are put on. As a specimen tree it is as vigorous as the Norway spruce and more tidy with tiny bevel-tipped dark glossy leaves. It is still a neat, conic tree when 30 m tall but by then it is growing very slowly and has a tendency to die back at the top.

Oriental spruce

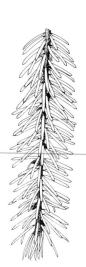

Serbian spruce

'Aurea'. In the summer this can be distinguished only by the odd leaf retaining some yellow, but in May it is superb. The slender new shoots pour out bright gold all over the dense, dark and shapely crown.

Picea pungens f. glauca Blue Colorado spruce

This 'forma' of the Colorado spruce derives from one tree selected from the wild, where the trees vary from dark green to bluish, and grown in a garden at Harvard, Massachusetts. Shoots were brought by Anthony Waterer to his nursery at Knaphill in 1877. It makes quite a robust, fairly narrow conic tree with level branches and rigid upstanding leaves blue-grey on both sides on stout orange or brown shoots. It is very hardy and withstands heat and drought but outside cool damp regions it loses its decorative value with age. It sheds leaves when they are only two years old and so becomes twiggy and thin, often due to a profusion of Green spruce aphid. In more favourable sites it grows well-furnished and highly attractive, to 23 m or more, and is a very good specimen tree. Elsewhere it is fine for small-scale plantings where it can be removed when it outgrows other small trees, at about which time it will be starting to deteriorate.

'Hoopesii'. This is so startlingly blue-white that it must be mentioned although seen so far mostly in the USA where some are bushy conic trees to 3 m and may qualify as trees one day. It is now available in Britain.

'Koster'. This is the most frequently seen form and is a mixture of several. The shoots are purple, brown or orange and the leaves brighter blue-white than in *f. glauca* although not as strikingly so as 'Hoopesii'. It grows in the same manner as *f. glauca* in the different regions but more slowly, and few are yet 20 m tall.

Picea sitchensis Sitka spruce

This native of the North American West Coast, from Alaska to California, is the standard species for maximum timber production in all western mountainous areas of run-down peaty soils, and no other conifer has ever been found to challenge it. The wavy leading shoots can be seen 1·5 m long and whole hillsides of 1 m leaders project from hitherto barren slopes swept by sea-winds. Obviously the tree has great value for shelter in some exposed places where other trees are hard to grow. It is, however, a tree strictly for the wet western and northern areas; anywhere else it will be thin and poor except in an occasional spring-fed dell. From Devon to Sutherland by way of Perth and Aberdeen there are occasional monster Sitkas towering to 45 or 50 m with boles 2 m through and growing fast. In Somerset one is 43 m × 1 m in 45 years' growth. For a monumental specimen tree of great height, keeping a conic top and windfirm, only the Sequoias are in the same class. As a young tree shooting upwards it is a little open and gawky at the top but the lower crown is better covered and the dark blue foliage, bright white beneath, is attractive.

In the specified areas, a large garden should make room for a specimen somewhere, probably around the edge. In extensive gardens and parks a small group will be a feature. In the Scone Palace Pinetum near Perth a square of four was planted in 1851 with a side of about 30 m. Now 45 m tall and 1·9 m through almost uniformly, they are a stirring sight. The foolish prejudice against this tree should be forgotten. Forests of Sitka spruce thrive where few trees will grow, bursting with promise. Any tree in full vigour growing more than 1 m every year is pleasing to see, even were the foliage not as lovely as that of the soft dark-blue Sitka. How fortunate that the Sitka spruce produces timber so fast and that our forests, more productive than any others in the world on their latitudes, look so well in the process.

Picea smithiana Morinda spruce

This tree from the western Himalayas could be regarded as a giant Brewer spruce, although weeping in a much less exaggerated way when young. The foliage differs from that of the flat-leafed Brewer spruce in that the long leaves are nearly square in cross-section. These spread all round stout shoots and, with the vigorous early growth, make it a superior specimen to the Brewer for at least twenty years. It starts well even in the drier warmer eastern parts, given a damp woodland soil, but in these areas it may achieve 28 m then become thin in the struggle to stay alive and slowly die. In the Coniferous Areas it remains well furnished, weeping more with age, and several trees from the New Forest to Easter Ross are 37 m or more tall.

Morinda spruce

Pinus ayacahuite Mexican white pine

This five-needled pine is one of the trees that was introduced by Theodor Hartweg on his first tour of Mexico in 1839-1840. As a foliage pine with blue needles it is not as good as its close relative, the Bhutan pine (p. 175) or its hybrid with that species, the Holford pine (p. 169) but is worth growing for its cones. These are freely borne from an age of about 20, on stout 2 cm stalks, and are long, tapering almost from the base to a narrow apex, heavy, firm and leathery, becoming woody. For a year they are bright blue-green turning to pale orange and much daubed with resin. A few trees bear cones only 15 cm long but 25–30 cm is more usual and 40 cm may be seen. The scales around the stalk are strongly reflexed, as are all the scales in some of the bigger cones; but more usually the remainder are straight, pointing somewhat outwards.

The tree grows very vigorously for many years on acid soils in good drainage, with a conic crown broad at the base in the first 30 years and long, level but sinuous branches. In older trees these may be shed and the upper crown can be a shapely, narrow and dense cone to over 25 m tall.

On less acid loam or clay, the growth rate falls earlier and the life-span is shorter. In either case a measure of shelter is of great benefit. The shoot is pale brownish-green thinly covered with fine pale pubescence and is more slender than the stout, blue-white bloomed, glabrous shoot of the Bhutan pine. The needles are shorter, about 15 cm.

Pinus bungeana Lacebark pine

'Lacebark' is not a good description of this tree at any stage but at least it calls attention to the feature for which it is grown. Mottled by pale patches from shed scales almost from the start, the bark becomes more colourful with age until a clean bole 30 cm through has a smooth background of blue-grey or pink, and where a scale has been shed will be a patch of yellow, brown, red-brown or dark purple-red. The crown has many nearly erect straight slender branches and may be an ovoid, pointed bush or variously conic. The foliage is good; rich dark shiny green leaves in threes, sparsely borne but each bundle closely held together on smooth olive or grey-green shoots with short, curved lateral shoots spreading perpendicularly.

This pine from northern and central China grows rather slowly but is very hardy and not fussy about its soil, given good drainage. It is so attractive and unusual that it is an ornament to any group of small trees or large shrubs.

Pinus cembra Arolla pine

An alternative name for this is 'Swiss stone pine', merely adding to the popular confusion that already surrounds the true Stone pine. As hardy as any tree, the Arolla pine is a snow-line tree in the Alps and planted to control avalanches. It will grow at only about 30 cm a year but over a long period of time, and can be 28 m tall and still have a conic top to its neatly columnar crown with short, level branches. The leaves are in bundles of five, densely covering the thickly hairy orange-brown shoot. Blackish from a distance, the needles are dark shiny green on the outer surfaces and blue-white on the inner. The cones are deep blue, squat cylindric, 8×6 cm, and near the top of the tree which has to be some 40 years old to fruit, if it will at all. The cones are shed when still unopened so may be found in good condition before rodents eat the seeds out. When this happens the seedless cones are curious and attractive, each seed leaving a smooth white cavity. This is a neat, tough tree able to grow above chalk or in peat or poor sands.

Pinus coulteri Coulter pine; Big-cone pine

This pine was sent by David Douglas in 1832 and grows in the hot dry mountains from San Bernardino, behind Los Angeles, to the Coast Range. Two specimens in Herefordshire were over 28 m × 1·1 m when they died after 1960 and may have been from Douglas's seed. The oldest tree now dates from after 1900. The Coulter pine may therefore be short-lived but it grows very rapidly and one at Wisley in Surrey, 22 years old, is 20 × 0.8 m. It is gaunt for some years with the leading shoot 1 m long, hence the whorls of branches are 1 m apart and with few branches per whorl, but it soon makes a broad conic crown, open but well furnished on the outside. The appeal of this tree apart from its early robust growth lies in both the foliage and the cone. The stout blue-white shoots bear stout, stiff grey needles 25–30 cm long around their tips, separated from those of the previous year by 30 cm or so of shoot covered in brown bracts. From about the tenth year it bears the most massive cones of any tree, sporadically but they become more numerous as it gets older. They may weigh 2 kg and be 35 cm long and are long-ovoid, pale shiny brown with each scale ending in a broad-based, up-curved, stout but exceedingly sharp spine. This tree can be grown anywhere in the southern half of the British Isles on well-drained neutral or acid soils and, while not one for sitting under when it is shedding cones, it makes a boldly foliaged specimen.

Pinus densiflora Japanese red pine

This makes an attractive young tree with slender dark green needles on slender bright green shoots. It is a pleasant variation on the Scots pine which it

resembles in cone and dark red scaly bark but is the better furnished and more shapely with its narrow conic deep green crown. It will grow on very poor soils and needs only good drainage in order to flourish.

'Umbraculifera' is rare here, more often seen in gardens in the north-eastern USA. It makes an upright bush on a 20 cm bole and may slowly achieve 8 m. The main feature is the bark which is prominent because of the open crown and the half-dozen or so stems. It is bright orange-red with patches of dark brown scales.

'Aurea' is scarcely known here yet, but young plants are exceptionally bright gold and neat.

Pinus × holfordiana Holford pine; Westonbirt hybrid pine

At Westonbirt in Gloucestershire, Sir George Holford extracted seeds in 1904 from the extra-large cones that distinguish Veitch's form of the Mexican white pine, *P. ayacahuite*. Some of the plants raised were given to friends while others were planted in 1908 in four groups, three in the Arboretum and one in Silk Wood at Westonbirt. When these first coned, twenty years later, it was seen that they were hybrids with some features of the Bhutan pine, *P. wallichiana*, a specimen of which had been growing behind the Mexican white pine at that time.

Holford pines as found in a number of collections vary from the true form, which must be grafts or first cross seedlings from Westonbirt, to forms approaching each parent, and these forms will be second generation trees raised from seeds of Holford pines. The true form is very vigorous, and makes a broad-based conic crown with long, level, wandering lower branches and an upswept narrow top. The bole is often curved at the base and has orange-brown scaly bark. It is best to clean the bole of branches as soon as this is possible. The needless hang 15 cm long in bundles of five from a shoot which is pale green and covered in fine buff hairs. Cones can be 30 cm long, cylindric, tapered to the tip, orange becoming dark brown and very resinous. The original trees grow on about 1 m of loam or sand above limestone and have been much depleted by losses from Honey-fungus.

Pinus jeffreyi Jeffrey pine

One of John Jeffrey's many fine discoveries, this pine ranges from south Oregon at above 2000 m through California to Mexico. It is the only tree from these south-western parts able to grow well in the east, north of New York. In Britain it is also an exceptionally tough tree and maintains a nearly perfect conic narrow crown until 30 m tall. It grows fast on any well-drained non-limy soil and makes a very handsome specimen from the start. The stout blue-bloomed shoots bear hard 20 cm pale blue-grey needles in threes and cylindric acute red-brown buds. The cones are purple-brown in their first year, big heavy ovoids 12 cm long. In their second year they are pale brown and broad ovoid with a flat base, part of which is left on the tree when they are shed, opening out to 20 × 15 cm. Although unlikely to flourish within a city, this is worth a trial in a town park and in any garden needing a large, shapely pine with big cones.

Pinus koraiensis Korean pine

This is very like the Arolla pine but makes a more attractive young plant as it has brighter foliage, with more blue-white on the inner surface, held less densely crowded and more loosely. Some of the older trees are thin and unhealthy but this is not always so and one at Bodnant in north Wales is a fine tree which bears numerous heavy dark blue 15 cm cones.

Pinus leucodermis Bosnian pine

Although botanically a Black pine closely related to the Austrian, this tree from the Balkans is quite unlike those scaly-barked, sooty, rough trees and is singularly clean and smooth. Where a neat pine of moderate size is needed it is among the very best. It grows steadily on any well-drained soil, from pure chalk to strongly acid sand or peat, to make a beautifully regular ovoid crown of upswept branches on a sturdy bole with pale grey bark finely cracked into squares. With age the bark becomes paler and finely fissured and the branches smooth and grey. The shoots are at first bloomed pale grey then pale brown and the leaves, in pairs, are stiff, densely borne and dark green. The cones appear on quite young trees and are deep blue in the summer, in pairs on the tips of most of the shoots, ovoid, 7 cm long.

Pinus montezumae Montezuma pine

A well-grown specimen of this Mexican tree is the most spectacular of any pine, if not of any conifer. The form that does best here, but is rarely found in the wild, has a great, broad dome on level and radiating branches, with huge brushes of long, blue-grey needles standing straight out from stout, shining orange-brown shoots. The needles are in fives, crowded on to the outer third of the annual shoot, slender and 30–40 cm long. Young trees are gaunt for some years but grow very rapidly. Despite this foliage on a giant scale, the cone in Britain is of no account, prickly and 8 cm long. Fine Montezuma pines grow from Sussex to Ayrshire and in eastern Ireland, seldom harmed by cold winters, but in 1979 one in Devon was killed, and a warm, dry site is best, well sheltered from the north and east.

Pinus muricata Bishop pine

This tree grows in scattered relict colonies by the coast of California. The largest patch in the north includes the Pygmy Forest where soil conditions reduce the normally towering Coast redwoods and Douglas firs to some 10 m in height. But not the Bishop pines. They soar, narrow, shapely and blue to 28 m or more. In groves to the south, however, the Bishop pines are short, broadly domed and dark green. Theodor Hartweg sent the first seed from a southern source in 1846 and the early trees are of this form. A line of much younger trees at Muckross Abbey in County Kerry is entirely of narrow blue, obviously northern trees, to 30 m tall. Seed from these gave plants which have grown on exceptionally poor acid soil at the National Pinetum at Bedgebury, Kent, to 18 m in

19 years and some have had shoots over 2 m long. No conifer withstands the maritime blasts on our west coasts as well as the Bishop pine. It has rarely been seen to scorch from salt or frost. Either form will rapidly provide dense outer shelter although there may be a few losses from windblow, but for specimen trees or feature groups, the blue form is much to be preferred.

Bishop pine is like the closely related Monterey pine but has its much stouter needles in pairs. It has a similar very fissured bark but dark grey, and it holds whorls of cones even more tenaciously. The cones are smaller ovoids, less oblique and, unlike those of Monterey pine, the scales bear strong, sharp spines so are even more difficult to wrench from the branch. Like most of the south-western American pines, these are 'fire-climax' trees, dominant after fires. The cones hold viable seed for 60 years or so and release them only when the crown of the tree is on fire. The seeds fall to the ash-enriched soil and the stand regrows. To extract seed from cones picked in Britain, these require a spell in a warm oven.

Pinus nigra maritima Corsican pine

This is the best tree for the rapid production of commercial timber on southern heathlands and the features mainly responsible also give it a potential importance in amenity planting, particularly in city parks on difficult soils. It is not a tree to plant in vast numbers for amenity as it gives thin shelter and is dull en masse, but rather as a small group in a shelter-belt or better, as a roundel or clump. Rapid growth is well maintained and occurs not only on acid sands, but also on clay, gravel, shallow peat and very shallow soil over chalk. Moreover, the tree is tailor-made for forestry, never with a crooked bole, rarely forked, but with light, level branches through to the persistent long conic top. Hence Corsican pine makes a splendid and shapely specimen tree almost anywhere and many are more than 37 m × 1 m. In addition, this tree can tolerate more soot and pollution than most, and many Midland parks and gardens once planted with a range of conifers are now dominated by Corsican (and Austrian) pines twice the size of any

other survivors. The brown shoots bear long, twisted dark grey 15 cm needles in well-spread pairs, giving an open, airy crown. This tree makes a sparse root-system and does not transplant well. Best results come from July planting of three-year-old pot-grown trees.

Pinus nigra nigra Austrian pine

This is a rougher, darker, even tougher form of the Corsican pine. Although it can be a straight-boled narrow, conic tree it is more often heavily branched from low on the bole and has an irregular or bushy crown. The foliage is much more dense; the shorter, 12 cm, stiff, in-curved needles being well bunched in close whorls on the shoot. Austrian pines commonly ring Victorian gardens in and around towns, and they stand in lines and groups along railway embankments. This is the best tree, mixed with Sycamore, to give shelter on high, exposed ridges of chalk or limestone – but only because few other trees can compete there. Elsewhere, the Austrian pine is too coarse and grimy-looking to earn a place in a garden.

Austrian pine (var. nigra)

Pinus parviflora Japanese white pine

When Japan was first opened to collectors, the area available was very limited and mostly around Tokyo and Yokohama. The collectors were nurserymen and the plant-nurseries were full of the huge range of extreme cultivars that the

Japanese gardeners had been selecting for many hundreds of years. It was only to be expected that cultivars formed a large part of the first acquisitions and that the wild species in the interior had to await times of greater freedom of travel. The Japanese white pine was sent in 1861 and was much planted and became familiar as a low spreading tree with level branches holding layers of very blue and white twisted needles in fives. It is well suited to Japanese-style gardens and rock-gardens and hardly exceeds 10 m in height whilst bearing innumerable whorls of up to four erect ovoid cones, bright green in their first year. The wild form, however, was not sent until about 1880 and is not so often seen. It is a straight tree, which at Stourhead in Wiltshire is 27 m tall, with lighter branches, similarly level and bearing layers of less twisted, much greener needles, and fewer cones. The garden form is a decorative little tree which grows well on any acid well-drained soil.

Pinus peuce Macedonian pine

This five-needled pine is singularly consistent and healthy. It grows at a steady rate of about 45 cm a year, whether on the richest soils and in the shelter of a Sussex garden or on windswept slopes at 600 m on a mountain in north Wales. It goes on, always columnar with a conic top, to make a well-foliaged, densely crowned tree. The oldest, now more than 100 years old, are over 25 m tall and still growing. It is very rare to see a Macedonian pine in anything but vigorous good health even if the trees all around are thinning and dying. The bark is either very pale grey or purplish-grey, shallowly divided into small squares. While most specimens are evenly branched, a few have many heavy branches low on the bole and these should have been cleaned up the bole for 2 m many years ago. The leaves are bright green when fresh, on outer surfaces, blue-white on inner, and are densely borne in bundles of five on smooth green shoots. The cones are numerous on trees 20 years or more old, slightly curved, tapered cylinders 10–15 cm long, with convex scales. This is a tree of some distinction and adds greatly to any group, being completely reliable as a single specimen in almost any soil.

Pinus pinea Stone pine

This is the pine with the wide umbrella crown on a sinuous orange, platy-barked bole, common around the Mediterranean. Despite coming from a warmer climate, it is very hardy, growing at least to the Scottish border on the east side. It looks best as a small group in a wide open space. For a few years the seedlings are remarkably attractive with long, soft, flat 'primordial leaves' which are silvery-blue. They are then upright bushy plants and when about 1·3 m high the shiny, dark green adult needles begin to take over. At about 20 years old the tree is almost globose on a short stem and it begins to bear cones. These are big, heavy and woody, nearly spherical, 10×10 cm, pale shining brown. A well-drained sandy soil may suit the Stone pine best but there are good specimens also on gravels and heavier soils. The male flowers cluster around a long basal sector of the new shoots, ovoids 1·3 cm long and quite a good orange-brown before they shed pollen.

Pinus ponderosa Western yellow pine; Ponderosa pine

From the Black Hills of South Dakota to the Coast Range, from the southern Fraser River Valley in British Columbia to Mexico, and throughout the Rocky Mountain system, there are Ponderosa pines. David Douglas sent it first, in 1827, from the Washington-Oregon border, then from 1850 several collectors sent seed from California and south Oregon. Trees from any of these last areas make grand specimens throughout the British Isles. In Dakota and all the eastern ranges, it is a rather different tree, var. *scopulorum*. Only the Western form makes a sturdy, straight tree to 35 m in several gardens and even at that size it can be regularly conic to a single stout leading shoot. The needles are greyish or yellowish-green, in threes, stiff or slightly drooped and 20 cm long on stout shiny brown shoots. The bark is sometimes black but with age it usually develops into long plates, pink or yellowish and very scaly. Ponderosa pine will not grow well in limy or chalky soils but grows fast in any well-drained acid soils. Young trees add greatly to any group, with their shapely crowns and bold foliage, and big specimens are full of character, with imposing boles and good crowns. The cones vary much in size, approaching at their biggest the size of those of its close relative, Jeffrey pine (p. 70) but never so broad at the base and usually only 8 × 5 cm ovoids. As in Jeffrey pine each scale has a small downward-pointing prickle.

Pinus radiata Monterey pine (*P. insignis*)

The old name 'insignis pine' means 'remarkable pine' and in some ways this is one of the most remarkable trees in the world. Confined to a few thousand hectares around Carmel in Monterey County and a smaller area around Cambria, 100 km to the south, the Monterey pine is mostly only some 20 m × 40 cm, infested with dwarf mistletoe and short-lived. In San Francisco on an irrigated lawn one is 15 m after five years. In New Zealand one was 61 m in 41 years, the youngest recorded conifer to achieve 60 m. In Somerset one grew a leading shoot 2·5 m long in a year and almost anywhere in western Britain annual growth of 1·5 m can be seen and trees 30 m tall are commonplace. The great domes of dense foliage, dark from a distance but bright green closer to hand, are part of the accepted scenery of Devon and Cornwall and nearly as frequent by all western coasts. Big rough trees are common inland in Kent but less frequent north along the eastern side of the country to Northumberland and Perthshire where this tree is scarce and not so big.

Young trees of good form are highly decorative, brilliant green, with regularly whorled narrow conic crowns and very long leaders. The bark is soon very coarsely ridged and deeply fissured scaly dark grey, heavy branches are ringed by whorls of big, thickly woody ovoid-oblique cones, and pale green slender shoots bear dense tufts of slender bright green needles in bunches of three. On shallow soil over chalk, growth will be as fast as elsewhere but after some 30 years the foliage will become yellow and the tree will soon die. Otherwise, any well-drained soil, however sandy, gives good results.

In western coastal areas exposed to sea-winds this pine is invaluable for the quick provision of good shelter. In spells of freezing winds the needles may scorch brown (unlike those of the Bishop pine, p. 170) but the following spring new shoots will sprout as usual. The rough, branchy aspect of so many Monterey pines does not matter in a shelter-belt by the sea, and the snaggy bare lower crown can be hidden from the interior of park or garden by other trees. On its own, however, the branchy tree will droop heavy branches and remain locally densely foliaged as a huge, apparently ancient, highly picturesque feature. If a tidier and less spreading specimen is preferred, early pruning high up the bole will usually give a splendid tree but some may like to collect cones from one of the narrow conic trees occasionally seen, warm them until the seeds can be shaken out, and raise their own trees.

Monterey pine

Pinus sylvestris Scots pine

Our one native pine grows wild in woods from the little islands in Loch Maree, Wester Ross, south and east, through Glenfinnan for example, to the

Black Wood of Rannoch. It must, of course, have migrated through England to reach those places, to be finally eliminated by the improving climate and subsequent arrival of species more successful there. In England it is thus a 'secondary native' and the first re-introduction known appears to be the planting of a few trees in north-eastern Hampshire, some of which still survive at Eversleigh, soon after 1660. It was first planted in the New Forest after 1770 with trees from Morayshire. When the light sandy areas of Bagshot Sands and Lower Greensand in south-eastern England had been cleared of their woodland cover by early settlers and had degenerated into sandy heaths subject to fires, the Scots pine spread rapidly through them and became a dominant feature of the West Surrey Desert and its extension through the Army-owned lands from Aldershot to Chobham and into Berkshire.

Heathland sites preserved for Dartford warblers, smooth snakes and natterjack toads, as well as numerous plants, are under constant threat from the advance of Scots pine and conservation in these parts is largely a matter of felling pines. They not only shade out the Heather but they are surprisingly thirsty trees in summer and winter, and dry out the bogs needed for the toads and many other forms of wildlife.

Lancelot Brown used the Scots pine in landscaping, frequently planting groups on the tumps and knolls raised with the spoils from his lakes. In Brown's time, the mid-eighteenth century, relatively few conifers were known and none of the fine species from western North America, so his choice was very limited, but the Scots pine was a good one as it makes some of the best clumps for distant viewing. It grows fast when young, adding annual shoots of around 1 m whether growing on poor acid sand or on quite heavy clay, and if the bole is cleaned of low branches early in life it can make a reasonable specimen tree of moderate size. However, it lacks the stature, shape and presence required in a single specimen on a large scale.

In young trees the bark is pale orange-brown flaking in tiny papery scales. In old trees the bark on upper branches is reddish-orange but on the bole it is variable. Some trees have smooth flat big scales, pink-brown or dark red-brown, while others have dark red scaley thick ridges.

'Aurea' Golden Scots pine. This tree is very slow-growing with a tendency to be bushy. It is a miserable, unhealthy-looking plant in the summer and autumn, an inferior Scots pine with greyish, yellow-tinged, dull foliage. As winter approaches, however, the leaves turn bright gold and the tree stands out until early spring as a splash of fine colour. There are better golden conifers, but none is a pine, so this deserves a place either in a winter-garden where it will be little seen in summer or at a moderate distance and in front of dark evergreens.

'Fastigiata' Erect Scots Pine. This neat little tree is strangely rare in British gardens where only three specimens of any significant age or size have been found. In several collections in the Eastern USA there may be twice this number in one group alone. It remains a tightly erect, well-foliaged tree until 8–10 m tall, after which one, so far, in Britain, has tended to splay out a little. This is a first-class tree as a feature in a small-scale planting in any situation and on any soil and should surely become popular once it is known more widely. It needs practically no room and after some years of moderate growth it becomes very slow.

Pinus thunbergii Japanese black pine

This tree makes an excellent, neat dark narrow tree for its first 30 years or so, with silky white-haired buds prominent amongst stiff dark paired needles in whorls. It is native to poor soils on the shore so is unusually tough and resistant to sea-winds, salt and difficult soils. It is strange that a tree so neat and upright in youth should become with age so gaunt, but old trees nearly all lean strongly and spread slender branches widely in a thin open crown. Another curious feature is the tendency to flower excessively; in some trees, every bundle of needles is replaced by a female flower. There may be 200 of them crowded on a length of shoot with no room for the cones to develop properly. This adds to the interest in growing such a peculiar tree.

Pinus wallichiana Bhutan pine

For no obvious reason this is the five-needle pine seen more than any other in the older gardens around towns. It is a good plant as a young tree but seldom as a specimen tree because as it ages, it starts losing branches and dies back at the top. It grows fast in youth, making leading shoots of 1 m, and may reach 20 m in 20 years but thereafter it is much slower. In rural areas it remains for many years well-foliaged and attractive with the long, 20 cm blue-grey needles in lax long whorls on a very whorled branch system in a fairly narrowly conic crown. Cones may be borne within ten years from seed and soon after they are numerous, hanging from shoots all over the crown. They are bright green and blue-grey with much resin, cylindric, narrow and curved, 20–30 cm long.

Bhutan pine

They add much to the tree until its crown becomes thin, when the tree seems to be all cone and little foliage. Except where there is room for a big, widely-branching old specimen, the Bhutan pine from the Himalayas should be regarded as a short-term adornment, to be replaced in 30 years or whenever it becomes too thin and open to be attractive. It will grow on any normal soil but not on thin soils over chalk.

Podocarpus andinus Plum-fruited yew

Although often a large erect bush, this Chilean plant can be a tree with 2–3 boles or, less often, with a single bole, and to 20 m tall. The bark is nearly black and smooth, wrinkled horizontally. The branches are light and upswept. The leaves are densely held, soft, 5 cm long, bright fresh or slightly blued green above with two broad pale blue-grey bands beneath. This is a hardy and accommodating tree and should be more planted in gardens for it has very good foliage. It is too likely to become a bush to be worth a place as a specimen tree, but splendid for low shelter or as a different foliage in a group of shrubs, and a good change from the sombre Yew. It grows slowly on any soil and makes a very good hedge. Male and female plants both have slender erect heads of flowers at the tips of some shoots, yellow on the male, bright blue-grey on the female, and females bear 2 cm apple-green long-ovoid fruit in small bunches.

Pseudolarix amabilis Golden larch

The true larches have been extolled earlier (see under *Larix*) for their many great virtues, but only the three types listed on p. 163 recommend themselves for general planting and specimen trees. Fortunately the Golden larch from China is now on the market; it is quite rare in gardens because there have been periods when there were no plants in the trade. It is hardy, but not in its first few years of very slow growth, and large specimens are confined to the west and the south. The largest is in Cornwall and there are good trees at Kew and at Leonardslee and Sheffield Park in Sussex.

The Golden larch has bigger foliage than other larches, with 5–7 cm strap-like leaves in whorls on long, curved spurs which lengthen and broaden each year. The leaves are bright pale green, greying a little until, in autumn, they turn yellow, orange and red-brown. This autumn display is the brightest of any conifer and earns the tree a place in a planting. It needs full light for, when shaded, it makes a narrow, thinly foliaged tree but in the open it is a broad tree with long level branches, pale grey deeply fissured bark and an attractive appearance. Golden larch grows reasonably well on a variety of neutral and fairly acid soils, light and heavy.

Pseudotsuga menziesii Douglas fir

David Douglas sent the first seed in 1827 from near Portland, Oregon, and by a strange chance seeds in a small area between there and the Puget Sound have been found to give the best results with us of all the seeds tried from the western slopes, from British Columbia to California. At Quinault Lake in Washington there is a stand of Douglas fir unsurpassed by any group of trees, with clear boles 2·2 m in diameter running 60 m to the first branch and with top heights 85–90 m. Although it makes a solid, green, heavy screen or shelter in all parts of the British Isles, individual trees in the east are of poor shape after youth and become much broken.

In Sussex there are some trees to 45 m tall growing on a few centimetres of soil over pure white chalk but more often, after a good start, Douglas fir will become yellowish and thin; it also has a miserable, thin stage when 20 m or so tall on sands and clays in the east, particularly in the Weald. There are better trees for all such uses in these parts. In the Coniferous Areas, however, Douglas fir is luxuriant in foliage and very rapidly grows into an enormous tree usually of good shape and to a great height, but variable. In many such areas a group will include several with long fine spires to 50 m or more, together with others with huge boles and branches, much broken by snow and gales.

As a single specimen in the right areas and in some shelter on a damp site, the Douglas fir needs plenty of room and, for the best effect, a bole kept clean for 3 m or more. Single trees have heavy dense masses of foliage hanging from big branches, the leaves soft to the touch and fragrant when bruised. It is splendid as a group, cleaning its boles up in the interior to make an impressive grove. Cones are abundant in old trees, and unique to the Douglas firs as a group in the three-pronged projecting bracts.

Saxegothaea conspicua Prince Albert's yew

This very attractive little tree from Chile and the Argentine grows best from Dorset to Cornwall and in eastern Ireland, where it makes fountains of rich dark green elegant foliage to 18 m tall. In other southern counties, east to Kent and in western areas it tends to be slender and small. The bark is similar to that of the common yew but smoother and polished, mottled pink, brown and dark red. The outer shoots hang strung with rather scattered bunches of dense foliage on slender bright green shoots, striped white. The leaves unfold tinged purple and are 2 cm long, curved, hard, spine-tipped and broadly white-banded beneath. Powdery-blue, 1 cm ovoid female flowers are common through much of the year.

Shelter and a damp, acid soil are important for this tree and it will tolerate considerable shade but very little exposure.

Sciadopitys verticillata Japanese umbrella pine

This strange tree surviving only as a single species in Japan is in the Redwood Family. It is unique in having its leaves fused together in pairs, in whorls held by small scale-like leaves. The fused leaves are 10–12 cm long and deep, shining green. Young trees are upright and narrowly conic. They may need guidance to form a shapely tree for some have been allowed to become many-stemmed and bushy. In either case, the foliage is unusual and attractive, even in some shade. This tree will grow on any damp non-alkaline soil and although most luxuriant and usually biggest in the Coniferous Areas, the tallest, 23 m, is in mid-Kent at Benenden School. It is normally slow or very slow in growth, but here again, Kent has the best record; of the few dated specimens, none has grown faster than a line in the National Pinetum at Bedgebury where several are 12–13 m in 50 years. In contrast, one in a Cornish garden is 3 m in 80 years. There are several fine large specimens in the southern parts of Ireland.

Sequoia sempervirens Coast redwood

The tallest tree in the world is a Coast redwood 114 m high at Redwood Creek in north-west California where entire stands are 90 m tall. In the sea-fog areas of the foothills of the Coast Range the trees stand very close together, but groups in Britain need to be at wider spacing in our drier climate, and 8–12 m spacing will give superb rich deep red boles closer than other trees of similar size. Grown in the open, a single tree maintains a narrow, columnar crown of light branches. Growth will cease at a certain height depending on the exposure and hence on the height of surrounding trees. In much of Cornwall, crowns will flatten out at some 25 m and in the Midlands and eastern counties this happens at about 28–30 m. Only in deep valleys and high woods in the west and the north do some trees continue upwards to 35–40 m. Young trees on damp, deep soils make annual shoots of around 1·3 m and in the New Forest some are 25 m tall in 23 years. Growing at that speed, some trees are gaunt, open and too narrow, but the thriving ones are good to see with their long, rather pendulous broadly leafed deep green foliage, and deeply fissured, fibrous bark, either dark chestnut all over or, as in California, pale grey on the ridges.

   This tree is excellent for a short avenue of massive boles in the shelter of woodland but in open country, as along a drive between fields, it is too thin to be effective. Long avenues of Coast redwood would be dull and rather featureless since the tree does not have a formal shape.

'Adpressa' is a relatively slow and small variant in which the new shoots are slender and cream-coloured, and one-year leaves are small, banded bright blue-white beneath and with a single white band above. Good for a group of middle-sized trees, taking about 100 years to reach 22 m.

Coast redwood

Sequoiadendron giganteum Sierra redwood; Giant Sequoia; Wellingtonia; Big tree

The name 'Sierra redwood' is preferred by Californian foresters since this distinguishes it by origin from the Coast redwood which is nowhere nearer than 200 km, across the Central Valley. The Sierra redwood is the biggest tree in the world but not quite the tallest, the stoutest or the oldest. Its combination of heights of 60–85 m and bole diameters of 7–8 m gives volumes of timber found in no other trees. Small groves occur scattered along the southern parts of the western flanks of the Sierra Nevada. A few of the 72 groves are in private ownership; the rest are State Forest Parks or National Parks. No tree has been felled this century and all are closely protected. Although noted in 1833 by a traveller, J. Leonard, in a diary which remained obscure until recently, the Sierra redwood was re-found in 1850 and only brought to the notice of the world in 1853, a by-product of the 1849 gold-rush.

   The remarkable merits of this tree for plantings on a monumental scale, in avenues, lines, roundels and single specimens or groups have been pointed out earlier, on pages 46 and 47. Early growth can be variable and is not very rapid in height, 60–80 cm a year being more usual than 1 m, but is often, after a few years, extremely rapid in diameter. Typically, a group of five planted in 1960 in the New Forest has one superb specimen

11 m × 34 cm at 20 years old, but the others are still thin and around 6 m tall. Some old trees have layered branches or many big ones low on the bole and would have been good specimens had they been cleaned up when young, but mostly these trees look after themselves very well indeed. From Hampshire to Wester and Easter Ross and to County Tyrone there are immense trees now 100–136 years old, 45–52 m × 2.6–3.4 m, growing on almost every kind of soil except solid chalk. Honey-fungus kills a few trees here and there, and lightning strikes most of those in south-east England – every tree in some avenues – but it seems to have no other problems and never blows down. With our trees being half the height and a third of the diameter of the best specimens in California, but only one-thirtieth of their age ('Grizzly Giant' is reckoned to be 3400 years old), it is an open and intriguing question how long they will live here and what sort of sizes may one day be seen. Already ours are some of the biggest trees of any kind in all Europe.

'Aureum' is a slower, more upright form with dull yellow new shoots raised in County Cork from one of the earliest seed-lots in 1856. It is only a curiosity and has no place as a golden tree.

'Pendulum' is a freak with short branches emerging and continuing almost vertically downwards. A few specimens remain erect in the main stem, like the 32 m tree in the ravine at Bodnant in Gwynedd, but most of them arch over to make a hoop 10–12 m high like a grazing giraffe.

Taxodium ascendens Pond cypress

This tree comes from the areas of Swamp cypress in the south-eastern corner of its range, in Florida, Georgia and Alabama. Less hardy than the Swamp cypress, it is very rare north of Southern England. It grows slowly and only a few old trees are 20 m tall. The form always seen here is 'Nutans' in which the branch-tips curve downwards. In the wild all degrees of this variation occur. The bark is coarsely ridged and fibrous like a willow, warm brown turning pale grey on the ridges. The crown is narrowly conic. The shoots are shed with the leaves and new shoots emerge in early summer, bright pale green slender spikes from the down-curved branch-tips, and perpendicularly from along the branches even when quite stout, standing vertically. At this stage the tree is at its quaint best but through the summer it is delicately foliaged in light green and in late autumn it becomes a rich red-brown. Each leaf is only 8 mm long, slender and finely pointed and they arise in spirals from the shoot.

In a damp or waterside site, well-sheltered, this will make a small, interesting tree but it has neither the stature nor the hardiness for general use as a specimen tree.

Giant sequoia;
Sierra redwood

Weeping
giant sequoia

Taxodium distichum Swamp cypress

In its native range, the Swamp or Bald cypress grows by tidal creeks along the coast from Virginia to Mexico and in freshwater swamps along the Mississippi bottomlands north to Illinois. From that great range there could, no doubt, be sources of trees hardier than those we have, but still needing hot summers for the best growth. There are rather few north of the Midlands and in Ireland. Many of the best specimens, which reach 35 m × 1·3 m, stand beside lakes or streams but some are not even in a damp position. Only those by water or in flooding ground will grow the woody termite-hills known as 'knees' or pneumatophores, which arise from the roots and are thought to supply them with air. No Swamp cypress in Britain is known to be growing in tidal or even brackish water – few gardens run to this anyway. Growth, best around London and in East Anglia, is moderate for a tree reaching such large size. Seldom in noticeable leaf before mid-June, it is eventually a bright fresh green over a twiggy, bluntly conic crown until darkening, then in November turning foxy-brown before shedding leaves and shoots. Swamp cypresses look much better in groups than singly; among other conifers they look bare and untidy whereas a group repeats the shape of the tree and makes a feature of it. A group by a waterside is also much preferred to a line. It has substance and does not straggle, as well as being unspoiled by a tree or two of poor growth, which would be fatal to a line.

Taxus baccata Yew

The common Yew, native north to northern Argyll, has one of the strongest and most elastic timbers of any tree. This enables a very old, very hollow bole to hold together and support long branches, when other trees would collapse, until it is well over 1000 years old. It is much longer-lived than any other tree in Northern Europe. It is also very nearly indestructible and will happily tolerate intensive clipping, cutting and shaping while remaining clothed with green to the ground, since it is able to bear shade in a way that few trees can. All these features make Yew a tree without a rival for background work on an intimate scale in the garden. As a backing to the herbaceous border running away from the house, as a subject for topiary and for the alcoves behind marble statuary, as well as for screens and divisions within the garden and dense year-round shelter,

what owner with thoughts of succeeding generations would not choose the plant which can be most closely clipped and lasts for over 1000 years?

Churchyards in a crescent from Kent to Devon, Wiltshire, Gloucestershire, Herefordshire, Powys and Clwyd are the homes of hundreds of vast old yews, bigger than any known elsewhere in the world, from two to over three metres in diameter. The presence of big, ancient yews in so many churchyards was formerly attributed to very early planting, to give shelter to the path and the porch; to yield, where male, the 'palm' used still in Ireland; to symbolize eternal life and to grow bowstaves where they would not poison grazing cattle. But, as shown by stone vaulting over a root from the Tandridge yew, standing eight metres from the church wall today, in the Saxon foundations, the yews hugely pre-date even the original churches built 1000 years ago. Many are now believed to be 3000 years old or more. The shelter they give to the church arises from the church being sited to benefit from the big, evergreen crown and to appropriate the ancient aura of the pagan sacred ground. Bowstaves were imported from Spain as the duty payable on a cask of sherry, less knotty than the home-grown.

Yews will grow on chalk, on clays or on sands. They never grow fast but will grow anywhere, in severe exposure or in shade, in damp or in dry soils, and they never blow down. Upward growth is usually 15–25 cm a year at best, then slows to a few centimetres for perhaps 300 years when the tree may be 20 m tall. A few, in woods or close lines, are over 25 m and appear to have short leading shoots still, while really old trees have such spreading crowns that there is no leader at all but shoots 10–15 cm long may sprout from all parts. Growth in diameter is very variable. There are some yews of known date that have grown for 100 years at the standard rate of 0·8 cm diameter a year, while others have grown at much less than half this rate. Very old yews may add 1 cm in diameter in 20 years. Such rates can only be accurately discovered by the individual taking his own measurements, for early figures were so unreliable that some records spanning 100 years or more in the growth of a tree show each succeeding figure as *less* than the one before. Gilbert White, however, was probably accurate when in 1777 he recorded the girth of the Selborne Yew as 7 m at 1 m on the bole; it was exactly 7·6 m in diameter at that height 200 years later.

'Adpressa' is a female form with a central axis and wide-spreading level branches slightly upswept, from which hang shoots lined with tiny ovate-acute leaves. Too open for use as a screen, this form makes a pleasant variation in foliage and should be beside a path or building where the minute leaves will be seen. It can be 11 m tall.

Small-leafed yew, 'Adpressa'

'Adpressa Aurea' is a beautiful golden-leafed form of 'Adpressa' but more bushy and less open. In winter it is bright fresh yellow, in early summer a deeper slightly orange colour, and at all times among the best of golden foliages.

'Dovastoniana'. The West Felton Yew is a strange plant with a history to make it a talking-point in a garden. Mr Dovaston bought it from a pedlar for sixpence in 1777 to put by his well-head at West Felton, Shropshire. It grew strangely, with a good central stem and long level branches wandering out and hanging their foliage in curtains. It is still there, 17 m tall and 117 cm in diameter, with a good bole. It is male but a female shoot was found on it too. Every Dovaston Yew comes from this one and now a gold-leafed form is available.

'Fastigiata'. The Irish Yew is in every churchyard and every tree is derived from one of the two female erect trees found in 1780 on a hillside in County Fermanagh. In the far west this grows numerous slender conic tops to 16 m tall but eastwards it is broader and more squat. Avenues and lines are common in Cornish gardens and sometimes successful but mostly they are broken out of shape if in the open, and straggly and dull if in shade. The twelve at Dartington, Devon, are superb and cleverly spaced but these are clipped into shape.

Thuja koraiensis Korean thuja

This little tree grows at 20–25 cm a year into a narrowly conic plant with up-curved branches, heavily foliaged but often only close to the branch. The foliage may be fresh yellowish-green or deep blue-green bloomed silver and the underside of each scale-leaf is thickly coated pure white all over. An added attraction is that crushed foliage emits a strong scent of rich lemony fruit-cake with almonds. This is a valuable tree as a single specimen in a collection on a small scale where only little trees can be grown, such as in a shrubbery, where it adds distinction and interest. It will grow on any soil except, perhaps, pure chalk.

Thuja occidentalis Eastern thuja; Northern white cedar

The name 'Eastern thuja' conflicts with 'occidentalis' because when it was first discovered, in Virginia, this counted as a very 'western' tree. Another 250 years passed before the Western thuja ('Western red cedar') was found by the Pacific Coast, and it was some time after this that the name 'Eastern thuja' or 'Arborvitae' was used. This tree is of minor use as it grows slowly and soon keels over and dies. Meanwhile it is a shapely conic tree with thin foliage pale bright green in curved plates, able to grow in sodden soils.

'Lutea' is a far superior form, sturdy, upswept and with new foliage bright gold in curled fronds.

'Spiralis' is dark green and very narrowly conic-columnar. The branches are fine and nearly level and the tips bear spirally-set upright sprays. A splendid, formal small-scale tree, able to reach 12 m but taking some 60 years to do so.

Thuja orientalis Chinese thuja

This is a dull, thinly foliaged, upright gaunt tree of no possible use in a garden here (although useful in semi-arid regions).

'Elegantissima'. This is very upright with vertically held plates of foliage, narrowly conic when young and eventually broadly columnar. The foliage is bright yellow at the tips in early summer, duller yellow until the first frosts when it bronzes a little. A young plant is neat and attractive in very restricted areas like patios and yards and small beds, and bigger plants (they can be 8 m tall) look well on a wall or beside a house. It flourishes on alkaline soil and on mildly acid soil but is not happy in very acid sands.

Thuja plicata Western red cedar

This tree, introduced by John Jeffrey and William Lobb in 1854, ranges from south Alaska to north California and inland to Montana where, in Ross Creek Grove, some are 57 m tall while in Stanley Park, Vancouver, there are boles more than 3 m in diameter. It grows moderately well everywhere in the British Isles but very rapidly and to great size only in the Coniferous Areas where some are now 40 m × 150 cm. It is a good tree on soil immediately above chalk and on damp clay. It is very widely used in shelter plantings and is often the best tree to mix with larch and other deciduous trees in a shelter-belt to increase winter shelter. It will clip well to make a hedge and in damp weather will scent the air around with an aroma of apple, acid-drop or pineapple, as will a grove of trees. It makes an excellent grove or roundel as, grown close, it remains shapely with a fine clean bole whereas a single specimen will often grow a big branch or two low from the bole, level then sharply up-curved, and can become untidy. In the right areas and in good shelter,

however, it will grow into a big tree. It is much better as a line than in an avenue; in a line the trees can keep a wall of foliage but in an avenue the shade makes them thin and less attractive, with many bare twigs in the lower crown where they are most seen by anyone traversing it.

'Zebrina' is one of the very best of the large-growing golden conifers. The oldest are little over 70 years planted now, and while not a really fast-growing tree it is often 20 m tall, sometimes 25 m, and still growing steadily. There is considerable variation in the intensity of gold-barring on the foliage but in most trees it is bright gold and in some, more seen in Ireland, there is very little green between the bars. The shape is always regularly conic, whether broad or narrow, and the breadth is determined largely by the amount of shade, with trees fully in the open rather broad. It grows best in damp sheltered sites, whether clay or sand, and tolerates lime.

Western red cedar   shoot

Thuja standishii Japanese thuja

This cannot compete with *T. plicata* in any of the roles of that tree but it has a place for interest and variety in a collection or group of trees not intended to achieve great size. Its shoots are rounded and sprays hang from erect branch-tips and are often silvery with bloom on dark green. When crushed the foliage emits the most delicious, sweet scent in which lemon, eucalyptus and catchouc are combined. The crown is a broad cone with level branches up-curved towards their ends, and open inside. This displays the bark which is at first red-brown and stringy but in older trees has plates of smooth rich deep red. Old trees have distinctively yellow-green foliage and, since the shoots hang, they look unhealthy; only the good bark redeems it at that age, and the scented foliage.

Thujopsis dolabrata Hiba

This Japanese tree likes the wet western areas where there are many around 20 m tall but it is slow-growing anywhere and tends to be rather short-lived in dry warm regions. At its best the big, bright green reptilian scales make very handsome foliage especially in the tree-form, hanging in sprays from branches bent upwards near the good single bole. The commoner form has between 12 and 20 stems of fairly even size and makes a broad many-topped bush with thinner foliage. The Hiba is a good tree for a small-scale group of varied foliages. Young trees of either form are very dense and broad-conic.

Tsuga canadensis Eastern hemlock

Although a shapely, slender pale green tree through most of its wide range from Nova Scotia to Alabama, the Eastern hemlock is a poorly shaped, dark and dull tree here and cannot compete in any role, even as a hedge, with the splendid Western hemlock. In a few oddly placed regions, notably near Leith Hill in Surrey and in south Shropshire, it has managed to grow free from big, low branches and to make a tall tree, to 30 m. The bark is nearly black and is coarsely ridged. The leaves taper from near the base, unlike the parallel-sided leaves of the Western hemlock, and engagingly arrange themselves so that a line of leaves above the shoot lies upside-down showing the silvery bands and identifying the tree at once. For general use it should be avoided.

Tsuga heterophylla Western hemlock

In its native woods from southern Alaska to northern California this is an elegant narrowly conic tree, to 70 m tall in parts of Washington. It grows in the same form with us but even faster, and in the Coniferous Areas it will very soon be as tall as the Washington trees, many now being over 40 m and none more than 125 years old. It was introduced by John Jeffrey in 1851 but only two or three trees are known that were planted before 1860. It withstands considerable shade during early life and grows faster under well-thinned larch or oak than in the open. In the Coniferous Areas it keeps up a great rate of growth so far indefinitely and even in areas of dry warm summers it will grow for many years on sand or on clay at 1·3 m a year, but here it eventually becomes thin and fails at around 25 m. It cannot therefore be recommended away from the west and the north where it is among the very best trees for groves, roundels and screens and as a single specimen on the largest scale. There is hardly a tree of Western hemlock in these areas which does not taper regularly to a single long-spired tip or one with a misplaced branch. Single trees very rarely blow down or suffer damage from snow or gales. It makes an outstanding line of trees but the spacing of an avenue would be tricky in order to achieve a cathedral-nave effect from the boles without it being too shady and sombre.

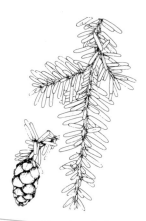

Western hemlock

Tsuga mertensiana Mountain hemlock

Growing, as this tree does, along the tree-line of the highest ranges from Alaska to California and on some inhospitable lavas where almost nothing else will grow, it should be remarkably tough. In fact it seems to thrive here only in the valleys of mid-Perthshire where on sheltered sites and good soils it has, after a slow start, grown reasonably quickly, and a few are now 30 m × 80 cm. Elsewhere it grows very slowly in every county and on almost any site, preferably on acid soil. It can be strongly recommended as a small tree of neat and attractive appearance. With a few bushy exceptions, it grows as a narrow cone of light level branches from which hang dense sprays of variably blue-grey foliage. In the wild, most are deep green but in gardens in Britain most are smoky-grey and some, grown as 'Glauca', are blue-white. The older leaves in all these forms become dark green or blackish so the interior of the crown is very dark and shows off the pale new foliage. The leaves spread from all round the shoot, unlike those in other hemlocks. Since the shoots tend to be short, in little bunches along the upper side of the branches, the small shoots look like the spurs of a cedar, and the blue-grey leaf adds to the resemblance to the Blue Atlas cedar. However, the leaves of the hemlock are flattened and soft, unlike the spined needles of a cedar. The bark is dark orange-brown and flakes in small papery scales, and the cones are much bigger than any other hemlock bears, more like spruce cones.

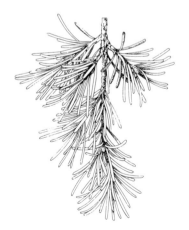

Mountain hemlock

Trees for Special Purposes

Fastigiate and Columnar Trees

The crowns of these two modes of growth may be similar in outline, with the same role in landscaping, but they differ in their structure. Fastigiate trees have strictly erect branches. A few, like the two poplars, 'Gigantea' and *alba* 'Pyramidalis', tend with age to open out and be broadest at the top, but many, like the Lombardy poplar, are columnar with a tapered, conic top. A few conifers have columnar crowns which arise not from erect branching but from level but very short branches, or downswept branches. They tend to have conic crowns until the lower branches fail to lengthen significantly, when they become columnar.

Thus a fastigiate crown is a special case among columnar crowns, and is the most common form.

Ginkgo

Sentry Ginkgo	*Ginkgo biloba* 'Fastigiata'

Conifers

Cedar	Fastigiate Red	*Thuja plicata* 'Fastigiata'
	Fastigiate Atlas	*Cedrus atlantica* 'Fastigiata'
	Incense	*Calocedrus decurrens*
	Pencil	*Juniperus virginiana* 'Cupressoides'
	White Fastigiate	*Thuja occidentalis* 'Fastigiata'
	Spiralis	*Thuja occidentalis* 'Spiralis'
Cypress	Italian	*Cupressus sempervirens*
Cypress	Lawson 'Columnaris'	*Chamaecyparis lawsoniana* 'Columnaris'
	'Ellwood's'	'Ellwoodii'
	'Fletcher's'	'Fletcheri'
	'Kilmacurragh'	'Kilmacurragh'
	'Lutea'	'Lutea'
	'Wissel'	'Wisselii'
	Monterey Fastigiate	*Cupressus macrocarpa* 'Fastigiata'
Fir	Alpine	*Abies lasiocarpa**
	Fastigiate Douglas	*Pseudotsuga menziesii* 'Fastigiata'†
	Fastigiate Silver	*Abies alba* 'Pyramidata'
	Red	*Abies magnifica*

Juniper	Chinese Golden	*Juniperus chinensis* 'Aurea'
	Syrian	*Juniper drupacea*
Pine	Chinese cowtail	*Cephalotaxus harringtonia* 'Fastigiata'
	Scots Fastigiate	*Pinus sylvestris* 'Fastigiata'
	Weymouth Fastigiate	*stobus* 'Fastigiata'†
Spruce	Black	*Picea mariana*
	Norway Fastigiate	*abies* Pyramidata'†
	Serbian	*omorika*
	White	*glauca**
Yew	Golden Irish	*Taxus baccata* 'Fastigiata Aurea'
	Irish	'Fastigiata'
	Standish's	'Standishii'

Broadleafed Trees

Alder	Fastigiate	*Alnus glutinosa* 'Pyramidalis'
Apple	Pillar	*Malus tschonoskii*
	van Eseltine	*Malus* 'van Eseltine'
Beech	Dawyck	*Fagus sylvatica* 'Dawyck'
Birch	Fastigiate	*Betula pendula* 'Fastigiata'
Cherry	Erect	*Prunus* 'Amanogawa'
	Hillier's Spire	× *hillieri* 'Spire'
Golden Rain, Fastigiate		*Koelreuteria paniculata* 'Fastigiata'
Hawthorn	Fastigiate	*Crataegus monogyna* 'Fastigiata'
Lime	American, Erect	*Tilia americana* 'Fastigiata'†
	Erect Broadleaf	*platyphyllos* 'Fastigiata'†
Locust	Fastigiate	*Robinia pseudoacacia* 'Fastigiata'
Maple	Lobel's	*Acer lobelii*
	Norway Erect	*platanoides* 'Columnare'†
		'Erectum'†
		'Fastigiatum'†
	Red Erect	*rubrum* 'Columnare'
	Sugar 'Newton Sentry'	*saccharum* 'Newton Sentry'†
	'Temple's Upright'	'Temple's Upright'†
	Sycamore Erect	*pseudoplatanus* 'Erectum'
Oak	Cypress	*Quercus robur* 'Fastigiata'
	Sessile Fastigiate	*petraea* 'Columna'
Poplar	Bolle's	*Populus alba* 'Pyramidalis'
	Female Lombardy	*nigra* 'Gigantea'
	Hybrid Balsam	*trichocarpa* × *balsamea* 'TT 32'
	Lombardy	*nigra* 'Italica'
Rowan	Fastigiate	*Sorbus aucuparia* 'Fastigiata'
Service tree Bastard, Erect		× *thuringiaca* 'Fastigiata'
Tulip-tree	Erect	*Liriodendron tulipifera* 'Fastigiatum'

*The most slender of all columnar trees in parts of their native ranges in the Rocky Mountains. Variable and slow in the British Isles; best results in northern Scotland.

†At present scarce or unknown in the British Isles, but fine trees in collections in north-eastern North America; should be grown here.

Trees with Yellow-Variegated Foliage (including cream)

Conifers

Cedar, Incense	*Calocedrus decurrens* 'Aureovariegata'
Cypress, Lawson	*Chamaecyparis lawsoniana* 'Aureomaculata'
Yew	*Taxus baccata* (many cultivars)

Broadleafed Trees

Beech	*Fagus sylvatica* 'Luteovariegata'
Box	*Buxus sempervirens* 'Aureovariegata'
	'Marginata'
Horse Chestnut	*Aesculus hippocastanum* 'Hampton Court'
Holly	*Ilex aquifolium* 'Golden Queen' etc
Highclere	× *altaclerensis* 'Golden King' 'Lawsoniana'
Maple Ash-leafed	*Acer negundo* 'Elegans'
Oak Common	*Quercus robur* 'Variegata'
Red	*rubra* 'Aurea'
Turkey	*cerris* 'Variegata'
Plane London	*Platanus* × *acerifolia* 'Suttneri'
Poplar Balsam	*Populus* × *candicans* 'Aurora'
Privet Chinese	*Ligustrum lucidum* 'Excelsum Superbum'
Tulip-tree	*Liriodendron tulipifera* 'Aureomarginatum'

Trees with White-Variegated Foliage

Conifers

Cypress Lawson	*Chamaecyparis lawsoniana* 'Albovariegata'
Sawara	*pisifera* 'Plumosa Argentea'
Juniper	*Juniperus chinensis* 'Variegata'

Broadleafed Trees

Beech	*Fagus sylvatica* 'Albovariegata'
Chestnut Sweet	*Castanea sativa* 'Albomarginata'
Dogwood	*Cornus controversa* 'Variegata'
Elm English	*Ulmus procera* 'Argenteovariegata'
	'Silvery Gem'

Holly		*Ilex aquifolium*	'Perry's Weeping'
			'Handsworth New Silver'
Maple	Ash-leafed	*Acer negundo*	'Variegatum'
	Drummond's	*platanoides*	'Drummondii'
	Snake-bark	*rufinerve*	'Albolimbatum'
	Sycamore	*pseudoplatanus*	'Variegatum'
Privet	Chinese	*Ligustrum lucidum*	'Tricolor'

Trees with Purple Foliage

Conifers

| Japanese red cedar | *Cryptomeria japonica* | 'Elegans' (winter) |

Broadleafed Trees

Apple		*Malus* × *purpurea* (forms)	
Beech		*Fagus sylvatica*	'Purpurea' 'Rivers' 'Purple'
Birch		*Betula pendula*	'Purpurea'
Maple	Japanese	*Acer palmatum*	'Atropurpureum'
	Norway	*platanoides*	'Crimson King'
			'Goldsworth Purple'
			'Faasen's Black'
	Sycamore	*pseudoplatanus*	'Atropurpureum'
			'Spaethiii'
Oak	Common	*Quercus robur*	'Atropurpurea'
	Sessile	*petraea*	'Purpurea'

Trees with Golden Foliage

Conifers

Cedar	Atlas	*Cedrus atlantica*	'Aurea'
	Lebanon	*libani*	'Aurea'
	White	*Thuja occidentalis*	'Lutea'
			'Rheingold'
Cypress	Cripps's	*Chamaecyparis obtusa*	'Crippsii'
	Hinoki		'Tetragona Aurea'
	Lawson	*lawsoniana*	'Hillieri'
			'Lutea'
			'Lanei'
			'Stewartii'
			'Winston Churchill'

Leyland	*Cupressocyparis leylandii*	'Castlewellan'; 'Golconda'; 'Robinson's Gold'
Monterey	*Cupressus macrocarpa*	'Donard Gold' 'Goldcrest' 'Gold Pillar' 'Lutea'
Sawara	*Chamaecyparis pisifera*	'Aurea' 'Filifera Aurea' 'Plumosa Aurea'

Juniper	Golden Chinese	*Juniperus chinensis*	'Aurea'
Pine	Golden Scots	*Pinus sylvestris*	'Aurea'
	Japanese	*densiflora*	'Aurea'
Thuja		*Thuja plicata*	'Zebrina'
Yew	Common	*Taxus baccata*	'Semperaurescens' 'Adpressa Aurea'
	Irish		'Fastigiata Aurea' 'Standishii'

Broadleafed Trees

Alder		*Alnus glutinosa*	'Aurea'
		incana	'Aurea'; 'Coccineis-ramulis'
Ash		*Fraxinus excelsior*	'Jaspidea'
Beech		*Fagus sylvatica*	'Zlatia'
Catalpa		*Catalpa bignonioides*	'Aurea'
Elm, English		*Ulmus procera*	'Louis van Houtte'
	Wych	*glabra*	'Lutescens'
Honey-locust		*Gleditsia triacanthos*	'Sunburst'
Locust		*Robinia pseudoacacia*	'Frisia'
Maple	Ash-leafed	*Acer negundo*	'Auratum'
	Cappadocian	*cappadocicum*	'Aureum'
	Field	*campestre*	'Postelense'
	Japanese	*palmatum*	'Aureum'
	Moon	*japonicum*	'Aureum'
	Sycamore	*pseudoplatanus*	'Corstorphinense' 'Worleei'
Oak	Common	*Quercus robur*	'Concordia'
Poplar	Black Italian	*Populus*	'Serotina Aurea'
	White	*alba*	'Richardii'

Small Trees

Recommended for year-round attraction

Birch	Black	*Betula nigra*
	Himalayan	*utilis*
	Kashmir	*jacquemontii*
	Transcaucasian	*medwediewii*
Cherry	Tibetan	*Prunus serrula*
Fir	Arizona cork	*Abies lasiocarpa* var. *arizonica*
Holly	Perry's Weeping	*Ilex aquifolium* 'Perry's Weeping'
	Pyramidal	'Pyramidalis'
	Silver	'Handsworth New Silver'
	Wilson's	*Ilex × altaclerensis* 'Wilsonii'
Magnolia	Shining	*Magnolia × loebneri*
Maple	Coral-bark	*Acer palmatum* 'Senkaki'
	Hers's	*hersii*
	Moose-bark	*pensylvanicum*
	Paper-bark	*griseum*
	Red Snake-bark	*capillipes*
Myrtle	Orange-bark	*Myrtus luma*
Privet	Chinese	*Ligustrum lucidum*
Rowan	Beissner's	*Sorbus aucuparia* 'Beissneri'
Strawberry tree	Cyprus	*Arbutus andrachne*
Spruce	Brewer	*Picea brewerana*
	Serbian	*omorika*

Recommended for spring–summer–autumn
(flower, foliage, fruit or autumn colour in some cases. Little or no merit in winter.)

Acacia	Rose	*Robinia hispida*
Apple	Hupeh crab	*Malus hupehensis*
	John Downie	'John Downie'
	Pillar	*tschonoskii*
	van Eseltine	'van Eseltine'
Cherry	Sargent	*Prunus sargentii*
Empress tree		*Paulownia tomentosa*
Golden rain tree		*Koelreuteria paniculata*
Magnolia	Big-leaf	*Magnolia macrophylla*
	Willow-leaf	*salicifolia*
	Sprenger's	*sprengeri diva*
Maple	Golden Ash-leafed	*Acer negundo* 'Auratum'
	Japanese Golden	*japonicum* 'Aureum'
	Vine-leafed	'Vitifolium'
	'Osakazuki'	*palmatum* 'Osakazuki'
	Trident	*buergeranum*
	Variegated Ash-leafed	*negundo* 'Variegatum'
Pear	'Chanticleer'	*Pyrus calleryana* 'Chanticleer'

	Willow-leafed	*salicifolia*
Rowan	'Embley'	*Sorbus commixta* 'Embley'
	'Joseph Rock'	'Joseph Rock'
	Sargent's	*sargentiana*
	Vilmorin's	*vilminiana*
Snowbell tree		*Styrax japonica*
Sorrel-tree		*Oxydendrum arboreum*
Thorn	Carriere's	*Crataegus* × *lavallei*
	Broad-leafed Hybrid	× *prunifolia*
	Washington	*phaenopyrum*
Willow	Bay	*Salix pentandra*
	Dragon's Claw	*matsudana* 'Tortuosa'

Recommended for flowering-season only

Some trees are spectacular for their flowers but otherwise of no merit, including the following:

Cherry	Japanese	All the 'Sato' cherries. Autumn colours can redeem 'Hokusai' 'Kanzan' and sometimes 'Tai-haku'
	Yoshino	*Prunus yedoensis*
Crab apple	Japanese	*Malus floribunda*
	Purple	'Profusion' is best.
Laburnum	Adam's	+ *Laburnocytisus adamii*
	Common	*Laburnum anagyroides*
	Scotch	*alpinum*
	Voss's	× *watererana* 'Vossii'

Trees for Autumn Colour

Large

Beech	Oak, Common	Roblé beech
Cherry, wild	Oak, Red	Tulip-tree
Hornbeam	Oak, Scarlet	Willow, Crack
Lime, Silver pendent	Poplar, Balsam	Wing-nut Caucasian
Maple, Field	Poplar, Grey	Wing-nut, Hybrid
Maple, Norway	Rauli	Zelkova, Caucasian

Medium

Apple	Pillar	*Malus tschonoskii*
Ash	Green	*Fraxinus pennsylvanica*
	Golden	*excelsior* 'Jaspidea'
	Raywood	*oxycarpa* 'Raywood'
Birch	Himalayan	*Betula utilis*
	Cherry	*lenta*
	Silver	*pendula*
	Yellow	*lutea*

Buck-eye	Hybrid	*Aesculus* × *hybrida*
	Yellow	*flava*
Cherry	Bird	*Prunus padus*
	Sargent	*sargentii*
Golden rain		*Koelreuteria paniculata*
Hickory	Butternut	*Carya cordiformis*
	Mockernut	*tomentosa*
	Pignut	*glabra*
	Shagbark	*ovata*
	Shell-bark	*laciniosa*
Honey-locust		*Gleditsia triacanthos*
Horse chestnut	Japanese	*Aesculus turbinata*
Katsura		*Cercidiphyllum japonicum*
Keaki		*Zelkova serrata*
Maple	Cappadocian	*Acer cappadocicum*
	Italian	*opalus*
	Red	*rubrum*
	Sugar	*saccharum*
Oak, Pin		*Quercus palustris*
Pear, Chanticleer		*Pyrus calleryana* 'Chanticleer'
Sassafras		*Sassafras albidum*
Service tree	Wild	*Sorbus torminalis*
Sweet-gum		*Liquidambar styraciflua*
	Chinese	*formosana*
Tupelo		*Nyssa sylvatica*
Varnish-tree	Japanese	*Rhus verniciflua*
Whitebeam		*Sorbus aria*
Yellow-wood		*Cladrastis lutea*
Sorrel-tree		*Oxydendrum arboreum*

Small

Birch	Transcaucasian	*Betula medwediewii*
Cherry	'Hokusai'	*Prunus* 'Hokusai'
Ironwood	Persian	*Parrotia persica*
Maple	Amur	*Acer ginnala*
	Coral-bark	*palmatum* 'Senkaki'
	Hers's	*hersii*
	Hornbeam	*carpinifolium*
	Japanese	*japonicum* 'Vitifolium'
	Moose-bark	*pensylvanicum*
	Nikko	*nikoense*
	Paper-bark	*griseum*
	Red snake-bark	*capillipes*
	Smooth Japanese	*palmatum* 'Osakazuki'
	Trident	*buergeranum*
	Vine-leaf	*cissifolium*

Rowan	Chinese	*Sorbus commixta*	'Embley'
	Japanese		*commixta*
	Joseph Rock		'Joseph Rock'
	Sargent's		*sargentiana*
	Vilmorin's		*vilmoriniana*
Thorn	Broad-leafed Cockspur	*Crataegus* × *prunifolia*	

Glossary

Acuminate Tapering to a fine point.

Abruptly-acuminate Round or blunt towards the end then suddenly drawn out to a fine point.

Long-acuminate Tapering gradually to a fine long point.

Acute Ending in a sharp point; narrower than 'obtuse'.

Anther The tip of the stamen bearing the pollen.

Axil The angle between the upper side of a leaf-stalk and the shoot bearing it, or between the upper side of a vein and the midrib.

Axis The line of the main stem from base to end.

Basal The segment nearest the stalk or shoot.

Blade The broad part of a leaf or leaflet: the leaf excluding the petiole.

Bloomed Covered partially or wholly with an obscuring pale colour, usually grey, white, lilac or blue.

Chimaera A plant formed of the tissues of two different forms or species, e.g. + *Laburnocytisus adamii* (p. 99).

Columnar Tall with vertical sides; cylindric. This and 'Conic' are the correct desciptions for plants often loosely described as 'Pyramidal'.

Compound (leaf) Composed of leaflets, either on each side of a central stalk (rachis) or radiating from a central point.

Doubly compound With leaflets which are themselves compound.

Conic Tapering from a circular base straight to the tip.

Conic-ovoid Tapering from a circular base by convex curve to the tip; egg-shaped with a conic tip.

Cordate Heart-shaped; leaf or petal with a rounded lobe at each side of the joint with the stalk.

Crenate (toothing) With broad-based, rounded teeth.

Cultivar See pp. 14–15.

Cuneate (leaf) With wedge-shaped base tapering evenly to the stalk.

Long cuneate With wedge-shaped base tapering more gradually to the stalk.

Decurved With the distal end curving downwards towards the tip.

Decussate ('opposite and decussate') Leaves arranged in opposite pairs, each at right-angles to the pair above and the pair below.

Distal (end) the free end opposite to basal end.

Doubly-toothed With teeth that are themselves finely toothed.

Elliptic Longer than broad, and broadest in the middle, curving to each end (cf. *ovate*; *obovate*).

Entire (margin) Without lobes or teeth.

Falcate (leaf) Curved and tapering, like the blade of a scythe.

Fastigiate A crown with branches almost vertical; strictly upright.

Forward (lobes or teeth) Pointing away from the base.

Fruit The seed together with the structure bearing or enclosing it (e.g. acorn plus cup; nut plus husk; pea plus pod).

Fusiform Spindle-shaped; long and narrow, tapering at each end.

Glabrous Without hairs or down; smooth.

Glaucous Pale whitish-green, grey-white or bluish-white.

Globose Roughly globular; approximately spherical.

Inflorescence The structure bearing the flowers; flower-head.

Juvenile (foliage) Leaves which in early years are in a markedly different form from the adult leaves, most prominent in eucalypts.

Lanceolate Spear-shaped; slender ovate-acuminate. Broadest towards the base.

Lateral (buds and shoots) On the side of the main shoot; not terminal.

Leader Leading shoot; the dominant central shoot or axis which should be on every young tree and is vital in conifers.

Lenticel Small corky pore appearing as pale spot on young shoots, in the case of some older trees enlarging and forming bands on the bark.

Lobe Segment of a leaf or petal, divided from adjacent segments.

Lobulate With small lobes.

Mat Non-shiny; dull.

Midrib The main vein, central in many leaves, from which smaller veins branch.

Mucronate With a minute point on the apex.

Node The point on a shoot where growth ceased at the end of a year and restarted the next, usually marked by scars of bud-scales in a ring, and often by a pair or cluster of buds, or shoots. In many conifers, e.g. pines, spruces and silver firs, the node is marked by whorls of main branches. The point on a stem from which pairs of leaves arise.

Nodule An outgrowth on the roots of some trees, e.g. alders and laburnums, in which certain bacteria grow, fed by the tree and able to use the nitrogen in the air in their growth, which the tree itself cannot.

Nutlet A seed which is hard and nut-like but small, as in maples.

Obovate Ovate with the broadest part in the outer half.

Obtuse With a point broader than a right-angle; bluntly pointed.

Ovate (Two-dimensional) Egg-shaped; broadest towards the base.

Ovate-acuminate Egg-shaped lower part, tapering to a long tip in the upper part.

Ovoid (Three-dimensional) Egg-shaped, as in many bulbs.

Panicle A flower-head with a central stem bearing branches.

Pedicel The stalk of a flower or fruit.

Petiole The stalk of a leaf.

Photosynthesis The process taking place in green tissues, in which the energy of sunlight is used in the green dye, chlorophyll, to make sugars and starch from water and carbon dioxide.

Pinnate (leaf) With pairs of leaflets each side of a common stalk; a form of compound leaf.

Pistil The female organs of a flower.

Plane Flat; not buckled or ridged.

Pubescent Covered in fine hairs; downy.

Raceme An inflorescence with a central stem and lateral stalks with flowers which open in succession from base to tip.

Rachis The central stalk of a compound leaf.

Recurved With the distal end curving upwards towards the tip.

Remote (toothing or lobing) Widely spaced; scattered.

Semi-double A flower with more petals than normal but not fully double, when stamens are replaced by petals.

Semi-evergreen The state in which a proportion of leaves remain green in autumn and through the winter, when the rest have been shed.

Serrate (toothing) With numerous sharp teeth like a saw.

Serrulate Very finely serrated.

Sessile Without a stalk; borne directly on the shoot or branch.

Spur A short shoot which bears leaves each year, increasing in length only a little or not at all.

Stamen The male organ of a flower bearing the pollen.

Stigma The part of the female organ of a flower which traps the pollen on its sticky surface.

Stipule An appendage at the base of the petiole, usually strap-like but sometimes leafy.

Striated Marked with lines or spots or streaks.

Sucker A shoot growing up directly from the root-system, often at a considerable distance from the bole; or a sprout on a bole.

Terminal At the tip of a shoot or leaf.

Tomentose Densely covered in hairs.

Trifoliate Bearing leaves of three leaflets.

Truncate Abruptly ended; cut across.

Type tree The wild species as opposed to a variety of it.

Umbel An inflorescence in which flower-stalks radiate from a common point.

Whorl A number of branches, shoots or leaves arising from a common point on the stem.

Notable Tree Collections Open to the Public

Most of the following are open all the year round, others at well-advertised times.

England

Avon	Botanic Garden, Bath Victoria Park, Bath
Bedfordshire	Woburn Abbey Wrest Park, Silsoe
Berkshire	Windsor Great Park (Savill, Valley Gardens; Botany Bay; Totem Pole Ride; Breakheart Hill etc.) University of Reading campus (Whiteknights Park)
Buckinghamshire	Ascott House, Wing, nr Leighton Buzzard Cliveden, Maidenhead Stowe Park
Cambridgeshire	Anglesea Abbey, nr Cambridge University Botanic Garden, Cambridge Clare College Garden, Cambridge Emmanuel College Garden, Cambridge
Cheshire	Jodrell Bank Ness Botanic Gardens, Wirral Tatton Park, Knutsford
Cornwall	Antony House, Tor Point Caerhays Castle, Gorran, St Austell Chyverton, Zelah Cotehele House, Calstock Glendurgan Garden, Helford River Mount Edgcumbe, nr Plymouth Pencarrow Gardens, Bodmin Trelissick Garden, nr Truro Trengwainton Garden, Penzance

Cornwall contd	Tresco Abbey Gardens, Isles of Scilly
	Trewidden, Penzance
	Trewithen Gardens, Probus, nr Truro
Cumbria	Aira Force, Ullswater
	Fallbarrow Park, Bowness
	Holker Hall, Cark-in-Cartmel
	Hutton-in-the-Forest, Penrith
	Lingholm, Keswick
	Monk Coniston
	Patterdale Hall, Ullswater
	Wray Castle, Ambleside
Derbyshire	Chatsworth House, Bakewell
	Elvaston Castle, SE of Derby
	Melbourne Hall
Devon	Arlington Court, Barnstaple
	Bicton Arboretum, East Budleigh
	Cockington Court, nr Torquay
	Dartington Hall, Totnes
	Killerton, nr Exeter
	Knightshayes Court, nr Tiverton
	Knowle Park, Sidmouth
	Powderham Castle, nr Exeter
	Saltram House, Plympton
	University of Devon campus, Exeter
Dorset	Abbotsbury
	Forde Abbey, nr Chard
	Minterne, Dorchester
Durham	Raby Castle, Staindrop, nr Darlington
	University Botanic Garden
Essex	Langleys, Great Waltham
Gloucestershire	Batsford Park Arboretum, Moreton-in-Marsh
	Colesbourne
	Hester Park, Cheltenham
	Sezincote, Moreton-in-Marsh
	Speech House, Coleford
	Stanway House, Winchcombe
	Stratford Park, Stroud
	Westonbirt Arboretum, Tetbury
Hampshire	Ashfield Chase, Petersfield
	Bolderwood, New Forest

Exbury Gardens, nr Southampton
Hillier Arboretum, Ampfield
Hollycombe House Woodland Gardens, Liphook
Jenkyn Place, Bentley
Longstock Park Gardens, nr Stockbridge
Osborne House, nr Newport, I.o.W.
Rhinefield Terrace, New Forest
Stratfield Saye, Reading
Ventnor Botanic Garden, I.o.W.

Herefordshire	Croft Castle, Leominster
	Eastnor Castle, nr Ledbury
	Hergest Croft Gardens, Kington
	Queenswood, Hope-under-Dinmore
	Whitfield House, Thruxton
Hertfordshire	Avenue House, Barnet
	Bayfordbury
	The Beale Arboretum, West Lodge Hotel, Barnet
Kent	National Pinetum, Bedgebury
	Knole Park, Sevenoaks
	Mote Park, Maidstone
	Sandling Park, nr Hythe
	Scotney Castle Garden, Lamberhurst
Leicestershire	Victoria Park, Leicester
	Exton Park (Rutland)
Lincolnshire	Belton Park, Grantham
	Brocklesby Park, Limber
London	Battersea Park
	Cannizaro Park, Wimbledon
	Chiswick House
	Greenwich Park
	Hyde Park
	Kensington Gardens
	Regents Park
	Victoria Park, Bethnal Green
Merseyside	Calderstones Park, Liverpool
Middlesex	Syon House, Isleworth
	Myddleton House, Enfield
	Osterly Park, Hounslow
Norfolk	Lyndford Arboretum, Mundford

Norfolk contd	Ryston, nr King's Lynn
	Sandringham
	Talbot Manor, Fincham
Northamptonshire	Althorp
	Deene Park, nr Corby
Northumberland	Alnwick Castle
	Belsay Castle, Morpeth
	Blagdon, Newcastle
	Cragside, Rothbury
	Howick Gardens, Craster, Alnwick
Nottinghamshire	Clumber Park, Worksop
Oxfordshire	Blenheim Palace, Woodstock
	Nuneham Arboretum, nr Oxford
	Oxford Botanic Garden
	Pusey House Gardens, nr Faringdon
	University Parks, Oxford
Shropshire	Hodnet Hall
	Oakley Park, Ludlow
	Walcot Park, Lydbury
	Weston Park, nr Shifnal
Somerset	Bath Botanic Garden and parks (Avon)
	Clapton Court
	Cricket Wildlife Park
	Nettlecombe Court, Willaton
Staffordshire	Alton Towers
	Biddulph Grange
	Sandon Park, Stafford
	Trentham Park, nr Stoke
Suffolk	Abbey Garden, Bury St Edmunds
	East Bertholt Place
	Hardwicke Park, Bury St Edmunds
	Ickworth, Horringer
	Ipswich Arboretum and Christchurch Park
	Somerleyton Hall, nr Lowestoft
Surrey	Kew Royal Botanic Garden
	Knaphill Nurseries, nr Woking
	London University B.G., Englefield Green
	Nonsuch Park, Epsom
	Riverside and Towpath Gardens, Richmond

	Winkworth Arboretum, Godalming
	Royal Horticultural Society Garden, Wisley
	Tilgates, Bletchingly
Sussex	Alexandra Park, St Leonards
	Borde Hill, Haywards Heath
	Cowdray Park, Midhurst
	Goodwood Park, Chichester
	The High Beeches, Handcross
	Highdown, Goring
	Leonardslee, Lower Beeding, nr Horsham
	Muntham House, Findon (Crematorium)
	Nymans Garden, Handcross
	Petworth House
	Sheffield Park, nr Uckfield
	Tilgate Park, Crawley
	Wakehurst Place, Ardingly
	West Dean Gardens, nr Chichester
	Woolbeding, nr Midhurst
Warwickshire	Birmingham Botanic Garden
	Jephson Park, Leamington Spa
Wiltshire	Bowood Gardens, Calne
	Corsham Court, Chippenham
	Lacock Abbey, nr Chippenham
	Longleat House, Warminster
	Stourhead, nr Mere
	Wilton House, Salisbury
Worcestershire	Burford House, Tenbury Wells
	Hewell Grange, Bromsgrove
	Madresfield Court, Malvern
	Spetchley Park, Pershore
Yorkshire	Castle Howard, nr Malton (being planted)
	Harlow Carr, Ripon
	Newby Hall, Ripon
	Studley Royal, Ripon
	Thorp Perrow Arboretum, Bedale

Wales

Anglesey	Plas Newydd, Llanfair p.g.
Glamorgan	Bute Park, Cardiff
	Dyffryn Garden, St Nicholas, Cardiff

Glamorgan contd	Margam Park, nr Port Talbot
	Roath Park, Cardiff
	St Fagan's Castle, Cardiff
Gwent	Tredegar Park, Newport
Gwynedd	Bodnant Garden, Tal-y-Cafn
	Penrhyn Castle, Bangor
	Portmeirion, Portmadoc
Powys	Evancoyd, Presteigne
	Leighton Woods (Redwood Grove, Royal Forestry Society), Welshpool
	Gliffaes Country House Hotel, Crickhowell
	Powis Castle, Welshpool
	Stanage Park, Knighton

Isle of Man

Laxey Glen
St Helen's
St John's

Scotland

Aberdeen	Balmoral Castle, Ballater
	Drum Castle, Peterculter
	Haddo House, Methlick
Angus	Camperdown Park, Dundee
	Cortachy Castle, Kirriemuir
	Glamis Castle
Argyll	Ardanaiseig, Oban
	Benmore Gardens, Dunoon
	Crarae Garden and Forest Garden, Furnace
	Inverary Castle
	Kilmun Forest Garden, Benmore
	Kilmory Castle
	Stonefield Hotel, Arduaine, Oban
	Strone House, Cairndow
Ayrshire	Auchincruive, Ayr
	Blairquhan, Maybole
	Culzean Castle, Maybole
	Glenapp Castle Gardens, Ballantrae
	Kelburn Castle, Fairlie
	Kilkerran, Maybole
	Roxelle Park, Ayr

Bute	Brodick Castle, Isle of Arran
Dumfries	Castle Milk, Lockerbie Drumlanrig Castle, nr Thornhill
Easter Ross	Castle Leod, Strathpeffer Fairburn, Muir of Ord
East Lothian	Haddington House Smeaton House, East Linton Tyninghame, East Linton Whittingehame, Haddington
Edinburgh	Royal Botanic Garden
Fife	University B.G., St Andrews
Inverness-shire	Armadale Castle, Isle of Skye Balmacaan, Drumnadrochit Moniac Glen, nr Beauly Torosay Castle, Isle of Mull
Kincardineshire	Crathes Castle Fasque House, Glendye Inchmarlo, Banchory
Midlothian	Carberry Tower, Musselburgh
Kirkcudbrightshire	Threave Castle Gardens, Castle Douglas
Morayshire	Innes House, Fochabers
Nairn	Cawdor Castle, Cawdor
Peebles	Dawyck Arboretum, Stobo
Perthshire	Blair Castle, Blair Atholl Blairhoyle, Lake of Menteith Dunkeld House Hotel, Dunkeld The Hermitage, Inver, Dunkeld Scone Palace, Perth
Roxburghshire	The Monteviot Pinery
Stirlingshire	Culcreuch Castle, Fintry
Sutherlandshire	Dunrobin Castle
Wester Ross	Dundonnell, Little Loch Broom Inverewe Garden, Poolewe Lael Forest Garden, Ullapool Leckmelm House, Ullapool
West Lothian	Hopetoun House, nr Edinburgh
Wigtownshire	Castle Kennedy Gardens, Stranraer Logan B.G.

Northern Ireland

County Armagh	Gosford Castle, Markethill
County Down	Castlewellan, Newcastle
	Bangor Castle, Belfast
	Mount Stewart, Newtownards
	Rowallane Garden, Saintfield
	Tullymore Park, Newcastle
County Tyrone	Drum Manor

Republic of Ireland

County Cork	Annesgrove, Castletownroche
	Ashbourne House Hotel
	Fota Island
	Illnacullin, Gairnish
Co Dublin	Glasnevin Botanic Garden
Co Kerry	Dunloe Castle Hotel, Killarney
	Killarney Castle
	Muckross Abbey, Killarney
	Rossdohan, Sneem
Co Kilkenny	Woodstock Country Park, Inistioge
Co Leix	Emo Court, Emo
Co Limerick	Adare Manor
	Curragh Chase, Asheaton
Co Offaly	Birr Castle
Co Waterford	Mount Congreve, Waterford
Co Westmeath	Tullynally Castle, Mullingar
Co Wexford	John F. Kennedy Arboretum, New Ross
	Johnstown Castle
Co Wicklow	Avondale Forest School, Rathdrum
	Charleville, Enniskerry
	Glencormac (Avoca Handweavers) Kilmacanogue, Bray Charleville, Enniskerry
	Kilmacurragh, Rathdrum
	Mount Usher, Ashford
	Powerscourt, Enniskerry

Index

Abbotsbury, Dorset 92, 198
Abele 114
Abies 148–52
  alba 50, 148
    'Pyramidata' 185
  amabilis 148
  concolor 149
    var. *Lowiana* 149
      'Violacea' 149
  bracteata 149
  cephalonica 150
    var. *apollinis* 150
  delavayi var. *forrestii* 150
  forrestii 150
  grandis 49, 150
  Holophylla 151
  homolepis 151
  koreana 151
  lasiocarpa var. *arizonica* 151,
    185, 190
  magnifica 151, 185
  mariesii 151
  nordmanniana 151
  numidica 151
  pectinata 148
  pindrow 152
  procera 50, 152
  veitchii 152
  venusta 149
Acacia dealbata 55
Acacia, False 130
Acanthopanax ricinifolius 97
Acer 55–67
  buergeranum 55, 190, 192
  campestre 56
    'Postelense' 189
  capillipes 56, 190, 192

  cappadocicum 57, 192
    'Aureum' 57, 189
  carpinifolium 57, 192
  cissifolium 58, 192
  crataegifolium 58
  dasycarpum 64
  ginnala 58, 192
  griseum 190, 192
  hersii 34, 59, 190, 192
  japonicum 60
    'Aureum' 189, 190
    'Vitifolium' 60, 190, 192
  lobelii 60, 186
  macrophyllum 60
  negundo 61
    'Auratum' 61, 189, 190
    'Elegans' 187
    'Variegatum' 61, 188,
      190
    'Violaceum' 61
  nikoense 61, 192
  opalus 192
  palmatum
    'Atropurpureum' 188
    'Aureum' 189
    'Osakazuki 190, 192
    'Senkaki' 190, 192
  pensylvanicum 190, 192
  platanoides 45, 62
    'Columnare' 62, 186
    'Crimson King' 188
    'Drummondii' 62, 189
    'Erectum' 62, 186
    'Faasen's Black' 62, 188
    'Fastigiatum' 186
    'Globosum' 62
    'Goldsworth Purple' 62,

    188
    'Pyramidale' 62
    'Schwedleri' 62
  pseudoplatanus 45, 62
    'Atropurpureum' 188
    'Brilliantissimum' 63
    'Corstorphinense' 189
    'Erectum' 186
    'Prinz Handjery' 63
    'Spaethi' 188
    'Variegatum' 188
    'Worleei' 189
  rubrum 63, 192
    'Columnare' 186
  rufinerve 64
  saccharinum 45, 64
    'Laciniatum' 65
  saccharum 65, 192
  trautvetteri 66
  x zoeschense 67
Adam's laburnum 99
Aesculus 67–9
  flava 53, 67, 192
  hippocastanum 45, 49, 67
    'Baumannii' 68
    'Hampton Court' 68, 187
  x hybrida 192
  indica 68
    'Sidney Pearce' 69
  turbinata 69, 192
Ailanthus altissima 69
Alder 69–71
  Caucasian 5, 71
  Common 70
  Cut-leaf 70
  Golden 37, 70
  Grey 5, 70

Italian 51, 69
Japanese 70
Oregon 71
Red 71
Alder whitebeam 133
Alerce 161
Algerian fir 152
Algerian oak 123
Alligator juniper 162
Almond 5
Alnus 69–71
  cordata 51, 69
  firma 70
  glutinosa 70
    'Aurea' 70, 189
    'Imperialis' 70
    'Laciniata' 70
    'Pyramidalis' 186
  incana 70
    'Aurea' 71, 189
    'Pendula' 71
    'Ramulis Coccineis' 33, 71
  rubra 71
  subcordata 71
Alpine fir 8
American lime 139
Amur maple 58
Antarctic beech 107
Apple 104–06
  Cherry 105
  Hupeh crab 104
  Japanese crab 104
  Magdeburg 105
  Pillar xi, 105
  Purple crab 105
Araucaria araucana 51, 153
Arbutus 72–3
  andrachne 72, 190
  x *andrachnoides* 72
  menziesii 40, 72
  unedo 40, 73
Arizona fir 151
Armenian oak 128
Arolla pine ix, 5, 168
Ash 90–1
  Caucasian 5, 91
  Common 3, 45, 91

Flowering 91
Golden 91
Manna 91
Narrow-leafed 91
One-leafed 91
Weeping 91
Ashford Chase, Sussex 102
Ash-leafed maple 15, 61
Aspen 3
Australia pine 5, 171

Bamboo oak 127
Banister, John 5
Banks, Sir Joseph 6
Battersea Park, London 97, 199
Bay 5
Bay willow 132
Beautiful fir 8, 148
Beech 44, 49, 88–90
  Antarctic 107
  Black 109
  Chinese 88
  Common 88
  Copper 90
  Cut-leafed 89
  Dawyck 51
  Dombey's southern 108
  Fastigiate 89
  Fern-leafed 15, 89
  Golden 90
  Moore's southern 108
  Mountain 109
  Oak-leafed 89
  Oriental 88
  Purple 90
  Red 108
  Weeping x, 15, 90
Betula 73–6
  ermanii 73
  jacquemontii 73, 190
  lenta 74, 191
  lutea 74, 191
  maximowicziana 52, 74
  medwediewii 74, 190, 192
  nigra 75, 190
  papyrifera 75
  pendula 75, 191

'Darlecarlica' 76
'Fastigiata' 186
'Purpurea' 188
platyphylla var. *szechuanica* 76
utilis 73, 190, 191
verrucosa 75
Bhutan pine 6, 175
Bicton Arboretum, Devon 153, 198
Big-cone pine 169
Big shell-bark hickory 78
Big tree 177
Birch 73–6
  Black 75
  Cherry 74
  Cut-leaf 76
  Erman's 73
  Hamalayan 73
  Jacquemont's 73
  Kashmir 73
  Monarch 52, 74
  Paper-bark 6, 75
  River 75
  Silver 42, 75
  Swedish 76
  Szechuan 76
  Tanscaucasain 74
  Yellow 74
Bird cherry 116
Bishop pine 7, 34, 42, 43, 170
Bitternut 77
Black beech 109
Black birch 75
Black gum 109
Black Italian poplar viii, 45
Black mulberry 5, 106
Black pine, Japanese 174
Black walnut 49, 96
Blue Atlas cedar 50, 154
Blue Colorado spruce 8, 167
Blue gum 8, 33, 48
Bolle's poplar x, 114
Borde Hill, Sussex 143, 200
Bosnian pine 52, 170
Botanic Garden, Bath 115, 200

Botanic Garden,
Cambridge 96, 197
Box-elder 61
Bradford pear xii, 120
Brewer spruce xii, 51, 165
Broad-leafed kindling-bark 85
Broad-leafed lime 46, 142
Butternut 96
Butt-rot (*Fomes annosus*) 48
Buxus semperivirens
'Aureovariegata' 187
'Marginata' 187
Cabbage tree xii
Caerhays Castle, Cornwall
104, 197
Californian laurel 145
Calocedrus decurrens 52, 153,
185
'Aureovariegata' 187
'Variegata' 154
Campell's magnolia 103
Cappadocian maple 40, 57
Carpinus betulus 76
'Columnaris' 77
'Fastigiata' 53, 76
japonica 77
Carya 77–8
cordiformis 77, 192
glabra 192
laciniosa 78, 192
ovata 77, 192
tomentosa 78, 192
Castanea sativa 45, 78
'Albomarginata' 187
Castle Kennedy,
Wigtownshire 153, 203
Castor Aralia 97
Catalpa 79–80
bignonioides 79
'Aurea' 79, 189
x *erubescens* 80
x *hybrida* 80
ovata 80
speciosa 79
Catalpa 79–80
Hybrid 80
Northern 79
Southern 79

Western 5
Yellow 80
Caucasian alder 5, 71
Caucasian ash 5, 91
Caucasian fir 151
Caucasian lime x, 140
Caucasian oak 127
Caucasian wing-nut 5, 37,
119
Caucasian zelkova 5, 50, 145
Cedar 154–5
Blue Atlas ix, 50, 154
Chinese 80
Incense 52, 153
Japanese red 158
of Lebanon 48, 155
of Lebanon, Golden 155
Northern white 180
Western red 50, 181
Cedrela 80
Cedrus 154–5
atlantica var. *glauca* 50, 154
'Aurea' 154, 188
'Fastigiata' 154, 185
deodara 154
libani 48, 155
'Aurea' 155, 188
Cephalotaxus harringtonia
'Fastigiata' 186
Cercidiphyllum japonicum 51,
80, 192
Cercis siliquastrum 81
Chamaecyparis 155–8
lawsoniana
'Albovariegata' 187
'Allumii' 156
'Aureomaculata' 187
'Columnaris' 156, 185
'Ellwoodii' 156, 185
'Erecta Viridis' 155
'Fletcheri' 156, 185
'Green Pillar' 156
'Green Spire' 156
'Hillieri' 188
'Intertexta' 156
'Kilmacurragh' 185
'Lane's Golden' 156, 188
'Lutea' 156, 185, 188

'New Silver' 156
'Pembury Blue' 156
'Pottenii' 157
'Stewartii' 157, 188
'Triumph of
Boskoop' 157
'Westermannii' 157
'Winston Churchill' 18,
188
'Wisselii' 52, 157, 185
nootkatensis 157
'Pendula' 158
obtusa 158
'Aurea' 158
'Crippsii' 158, 188
'Tetragona Aurea' 158,
188
pisifera 158
'Argentea' 187
'Aurea' 158, 189
'Filifera Aurea' 189
'Plumosa' 187
'Plumosa Aurea' 189
'Squarrosa' 158
Chequers tree 137
Cherry apple 105
Cherry birch 74
Cherry, Bird 3, 116
Cherry, Double-flowered
sour 116
Cherry, Manchurian 116
Cherry, Rose-bud 119
Cherry, Sargent 117
Cherry, Sato 117
Cherry, Sheraton 117
Cherry, Tibetan 117
Cherry, Wild 3, 116
Cherry, Winter 119
Chestnut
Horse 45, 49, 67
Indian horse 68
Japanese horse 69
Spanish 78
Sweet 9, 45, 78
Chestnut-leafed oak 5, 33, 50,
124
Chile pine 153
Chinese beech 88

Chinese cedar 80
Chinese cork oak 129
Chinese elm 143
Chinese euodia 87
Chinese evergreen
    magnolia 103
Chinese fir 159
Chinese liquidambar 100
Chinese necklace poplar 115
Chinese privet 5, 100
Chinese stuartia 138
Chinese stuartia 138
Chinese sweet gum 53, 100
Chinese thuja 5, 181
Chinese tulip-tree 6, 102
Chinese whitebeam 134
Chusan palm xi, 6, 142
Cider gum 33, 86
Cladrastis lutea 192
Cliveden, Buckinghamshire
    96, 197
Coast redwood vii, 8, 33, 50,
    177
Cockspur, Broad-leafed
    hybrid 83
Cockspur thorn 82
Coffin juniper 162
Coigue 108
Collinson, Peter 5
Common alder 70
Common ash 90
Common beech 88
Common lime 46, 140
Common oak 44, 128
Common silver fir 50, 148
Common walnut 97
Compton, Henry 5, 61
Copper beech 90
Cork fir 151
Cornish elm 3, 4, 44, 144
Cornus controversa 81
    'Variegata' 82, 187
Corsican pine vii, 41, 171
Corylus colurna 52, 82
Coulter pine 169
Cox's juniper xi, 162
Crab apple 104–6
    Hupeh 104

Japanese 104
'John Downie' 104
Magdeburg 105
Purple 105
Crack willow 3, 131
Crataegus 82–3
    x *carrieri* 82
    'coccinea' 82
    coccinioides 82
    crus-galli 82
    x *lavallei* 82, 191
    mollis 82
    monogyna 'Fastigiata' 186
    pedicellata 82
    phaenopyrum 83, 191
    x *prunifolia* 83, 191, 193
    sumbollis 82
Crimean lime 140
Crimean pine viii
Cryptomeria japonica 6, 158
    'Elegans' 159, 188
    'Lobbii' 159
Cucumber tree 103
Cunninghamia lanceolata 6,
    159
x *Cupressocyparis leylandii* 52
    159–61
    'Castlewellan' 160, 189
    'Golconda' 160
    'Haggerston Grey' 159, 160
    'Leighton Green' 159, 160
    'Naylor's Blue' 159, 160
    'Robinson's Gold' 160, 189
    'Stapehill' 20, 160
    'Stapehill' 21, 160
Cupressus
    arizonica var. *bonita* 160
    glabra 52, 160
        'Pyramidalis' 160
    macrocarpa 160
        'Donard Gold' 161, 189
        'Fastigiata' 185
        'Lutea' 161, 189
        'Goldcrest' 189
        'Gold Pillar' 189
    sempervirens 161, 185
Cut-leaf alder 70
Cut-leaf beech 89

Cut-leaf lime 142
Cypress
    Bald 178
    Cripps's 158, 188
    Hinoki 54, 158, 188
    Italian ix, 5, 161
    Lawson 11, 15, 54, 155,
        188
    Leyland viii, 33, 52, 159
    Monterey 34, 43, 54, 160
    Nootka ix, 7, 157
    Pond xii, 178
    Sawara 158
    Smooth Arizona ix, 52, 160
    Swamp viii, 5, 37, 151,
        178
    Wissel 52
    Yellow 157
Cypress oak ix, 51, 128
Cyprus strawberry tree 72
Daimyo oak 124
David, Father 6, 84
Davidia involucrata 84
    var. *vilmoriniana* 84
Dawn redwood ix, 33, 37, 51,
    164
Dawyck beech 51
Dawyck, Peebles-shire 89
Deciduous cemellia 137
Delavay, Father 6
Deodar 6, 154
Dogwood, Table 81
Dombey's southern beech 108
Douglas, David 7, 8, 152,
    169, 172, 176
Douglas fir 6, 7, 8, 17, 34,
    46, 50, 176
Dove tree 84
Downy birch 3
Downy euodia 87
Downy Japanese maple 60
Dragon's claw willow 132
Drimys winteri 84
Durmast oak 128
Dutch elm 145
Eastern hemlock 182
Eastern thuja 180
Elm 4, 46, 143–5

Chinese 143
Cornish 3, 4, 44, 144
Dutch 145
English 145
Huntingdon 44, 145
Jersey 144
Siberian 143
Wych 3, 44, 144
Empress tree 111
English elm 145
Erect Scots pine 174
Erman's birch 73
Eucalyptus 85–7
 dalrympleana 85
 de Beauzenvillei 87
 globulus 48, 86
 gunnii 86
 johnstoni 86
 mitchelliani 86
 nicholii 86
 niphophila 86
 nitens 87
Eucommia ulmoides 87
Euodia 87
 danielli 87
 hupehensis 43, 87
 velutina 87
Euodia 87
 Chinese 87
 Downy 87
Euonymus
 Fimbriatus 88
 lucidus 88
European hop-hornbeam 110
European larch 4, 5, 9, 34,
 46, 163
European silver fir 148
Evergreen magnolia, Chinese
 103
Evergreen oak, Japanese 122

Fagus 88–91
 orientalis 88
 sylvatica 44, 49, 88
 'Albovariegata' 187
 'Asplenifolia' 89
 'Cockleshell' 90
 'Cupraea' 90

'Dawyck' 51, 89, 186
'Heterophylla' 89
'Laciniata' 89
'Luteovariegata' 187
'Pendula' 90
'Purpea' 90, 188
'Quercifolia' 89
'Riversii' 90
'Rivers's Purple' 90, 188
'Rotundifolia' 90
'Zlatia' 90, 189
False acacia 130
Farges, Father 6, 84
Fastigiate beech 89
Fastigiate hornbeam 53
Fern-leaf beech 15, 89
Field maple 3, 40, 56
Fig 4
Fir 148–50
 Algerian 152
 Alpine 8
 Arizona 151
 Beautiful 8, 148
 Caucasian 151
 Chinese 159
 Common silver vii, 148
 Cork 151
 Douglas 6, 7, 8, 17, 34, 46,
 50, 176
 European silver 148
 Forrest's 150
 Grand 7, 8, 34, 46, 50,
 176
 Grecian 150
 Korean 151
 Low's viii, 8, 41, 149
 Manchurian 151
 Maries's 151
 Nikko 151
 Noble 152
 Pindrow 152
 Red vii, 7, 8, 148, 151
 Santa Lucia 8, 149
 Shasta 8
 Veitch's silver 152
Fitzroya
 cupressoides 7, 161
 patagonica 161

Flowering ash 91
Forrest, George 6
Forrest's fir 150
Fortune, Robert 6
Fraser, John 5
Fraxinus 90–1
 angustifolia 91
 excelsior 45, 90
 'Aurea' 91
 'Diversifolia' 91
 'Jaspidea' 91, 189, 191
 'Pendula' 91
 ornus 91
 oxycarpa 91
 'Raywood' 91, 191
 pensylvanica 191

Gean 116
Giant Sequoia xii, 7, 40, 46,
 47, 177
Ginkgo biloba 5, 11, 41, 42,
 51, 146
 'Fastigiata' 147, 185
Gleditsia triacanthos 91, 192
 'Sunburst' 92, 189
Glossy privet 100
Golden alder 37, 70
Golden ash 91
Golden-barred thuja 51
Golden beech 90
Golden black poplar 45, 115
Golden catalpa 79
Golden cedar of Lebanon 155
Golden Chinese juniper 161
Golden larch 6, 51, 175
Golden raintree 99
Golden Scots pine 74
Govan, Dr 6
Grand fir 7, 8, 34, 49, 150
Grecian fir 150
Greenwich Park, London 87,
 199
Grey alder 5, 70
Grey-budded snake-bark
 maple 56, 64
Grey poplar 44, 45
Gum trees 85–7
 Black 109

Blue 8, 33, 48, 86
Cider 8, 33, 86
Chinese sweet 53, 100
Pepper 86
Snow 86
Shining 33, 87
Sweet 37, 41, 53
Gutta-percha tree 87
Gymnocladus dioicus 92

Handkerchief tree 84
Hartweg, Theodore 7, 8, 168
Haw, Scarlet 82
Hawthorn 3
Hawthorn maple 58
Hazel, Turkish x, 5, 52, 82
Hemlock 182–3
    Eastern 182
    Mountain 7, 40, 182
    Western vii, 7, 34, 42, 48,
        182
Hemsley's storax 138
Henry, Augustine 6
Hers's maple 59
Hiba 182
Highclere hybrid hollies 94
Hickory 77–8
    Big shell-bark 78
    Shagbark 77
Himalayan birch 73
Halesia
    carolina 92
    monticola 92
        'Rosea' 92
Hodgins's holly 42, 44, 94
Holford pine 169
Holly 94–6
    Common 3, 95
    Highclere hybrids 94
    Hodgins's 42, 44, 94
    Lawson's 95
    Madeira 94
    Weeping 96
    Wilson's 95
Holm oak 4, 5, 44, 126
Hondo spruce 165
Honey locust 11, 43, 91
Hop-hornbeam,

European 110
Hornbeam 3, 41, 76–7
    Fastigiate (Pyramidal) xi,
        53, 76
    Japanese 77
Hornbeam maple 57
Horse chestnut 45, 49, 67–9
    Indian 68
    Japanese 69
Hungarian oak vii, 48, 124
Huntingdon elm 145
Hupeh crab apple 104
Hupeh rowan 134
Hybrid catalpa 180
Hybrid larch 34, 163
Hybrid strawberry tree 72
Hybrid wing-nut 33, 120

Idesia polycarpa 92
Ilex 94–6
    x *altaclerensis* 94
        'Camelliifolia' 94
        'Golden King' 95, 187
        'Hendersonii' 95
        'Heterophylla' 94
        'Hodginsii' 94
        'Lawsoniana' 94, 187
        'Nobilis' 95
        'Wilsonii' 95, 190
    aquifolium 95
        'Bacciflava' 95
        'Golden Queen' 95, 187
        'Handsworth New
            Silver' 95, 188, 190
        'Laurifolia' 96
        'Pendula' 96
        'Perry's Weeping' 95,
            188, 190
        'Pyramidalis' 96, 190
    perado 94
Incense cedar 52, 153
Indian bean tree 43, 79
Insignis pine 173
Irish yew 180
Italian alder 51, 69
Italian cypress ix, 161
Italian maple 40
Ivy 26

Jacquermont's birch 73
Japanese alder 70
Japanese black pine 174
Japanese chestnut oak 122
Japanese crab apple 104
Japanese evergreen oak 122
Japanese hornbeam 77
Japanese horse chestnut 69
Japanese larch 163
Japanese maples 140
Japanese red cedar 158
Japanese red pine 169
Japanese thuja 181
Japanese umbrella pine 176
Japanese walnut 96
Japanese white pine 171
Jeffrey, John 7, 170, 181
Jeffrey pine 7, 49, 170
Jersey elm 144
Judas tree 5, 81
Juglans 96–7
    ailantifolia 96
    cinerea 96
    microcarpa 96
    nigra 49, 96
    regia 97
    rupestris 96
Juniper 161–3
    Alligator 162
    Coffin 162
    Cox's xi, 162
    Golden Chinese 161
    Meyer's 162
    Syrian xii, 162
    Wallich's 163
Juniperus 161–3
    chinensis 'Aurea' 161, 186,
        189
    deppeana var. *pachyphloea*
        162
    drupacea 162, 185
    recurva var. *coxii* 162
    squamata 'Meyeri' 162
    virginiana 'Cupressoides'
        185
    wallichiana 163

Kalopanax pictus 97

var. *maximowiczii* 97
Kashmir birch 73
Katsura tree 41, 51, 80
Kentucky coffee tree 92
Kerr, John 6
Killerton, Devon 100, 198
Knaphill Nurseries, Surrey 8,
    15, 90, 124, 167, 200
Koelreuteria paniculata 99,
    190, 192
    'Fastigiata' 186
Korean fir 151
Korean pine 170
Korean thuja 180

+*Laburnocytisus adamii* 99,
    191
Laburnum 99–100
    Adam's 99
    Voss's hybrid 100
Laburnum
    alpinum 191
    anagyroides 191
    watere ana 'Vossii' 100,
        191
Lacebark pine 168
Ladder-leaf rowan 136
Larch 163–4
    European 4, 5, 9, 34, 46,
        163
    Golden 6, 51, 175
    Hybrid 34, 163
    Japanese 163
Larix 163–4
    decidua 46, 163
    x *eurolepis* 163
    europaea 163
    kaempferi 163
Laurel, Californian 145
Lawson cypress 11, 15, 155
Lebanon oak 126
Leighton Hall, Powys 159,
    201
Leyland cypress viii, 33, 52,
    159
Libocedrus decurrens 153
Ligustrum lucidum 100, 190
    'Excelsum Superbum' 187

'Tricolor' 188
Likiang spruce 165
Lime 139–42
    American 139
    Broad-leafed 46, 142
    Caucasian x, 140
    Common 46, 48, 140
    Mongolian 140
    Oliver's 53, 141
    Silver 142
    Silver pendent x, 48, 141
    Von Moltke's 140
Linden *see Lime*
Liquidambar 100–1
    formosana 53, 100, 192
    styraciflua 53, 101, 192
Liriodendron 102–3
    chinense 102
    tulipifera 49, 102
        'Aureomarginatum' 103,
            187
        'Fastigiatum' 103, 186
Lobb, William 7, 8, 181
Lobel's maple 40, 60
Locust tree 42, 130
Lombardy poplar vii, 52
London plane 41, 42, 44, 47,
    113
    'Augustine Henry' 47
Louisiana oak 127
Low's fir viii, 8, 41, 149
Lucombe oak 126

Macedonian pine 52, 172
Madrona 72
Magdeburg apple 105
Magnolia 103–4
    acuminata 103
    campbellii 103
        'Charles Raffill' 103
    delavayi 103
    denudata 103
    x *soulangiana* 103
    x *loebneri* 104, 190
    marcrophylla 190
    salicifolia 190
    sprengeri 190
        var. *diva* 104

var. *elongata* 104
Magnolia 103–4
    Campbell's 103
    Chinese evergreen 103
Maidenhair tree ix, 146
Malus 104–6
    floribunda 104, 106, 191
    hupehensis 104, 190
    'John Downie' 104, 190
    x *magdeburgensis* 105
    x *purpurea* 105, 188
        'Liset' 105
        'Royal Red' 105
        'Profusion' 105, 191
    trilobata 105
    tschonoskii 105, 186, 190,
        191
    'Van Eseltine' 106, 186,
        190
Manchurian cherry 116
Manchurian fir 151
Manna ash 91
Maple 55–67
    Amur 58
    Ash-leaf 15, 61
    Cappadociano 40, 57
    Downy Japanese 60
    Field 3, 40, 56
    Great 62
    Grey-budded snake-bark 64
    Hawthorn 58
    Hers's 59
    Hornbeam 57
    Lobel's 40, 60
    Nikko 40, 61
    Norway 5, 9, 45, 62
    Oregon 60
    Red 5, 37, 63
    Red snake-bark 56
    Silver 45, 64
    Sugar 65
    Trautvetter's 66
    Trident 55
    Vine-leaf 58
    Zoeschense 40, 67
Maries, Charles 6
Maries's fir 151
Matthew, J. D. 7

Menzies, Archibald 7, 8
Metasequoia glyptostroboides
    51, 164
Mexican white pine 8, 168
Meyer's juniper 162
Michaux, André 5
Michelia doltsopa 106
Mimosa 55
Mirbeck's oak 123
Mockernut 78
Monarch birch 52, 74
Mongolian linden 140
Monkey-puzzle tree 7, 40, 51,
    153
Monterey cypress 34, 43, 160
Monterey pine viii, 33, 34,
    43, 173
Montezuma pine 8, 170
Moore's southern beech 108
Morinda spruce 6, 167
Morus 106–7
    alba 107
    nigra 106
Mote Park, Maidstone 97,
    199
Mottisfont Abbey,
        Hampshire 113
Mountain ash 133
Mountain hemlock 7, 40, 182
Muckross Abbey, Co.
        Kerry 170, 203
Mulberry 106–7
    Black 5, 106
    White 5, 107
Myrtle, Oregon 145
Myrtus luma 107, 190

Narrow-leafed ash 91
National Pinetum, Bedgebury,
        Kent 162, 165, 170,
        177, 199
Nikko fir 40, 151
Nikko maple 61
Noble fir 7, 50, 152
Nootka cypress ix, 7, 157
Northern catalpa 79
Northern white cedar 180
Norway maple 5, 9, 45

Norway spruce 4, 5, 40, 164
Nothofagus 107–9
    antarctica 107
    dombeyi 108
    fusca 108
    moorei 108
    obliqua 108
    procera 53, 109
    solandri 109
Nymans Garden, Sussex 108,
    109
Nyssa sylvatica 53, 109, 192

Oak 122–30
    Algerian 123
    Armenian 128
    Bamboo 127
    Black 130
    Caucasian 127
    Chinese cork 129
    Chestnut 122
    Chestnut-leafed 5, 33, 50,
        124
    Common 44, 128
    Cypress ix, 128
    Daimyo 124
    Durmast 128
    Holm 5, 44, 126
    Hungarian vii, 48, 124
    Japanese evergreen 122
    Lebanon 126
    Lucombe 126
    Ludwig's 127
    Mirbeck's 123
    Pin 53, 128
    Quercitron 130
    Red 129
    Sawtooth 122
    Scarlet 124
    Sessile 44, 50, 128
    Turkey 46, 50, 124
    White 123
Oak-leafed beech 89
Oldham, Charles 6
Oliver's lime 53, 141
One-leafed ash 91
Oregon alder 71
Oregon maple 60

Oregon myrtle 145
Oriental beech 88
Oriental plane 5, 41, 114
Ostrya carpinifolia 110
Oxydendrum arboreum 110,
    191, 192

Pacific strawberry tree 72
Pagoda tree 5, 133
Palm, Chusan xi, 6, 142
Paper-bark birch 6, 75
Parrotia persica 111, 192
Paulownia tomentosa 6, 34,
    111, 190
Peach 5
Pear 120
    Bradford xii, 120
    Willow-leafed 120
Persian ironwood 111
Picea 164–8
    abies 164
    brachytyla 164
    brewerana 51, 165, 190
    glauca 186
    jezoensis var. *hondoensis* 165
    likiangensis 165
    mariana 186
    omorika 52, 166, 186, 190
    orientalis 166
        'Aurea' 166
    pungens f. *glauca* 167
        'Hoopesii' 167
        'Koster' 167
    sitchensis 50, 167
    smithiana 167
Picrasma quassioides 113
Pillar apple xi, 105
Pin oak 53, 128
Pindrow fir 152
Pine 164–8
    Aleppo 42
    Arolla ix, 5, 168
    Austrian 5, 43, 117
    Bhutan 6, 175
    Big-cone 169
    Bishop 7, 34, 42, 43, 170
    Bosnian 52, 170
    Chile 153

Corsican vii, 40, 171
Coulter 7, 169
Erect Scots 174
Golden Scots 174
Holford 169
Japanese black 174
Japanese red 169
Japanese umbrella 176
Japanese white 171
Jeffrey 7, 170
Korean 170
Lacebark 168
Macedonian 52, 172
Maritime 5, 42
Mexican white 8, 168
Monterey viii, 7, 33, 42, 43, 173
Montezuma 8, 170
Ponderosa 172
Scots 42, 173
Stone 5, 172
Swiss stone 168
Western yellow viii, 50, 172
Westonbirt hybrid 169
Pinus 164–8
  ayacahuite 168, 169
  bungeana 168
  cembra 168
  coulteri 169
  densiflora 169
    'Aurea' 169, 189
    'Umbraculifera' 169
  x *holfordiana* 169
  jeefreyi 49, 170
  koraiensis 170
  leucodermis 52, 170
  montezumae 170
  muricata 170
  nigra maritima 171
  nigra nigra 43, 171
  parviflora 171
  peuce 52, 172
  pinea 172
  ponderosa 50, 172
  radiata 173
  strobus 'Fastigiata' 185
  sylvestris 173

  'Aurea' 174, 189
  "Fastigiata" 174, 186
  thunbergii 43, 174
  wallichiana 175
Pittosporum tenuifolium 113
Plane 113–14
  London 41, 42, 113
  Oriental 5, 41, 114
Platanaus 113–14
  x *acerifolia* 44, 47, 113
    'Augustine Henry' 113
    'Pyramidalis' 113
    'Suttneri' 114, 187
  orientalis 114
    'Digitata' 114
Plum-fruited yew 175
Podocarpus andinus 175
Pond cypress xii, 178
Ponderosa pine 172
Poplar 114–15
  Black Italian viii, 45
  Bolle's x, 114
  Chinese necklace 115
  Golden black 45, 115
  Grey 4, 44, 45, 114
  Lombardy vii, 52
  Robusta 33, 37, 41, 102, 115
  White 4, 44, 114
Populus 114–15
  alba 114
    'Richardii' 114, 189
    'Pyramidalis' 114, 186
  x *candicans* 'Aurora' 114, 187
  canescens 45, 114
  deltoides 15
  lasiocarpa 115
  nigra 115
    'Gigantea' 115, 186
    'Italica' 52, 186
    'Robusta' 115
    'Serotina' 41, 45
    'Serotina Aurea' 45, 115, 189
  trichocarpa x *balsamea* 'TT32' 186
Prickly castor-oil tree 97

Pride of India 99
Prince Albert's yew 176
Privet 100
  Chinese 6, 100
  Glossy 100
Prunus 117–19
  'Accolade' 116
  avium 116
    'Plena' 116
  cerasus 'Rhexii' 116
  'Hally Jolivette' 119
  x *hillieri* 'Spire' 186
  'Kursar' 119
  maackii 116
  padus 116, 192
    'Colorata' 117
    'Watererl' 117
  sargentii 117, 190, 192
  serrula 117, 190
  serrulata 117
    'Amonogawa' 118, 186
    'Fugenzo' 118
    'Hokusai' 118, 191
    'Kanzan' 14, 116, 118, 191
    'Okiku' 118
    'Pink Pernection' 118
    'Shimidsu' 118
    'Shirofugen' 118
    'Shirotae' 118
    'Tai Haku' 119, 191
    'Ukon' 119
  subhirtella 119
    'Autumnalis' 119
    'Pendula' 119
    'Rosea' 119
  yedoensis 191
Pseudolarix amabilis 51, 175
Pseudotsuga menziesii 46, 50, 176
  'Fastigiata' 185
Pterocarya 119–20
  fraxinifolia 119
  x *rehderana* 120
Purple beech 90
Purple crab apple 105
Pusey House, Oxfordshire 113, 200

Pyramidal hornbeam xii, 53, 76
Pyrus 120
  calleryana 'Bradford' 120
    'Chanticleer' 120, 190, 192
  elaeagrifolia 120
  salicifolia 190

Quassia tree 113
Quercus 122–30
  acuta 122
  acutissima 122
  alba 123
  canariensis 123
  castaneifolia 50, 124
  cerris 46, 50, 124
    'Variegata' 187
  coccinea 124
    'Splendens' 124
  dentata 124
  frainetto 48, 124
  x *hispanica*
    'Lucombeana' 126
  ilex 126
  libani 126
  x *ludoviciani* 127
  macranthera 127
  myrsinifolia 127
  palustris 53, 128, 192
  pendunculata 128
  petraea 44, 50, 128
    'Columna' 128, 186
  pontica 128
  robur 44, 128
    'Atropurpurea' 188
    'Concordia' 189
    'Fastigiata' 51, 128, 186
    'Purpurea' 188
    'Variegata' 187
  rubra 129
    'Aurea' 187
  suber 129
  variabilis 129
  velutina 130
    'Rubrifolia' 130

Railway poplar x

Rauli 7, 9, 33, 53, 109
Red alder 71
Red beech 108
Red cedar, Japanese 158
Red cedar, Western 181
Red fir vii, 7, 8, 148
Red maple x, 5, 63
Red oak 129
Red pine, Japanese 169
Red snake-bark maple 56
Redwood
  Coast vii, 8, 33, 46, 50, 177
  Dawn ix, 33, 37, 51, 164
  Sierra 42, 46, 177
Rhus verniciflua 130, 192
River birch 75
Robinia
  hispida 190
  pseudoacacia 130
    'Frisia' 130, 189
    'Fastigiata' 186
Roblé 7, 33, 108
Robusta poplar 33, 37, 115
Roche's Arboretum, West Dean 39
Rock, Joseph 6
Rose-bud cherry 119
Rowan 3, 42, 133–7
  Hupeh 134
  Ladder-leaf 136
  Sargent 136
  Scarlet xii, 133
  Vilmorin xii, 137

Salix 130–2
  alba 130
    'Argentea' 130
    'Britzensis' 130
    'Tristis' 131
  caprea 131
  x *chrysocoma* 52, 131
  fragilis 131
  matsudana 'Tortuosa' 132, 191
  pentandra 132, 191
  x *rubens* 131
Sallow 3, 42, 131

Santa Lucia fir 7, 149
Sargent, Charles 6
Sargent cherry 117
Sargent rowan 136
Sargent spruce 164
Sassafras albidum 132, 192
Sato cherries 117
Sawtooth oak 122
Saxegothaea conspicua 7, 176
Scarlet haw 82
Scarlet oak 124
Scarlet rowan xii, 133
Scholar's tree 133
Sciadopitys verticillata 176
Scone Place Pinetum, Perth 167, 203
Scots pine 173
Sentinel ginko 147
Sequoia sempervirens 46, 50, 177
  'Adpressa' 177
Sequoiadendron giganteum 7, 40, 46, 47, 177
  'Aureum' 178
  'Pendulum' xii, 178
Serbian spruce ix, 40, 52, 166
Service tree, True 134
Service tree, Wild 137
Sessile oak 3, 44, 50, 128
Shagbark hickory 77
Shasta fir 8
Sheffield Park, Sussex 110, 175, 200
Sheraton cherry 117
Shining gum 33, 87
Siebold, Phillipp von 6
Sierra redwood 42, 46
Silver birch 42, 75
Silver fir, Common 148
Silver fir, European 5, 148
Silver lime 142
Silver maple 45, 64
Silver pendent lime x, 48, 141
Silver wattle 55
Silver willow 130
Sitka spruce 7, 8, 34, 43, 50, 167
Slindon, Sussex 88

Small-leafed lime vii, 46, 139
Small-leafed yew 180
Smooth Arizona cypress ix,
     52, 161
Snowdrop tree 5, 92
Sophora japonica 133
   'Pendula' 133
Sorbus 133–7
   alnifolia 133
   aria 192
   auaparia 133
   'Beissneri' 133, 190
   'Fastigiata' 186
   'Sheerwater Seedling' 133
   'Xanthocarpa' 133
   commixta 133, 193
      'Embley' 134, 191, 193
   cuspidata 134
   discolor 134
   domestica 134
   esserteauiana 136
   folgneri 134
   hupehensis 134
   'Joseph Rock' 136, 191,
      193
   mitchellii 134
   pohuashanensis 136
   sargentiana 136, 191, 193
   scalaris 136
   thibetica 134
      'John Mitchell' 134
   x *thuringiaca* 'Fastigiata'
      186
   torminalis 137, 192
   vilmoriniana 137, 191, 193
Sorrel-tree 40, 110
Sourwood 10
Southern beech,
      Dombey's 108
Southern beech, Moore's 108
Southern catalpa 79
Spanish chestnut 78
Spruce 164–7
   Brewer xii, 165
   Blue Colorado 8, 167
   Hondo 165
   Likiang 165
   Morinda 6, 167

Norway 40, 164
Oriental 166
Sargent 6, 164
Serbian ix, 40, 166
Sitka 7, 8, 34, 43, 50, 167
Spur-leaf 139
Stone pine 172
Storax
   Big leaf 138
   Hemsley's 138
Stourhead, Wilsthire 172,
      201
Strawberry tree xi, 3, 40,
      44, 73
   Cyprus 72
   Hybrid 72
   Pacific 72
Stuartia
   Pseudocamellia 137
   sinensis 138
Styrax
   hemsleyana 138
   japonica 191
   obassia 138
Sugar maple 65
Swamp cypress viii, 5, 37, 43,
      51
Sweet buck-eye 67
Sweet chestnut 4, 9, 45, 78
Sweet gum, Chinese 53, 100
Sweet gum 37, 41, 53, 101
Swiss stone pine 168
Sycamore 4, 42, 44, 45, 62
Syrian juniper xii, 162

Table dogwood 81
Taxodium
   ascendens 178
   distichum 51, 178
Taxus baccata 179, 187
   'Adpressa' 180
   'Adpressa Aurea' 180, 189
   'Dovastoniana' 180
   'Fastigiata' 180, 186, 189
   'Fastigiata Aurea' 186
   'Semperaurescens' 189
   'Standishii' 186, 189
Textracentron sinense 139

Texan walnut 96
Thorn, Carrière's hybrid 82
Thorn, Cockspur 82
Thorn, Washington 83
Thuja 180–1
   koraiensis 180
   occidentalis 180
      'Fastigiata' 185
      'Lutea' 180, 188
      'Rheingold' 180, 188
      'Spiralis' 181, 185
   orientalis 181
      'Elegantissima' 181
   plicata 50, 181
      'Fastigiata' 185
      'Zebrina' 51, 181, 189
   standishii 181
Thuja 180–1
   Chinese 6, 181
   Eastern 180
   Japanese 181
   Korean 180
Thujopis dolabrata 182
Tibetan cherry 117
Tilia 139–42
   americana 139
   cordata 46, 49, 139
      'Fastigiata' 186
      'Green Spire' 140
   euchlora 140
   x *europaea* 46, 48, 140
   x *moltkei* 140
   mongolica 140
   oliveri 53, 141
   petiolaris 48, 141
   platyphyllos 46, 142, 186
      'Laciniata' 142
   tomentosa 142
Totworth Court,
      Gloucestershire 113
Trachycarpus fortunei 142
Tradescant, John 63
Transcaucasian birch 74
Trautvetter's maple 66
Tree of Heaven 5, 34, 43, 69
Trident maple 55
True service tree 134
Tsuga 182–3

canadensis 182
heterophylla 182
mertensiana 182
  'Glauca' 183
Tsuga heterophylla 48
Tulip-tree xi, 41, 49, 102
  Chinese 6, 102
Tupelo 53, 109
Turkey oak 46, 50, 124
Turkish hazel x, 5, 52, 82

Ulmus 143–5
  carpinifolia 144
    'Cornubiensis' 144
    'Sarniensis' 50, 144
  glabra 144
    'Camperdown' 144
    'Lutescens' 145
    'Pendula' 145
  x *hollandica* 145
    'Hollandica' 145
    'Vegeta' 145
  parvifolia 143
  procera 145
    'Argenteovariegata' 187
    'Louis van Houtte' 189
    'Lutescens' 189
    'Silvery Gem' 187
  pumila 143
    'Sapporo Autumn
      Gold' 144
Umbellularia californica 145
Umbrella pine, Japanese 176

Varnish tree 130
Veitch, John Gould 6
Veitch J. H. 6
Veitch's Nuseries 6
Veitch's silver fir 152
Victoria Park, London 83,
  199
Vilmorin rowan xii, 137
Vine-leaf maple 58

Von Moltke's lime 140
Voss's hybrid laburnum 100

Wakehurst Place, Sussex 102,
  140
Wallich's juniper 163
Walnut 106–7
  Black 49, 96
  Common 4, 97
  Japanese 96
  Texan 96
Ward, Kingdon 6
Washington thorn 83
Waterer, Anthony 8, 167
Wattle, Silver 55
Weeping ash 91
Weeping beech x, 15, 90
Weeping Sally 86
Weeping willow 15, 37, 52
Wellingtonia 177
West Felton yew xi
Western hemlock vii, 7, 34,
  42, 48, 282
Western red cedar 50, 181
Western yellow pine viii, 7,
  50, 172
Westonbirt, Gloucestershire
  21–2, 39, 80, 104, 111,
  153, 198
Westonbirt hybrid pine 169
Wheatley elm 50, 144
White cedar, Northern 180
White fir 149
White mulberry 5, 107
White oak 123
White pine, Japanese 171
White poplar 4, 44, 114
White willow 130
Whitebeam
  Alder 133
  Himalayan 134
  Chinese 134
Whittingehame, East Lothian

86
Wild cherry 3, 116
Wild service tree 137
Willow 130–2
  Babylon 131
  Bay 132
  Crack 3, 37, 131
  Dragon's Claw 132
  Goat 131
  Silver 130
  Weeping 15, 37, 52, 131
  White 37, 130
Willow-leafed pear 120
Wilson, Ernest 6, 7, 84, 136,
  138, 141
Wing-nut
  Caucasian 5, 37, 119
  Hybrid 33, 120
Winkworth Arboretum,
  Surrey 110, 200
Winter cherry 119
Winter's bark 84
Wisley (RHS Garden),
  Surrey 134, 200
Wissel cypress 52
Wych elm 3, 144

Yellow birch 74
Yellow buck-eye 53, 67
Yellow catalpa 80
Yellow cypress 157
Yellow pine, Western viii, 172
Yew 3, 179–80
  Irish 180
  Plum-fruited 175
  Prince Albert's 176
Yulan lily 103

Zelkova 145–6
  acuminata 146
  carpinifolia 5, 50, 145
  serrata 146, 192
Zoeschen maple 40, 67